8.30

THE LOEB CLASSICAL LIBRARY

FOUNDED BY JAMES LOEB, LL.D.

EDITED BY

E. H. WARMINGTON, M.A., F.R.HIST.SOC.

SALLUST

SALLUST

WITH AN ENGLISH TRANSLATION BY

J. C. ROLFE

PROFESSOR OF LATIN IN THE UNIVERSITY OF PENNSYLVANIA

LONDON

WILLIAM HEINEMANN LTD

CAMBRIDGE, MASSACHUSETTS

HARVARD UNIVERSITY PRESS

MCMLXXI

American ISBN 0–674–99128–1
British ISBN 0 434 99116 3

First printed 1921
Reprinted and Revised 1931
Reprinted 1947, 1955, 1960, 1965, 1971

Printed in Great Britain

CONTENTS

PREFACE

TO THE SECOND IMPRESSION

The part of the Introduction dealing with the manuscripts has been re-written in the light of the new classification of Axel W. Ahlberg (*Prolegomena in Sallustium, Göteberg,* 1911), which was followed by him in his Teubner text (Leipzig, 1919) and, except in some minor details, by B. Ornstein in the Budé *Salluste* (Paris, 1924); and the critical notes have been made to conform to that classification. Some changes have been made also in the section on the "pseudo-Sallustian" works, to which a good deal of attention has been devoted during the past decade Finally, some errors have been corrected and a few additions made to the bibliography.

John C. Rolfe.

May 15, 1928.

PREFACE

TO THE FIRST IMPRESSION

In the absence of an entirely satisfactory text of Sallust, the translator has made his own. In some points of orthography, for example in the assimilation of prepositions, he has not followed the manuscripts, but has aimed rather at uniformity.

A complete translation of Sallust was submitted, including all the fragments on the basis of Maurenbrecher's edition of the *Histories*, but the General Editors decided, partly from considerations of space and partly because of the slight interest of the shorter bits, that only the complete *Orations* and *Letters* should be printed. To these have been added the Pseudo-Sallustian works mentioned on p. xviii of the Introduction.

In not a few instances, perhaps oftener than a more gifted translator would have found necessary, Sallust's sententious brevity has been sacrificed to clearness.

JOHN C. ROLFE.

October, 1920.

INTRODUCTION

The Life and Works of Sallust

GAIUS SALLUSTIUS CRISPUS was born in 86 B.C. at Amiternum, a town in the Sabine territory about fifty-five miles north-east of Rome at the foot of the Gran Sasso d'Italia. It was not far from Reate, the native place of Varro and of the Emperor Vespasian. The family does not make its appearance in history before the end of the seventh century of the city, and it was evidently of plebeian origin, since Sallust held the office of tribune of the commons. The author of the *Invective against Sallust* declares that the historian was wild and dissipated in his youth and that his conduct hastened his father's end; Sallust's own words, however, in *Cat.* iii. 3–5, imply that his only fault was ambition, and he certainly applied himself to his studies sufficiently to acquire a good education. One of his teachers was the celebrated Ateius Philologus (Suet. *Gramm.* x.).

Accusations of the most outrageous kind were so freely bandied about in Roman political circles that one might naturally attribute many of those made against Sallust to malicious gossip, especially since we are informed that one Lenaeus, a freedman of

Pompey the Great, assailed the historian in a bitter satire because of his criticisms of Pompey.[1] The best authenticated charge against him is that of an intrigue with the wife of Milo, made by Gellius on the authority of Varro.[2] Varro, however, was a Pompeian and was probably not over-critical in examining the authenticity of a bit of scandal about a prominent Caesarian.

According to his own statement,[3] Sallust must have entered upon a political career at Rome at an early age. He attained the quaestorship and thus gained admission to the senate,[4] but in what year this happened is uncertain. In 52 B.C. he was tribune of the commons and took sides with his two colleagues, Quintus Pompeius and Titus Munatius Plancus, against Cicero and Milo after the murder of Clodius.[5] In 50 B.C. he fell a victim to the partisan activity of the censor Appius Claudius Pulcher,[6] and was expelled from the senate; the charges made against him on that occasion need not be taken too seriously. Mommsen thought that Cicero addressed *Ad Fam.* 2. 17 to C. Sallustius,[7] and that therefore the historian was *legatus pro praetore* to Bibulus in Syria during the year 50–51.

[1] Suet. *Gramm.* 15.   [2] Gell. 17. 18.
[3] *Cat.* iii. 3.   [4] *Inv. in Sall.* vi. 17.
[5] Ascon. *pro Mil.* 33 (p. 37, l. 18, Clark).
[6] Cassius Dio, 40. 63. 4.
[7] *Hermes*, 1. 171 ; *Röm. Forsch.* 2, p. 434, l. 42. C. is a conjecture of Mommsen's ; all the manuscripts read *Canini Salustio*.

INTRODUCTION

In 49 B.C. Caesar reappointed Sallust to a quaestorship, and thus made him once more a member of the senate. In 48 he commanded one of Caesar's legions in Illyricum, but did not distinguish himself, being defeated by Octavius and Libo.[1] The following year he was sent to quiet the mutinous legions in Campania and was again unsuccessful,[2] narrowly escaping death at the hands of the troops. In 46, now a praetor, he sailed to the island of Circina, to seize the enemy's stores;[3] this time he succeeded in accomplishing his mission, which contributed in no small degree to Caesar's ultimate success. As a reward for his services he was appointed proconsular governor of the province of Numidia and Africa,[4] and there ended his political career.

On his return to Rome Sallust was tried for extortion, but was acquitted, doubtless through Caesar's influence, although the charge that he gave Caesar a bribe of two million sesterces rests only on the doubtful authority of the *Invective*.[5] Whether the accusation of extortion was well founded or not, it is certain that Sallust became very wealthy and that he was the owner of the magnificent *horti Sallustiani*, which were afterwards the property of Nero, Vespasian, Nerva, and Aurelian.

After the assassination of Caesar, Sallust went into retirement and devoted himself to the writing

[1] Orosius, 6. 15. 8. [2] Cassius Dio, 42. 52.
[3] *Bell. Afr.* 8 and 34. [4] *Bell. Afr.* 97.
[5] vii. 19.

of history. He is reported to have married Cicero's divorced wife Terentia,[1] and he adopted his sister's grandson, the Sallustius Crispus to whom Horace addressed one of his Odes,[2] afterwards a trusted friend of the Emperor Augustus.[3] It is therefore probable that he had no son of his own. He died in 35–34 B.C.

Sallust devoted his attention to a comparatively new branch of historiography, the historical monograph. He seems to have made careful and conscientious preparation for his work. Suetonius tells us[4] that Ateius Philologus supplied him with an outline of the whole of Roman history, and his careful study of Thucydides and Cato is apparent; Lenaeus, indeed, called him " an ignorant pilferer of the language of the ancients and of Cato in particular."[5] Sallust professes complete impartiality, and while his leaning towards the popular party is obvious, his fairness is shown by his treatment of Metellus and Marius in the *Jugurtha*. His first work was an account of the conspiracy of Catiline, which has come down to us under three titles, *Catilina*, *Bellum Catilinae*, *Bellum Catilinarium*.[6] The reason which he himself gives for the choice of the theme is " the novelty of the crime and the danger to which

---

[1] Hieronymus, *adv. Jov.* 1.   [2] 2. 2.
[3] Tacitus, *Ann.* 3. 30.   [4] *De Gramm.* 10.
[5] Suet. *De Gramm.* 15. Asinius Pollio also accused him of imitating Cato (*Gramm.* 10).
[6] For a full discussion of the question see Ahlberg, *Prolegomena*, pp. 155 ff.; cf. note 3, p. xiv.

the state was exposed," [1] but it has been suspected that he had the underlying motive of clearing Caesar, as well as Gaius Antonius, the uncle of Mark Antony, from the suspicion of complicity in the plot; some have even regarded this as his main purpose. The exact time when the *Catiline* was written is uncertain, but the language of the eulogy of Caesar [2] indicates that it was not published until after the death of the dictator. Some scholars maintain that it was issued immediately after the assassination, while others assign it to the year 40 B.C.

Sallust had an abundance of written records on which to base his account, such as decrees of the senate, Cicero's published speeches, and the histories of Cicero's consulship. He could also draw upon his personal recollection of the events and on the testimony of his contemporaries. Yet the monograph is inaccurate in many of its details, in particular in assigning the beginning of the conspiracy to the year 64, instead of to 63, thus prolonging the events of a few months to the duration of more than a year, with inevitable distortion of the facts. The principal aim seems to have been to make the account interesting and vivid, and in that Sallust unquestionably succeeded; from the literary point of view the *Catiline* must always take a high rank. The character sketches of Sempronia, Cato, and Caesar, with the speeches of the last two, are especially fine.

---

[1] *Cat.* iv. 4.   [2] *Cat.* liv. especially 1–4.

In fact, the orations in all of Sallust's works were greatly admired in antiquity, and collections of them were made for use in the schools of rhetoric; yet he is not mentioned by Cicero among the great speakers of the day, and Quintilian[1] expressly warns orators against taking him as a model. It was probably Sallust's own speeches, and not those which he puts into the mouths of his characters, to which Cassius Severus referred when he said "orationes Sallustii in honorem historiarum leguntur."[2] The addresses in Sallust's works are introduced by such phrases as "hoc modo disseruit," "huiuscemodi orationem habuit," and the like, and hence do not purport to give the exact words of the speakers. They are carefully composed and their sentiments are adapted to those who are represented as delivering them, but the language is that of Sallust himself.

Sallust's second work was an account of the war with Jugurtha, entitled *Bellum Iugurthinum*.[3] The contest with the Numidian prince doubtless attracted Sallust's attention because of his acquaintance with the scene of the conflict. He himself says that he selected it "because of its perilous nature and shifting fortunes, and because it marked the beginning

---

[1] 4. 2. 45.   [2] Sen. Rhet. *Contr.* 3. pr. 8, p. 243 к.
[3] Quint. 3. 8. 9. The title *De Bello Iugurthino* is also found. The *Catiline* and the *Jugurtha* are collectively referred to as *Bella*, and the title of the latter influenced that of the former, which for three centuries was usually *Catilina*; after that, *Bellum Catilinae* or (in the grammarians) *B. Catilinarium.*

of successful resistance to the dominant power of the nobles." [1] Besides the information which he himself had gathered in Numidia, Sallust had the benefit of a number of literary sources, such as the *History* of Sisenna,[2] and the *Memoirs* of Sulla, Marcus Aemilius Scaurus, and Publius Rutilius Rufus. He also made use of Punic sources, which he had caused to be translated for his benefit.[3] Nevertheless, judged by modern standards, the *Jugurtha* is rather like an historical novel of the better class than like sober history. Chronology is to a great extent disregarded, and in place of exact dates we have such vague expressions as "interea," "iisdem temporibus," "paucos post annos," and the like. Sallust even ventures upon shifts in the sequence of events, in order to make a better rounded tale. As a literary masterpiece the work takes high rank.

The *Jugurtha* was written after the *Catiline* and published in 41 B.C., if the earlier date assigned to the *Catiline* is the correct one ; in any event, not far from that time. It was followed by Sallust's most extensive work, the *Historiae,* which in five books recounted the events of about twelve years, from 78 to 67 B.C. The work formed a continuation of Sisenna's *History,* which ended with the death of Sulla. If, like Sallust's other works, the *Historiae* had a secondary motive, it was still further to discredit the party of the nobles and to show Pompey's

---

[1] *Jug.* v. 1.   [2] Cited *Jug.* xcv. 2.   [3] *Jug.* xvii. 7.

unfitness to be entrusted with the rule of the state.

The greater part of the *Historiae* has perished. Four complete speeches and two letters are preserved in a collection made apparently in the second century for use in the schools of rhetoric. The work was frequently cited by grammarians and other ancient writers, and from this source numerous small fragments have been recovered. Three longer passages are transmitted in a more or less mutilated form in manuscript. These are the *fragmentum Vaticanum*, of two leaves containing eight columns and belonging to the Third Book; the *fragmentum Berolinense*, of one leaf containing a bit of the Second Book; and the *fragmentum Aurelianense*, two pieces of a palimpsest, one consisting of two leaves and the other of eight complete and two mutilated columns, discovered by Hauler in *Codex Orleanensis*, 169. The former of these supplements the *frag. Berolinense*, and with it gives an account of the consulship of Lucius Octavius and Gaius Aurelius Cotta,[1] while the latter is of varied contents. Still other brief extracts from the *Histories* have been recovered from the account of the First Civil War written by Julius Exsuperantius in the latter part of the fourth and the beginning of the fifth centuries, and based upon Sallust.

The proper arrangement of the fragments and

[1] 75 B.C.

their interpretation are matters of considerable uncertainty and difference of opinion, but the labours of De Brosse, Kritz, Dietsch, and Maurenbrecher [1] have gone far towards solving the problem.

The style of Sallust is quite unlike that of Caesar and Cicero. His model in the writing of history was Thucydides, whose brevity of expression he also imitated and, according to Seneca Rhetor,[2] even surpassed. He is also highly rhetorical and his language is decidedly archaistic, so much so that he was accused of pilfering from the works of Cato the Censor.[3] His reputation in antiquity was very high, although it was based for the most part on his last and greatest work, the *Histories*. Quintilian's opinion,[4] "nec opponere Thucydidi Sallustium verear," does more credit to his patriotism than to his critical acumen, but Martial's less extravagant verdict,[5] "primus Romana Crispus in historia," was true at the time when it was written. Sallust was criticized by Asinius Pollio and Livy, but his admirers and imitators far outnumbered his detractors. Tacitus, who deprived him of the first rank assigned him by Martial, speaks of him as "rerum Romanarum florentissimus auctor," [6] and paid him the still higher compliment of imitation. In Hadrian's time Sallust was even translated into Greek by a certain Zenobius, and his archaic

---

[1] See Bibliographical Note, p. xxii.

[2] *Contr*. 9. 1. 13 ; Kiessling (Index, *s.v.* " Thucydides ") understands the comparison to be with Demosthenes.

[3] Suet. *Gramm*. 10. 15.; *Aug*. 86. 3.

[4] 10. 1. 101.   [5] 14. 191.   [6] *Ann*. 3. 30.

diction made him a favourite writer with Fronto and his school. Towards the end of the second century Aemilius Asper wrote a commentary on the works of Sallust, and in the fourth century St. Augustine calls him " nobilitatae veritatis historicus." [1] The influence of his style is seen in Ammianus Marcellinus, Dictys Cretensis, Hegesippus, Sulpicius Severus, Lactantius, Hilarius, Julius Exsuperantius and others, and it continued into the Middle Ages.

The Doubtful Works

In codex Vaticanus 3864 (*V*) the excerpts from the *Historiae* [2] are followed in the same handwriting by two anonymous *suasoriae*, or pleas, addressed to Julius Caesar, in both of which advice is given to the dictator as to the proper conduct of the government. We also find in our manuscripts, sometimes in company with genuine works of Cicero and sometimes with the *Bella* of Sallust, an *Invective against Cicero* ascribed to Sallust and a reply purporting to be that of Cicero.

The first *suasoria* has generally been called an " oration " and therefore [3] precedes the second, which was termed a letter. But the dramatic date of the former is 46 B.C., and that of the latter, 49 or 50 B.C. The former date is the

---

[1] *De Civ. Dei*, 1. 5.   [2] See p. xvi.
[3] Through the influence of the title *Orationes et Epistulae* of codex *V*.

one generally accepted, but Post[1] maintains that the letter was written before Caesar crossed the Rubicon. The question of their authorship is reviewed and discussed, with a full bibliography, by H. Last,[2] who is inclined to admit the genuineness of the first *suasoria*, but denies that of the second, which he believes to contain proof that it was not written by Sallust or by a contemporary of his. The genuineness of both is upheld by L. Post,[3] Kurfess,[4] and others.[5]

The *Invective against Cicero* has generally been regarded as spurious, and as a specimen of the pamphleteer literature of the period following the death of Caesar.[6] But Kurfess, who once argued against its genuineness,[7] now believes that it was written by Sallust as a political pamphlet and published and circulated anonymously.[8] It is generally agreed that its dramatic date is 54 B.C. Quintilian, who quotes from it,[9] regarded it as a genuine work of Sallust. The *suasoriae*, however, are not referred

[1] *Class. Weekly* xxi. (1928), p. 19.
[2] *Class. Quarterly*, xvii. (1923), pp. 87 ff. and 151 ff.; xviii. (1924), p. 83.
[3] *l.c.*
[4] *Sallustii Crispi Epistulae ad Caesarem Senem de Re Publica*, Leipzig, 1924.
[5] See Last, *l.c.*
[6] Schanz, *Rom. Lit.* 1², p. 234.
[7] *Mnemosyne*, xl. (1912), pp. 364 ff., and *Sallustii Crispi in Ciceronem et invicem Invectivae*, Leipzig, 1914.
[8] *Jahresb. des Phil. Vereins zu Berlin*, 48 (1922), 66 ff., and *Bursians Jahresb.* 1922, p. 61.
[9] iv. 1. 68 ; ix. 3. 89.

to by the ancient writers, unless Gellius xvii. 18 be an exception; not even by the grammarians, who so frequently quote Sallust.

The *Invective against Sallust*, although it purports to be a reply to the attack upon Cicero, does not observe the same time limits but covers the entire life of Sallust. It is probably an exercise from the schools of rhetoric, composed by a writer of small ability and inferior Latinity[1] at a late period which cannot be determined with certainty.

THE MANUSCRIPTS

The number of manuscripts of the *Catiline* and *Jugurtha* is very great. Roth[2] was the first to submit them to a critical examination, on the basis of which he divided them into two classes. These are:

(1) The *codices mutili*, marked by an extensive lacuna in the *Jugurtha* (ciii. 2, "quinque" ... cxii. 3, "et ratam"). In some instances the lacuna has been filled by a later hand.

(2) The *codices integri*, in which the lacuna is filled by the first hand, either in the proper place or at the end. Some of these manuscripts have a phrase

---

[1] *Angusti et pusilli rhetoris posterioris aetatis*, Kurfess, *Mnemosyne*, **xl.** (1912); for examples of his *impurus sermo*, see *ibid.* p. 377. Kurfess also shows that the author of the second *Invective* was a servile imitator of the writer of the first one.

[2] *Rhein. Mus.* ix. pp. 129 ff.

("neque muniebantur ea," *Jug.* xliv. 5) which is not found in any other codices, and of these Dietsch made a third class. The usual division, however, is a twofold one, although Wirz[1] is right in not recognizing the *mutili* and *integri* as classes, except for convenience. As a whole the *mutili* are older and better than the *integri*. A careful examination of the manuscripts has recently been made by Ahlberg (see Preface), and his classification, while probably not definitive,[2] will doubtless be the standard for some years to come. He makes use of the following *codices mutili*:

Codex Parisinus, 16024 (*P*), formerly Sorbonnensis, 500, of the Tenth century.

Codex Parisinus, 16025 (*A*), formerly Sorbonnensis, 1576, of the Tenth century (*P*¹ of former editions).[3]

Codex Parisinus, 6085 (*C*), of the latter part of the Tenth or the early Eleventh century. After the end of the *Jugurtha* the speech of Bocchus (ch. 110) is added by the first hand, and the entire lacuna is supplied by a later hand (*P*² of former editions).

Codex Basileensis, A.N. iv. 11 (*B*), of the Eleventh

---

[1] *C. Sallusti Crispi libri qui est de bello Iugurthino partem extremam* . . . recensuit H. Wirz, Zürich, 1897.

[2] See O. Schulthess, *Das humanistische Gymn.* xxvi. (1915), p. 92.

[3] Ornstein (see Preface) follows this earlier nomenclature.

century. *Jug.* 110 is added at the end by the
first hand, as in *C* (*B* of former editions).

Codex Palatinus, 889 (*N*), formerly Nazarianus, of
the early part of the Eleventh century.

Codex Palatinus, 887 (*K*), formerly owned by the
humanist Kemnatus; of the Eleventh century.
It ends with *Jug.* 102. 11, but the rest is supplied
by a later hand.

Codex Berolinensis, 205 (*H*), formerly Philippicus,
1902, of the Eleventh century. The lacuna is
supplied a little later by a second hand.

Codex Monacensis, 4559 (*M*), of the Eleventh or
Twelfth century. Besides the lacuna, *Jug.* 28. 1,
pecunia . . . 31. 12, *sunt ii qui* (= folia 23^b and
24^a) is supplied by a later hand (*M*^{2} of former
editions).

Codex Turicensis, bibl. reip. c. 143, a (*T*), of the
latter part of the Eleventh century. The lacuna
is supplied by a later hand.

Codex Parisinus, 10195 (*D*), formerly Echternacensis,
of about the same date as *T*. The lacuna is
supplied by a later hand.

Codex Hauniensis, 25 (*F*), formerly Fabricianus, of
the same time as *T* and *D*. The latter part of
the *Jugurtha* (103. 2 to the end) is supplied by a
later hand.

All these manuscripts contain corrections, of
which P^2 and A^2 are of the greatest value, since
they are but little later than the first hand.

INTRODUCTION

The following *codices mutili* are also used in connection with the lacuna, which was supplied by a hand not much later than the first:

Codex Parisinus, 5748 (*Q*), of the Eleventh century. (*P*[4] of earlier editions.)

Codex Vaticanus, 3325 (*R*) of the latter part of the Twelfth century. (Formerly *V*[1] or *v*.)

The following *codices integri* are used:

Codex Leidensis Vossianus Lat. 73 (*l*), of the Eleventh century. The latter part is badly damaged and ends with *praeterea, Jug.* 109. 4.

Codex Lipsiensis, bibl. sen. rep. I, fol. 4 (*s*), of the Eleventh century.

Codex Parisinus, 6086 (*n*), of the Eleventh century.

Codex Monacensis, 14777 (*m*), of the Eleventh century. Ends with *Volux adveniens, Jug.* 106. 1.

And in connection with the lacuna:

Codex Palatinus, 883 (*π*), of the Twelfth century.

Of the *codices mutili P, A, C, B* are descended from a common archetype (*X*), *M, T, D, F* from another (*Γ*), and *N, K, H, Γ* from a third (*Y*). Of the *codices integri l* and *s* are most closely related to *X, m* and *n* to *Y*.

Codex Vaticanus, 3864 (*V*) is useful for a part of the *Catiline* and the *Jugurtha*, since it contains a collection of Speeches and Letters from all the works of Sallust. This manuscript, of the Tenth

century, is highly esteemed by Hauler [1] and Ahlberg, [2] who regard it as an earlier recension than the archetype of the *codices mutili*. It also contains the two *suasoriae*.

Sallust is quoted for various reasons by many ancient writers, and these *testimonia* are sometimes of value in the criticism of his text, especially those of Fronto and St. Augustine, and of the grammarians Arusianus and Priscian.

For the manuscripts of the *Invectives* see p. 492, note 1.

For the manuscripts of the *Invectives* see p. 492, note 1.

BIBLIOGRAPHICAL NOTE

The *Editio princeps* of Sallust was published in 1470. Other early editions are those of Glareanus, Basle, 1538; Carrio, Antwerp, 1580; Gruter, Frankfurt, 1607; Corte, Leipzig, 1724; Havercamp, Amsterdam, 1742.

More recent editions are those of Kritz, three volumes, Leipzig, 1828–1853; Gerlach, Basle, 1832, 1852, Stuttgart, 1870; Dietsch, Leipzig, 1859; Jordan, Berlin, 1866, 1876, 1887; Eussner, Leipzig, 1887; Ahlberg, Leipzig, 1919; Ornstein and Roman, Paris, 1924.

Of editions with commentaries may be mentioned: Fabri, Nuremberg[2], 1845; Kritz, Leipzig, 1856; Jacobs, Berlin[10], 1894 (by H. Wirz); Schmalz[10], Gotha, 1919; Capes, Oxford, 1889; Merivale,

---

[1] *Wiener Studien*, xvii. pp. 122 ff.
[2] *Prolegomena*, p. 104.

INTRODUCTION

London, 1884; and of the *Histories*, B. Maurenbrecher, Leipzig, 1891–93.

The translations of Sallust into various languages of modern Europe are exceedingly numerous, among them German versions by Cless (Stuttgart, 1855) and Holzer (Stuttgart, 1868), and French translations by De Brosses (Paris, 1837) and Roman (Paris, 1924). The earliest English rendering seems to be Alexander Barclay's *Historye of Jugurth,* published in 1557 together with *The Conspiracie of Catiline* of Constantius Felicius Durantinus. Later versions are those of John Mair, Dublin, 1788; William Rose, London, 1751, and often reprinted; John Watson, Bohn Library, 1852.

SALLUST

[1970] We now have the complete edition by A. Kurfess, in the Teubner series, this being a second edition of that by A. W. Ahlberg (1911, 1915), Leipzig 1954; in the Budé series A. Ernout, Paris, 1947; and in the Penguin series a translation by S. A. Handford, Harmondsworth, 1963.

The *Catilinarian Conspiracy* has been edited by A. T. Davis, Oxford, 1967. The Letters etc. attributed to Sallust have been re-edited by A. Kurfess, Leipzig, (Teubner, 1962); by A. Ernout (Budé, 1962); and by P. Cagusi (Cagliari, 1958). Very useful is A. D. Leeman, *A Systematic Bibliography of Sallust*, 1870–1950.

SIGLA

$V =$ cod. Vaticanus, 3864.
$P =$ cod. Parisinus, 16024.
$A =$ cod. Parisinus, 16025.
$C =$ cod. Parisinus, 6085.
$B =$ cod. Basileensis, A. N. iv. 11.
$X =$ the archetype of P, A, C, B.
$N =$ cod. Palatinus, 889.
$K =$ cod. Palatinus, 887.
$H =$ cod. Berolinensis, 205.
$M =$ cod. Monacensis, 4559.
$T =$ cod. Turicensis, bibl. reip. C. 143a.
$D =$ cod. Parisinus, 10195.
$F =$ cod. Hauniensis, 25.
$\Gamma =$ the archetype of M, T, D, F.
$Y =$ the archetype of N, K, H, Γ.
$l =$ cod. Leidensis Voss. Lat. 73.
$s =$ cod. Lipsiensis, bibl. sen. rep. I. fol. 4.
$n =$ cod. Parisinus, 6086.
$m =$ cod. Monacensis, 14777.
$Q =$ cod. Parisinus, 5748.
$R =$ cod. Vaticanus, 3325.
$\pi =$ cod. Palatinus, 883.
$P^1A^1 =$ the first hand; P^2A^2, the second hand.
$Ah =$ Ahlberg, *Sallust*, Leipzig, 1919.
$Or =$ Ornstein, *Salluste*, Paris, 1924.

SALLUST
THE WAR WITH CATILINE

C. SALLUSTI CRISPI

BELLUM CATILINAE

I. Omnis homines qui sese student praestare ceteris animalibus summa ope niti decet ne vitam silentio transeant veluti pecora, quae natura prona 2 atque ventri oboedientia finxit. Sed nostra omnis vis in animo et corpore sita est; animi imperio, corporis servitio magis utimur; alterum nobis cum dis, 3 alterum cum beluis commune est. Quo mihi rectius videtur ingeni quam virium opibus gloriam quaerere, et, quoniam vita ipsa qua fruimur brevis est, memo- 4 riam nostri quam maxume longam efficere; nam divitiarum et formae gloria fluxa atque fragilis est, virtus clara aeternaque habetur.

5 Sed diu magnum inter mortalis certamen fuit vine corporis an virtute animi res militaris magis pro- 6 cederet. Nam et prius quam incipias, consulto, et 7 ubi consulueris, mature facto opus est. Ita utrumque per se indigens alterum alterius auxilio eget.

SALLUST

THE WAR WITH CATILINE

I. It behooves all men who wish to excel the other animals to strive with might and main not to pass through life unheralded, like the beasts, which Nature has fashioned grovelling and slaves to the belly. All our power, on the contrary, lies in both mind and body; we employ the mind to rule, the body rather to serve; the one we have in common with the Gods, the other with the brutes. Therefore I find it becoming, in seeking renown, that we should employ the resources of the intellect rather than those of brute strength, to the end that, since the span of life which we enjoy is short, we may make the memory of our lives as long as possible. For the renown which riches or beauty confer is fleeting and frail; mental excellence is a splendid and lasting possession.

Yet for a long time mortal men have discussed the question whether success in arms depends more on strength of body or excellence of mind; for before you begin, deliberation is necessary, when you have deliberated, prompt action. Thus each of these,[1] being incomplete in itself, requires the other's aid.

[1] Namely, mind and body.

II. Igitur initio reges—nam in terris nomen imperi id primum fuit—divorsi pars ingenium, alii corpus exercebant; etiam tum vita hominum sine cupiditate agitabatur; sua cuique satis placebant. 2 Postea vero quam in Asia Cyrus, in Graecia Lacedaemonii et Athenienses coepere urbis atque nationes subigere, lubidinem dominandi causam belli habere, maxumam gloriam in maxumo imperio putare, tum demum periculo atque negotiis compertum est in bello plurumum ingenium posse. 3 Quodsi regum atque imperatorum animi virtus in pace ita ut in bello valeret, aequabilius atque constantius sese res humanae haberent, neque aliud alio ferri neque mutari ac misceri omnia cerneres. 4 Nam imperium facile eis artibus retinetur quibus 5 initio partum est. Verum ubi pro labore desidia, pro continentia et aequitate lubido atque superbia invasere, fortuna simul cum moribus immutatur. 6 Ita imperium semper ad optumum quemque a minus bono transfertur.

7 Quae homines arant, navigant, aedificant, virtuti 8 omnia parent. Sed multi mortales dediti ventri atque somno indocti incultique vitam sicuti peregrinantes transiere;[1] quibus profecto contra naturam corpus voluptati, anima oneri fuit. Eorum ego vitam mortemque iuxta aestumo, quoniam de utraque sile- 9 tur. Verum enimvero is demum mihi vivere atque

---

[1] transiere, *K*, *M* (g *written above*) *m*; *Prisc.* iii. 433. 31 κ; *Nonius, p.* 419 м (677 Linds.); transierunt, *Donat. Ter. Ph.* 605 (*cod. O*); transire, *A*[1]; transigere, *N* (g *deleted*), *F. Serv. Ge.* i. 3, *Donat.*; transegere, *A*[2] *and the other mss.*

II. Accordingly in the beginning kings (for that was the first title of sovereignty among men), took different courses, some training their minds and others their bodies. Even at that time men's lives were still free from covetousness; each was quite content with his own possessions. But when Cyrus in Asia and in Greece the Athenians and Lacedaemonians began to subdue cities and nations, to make the lust for dominion a pretext for war, to consider the greatest empire the greatest glory, then at last men learned from perilous enterprises that qualities of mind availed most in war.

Now if the mental excellence with which kings and rulers are endowed were as potent in peace as in war, human affairs would run an evener and steadier course, and you would not see power passing from hand to hand and everything in turmoil and confusion; for empire is easily retained by the qualities by which it was first won. But when sloth has usurped the place of industry, and lawlessness and insolence have superseded self-restraint and justice, the fortune of princes changes with their character Thus the sway is always passing to the best man from the hands of his inferior.

Success in agriculture, navigation, and architecture depends invariably upon mental excellence. Yet many men, being slaves to appetite and sleep, have passed through life untaught and untrained, like mere wayfarers; in these men we see, contrary to Nature's intent, the body a source of pleasure, the soul a burden. For my own part, I consider the lives and deaths of such men as about alike, since no record is made of either. In very truth that man alone lives and makes the most of life, as it

5

frui anima videtur, qui aliquo negotio intentus praeclari facinoris aut artis bonae famam quaerit. Sed
in magna copia rerum aliud alii natura iter ostendit.

III. Pulchrum est bene facere rei publicae, etiam
bene dicere haud absurdum est; vel pace vel bello
clarum fieri licet. Et qui fecere et qui facta aliorum
2 scripsere, multi laudantur. Ac mihi quidem, tametsi
haud quaquam par gloria sequitur scriptorem et
actorem[1] rerum, tamen in primis arduum videtur res
gestas scribere; primum quod facta dictis exaequanda
sunt, dehinc quia plerique quae delicta reprehen-
deris malivolentia et invidia dicta putant; ubi de
magna virtute atque gloria bonorum memores, quae
sibi quisque facilia factu putat, aequo animo accipit,
supra ea veluti ficta pro falsis ducit.

3 Sed ego adulescentulus initio sicuti plerique studio
ad rem publicam latus sum, ibique mihi multa advorsa fuere. Nam pro pudore, pro abstinentia, pro
4 virtute audacia, largitio, avaritia vigebant. Quae
tametsi animus aspernabatur insolens malarum artium, tamen inter tanta vitia imbecilla aetas ambi-
5 tione corrupta tenebatur; ac me cum ab reliquorum
malis moribus dissentirem, nihilo minus honoris

---

[1] auctorem, *PB* (u *erased*) *H, Gell.* iv. 15. 2 (*codd. PV*),
Charis. i. 215. 27 к ; actorem, *the other mss. and Gell. RV*[3].

seems to me, who devotes himself to some occupation, courting the fame of a glorious deed or a noble career. But amid the wealth of opportunities Nature points out one path to one and another to another.

III. It is glorious to serve one's country by deeds; even to serve her by words is a thing not to be despised; one may become famous in peace as well as in war. Not only those who have acted, but those also who have recorded the acts of others oftentimes receive our approbation. And for myself, although I am well aware that by no means equal repute attends the narrator and the doer of deeds, yet I regard the writing of history as one of the most difficult of tasks: first, because the style and diction must be equal to the deeds recorded; and in the second place, because such criticisms as you make of others' shortcomings are thought by most men to be due to malice and envy. Furthermore, when you commemorate the distinguished merit and fame of good men, while every one is quite ready to believe you when you tell of things which he thinks he could easily do himself, everything beyond that he regards as fictitious, if not false.[1]

When I myself was a young man, my inclinations at first led me, like many another, into public life, and there I encountered many obstacles; for instead of modesty, incorruptibility and honesty, shamelessness, bribery and rapacity held sway. And although my soul, a stranger to evil ways, recoiled from such faults, yet amid so many vices my youthful weakness was led astray and held captive by ambition; for while I took no part in the evil practices of the others, yet the desire for preferment made me

[1] cf. Thuc. i. 35

cupido eadem qua ceteros fama atque invidia vexabat.

IV. Igitur ubi animus ex multis miseriis atque periculis requievit et mihi reliquam aetatem a re publica procul habendam decrevi, non fuit consilium socordia atque desidia bonum otium conterere, neque vero agrum colundo aut venando servilibus officiis 2 intentum aetatem agere; sed a quo incepto studioque me ambitio mala detinuerat, eodem regressus statui res gestas populi Romani carptim, ut quaeque memoria digna videbantur, perscribere; eo magis, quod mihi a spe, metu, partibus rei publicae animus 3 liber erat. Igitur de Catilinae coniuratione quam 4 verissume potero paucis absolvam; nam id facinus in primis ego memorabile existumo sceleris atque 5 periculi novitate. De cuius hominis moribus pauca prius explananda sunt, quam initium narrandi faciam.

V. L. Catilina, nobili genere natus, fuit magna vi et animi et corporis, sed ingenio malo pravoque. 2 Huic ab adulescentia bella intestina, caedes, rapinae, discordia civilis grata fuere, ibique iuventutem suam 3 exercuit. Corpus patiens inediae, algoris, vigiliae 4 supra quam cuiquam credibile est. Animus audax, subdolus, varius, cuius rei lubet simulator ac dissimulator, alieni appetens, sui profusus, ardens in cupidi- 5 tatibus; satis eloquentiae, sapientiae parum. Vastus

---

[1] As being purely corporeal; see p. 2, l. 5: *animi imperio, corporis servitio magis utimur.*

8

the victim of the same ill-repute and jealousy as they.

IV. Accordingly, when my mind found peace after many troubles and perils and I had determined that I must pass what was left of my life aloof from public affairs, it was not my intention to waste my precious leisure in indolence and sloth, nor yet by turning to farming or the chase, to lead a life devoted to slavish employments.[1] On the contrary, I resolved to return to a cherished purpose from which ill-starred ambition had diverted me, and write a history of the Roman people, selecting such portions as seemed to me worthy of record; and I was confirmed in this resolution by the fact that my mind was free from hope, and fear, and partisanship. I shall therefore write briefly and as truthfully as possible of the conspiracy of Catiline; for I regard that event as worthy of special notice because of the extraordinary nature of the crime and of the danger arising from it. But before beginning my narrative I must say a few words about the man's character.

V. Lucius Catilina, scion of a noble family, had great vigour both of mind and of body, but an evil and depraved nature. From youth up he revelled in civil wars, murder, pillage, and political dissension, and amid these he spent his early manhood. His body could endure hunger, cold and want of sleep to an incredible degree; his mind was reckless, cunning, treacherous, capable of any form of pretence or concealment. Covetous of others' possessions, he was prodigal of his own; he was violent in his passions. He possessed a certain amount of eloquence, but little discretion. His

9

animus immoderata, incredibilia, nimis alta semper cupiebat.

6 Hunc post dominationem L. Sullae lubido maxuma invaserat rei publicae capiundae, neque id quibus modis adsequeretur, dum sibi regnum
7 pararet, quicquam pensi habebat. Agitabatur magis magisque in dies animus ferox inopia rei familiaris et conscientia scelerum, quae utraque eis artibus
8 auxerat quas supra memoravi. Incitabant praeterea corrupti civitatis mores, quos pessuma ac divorsa inter se mala, luxuria atque avaritia, vexabant.

9 Res ipsa hortari videtur, quoniam de moribus civitatis tempus admonuit, supra repetere ac paucis instituta maiorum domi militiaeque, quo modo rem publicam habuerint quantamque reliquerint, ut paulatim immutata ex pulcherrima atque optuma pessuma ac flagitiosissuma facta sit, disserere.

VI. Urbem Romam, sicuti ego accepi, condidere atque habuere initio Troiani, qui Aenea duce profugi sedibus incertis vagabantur, cumque eis Aborigines, genus hominum agreste, sine legibus,
2 sine imperio, liberum atque solutum. Hi postquam in una moenia convenere, dispari genere, dissimili lingua, alii alio more viventes, incredibile memoratu est quam facile coaluerint; ita brevi multitudo dis-
3 persa atque vaga concordia civitas facta erat. Sed

---

[1] Sulla was dictator from 82 to 79 B.C.
[2] The emphasis given by *ego* shows that Sallust is offering his personal view of the matter, and in fact his version differs from all other extant traditions.

disordered mind ever craved the monstrous, incredible, gigantic.

After the domination of Lucius Sulla[1] the man had been seized with a mighty desire of getting control of the government, recking little by what manner he should achieve it, provided he made himself supreme. His haughty spirit was goaded more and more every day by poverty and a sense of guilt, both of which he had augmented by the practices of which I have already spoken. He was spurred on, also, by the corruption of the public morals, which were being ruined by two great evils of an opposite character, extravagance and avarice.

Since the occasion has arisen to speak of the morals of our country, the nature of my theme seems to suggest that I go farther back and give a brief account of the institutions of our forefathers in peace and in war, how they governed the commonwealth, how great it was when they bequeathed it to us, and how by gradual changes it has ceased to be the noblest and best, and has become the worst and most vicious.

VI. The city of Rome, according to my understanding,[2] was at the outset founded and inhabited by Trojans, who were wandering about in exile under the leadership of Aeneas and had no fixed abode; they were joined by the Aborigines, a rustic folk, without laws or government, free and unrestrained. After these two peoples, different in race, unlike in speech and mode of life, were united within the same walls, they were merged into one with incredible facility, so quickly did harmony change a heterogeneous and roving band into a commonwealth. But when this new community had grown

postquam res eorum civibus, moribus, agris aucta,
satis prospera satisque pollens videbatur, sicuti
pleraque mortalium habentur, invidia ex opulentia
4 orta est. Igitur reges populique finitumi bello tempt-
tare, pauci ex amicis auxilio esse ; nam ceteri metu
5 perculsi a periculis aberant. At Romani domi militiaeque intenti festinare, parare, alius alium hortari,
hostibus obviam ire, libertatem, patriam parentisque
armis tegere. Post ubi pericula virtute propulerant,
sociis atque amicis auxilia portabant, magisque
dandis quam accipiundis beneficiis amicitias parabant.
6   Imperium legitumum, nomen imperi regium habebant. Delecti, quibus corpus annis infirmum,
ingenium sapientia validum erat, rei publicae con-
sultabant ; ei vel aetate vel curae similitudine patres
7 appellabantur. Post ubi regium imperium, quod
initio conservandae libertatis atque augendae rei
publicae fuerat, in superbiam dominationemque se
convortit, immutato more annua imperia binosque
imperatores sibi fecere ; eo modo minume posse
putabant per licentiam insolescere animum humanum.

   VII. Sed ea tempestate coepere se quisque magis
extollere magisque ingenium in promptu habere.
2 Nam regibus boni quam mali suspectiores sunt
3 semperque eis aliena virtus formidulosa est. Sed
civitas incredibile memoratu est adepta libertate

---

1 Such as the Sabini, Aequi, Rutuli, and Volsci.
2 The consuls, first chosen in 509 B.C., according to the
traditional chronology.

in numbers, civilization, and territory, and was beginning to seem amply rich and amply strong, then, as is usual with mortal affairs, prosperity gave birth to envy. As a result, neighbouring kings and peoples [1] made war upon them, and but few of their friends lent them aid; for the rest were smitten with fear and stood aloof from the danger. But the Romans, putting forth their whole energy at home and in the field, made all haste, got ready, encouraged one another, went to meet the foe, and defended their liberty, their country, and their parents by arms. Afterwards, when their prowess had averted the danger, they lent aid to their allies and friends, and established friendly relations rather by conferring than by accepting favours.

They had a constitution founded upon law, which was in name a monarchy; a chosen few, whose bodies were enfeebled by age but whose minds were fortified with wisdom, took counsel for the welfare of the state. These were called Fathers, by reason either of their age or of the similarity of their duties. Later, when the rule of the kings, which at first had tended to preserve freedom and advance the state, had degenerated into a lawless tyranny, they altered their form of government and appointed two rulers with annual power,[2] thinking that this device would prevent men's minds from growing arrogant through unlimited authority.

VII. Now at that time every man began to lift his head higher and to have his talents more in readiness. For kings hold the good in greater suspicion than the wicked, and to them the merit of others is always fraught with danger; still the free state, once liberty was won, waxed incredibly strong

quantum brevi creverit; tanta cupido gloriae in-
4 cesserat. Iam primum iuventus, simul ac belli
patiens erat, in castris per laborem usum militiae [1]
discebat magisque in decoris armis et militaribus
equis quam in scortis atque conviviis lubidinem
5 habebant. Igitur talibus viris non labor insolitus,
non locus ullus asper aut arduus erat, non armatus
6 hostis formidulosus; virtus omnia domuerat. Sed
gloriae maximum certamen inter ipsos erat; se
quisque hostem ferire, murum ascendere, conspici
dum tale facinus faceret, properabat; eas divitias,
eam bonam famam magnamque nobilitatem putabant. Laudis avidi, pecuniae liberales erant; glo-
7 riam ingentem, divitias honestas volebant. Memorare possem quibus in locis maximas hostium
copias populus Romanus parva manu fuderit, quas
urbis natura munitas pugnando ceperit, ni ea res
longius nos ab incepto traheret.

VIII. Sed profecto fortuna in omni re dominatur;
ea res cunctas ex lubidine magis quam ex vero
2 celebrat obscuratque. Atheniensium res gestae,
sicuti ego aestumo, satis amplae magnificaeque
fuere, verum aliquanto minores tamen quam fama
3 feruntur. Sed quia provenere ibi scriptorum magna
ingenia, per terrarum orbem Atheniensium facta pro
4 maximis celebrantur. Ita eorum qui ea [2] fecere

---

[1] usum militiae, *T, Veget.* i. 4 (*Qπ*); usu militiae, *P*[1];
usum militiam, *P*[2]*M*; et usum militiam, *H*; usu militiam,
the other mss. and Veget. (*M*).

[2] ea, *mss.* ("*added later in P,*" *Ahlb.*); *omitted by Hieron.
vit. Hilarion.* 1; *Aug. Civ. D.* xviii. 2, *Ah, Or.*

and great in a remarkably short time, such was the thirst for glory that had filled men's minds. To begin with, as soon as the young men could endure the hardships of war, they were taught a soldier's duties in camp under a vigorous discipline, and they took more pleasure in handsome arms and war horses than in harlots and revelry. To such men consequently no labour was unfamiliar, no region too rough or too steep, no armed foeman was terrible; valour was all in all. Nay, their hardest struggle for glory was with one another; each man strove to be first to strike down the foe, to scale a wall, to be seen of all while doing such a deed. This they considered riches, this fair fame and high nobility. It was praise they coveted, but they were lavish of money; their aim was unbounded renown, but only such riches as could be gained honourably. I might name the battlefields on which the Romans with a mere handful of men routed great armies of their adversaries, and the cities fortified by nature which they took by assault, were it not that such a theme would carry me too far from my subject.

VIII. But beyond question Fortune holds sway everywhere. It is she that makes all events famous or obscure according to her caprice rather than in accordance with the truth. The acts of the Athenians, in my judgment, were indeed great and glorious enough, but nevertheless somewhat less important than fame represents them. But because Athens produced writers of exceptional talent,[1] the exploits of the men of Athens are heralded throughout the world as unsurpassed. Thus the merit of those who

---

[1] Such as Herodotus, Thucydides, and Xenophon.

virtus tanta habetur, quantum ea[1] verbis potuere
5 extollere praeclara ingenia. At populo Romano
numquam ea copia fuit, quia prudentissumus quisque
maxume negotiosus erat; ingenium nemo sine
corpore exercebat; optumus quisque facere quam
dicere, sua ab aliis benefacta laudari quam ipse
aliorum narrare malebat.

IX. Igitur domi militiaeque boni mores colebantur,
concordia maxuma, minuma avaritia erat, ius bo-
numque apud eos non legibus magis quam natura
2 valebat. Iurgia, discordias, simultates cum hostibus
exercebant, cives cum civibus de virtute certabant.
In suppliciis deorum magnifici, domi parci, in amicos
3 fideles erant. Duabus his artibus, audacia in bello,
ubi pax evenerat aequitate seque remque publicam
4 curabant. Quarum rerum ego maxuma documenta
haec habeo, quod in bello saepius vindicatum est in
eos qui contra imperium in hostem pugnaverant
quique tardius revocati proelio excesserant, quam
qui signa relinquere aut pulsi loco cedere ausi erant;
5 in pace vero, quod beneficiis magis[2] quam metu
imperium agitabant, et accepta iniuria ignoscere
quam persequi malebant.

X. Sed ubi labore atque iustitia res publica crevit,
reges magni bello domiti, nationes ferae et populi
ingentes vi subacti, Carthago aemula imperi Romani

---

[1] eam, *Fn, Hieron, l.c., Aug. l.c. (cf. Vopisc. Prob. 1. 1),
Ah. Or* ; ea, *the other mss.*
[2] magis *omitted in Pls.*

did the deeds is rated as high as brilliant minds have been able to exalt the deeds themselves by words of praise. But the Roman people never had that advantage, since their ablest men were always most engaged with affairs; their minds were never employed apart from their bodies; the best citizen preferred action to words, and thought that his own brave deeds should be lauded by others rather than that theirs should be recounted by him.

IX. Accordingly, good morals were cultivated at home and in the field; there was the greatest harmony and little or no avarice; justice and probity prevailed among them, thanks not so much to laws as to nature. Quarrels, discord, and strife were reserved for their enemies; citizen vied with citizen only for the prize of merit. They were lavish in their offerings to the gods, frugal in the home, loyal to their friends. By practising these two qualities, boldness in warfare and justice when peace came, they watched over themselves and their country. In proof of these statements I present this convincing evidence: firstly, in time of war punishment was more often inflicted for attacking the enemy contrary to orders, or for withdrawing too tardily when recalled from the field, than for venturing to abandon the standards or to give ground under stress; and secondly, in time of peace they ruled by kindness rather than fear, and when wronged preferred forgiveness to vengeance.

X. But when our country had grown great through toil and the practice of justice, when great kings had been vanquished in war, savage tribes and mighty peoples subdued by force of arms, when Carthage, the rival of Rome's sway, had perished root and

ab stirpe interiit, cuncta maria terraeque patebant,
2 saevire fortuna ac miscere omnia coepit. Qui
labores, pericula, dubias atque asperas res facile
toleraverant, eis otium, divitiae,[1] optanda alias, oneri
3 miseriaeque fuere. Igitur primo pecuniae, deinde
imperi cupido crevit; ea quasi materies omnium
4 malorum fuere. Namque avaritia fidem, probitatem
ceterasque artis bonas subvortit; pro his superbiam,
crudelitatem, deos neglegere, omnia venalia habere
5 edocuit. Ambitio multos mortalis falsos fieri subegit, aliud clausum in pectore aliud in lingua
promptum habere, amicitias inimicitiasque non ex
re sed ex commodo aestumare magisque voltum
6 quam ingenium bonum habere. Haec primo
paulatim crescere, interdum vindicari; post, ubi
contagio quasi pestilentia invasit, civitas immutata,
imperium ex iustissumo atque optumo crudele in-
tolerandumque factum.

XI. Sed primo magis ambitio quam avaritia
animos hominum exercebat, quod tamen vitium
2 propius virtutem erat. Nam gloriam, honorem,
imperium bonus et ignavus aeque sibi exoptant; sed
ille vera via nititur, huic quia bonae artes desunt,
3 dolis atque fallaciis contendit. Avaritia pecuniae
studium habet, quam nemo sapiens concupivit; ea
quasi venenis malis imbuta corpus animumque virilem
effeminat, semper infinita,[2] insatiabilis est, neque copia
4 neque inopia minuitur. Sed postquam L. Sulla
armis recepta re publica bonis initiis malos eventus

---

[1] divitiaeque, A^2CB, Ah.   [2] infinita et, *Gell.* iii. 1. 2, Ah.

branch, and all seas and lands were open, then Fortune began to grow cruel and to bring confusion into all our affairs. Those who had found it easy to bear hardship and dangers, anxiety and adversity, found leisure and wealth, desirable under other circumstances, a burden and a curse. Hence the lust for money first, then for power, grew upon them; these were, I may say, the root of all evils. For avarice destroyed honour, integrity, and all other noble qualities; taught in their place insolence, cruelty, to neglect the gods, to set a price on everything. Ambition drove many men to become false; to have one thought locked in the breast, another ready on the tongue; to value friendships and enmities not on their merits but by the standard of self-interest, and to show a good front rather than a good heart. At first these vices grew slowly, from time to time they were punished; finally, when the disease had spread like a deadly plague, the state was changed and a government second to none in equity and excellence became cruel and intolerable.

XI. But at first men's souls were actuated less by avarice than by ambition—a fault, it is true, but not so far removed from virtue; for the noble and the base alike long for glory, honour, and power, but the former mount by the true path, whereas the latter, being destitute of noble qualities, rely upon craft and deception. Avarice implies a desire for money, which no wise man covets; steeped as it were with noxious poisons, it renders the most manly body and soul effeminate; it is ever unbounded and insatiable, nor can either plenty or want make it less. But after Lucius Sulla, having gained control of the state by arms,[1] brought everything to a bad end

[1] See note on v. 6. He died in 78 B.C.

habuit, rapere omnes,[1] trahere, domum alius alius
agros cupere, neque modum neque modestiam
victores habere, foeda crudeliaque in civis facinora
5 facere. Huc accedebat quod L. Sulla exercitum
quem in Asia ductaverat, quo sibi fidum faceret,
contra morem maiorum luxuriose nimisque liberaliter
habuerat. Loca amoena, voluptaria facile in otio
6 ferocis militum animos molliverant. Ibi primum
insuevit exercitus populi Romani amare, potare ;
signa, tabulas pictas, vasa caelata mirari ; ea privatim et publice rapere, delubra spoliare, sacra
7 profanaque omnia polluere. Igitur ei milites, postquam victoriam adepti sunt, nihil reliqui victis
fecere. Quippe secundae res sapientium animos
fatigant, ne[2] illi corruptis moribus victoriae
temperarent.

XII. Postquam divitiae honori esse coepere et
eas gloria, imperium, potentia sequebatur, hebescere
virtus, paupertas probro haberi, innocentia pro mali-
2 volentia duci coepit. Igitur ex divitiis iuventutem
luxuria atque avaritia cum superbia invasere ; rapere,
consumere, sua parvi pendere, aliena cupere, pudorem, pudicitiam, divina atque humana promiscua,
nihil pensi neque moderati habere.

3 Operae pretium est, cum domos atque villas
cognoveris in urbium modum exaedificatas, visere
templa deorum, quae nostri maiores, religiosissumi

[1] Referring respectively to military and political power.

from a good beginning, all men began to rob and pillage. One coveted a house, another lands; the victors showed neither moderation nor restraint, but shamefully and cruelly wronged their fellow citizens. Besides all this, Lucius Sulla, in order to secure the loyalty of the army which he led into Asia, had allowed it a luxury and license foreign to the manners of our forefathers; and in the intervals of leisure those charming and voluptuous lands had easily demoralized the warlike spirit of his soldiers. There it was that an army of the Roman people first learned to indulge in women and drink; to admire statues, paintings, and chased vases, to steal them from private houses and public places, to pillage shrines, and to desecrate everything, both sacred and profane. These soldiers, therefore, after they had won the victory, left nothing to the vanquished. In truth, prosperity tries the souls even of the wise; how then should men of depraved character like these make a moderate use of victory?

XII. As soon as riches came to be held in honour, when glory, dominion,[1] and power[1] followed in their train, virtue began to lose its lustre, poverty to be considered a disgrace, blamelessness to be termed malevolence. Therefore as the result of riches, luxury and greed, united with insolence, took possession of our young manhood. They pillaged, squandered; set little value on their own, coveted the goods of others; they disregarded modesty, chastity, everything human and divine; in short, they were utterly thoughtless and reckless.

It is worth your while, when you look upon houses and villas reared to the size of cities, to pay a visit to the temples of the gods built by our forefathers,

4 mortales, fecere. Verum illi delubra deorum pie-
tate, domos suas gloria decorabant, neque victis
5 quicquam praeter iniuriae licentiam eripiebant. At
hi contra ignavissumi homines per summum scelus
omnia ea sociis adimere, quae fortissumi viri victores reliquerant; proinde quasi iniuriam facere id
demum esset imperio uti.

XIII. Nam quid ea memorem, quae nisi eis qui
videre nemini credibilia sunt, a privatis compluribus
2 subvorsos montis, maria constrata esse? Quibus
mihi videntur ludibrio fuisse divitiae; quippe quas
honeste habere licebat, abuti per turpitudinem pro-
3 perabant. Sed lubido stupri, ganeae ceterique cultus
non minor incesserat; viri muliebria pati, mulieres
pudicitiam in propatulo habere; vescendi causa terra
marique omnia exquirere, dormire prius quam somni
cupido esset, non famem aut sitim neque frigus
neque lassitudinem opperiri sed ea omnia luxu ante-
4 capere. Haec iuventutem, ubi familiares opes defe-
5 cerant, ad facinora incendebant. Animus imbutus
malis artibus haud facile lubidinibus carebat; eo pro-
fusius omnibus modis quaestui atque sumptui deditus
erat.

---

¹ Referring to Xerxes. Lucullus, called by Pompey
"Xerxes togatus," and Pompey himself cut through hills
to bring salt water into their fishponds, and villas built out
into the sea existed in Sallust's time at Baiae. See Horace,
Odes 3. 1. 33:

> *Contracta pisces aequora sentiunt*
> *iactis in altum molibus.*

most reverent of men. But they adorned the shrines of the gods with piety, their own homes with glory, while from the vanquished they took naught save the power of doing harm. The men of to-day, on the contrary, basest of creatures, with supreme wickedness are robbing our allies of all that those heroes in the hour of victory had left them; they act as though the one and only way to rule were to wrong.

XIII. Why, pray, should I speak of things which are incredible except to those who have seen them, that a host of private men have levelled mountains and built upon the seas?[1] To such men their riches seem to me to have been but a plaything; for while they might have enjoyed them honourably, they made haste to squander them shamefully. Nay more, the passion which arose for lewdness, gluttony, and the other attendants of luxury was equally strong; men played the woman, women offered their chastity for sale; to gratify their palates they scoured land and sea; they slept before they needed sleep; they did not await the coming of hunger or thirst, of cold or of weariness, but all these things their self-indulgence anticipated.[2] Such were the vices that incited the young men to crime, as soon as they had run through their property. Their minds, habituated to evil practices, could not easily refrain from self-indulgence, and so they abandoned themselves the more recklessly to every means of gain as well as of extravagance.

---

[2] They forestalled hunger and thirst by appetizers and even by emetics (cf. Sen. *Cons. ad Helv.* 10. 3, *vomunt ut edant, edunt ut vomant*), cold and weariness by baths and indolent habits.

23

XIV. In tanta tamque corrupta civitate Catilina, id quod factu facillumum erat, omnium flagitiorum atque facinorum circum se tamquam stipatorum ca-2 tervas habebat. Nam quicumque impudicus, ganeo, aleator,[1] manu, ventre, pene bona patria laceraverat, quique alienum aes grande conflaverat, quo flagitium 3 aut facinus redimeret, praeterea omnes undique parricidae, sacrilegi, convicti iudiciis aut pro factis iudicium timentes, ad hoc quos manus atque lingua periurio aut sanguine civili alebat, postremo omnes quos flagitium, egestas, conscius animus exagitabat, 4 ei Catilinae proxumi familiaresque erant. Quodsi quis etiam a culpa vacuus in amicitiam eius inciderat, cotidiano usu atque illecebris facile par similisque ceteris efficiebatur. Sed maxume adulescentium 5 familiaritates appetebat; eorum animi molles etiam[2] 6 et fluxi dolis haud difficulter capiebantur. Nam ut cuiusque studium ex aetate flagrabat, aliis scorta praebere, aliis canes atque equos mercari, postremo neque sumptui neque modestiae[3] suae parcere, dum 7 illos obnoxios fidosque sibi faceret. Scio fuisse non nullos qui ita existumarent, iuventutem quae domum Catilinae frequentabat parum honeste pudicitiam habuisse; sed ex aliis rebus magis, quam quod cuiquam id compertum foret, haec fama valebat.

XV. Iam primum adulescens Catilina multa nefanda stupra fecerat, cum virgine nobili, cum sacer-

---

[1] ganeo, aleator, *Wölfflin* ; adulter, ganeo, *mss.*
[2] etiam et, *PA¹l* ; et aetate, *Ysnm* ; aetate et, *A²CB*.
[3] modestiae, *mss.* ; molestiae, *Madvig, Advers. Crit.* 2. 291.

XIV. In a city so great and so corrupt Catiline found it a very easy matter to surround himself, as by a bodyguard, with troops of criminals and reprobates of every kind. For whatever wanton, glutton, or gamester had wasted his patrimony in play, feasting, or debauchery; anyone who had contracted an immense debt that he might buy immunity from disgrace or crime; all, furthermore, from every side who had been convicted of murder or sacrilege, or feared prosecution for their crimes; those, too, whom hand and tongue supported by perjury or the blood of their fellow citizens; finally, all who were hounded by disgrace, poverty, or an evil conscience—all these were nearest and dearest to Catiline. And if any guiltless man did chance to become his friend, daily intercourse and the allurements of vice soon made him as bad or almost as bad as the rest. But most of all Catiline sought the intimacy of the young; their minds, still pliable as they were and easily moulded, were without difficulty ensnared by his wiles. For carefully noting the passion which burned in each, according to his time of life, he found harlots for some or bought dogs and horses for others; in fine, he spared neither expense nor his own decency, provided he could make them submissive and loyal to himself. I am aware that some have believed that the young men who frequented Catiline's house set but little store by their chastity; but that report became current rather for other reasons than because anyone had evidence of its truth.

XV. Even in youth Catiline had many shameful intrigues—with a maiden of noble rank, with a priestess of Vesta[1]—and other affairs equally un-

---

[1] Fabia, half-sister of Terentia, Cicero's wife. Catiline was acquitted.

dote Vestae, alia huiuscemodi contra ius fasque.
2 Postremo captus amore Aureliae Orestillae, cuius
praeter formam nihil umquam bonus laudavit, quod
ea nubere illi dubitabat, timens privignum adulta
aetate, pro certo creditur necato filio vacuam domum
3 scelestis nuptiis fecisse. Quae quidem res mihi in
4 primis videtur causa fuisse facinus maturandi. Namque animus impurus, dis hominibusque infestus,
neque vigiliis neque quietibus sedari poterat; ita
5 conscientia mentem excitam vastabat. Igitur color[1]
ei exanguis, foedi oculi, citus modo modo tardus in-
cessus; prorsus in facie voltuque vecordia inerat.

XVI. Sed iuventutem, quam, ut supra diximus,
2 illexerat, multis modis mala facinora edocebat. Ex
illis testis signatoresque falsos commodare; fidem,
fortunas, pericula vilia habere, post ubi eorum famam
atque pudorem attriverat, maiora alia imperabat.
3 Si causa peccandi in praesens minus suppetebat,
nihilo minus insontis sicuti sontis circumvenire, iu-
gulare; scilicet, ne per otium torpescerent manus
aut animus, gratuito potius malus atque crudelis
erat.
4   Eis amicis sociisque confisus Catilina, simul quod
aes alienum per omnis terras ingens erat et quod
plerique Sullani milites largius suo usi rapinarum et
victoriae veteris memores civile bellum exoptabant,

---

[1] color, *mss.*; colos, *Probus, Catholica* 4. 15. 14 K and 4. 23. 34.

---

[1] This trenchant phrase seems to have originated with
Cicero, *Cat.* 1. 14, *cum morte superioris uxoris novis nuptiis
domum vacuefecisses*; *cf.* Livy 1. 46. 9, *cum domos vacuas
novo matrimonio fecissent.*

lawful and impious. At last he was seized with a passion for Aurelia Orestilla, in whom no good man ever commended anything save her beauty; and when she hesitated to marry him because she was afraid of his stepson, then a grown man, it is generally believed that he murdered the young man in order to make an empty house for this criminal marriage.[1] In fact, I think that this was his special motive for hastening his plot; for his guilt-stained soul, at odds with gods and men, could find rest neither waking nor sleeping, so cruelly did conscience ravage his overwrought mind. Hence his pallid complexion, his bloodshot eyes, his gait now fast, now slow; in short, his face and his every glance showed the madman.

XVI. To the young men whom he had ensnared, as I have described, he taught many forms of wickedness. From their number he supplied false witnesses and forgers; he bade them make light of honour, fortune, and dangers; then, when he had sapped their good repute and modesty, he called for still greater crimes. If there was no immediate motive for wrong doing, he nevertheless waylaid and murdered innocent as well as guilty;[2] indeed, he preferred to be needlessly vicious and cruel rather than to allow their hands and spirits to grow weak through lack of practice.

Relying upon such friends and accomplices as these, Catiline formed the plan of overthrowing the government, both because his own debt was enormous in all parts of the world and because the greater number of Sulla's veterans, who had squandered their property and now thought with longing of

[2] That is, through his pupils in crime.

opprimundae rei publicae consilium cepit. In Italia
nullus exercitus, Cn. Pompeius in extremis terris
bellum gerebat; ipsi consulatum petenti magna
spes, senatus nihil sane intentus; tutae tranquillae-
que res omnes, sed ea prorsus opportuna Catilinae.

XVII. Igitur circiter kalendas Iunias L. Caesare
et C. Figulo consulibus primo singulos appellare,
hortari alios, alios temptare; opes suas, imparatam
rem publicam, magna praemia coniurationis docere.
2 Ubi satis explorata sunt quae voluit, in unum omnis
convocat quibus maxuma necessitudo et plurumum
3 audaciae inerat.   Eo convenere senatorii ordinis
P. Lentulus Sura, P. Autronius, L. Cassius Longinus,
C. Cethegus, P. et Ser. Sullae Ser. filii, L. Vargunteius, Q. Annius, M. Porcius Laeca, L. Bestia, Q.
4 Curius; praeterea ex equestri ordine M. Fulvius
Nobilior, L. Statilius, P. Gabinius Capito, C. Cornelius; ad hoc multi ex coloniis et municipiis, domi
5 nobiles.   Erant praeterea complures paulo occultius
consili huiusce participes nobiles, quos magis dominationis spes hortabatur quam inopia aut alia neces-
6 situdo.   Ceterum iuventus pleraque, sed maxume
nobilium, Catilinae inceptis favebat, quibus in otio
vel magnifice vel molliter vivere copia erat, incerta
7 pro certis, bellum quam pacem malebant.   Fuere
item ea tempestate qui crederent M. Licinium

---

[1] He was at the time in Syria, having defeated Mithridates
in Pontus.   [2] 64 B.C.

their former pillage and victories, were eager for civil war. There was no army in Italy; Gnaeus Pompeius was waging war in distant parts of the world;[1] Catiline himself had high hopes as a candidate for the consulship; the senate was anything but alert; all was peaceful and quiet; this was his golden opportunity.

XVII. Accordingly, towards the first of June in the consulate of Lucius Caesar and Gaius Figulus,[2] he addressed his followers at first one by one, encouraging some and sounding others. He pointed out his own resources, the unprepared condition of the state, the great prizes of conspiracy. When he had such information as he desired, he assembled all those who were most desperate and most reckless. There were present from the senatorial order Publius Lentulus Sura, Publius Autronius, Lucius Cassius Longinus, Gaius Cethegus, Publius and Servius Sulla, sons of Servius, Lucius Vargunteius, Quintus Annius, Marcus Porcius Laeca, Lucius Bestia, Quintus Curius; also of the equestrian order, Marcus Fulvius Nobilior, Lucius Statilius, Publius Gabinius Capito, Gaius Cornelius; besides these there were many men from the colonies and free towns who were of noble rank at home. There were, moreover, several nobles who had a somewhat more secret connection with the plot, men who were prompted rather by the hope of power than by want or any other exigency. The greater part of the young men also, in particular those of high position, were favourable to Catiline's project; for although in quiet times they had the means of living elegantly or luxuriously, they preferred uncertainty to certainty, war to peace. There were also at that time some who believed that Marcus

Crassum non ignarum eius consili fuisse; quia Cn.
Pompeius invisus ipsi magnum exercitum ductabat,
cuiusvis opes voluisse contra illius potentiam crescere, simul confisum, si coniuratio valuisset, facile
apud illos principem se fore.

XVIII. Sed antea item coniuravere pauci contra
2 rem publicam, in quis[1] Catilina fuit; de qua quam
verissume potero dicam. L. Tullo et M'.[2] Lepido
consulibus P. Autronius et P. Sulla designati consules legibus ambitus interrogati poenas dederant.
3 Post paulo Catilina pecuniarum repetundarum reus
prohibitus erat consulatum petere, quod intra legi-
4 tumos dies profiteri nequiverat.[3] Erat eodem tempore Cn. Piso, adulescens nobilis, summae audaciae,
egens, factiosus, quem ad perturbandam rem publi-
5 cam inopia atque mali mores stimulabant. Cum hoc
Catilina et Autronius circiter nonas Decembris consilio communicato parabant in Capitolio kalendis
Ianuariis L. Cottam et L. Torquatum consules interficere, ipsi fascibus correptis Pisonem cum exercitu

---

[1] quis, *Diomedes* 1. 445. 23 κ ; quibus, *mss.*
[2] M., *mss.*
[3] nequiverat, *MT*[2]; nequiverit, *the other mss.*

---

[1] The so-called First Conspiracy of Catiline, in which
Catiline bore a subordinate part, if he was connected with it
at all. It owes its name to the fact that the second conspiracy was the direct outgrowth of the earlier one.
[2] 66 B.C.
[3] These included a fine, the loss of their office, and expulsion from the senate.

Licinius Crassus was not wholly ignorant of the plot; that because his enemy Gaius Pompeius was in command of a large army, he was willing to see anyone's influence grow in opposition to the power of his rival, fully believing meanwhile that if the conspirators should be successful, he would easily be the leading man among them.

XVIII. Now, even before that time a few men had conspired against the government, and among them was Catiline; of that affair[1] I shall give as true an account as I am able.

In the consulship of Lucius Tullus and Manius Lepidus,[2] the consuls elect, Publius Autronius and Publius Sulla, were arraigned under the law against bribery and paid the penalties.[3] A little later Catiline was charged with extortion and prevented from standing for the consulship, because he had been unable to announce his candidacy within the prescribed number of days.[4] There was at that same time a young noble called Gnaeus Piso, a man of the utmost recklessness, poor, and given to intrigue, who was being goaded on by need of funds and an evil character to overthrow the government. He revealed his plans to Catiline and Autronius; they in concert with him began, about the fifth of December, to make preparations to murder the consuls Lucius Cotta and Lucius Torquatus in the Capitol on the first of January; they then proposed that they themselves should seize the fasces[5] and dispatch Piso with an army to take possession of the two

[4] This was a *trinundinum*, or "three weeks."

[5] A bundle of rods with an axe projecting from their middle, carried by lictors before the higher magistrates at Rome. The axes were removed when the magistrates were within the city.

6 ad optinendas duas Hispanias mittere. Ea re cognita rursus in nonas Februarias consilium caedis
7 transtulerant. Iam tum non consulibus modo, sed
plerisque senatoribus perniciem machinabantur.
8 Quodni Catilina maturasset pro curia signum sociis
dare, eo die post conditam urbem Romam pessumum
facinus patratum foret. Quia nondum frequentes
armati convenerant, ea res consilium diremit.

XIX. Postea Piso in citeriorem Hispaniam quaestor pro praetore missus est adnitente Crasso, quod
eum infestum inimicum Cn. Pompeio cognoverat.
2 Neque tamen senatus provinciam invitus dederat,
quippe foedum hominem a re publica procul esse
volebat; simul quia boni complures praesidium in eo
putabant et iam tum potentia Pompei formidulosa
3 erat. Sed is Piso in provincia[1] ab equitibus Hispanis quos in exercitu ductabat iter faciens occisus
4 est. Sunt qui ita dicant, imperia eius iniusta, su-
5 perba, crudelia barbaros nequivisse pati; alii autem
equites illos Cn. Pompei veteres fidosque clientis
voluntate eius Pisonem aggressos; numquam His-
panos praeterea tale facinus fecisse, sed imperia
saeva multa antea perpessos. Nos eam rem in
medio relinquemus. De superiore coniuratione satis
dictum.

XX. Catilina ubi eos quos paulo ante memoravi
convenisse videt, tametsi cum singulis multa saepe

[1] provincia, *Ysm*; provinciam, *XNFln.*

---

[1] For a different account see Suetonius, *Jul.* 9.

Spanish provinces. Upon the discovery of their plot they postponed their murderous design until the fifth of February. At that time they plotted the destruction not merely of the consuls but of many of the senators, and had Catiline not been over-hasty in giving the senate the signal to his accomplices in front of the senate-house, on that day the most dreadful crime since the founding of the city of Rome would have been perpetrated. But because the armed conspirators had not yet assembled in sufficient numbers, the affair came to naught.[1]

XIX. Piso was afterwards, through the efforts of Crassus, who knew him to be a deadly enemy of Gnaeus Pompeius, sent to Hither Spain with praetorian powers, although he was only a quaestor. The senate, however, had been quite willing to give him the province, wishing to remove the shameless fellow to a distance from the seat of government; moreover, many of the aristocracy thought they had in him a safeguard against Pompey, whose power was even then becoming formidable. Now this Piso was slain, while marching through his province, by the Spanish cavalry under his command. Some say that the barbarians could not endure his rule, unjust, insolent, and cruel; others, that the horsemen, who were old and devoted retainers of Pompey, attacked Piso at his instigation. The latter point out that the Spaniards had never before committed such a crime, but had tolerated many cruel rulers in former days. We shall not attempt to decide this question, and enough has been said about the first conspiracy.

XX. When Catiline saw before him the men whom I mentioned a short time ago, although he had often had long conferences with them individually, he

33

egerat, tamen in rem fore credens univorsos appellare et cohortari, in abditam partem aedium secedit atque ibi omnibus arbitris procul amotis orationem huiuscemodi habuit.

2 " Ni virtus fidesque vostra spectata mihi forent,[1] nequiquam opportuna res cecidisset; spes magna,
3 dominatio in manibus frustra fuissent, neque ego per ignaviam aut vana ingenia incerta pro certis captarem. Sed quia multis et magnis tempestatibus vos cognovi fortis fidosque mihi, eo animus ausus est maxumum atque pulcherrumum facinus incipere, simul quia vobis eadem quae mihi bona malaque esse
4 intellexi; nam idem velle atque idem nolle, ea de-
5 mum firma amicitia est. Sed ego quae mente agitavi
6 omnes iam antea divorsi audistis. Ceterum mihi in dies magis animus accenditur, cum considero quae condicio vitae futura sit, nisi nosmet ipsi vindicamus
7 in libertatem. Nam postquam res publica in paucorum potentium ius atque dicionem concessit, semper illis reges, tetrarchae vectigales esse, populi, nationes stipendia pendere ; ceteri omnes, strenui, boni,[2] nobiles atque ignobiles, volgus fuimus sine gratia, sine auctoritate, eis obnoxii, quibus, si res publica valeret,
8 formidini essemus. Itaque omnis gratia, potentia, honos, divitiae apud illos sunt aut ubi illi volunt; nobis reliquere pericula, repulsas, iudicia, egestatem.
9 Quae quousque tandem patiemini, o fortissumi viri ?

---

[1] foret, *VP²n, Serv. Ge.* i. 260; forent, *XYlsm. See Ahlb. Proleg.* p. 169.
[2] boni mali, *Gudeman, omitting* strenui.

thought that it would be well to address and encourage the entire body. Accordingly, withdrawing to a private room of the house and excluding all witnesses, he made the following speech:

"If I had not already tested your courage and loyalty, in vain would a great opportunity have presented itself; high hopes and power would have been placed in my hands to no purpose, nor would I with the aid of cowards or inconstant hearts grasp at uncertainty in place of certainty. But because I have learned in many and great emergencies that you are brave and faithful to me, my mind has had the courage to set on foot a mighty and glorious enterprise, and also because I perceive that you and I hold the same view of what is good and evil; for agreement in likes and dislikes—this, and this only, is what constitutes true friendship. As for the designs which I have formed, they have already been explained to you all individually. But my resolution is fired more and more every day, when I consider under what conditions we shall live if we do not take steps to emancipate ourselves. For ever since the state fell under the jurisdiction and sway of a few powerful men, it is always to them that kings and potentates are tributary and peoples and nations pay taxes. All the rest of us, energetic, able, nobles and commons, have made up the mob, without influence, without weight, and subservient to those to whom in a free state we should be an object of fear. Because of this, all influence, power, rank, and wealth are in their hands, or wherever they wish them to be; to us they have left danger, defeat, prosecutions, and poverty. How long, pray, will you endure this,

Nonne emori per virtutem praestat quam vitam
miseram atque inhonestam, ubi alienae superbiae
10 ludibrio fueris, per dedecus amittere? Verum enimvero, pro deum atque hominum fidem victoria in
manu nobis[1] est, viget aetas, animus valet; contra
illis annis atque divitiis omnia consenuerunt. Tantum modo incepto opus est; cetera res expediet.

11 Etenim quis mortalium, cui virile ingenium est, tolerare potest, illis divitias superare, quas profundant in
extruendo mari et montibus coaequandis, nobis rem
familiarem etiam ad necessaria deesse? Illos binas
aut amplius domos continuare, nobis larem familia-
12 rem nusquam ullum esse? Cum tabulas, signa, toreumata emunt, nova diruunt, alia aedificant, postremo
omnibus modis pecuniam trahunt, vexant, tamen
13 summa lubidine divitias suas vincere nequeunt. At
nobis est domi inopia, foris aes alienum, mala res,
spes multo asperior; denique quid reliqui habemus
14 praeter miseram animam? Quin igitur expergiscimini? En illa illa quam saepe optastis libertas,
praeterea divitiae, decus, gloria in oculis sita sunt.
15 Fortuna omnia ea victoribus praemia posuit. Res,
tempus, pericula, egestas, belli spolia magnifica
16 magis quam oratio mea vos hortantur. Vel imperatore vel milite me utimini; neque animus neque
17 corpus a vobis aberit. Haec ipsa, ut spero, vobiscum

[1] nobis in manu, *Prisc.* iii. 364. 3 κ; vobis, *VP²A²C²Bn.*

[1] See note on chap. xiii. 1.

brave hearts? Is it not better to die valiantly,
than ignominiously to lose our wretched and dishonoured lives after being the sport of others' insolence? Assuredly (I swear it by the faith of gods
and men!) victory is within our grasp. We are in
the prime of life, we are stout of heart; to them,
on the contrary, years and riches have brought
utter dotage. We need only to strike; the rest
will take care of itself. Pray, what man with the
spirit of a man can endure that our tyrants should
abound in riches, to squander in building upon the
sea and in levelling mountains,[1] while we lack the
means to buy the bare necessities of life? That
they should join their palaces by twos or even more,
while we have nowhere a hearthstone? They amass
paintings, statuary and chased vases,[2] tear down
new structures and erect others, in short misuse and
torment their wealth in every way; yet, with the
utmost extravagance, they cannot get the upper
hand of their riches. But we have destitution at
home, debt without, present misery and a still more
hopeless future; in short, what have we left, save
only the wretched breath of life? Awake then! Lo,
here, here before your eyes, is the freedom for which
you have often longed, and with it riches, honour,
and glory; Fortune offers all these things as prizes to
the victors. The undertaking itself, the opportunity,
the dangers, your need, the splendid spoils of war,
speak louder than any words of mine. Use me
either as your leader or as a soldier in the ranks;
my soul and my body shall be at your service.
These very schemes I hope to help you carry out

---

[2] *Toreumata* is the Greek equivalent of *vasa caelata*,
xi. 6.

una consul agam, nisi forte me animus fallit et vos
servire magis quam imperare parati estis."

XXI. Postquam accepere ea homines quibus mala
abunde omnia erat, sed neque res neque spes bona
ulla, tametsi illis quieta movere magna merces videbatur, tamen postulavere plerique ut proponeret
quae condicio belli foret, quae praemia armis pete-
2 rent, quid ubique opis aut spei haberent. Tum
Catilina polliceri tabulas novas, proscriptionem
locupletium, magistratus, sacerdotia, rapinas, alia
omnia quae bellum atque lubido victorum fert.
3 Praeterea esse in Hispania citeriore Pisonem, in
Mauretania cum exercitu P. Sittium Nucerinum,
consili sui participes; petere consulatum C. Antonium, quem sibi collegam fore speraret, hominem
et familiarem et omnibus necessitudinibus circumventum; cum eo se consulem initium agundi fac-
4 turum. Ad hoc maledictis increpabat omnis bonos,
suorum unum quemque nominans laudare; ad-
monebat alium egestatis, alium cupiditatis suae,
compluris periculi aut ignominiae, multos victoriae
5 Sullanae, quibus ea praedae fuerat. Postquam
omnium animos alacris videt, cohortatus ut petiti-
onem suam curae haberent, conventum dimisit.

XXII. Fuere ea tempestate qui dicerent Catilinam
oratione habita cum ad iusiurandum popularis sceleris
sui adigeret,[1] humani corporis sanguinem vino per-
2 mixtum in pateris circumtulisse; inde cum post
exsecrationem omnes degustavissent, sicuti in

[1] adigeret, *Eugraph. Ter. Ph.* 35 ; adiceret, *mss.*

as your consul, unless haply I delude myself and you are content to be slaves rather than to rule."

XXI. When these words fell upon the ears of men who had misfortune of every kind in excess, but neither means nor any honourable hope, although disorder alone seemed to them an ample reward, yet many of them called upon him to explain the conditions under which war would be waged, what the prizes of victory would be, and what resources or prospects they would have and in what quarter. Thereupon Catiline promised abolition of debts, the proscription of the rich, offices, priesthoods, plunder, and all the other spoils that war and the license of victors can offer. He added that Piso was in Hither Spain, Publius Sittius of Nuceria in Mauretania with an army, both of whom were partners in his plot; that Gaius Antonius was a candidate for the consulship, and, he hoped, would be his colleague, a man who was an intimate friend of his and was beset by every sort of necessity; consul with him, he would launch his undertaking. Thereupon he heaped maledictions upon all good citizens, lauded each of his own followers by name; he reminded one of his poverty, another of his ambition, several of their danger or disgrace, many of the victory of Sulla, which they had found a source of booty. When he saw that their spirits were all aflame, he dismissed the meeting, urging them to have his candidacy at heart.

XXII. It was said at the time that when Catiline, after finishing his address, compelled the participants in his crime to take an oath, he passed around bowls of human blood mixed with wine; that when after an imprecation upon traitors all had tasted it, as

sollemnibus sacris fieri consuevit, aperuisse consilium
suum; atque eo dictitare fecisse,[1] quo inter se fidi
3 magis forent, alius alii tanti facinoris conscii. Non
nulli ficta et haec et multa praeterea existumabant
ab eis qui Ciceronis invidiam, quae postea orta
est, leniri credebant atrocitate sceleris eorum qui
poenas dederant. Nobis ea res pro magnitudine
parum comperta est.

XXIII. Sed in ea coniuratione fuit Q. Curius,
natus haud obscuro loco, flagitiis atque facinoribus
coopertus, quem censores senatu probri gratia move-
2 rant. Huic homini non minor vanitas inerat quam
audacia; neque reticere quae audierat, neque
suamet ipse scelera occultare; prorsus neque dicere
3 neque facere quicquam pensi habebat. Erat ei cum
Fulvia, muliere nobili, stupri vetus consuetudo; cui
cum minus gratus esset, quia inopia minus largiri
poterat, repente glorians maria montisque polliceri
coepit et minari interdum ferro, ni sibi obnoxia
foret; postremo ferocius agitare quam solitus erat.
4 At Fulvia insolentiae[2] Curi causa cognita tale
periculum rei publicae haud occultum habuit, sed

---

[1] *Some good mss. omit or expunge this phrase. Ritschl
proposed omitting the whole phrase and Selling to omit* dictitare. Idque eo dicitur fecisse, *Bergk*; atque eo dixisse eam
rem fecisse *"aut similiter," Madvig*; atque eo se fecisse,
Summers; atque eo ita fecisse, *fortasse* divinam rem, *Ah*; *Or*.

[2] insolentiae, *N corr.*; *the other mss. have* insolentia.

is usual in solemn rites, he disclosed his project; and his end in so doing was, they say, that they might be more faithful to one another because they shared the guilty knowledge of so dreadful a deed. Others thought that these and many other details were invented by men who believed that the hostility which afterwards arose against Cicero would be moderated by exaggerating the guilt of the conspirators whom he had put to death. For my own part I have too little evidence for pronouncing upon a matter of such weight.

XXIII. Now one of the members of the conspiracy was Quintus Curius, a man of no mean birth but guilty of many shameful crimes, whom the censors[1] had expelled from the senate because of his immorality. This man was as untrustworthy as he was reckless; he could neither keep secret what he had heard nor conceal even his own misdeeds; he was utterly regardless of what he did or said. He had an intrigue of long standing with Fulvia, a woman of quality, and when he began to lose her favour because poverty compelled him to be less lavish, he suddenly fell to boasting, began to promise her seas and mountains,[2] and sometimes to threaten his mistress with the steel if she did not bow to his will; in brief, to show much greater assurance than before. But Fulvia, when she learned the cause of her lover's overbearing conduct, had no thought of concealing such a peril to her country, but without mentioning the name of her informant she told a

[1] Probably Cn. Lentulus and L. Gellius, in 70 B.C.; see Livy, *Epit.* xcviii.
[2] *cf.* Terence, *Phormio* 68: *modo non montis auri pollicens,* a common proverbial expression; *maria* seems to be rarer in this sense.

sublato auctore de Catilinae coniuratione quae
quoque modo audierat compluribus narravit.

5 Ea res in primis studia hominum accendit ad
6 consulatum mandandum M. Tullio Ciceroni. Namque antea pleraque nobilitas invidia aestuabat[1]
et quasi pollui consulatum credebant, si eum quamvis egregius homo novus adeptus foret. Sed ubi
periculum advenit, invidia atque superbia post fuere.

XXIV. Igitur comitiis habitis consules declarantur M. Tullius et C. Antonius, quod factum primo
2 popularis coniurationis concusserat. Neque tamen
Catilinae furor minuebatur, sed in dies plura agitare,
arma per Italiam locis opportunis parare, pecuniam
sua aut amicorum fide sumptam mutuam Faesulas
ad Manlium quendam portare, qui postea princeps
3 fuit belli faciundi. Ea tempestate plurimos cuiusque
generis homines adscivisse sibi dicitur, mulieres
etiam aliquot, quae primo ingentis sumptus stupro
corporis toleraverant, post ubi aetas tantum modo
quaestui neque luxuriae modum fecerat, aes alienum
4 grande conflaverant. Per eas se Catilina credebat
posse servitia urbana sollicitare, urbem incendere,
viros earum vel adiungere sibi vel interficere.

XXV. Sed in eis erat Sempronia, quae multa
2 saepe virilis audaciae facinora commiserat. Haec
mulier genere atque forma, praeterea viro atque[2]
liberis satis fortunata fuit; litteris Graecis et Latinis

[1] aestimabat, *X (corr. B)* *n.*
[2] *Omitted by* A^1m, *Fronto*, p. 110 N., *Arus.* vii. 473. 28 K,
Eugr. Ter. Andr. 97; *Ah*; *Or.* *Ah would omit preceding* atque.

---

[1] Meaning one whose ancestors had held no curule office;
that is, had not been curule aedile, praetor or consul.

42

number of people what she had heard of Catiline's conspiracy from various sources.

It was this discovery in particular which aroused a general desire to confer the consulate upon Marcus Tullius Cicero; for before that most of the nobles were consumed with jealousy and thought the office in a way prostituted if a "new man,"[1] however excellent, should obtain it. But when danger came, jealousy and pride fell into the background.

XXIV. Accordingly, when the elections had been held Marcus Tullius and Gaius Antonius were proclaimed consuls, and this at first filled the conspirators with consternation. And yet Catiline's frenzy did not abate. On the contrary, he increased his activity every day, made collections of arms at strategic points in Italy, and borrowed money on his own credit or that of his friends, sending it to Faesulae to a certain Manlius, who afterwards was the first to take the field. At that time Catiline is said to have gained the support of many men of all conditions and even of some women; the latter at first had met their enormous expenses by prostitution, but later, when their time of life had set a limit to their traffic but not to their extravagance, had contracted a huge debt. Through their help Catiline believed that he could tempt the city slaves to his side and set fire to Rome; and then either attach the women's husbands to his cause or make away with them.

XXV. Now among these women was Sempronia, who had often committed many crimes of masculine daring. In birth and beauty, in her husband also and children, she was abundantly favoured by fortune; well read in the literature of Greece and

43

docta, psallere et[1] saltare elegantius, quam necesse
est probae, multa alia, quae instrumenta luxuriae
3 sunt. Sed ei cariora semper omnia quam decus atque
pudicitia fuit; pecuniae an famae minus parceret,
haud facile discerneres; lubido[2] sic accensa, ut
4 saepius peteret viros quam peteretur. Sed ea saepe
antehac fidem prodiderat, creditum abiuraverat,
caedis conscia fuerat, luxuria atque inopia praeceps
5 abierat. Verum ingenium eius haud absurdum;
posse versus facere, iocum movere, sermone uti vel
modesto vel molli vel procaci; prorsus multae
facetiae multusque lepos inerat.

XXVI. His rebus comparatis Catilina nihilo minus
in proxumum annum consulatum petebat, sperans,
si designatus foret, facile se ex voluntate Antonio
usurum. Neque interea quietus erat, sed omnibus
2 modis insidias parabat Ciceroni. Neque illi tamen
3 ad cavendum dolus aut astutiae deerant. Namque
a principio consulatus sui multa pollicendo per
Fulviam effecerat ut Q. Curius, de quo paulo ante
4 memoravi, consilia Catilinae sibi proderet. Ad hoc
collegam suum Antonium pactione provinciae per-

---

[1] *Omitted by Fronto, l.c. and Macrob.* iii. 14. 5 ; *Ah* ; *Or.*
[2] lubido, *P¹Ylsm* ; libidine, *X and m.* 2 *PKHTDFl.*

---

[1] See chap. xxiv. 2.
[2] In spite of his revolutionary designs.
[3] 62 B.C.   [4] See chap. xxiii. 3.   [5] Chap. xxiii.
[6] The Sempronian law of Gaius Gracchus provided that
two provinces should be assigned to the consuls in advance

Rome, able to play the lyre and dance more skil-fully than an honest woman need, and having many other accomplishments which minister to voluptuous-ness. But there was nothing which she held so cheap as modesty and chastity; you could not easily say whether she was less sparing of her money or her honour; her desires were so ardent that she sought men more often than she was sought by them. Even before the time of the conspiracy she had often broken her word, repudiated her debts, been privy to murder; poverty and extravagance combined had driven her headlong. Nevertheless, she was a woman of no mean endowments; she could write verses, bandy jests, and use language which was modest, or tender, or wanton; in fine, she possessed a high degree of wit and of charm.

XXVI. After making these preparations [1] Catiline nevertheless [2] became a candidate for the consulship of the following year, [3] hoping that if he should be elected he could easily do whatever he wished with Antonius. In the meantime he was not idle, but kept laying plots of all kinds against Cicero, who, however, did not lack the craft and address to escape them. For immediately after the beginning of his consulate, by dint of many promises made through Fulvia, [4] Cicero had in-duced Quintus Curius, the man whom I mentioned a little while ago, [5] to reveal Catiline's designs to him. Furthermore, he had persuaded his colleague Antonius, by agreeing to make over his province [6] to

of the elections, which were later apportioned by agreement or by lot. Cicero offered Antonius the rich province of Macedonia, in place of Gaul, which the fortune of the lot had given him.

pulerat ne contra rem publicam sentiret; circum se
praesidia amicorum atque clientium occulte habebat
5 Postquam dies comitiorum venit et Catilinae neque
petitio neque insidiae quas consulibus[1] in campo
fecerat prospere cessere, constituit bellum facere et
extrema omnia experiri, quoniam quae occulte temp-
taverat aspera foedaque evenerant. XXVII. Igitur
C. Manlium Faesulas atque in eam partem Etruriae,
Septimium quendam Camertem in agrum Picenum,
C. Iulium in Apuliam dimisit, praeterea alium alio,
2 quem ubique opportunum sibi fore credebat. Interea Romae multa simul moliri: consulibus[2] insidias
tendere, parare incendia, opportuna loca armatis
hominibus obsidere, ipse cum telo esse, item alios
iubere, hortari uti semper intenti paratique essent;
dies noctisque festinare, vigilare, neque insomniis
3 neque labore fatigari. Postremo ubi multa agitanti
nihil procedit, rursus intempesta nocte coniurationis
principes convocat per M. Porcium Laecam, ibique
4 multa de ignavia eorum questus, docet se Manlium
praemisisse ad eam multitudinem quam ad capiunda
arma paraverat, item alios in alia loca opportuna,
qui initium belli facerent, seque ad exercitum
proficisci cupere, si prius Ciceronem oppressisset;
eum suis consiliis multum officere.

XXVIII. Igitur perterritis ac dubitantibus ceteris,
C. Cornelius eques Romanus operam suam pollicitus

---

[1] consuli, A^2CBn; *Dietsch omitted.*
[2] *Omitted by Dietsch and some later editors.*

him, not to entertain schemes hostile to the public weal, and he also had surrounded himself secretly with a bodyguard of friends and dependents.

When the day of the elections came and neither Catiline's suit nor the plots which he had made against the consuls in the Campus Martius were successful, he resolved to take the field and dare the uttermost, since his covert attempts had resulted in disappointment and disgrace. XXVII. He therefore dispatched Gaius Manlius to Faesulae and the adjacent part of Etruria, a certain Septimius of Camerinum to the Picene district, and Gaius Julius to Apulia; others too to other places, wherever he thought that each would be serviceable to his project. Meanwhile he himself was busy at Rome with many attempts at once, laying traps for the consul, planning fires, posting armed men in commanding places. He went armed himself, bade others do the same, conjured them to be always alert and ready, kept on the move night and day, took no rest yet succumbed neither to wakefulness nor fatigue. Finally, when his manifold attempts met with no success, again in the dead of night he summoned the ringleaders of the conspiracy to the house of Marcus Porcius Laeca. There, after reproaching them bitterly for their inaction, he stated that he had sent Manlius on ahead to the force which he had prepared for war, and also other men to other important points to commence hostilities, explaining that he himself was eager to go to the front if he could first make away with Cicero, who was a serious obstacle to his plans.

XXVIII. Upon this the rest were terrified and hesitated; but Gaius Cornelius, a Roman knight,

et cum eo L. Vargunteius senator constituere ea
nocte paulo post cum armatis hominibus sicuti
salutatum introire ad Ciceronem ac de improviso
2 domi suae imparatum confodere.   Curius ubi intellegit quantum periculum consuli impendeat,
propere per Fulviam Ciceroni dolum qui parabatur
3 enuntiat.   Ita illi ianua prohibiti tantum facinus
frustra susceperant.

4   Interea Manlius in Etruria plebem sollicitare,
egestate simul ac dolore iniuriae novarum rerum
cupidam, quod Sullae dominatione agros bonaque
omnia amiserat, praeterea latrones cuiusque generis,
quorum in ea regione magna copia erat, non nullos
ex Sullanis coloniis, quibus lubido atque luxuria
ex magnis rapinis nihil reliqui fecerant.[1]

XXIX. Ea cum Ciceroni nuntiarentur, ancipiti
malo permotus, quod neque urbem ab insidiis privato
consilio longius tueri poterat, neque exercitus
Manli quantus aut quo consilio foret satis compertum
habebat, rem ad senatum refert, iam antea volgi
2 rumoribus exagitatam.   Itaque, quod plerumque
in atroci negotio solet, senatus decrevit darent
operam consules ne quid res publica detrimenti

---

[1] fecerat *PAB* (n *written above*), *Or* ; fecerant, *the other
mss., Ah.*

---

[1] The *salutatio*, or ceremonial call, paid to distinguished
men by clients and friends, took place soon after sunrise.
The meeting of the conspirators must have been prolonged
to the small hours.

offered his services and was joined by Lucius Vargunteius, a senator. These two men determined that very night, a little later, to get access to Cicero, accompanied by a band of armed men, as if for a ceremonial call[1] and taking him by surprise to murder the defenceless consul in his own house. When Curius learned of the great danger which threatened the consul, he hastened to report to Cicero through Fulvia the trap which was being set for him. Hence the would-be assassins were refused admission and proved to have undertaken this awful crime to no purpose.

Meanwhile Manlius in Etruria was working upon the populace, who were already ripe for revolution because of penury and resentment at their wrongs; for during Sulla's supremacy they had lost their lands and all their property. He also approached brigands of various nationalities, who were numerous in that part of the country, and some members of Sulla's colonies who had been stripped by prodigal and luxurious living of the last of their great booty.

XXIX. When these events were reported to Cicero, he was greatly disturbed by the twofold peril, since he could no longer by his unaided efforts protect the city against these plots, nor gain any exact information as to the size and purpose of Manlius's army; he therefore formally called the attention of the senate to the matter, which had already been the subject of popular gossip.[2] Thereupon, as is often done in a dangerous emergency, the senate voted "that the consuls should take heed

---

[2] This was on Oct. 20. Sallust differs from Cicero in placing the consular elections before Cicero's announcement to the senate (see chap. xxvi.), whereas they did not take place until Oct. 28.

3 caperet. Ea potestas per senatum more Romano
magistratui maxuma permittitur, exercitum parare,
bellum gerere, coercere omnibus modis socios atque
civis, domi militiaeque imperium atque iudicium
summum habere; aliter sine populi iussu nullius
earum rerum consuli ius est.

XXX. Post paucos dies L. Saenius senator in
senatu litteras recitavit, quas Faesulis adlatas sibi
dicebat, in quibus scriptum erat C. Manlium arma
cepisse cum magna multitudine ante diem VI ka-
2 lendas Novembris. Simul, id quod in tali re solet,
alii portenta atque prodigia nuntiabant, alii conventus fieri, arma portari, Capuae atque in Apulia
servile bellum moveri.
3   Igitur senati decreto Q. Marcius Rex Faesulas,
Q. Metellus Creticus in Apuliam circumque ea
4 loca missi — ei utrique ad urbem imperatores
erant, impediti ne triumpharent calumnia paucorum, quibus omnia honesta atque inhonesta
5 vendere mos erat—sed praetores Q. Pompeius
Rufus Capuam, Q. Metellus Celer in agrum Picenum, eisque permissum uti pro tempore atque
6 periculo exercitum compararent. Ad hoc, siquis
indicavisset de coniuratione, quae contra rem

---

¹ This decree seems not to have been resorted to before
the end of the Third Punic War (146 B.C.), before which
time a dictator was chosen. The right of the senate to pass
such a decree was not admitted by the popular party.
² The former had waged war successfully in Cilicia, while

that the commonwealth suffer no harm." The power which according to Roman usage is thus conferred upon a magistrate by the senate is supreme, allowing him to raise an army, wage war, exert any kind of compulsion upon allies and citizens, and exercise unlimited command and jurisdiction at home and in the field; otherwise the consul has none of these privileges except by the order of the people.[1]

XXX. A few days later, in a meeting of the senate, Lucius Saenius, one its members, read a letter which he said had been brought to him from Faesulae, stating that Gaius Manlius had taken the field with a large force on the twenty-seventh day of October. At the same time, as is usual in such a crisis, omens and portents were reported by some, while others told of the holding of meetings, of the transportation of arms, and of insurrections of the slaves at Capua and in Apulia.

Thereupon by decree of the senate Quintus Marcius Rex was sent to Faesulae and Quintus Metellus Creticus to Apulia and its neighbourhood. Both these generals were at the gates in command of their armies, being prevented from celebrating a triumph[2] by the intrigues of a few men, whose habit it was to make everything, honourable and dishonourable, a matter of barter. Of the praetors, Quintus Pompeius Rufus was sent to Capua and Quintus Metellus Celer to the Picene district, with permission to raise an army suited to the emergency and the danger. The senate also voted that if anyone should give information as to the plot which had been made against the state, he should, if a

the latter had won his surname by reducing Crete to submission. They could not enter the city without losing the *imperium*, without which a triumph could not be secured.

publicam facta erat, praemium servo libertatem et
7 sestertia centum, libero impunitatem eius rei et
sestertia ducenta, itemque decrevere uti gladia-
toriae familiae Capuam et in cetera municipia dis-
tribuerentur pro cuiusque opibus, Romae per totam
urbem vigiliae haberentur, eisque minores[1] magistratus praeessent.

XXXI. Quibus rebus permota civitas atque immutata urbis facies erat. Ex summa laetitia atque
lascivia, quae diuturna quies pepererat, repente
2 omnis tristitia invasit ; festinare, trepidare, neque
loco neque homini cuiquam satis credere, neque
bellum gerere neque pacem habere, suo quisque
3 metu pericula metiri. Ad hoc mulieres, quibus rei
publicae magnitudine belli timor insolitus incesserat,
adflictare sese, manus supplices ad caelum tendere,
miserari parvos liberos, rogitare, omnia pavere,[2]
superbia atque deliciis omissis sibi patriaeque
diffidere.

4   At Catilinae crudelis animus eadem illa movebat,
tametsi praesidia parabantur et ipse lege Plautia
5 interrogatus erat ab L. Paulo. Postremo dissimu-
landi causa aut sui expurgandi, sicut iurgio lacessitus

---

[1] maiores, *P.*

[2] rogitare omnia, omni rumore p., adripere omnia, *Fronto,*
p. 110 *N* ; *Ah* ; *Or.*

---

[1] See Index under *sestertius.*

[2] To relieve Rome of the danger of their presence.

[3] See Gellius 15. 13. 4. The term is used formally of all
below the curule magistrates (see note on chap. xxiii. 6) ;
namely, the plebeian aediles, quaestors, tribunes of the

slave, be rewarded with his freedom and a hundred thousand sesterces,[1] and if a free man, with immunity for complicity therein, and two hundred thousand sesterces[1]; further, that the troops of gladiators should be quartered on Capua and the other free towns according to the resources of each place;[2] that at Rome watch should be kept by night in all parts of the city under the direction of the minor magistrates.[3]

XXXI. These precautions struck the community with terror, and the aspect of the city was changed. In place of extreme gaiety and frivolity, the fruit of long-continued peace, there was sudden and general gloom. Men were uneasy and apprehensive, put little confidence in any place of security or in any human being, were neither at war nor at peace, and measured the peril each by his own fears. The women, too, whom the greatness of our country had hitherto shielded from the terrors of war, were in a pitiful state of anxiety, raised suppliant hands to heaven, bewailed the fate of their little children, asked continual questions, trembled at everything, and throwing aside haughtiness and self-indulgence, despaired of themselves and of their country.

But Catiline's pitiless spirit persisted in the same attempts, although defences were preparing, and he himself had been arraigned by Lucius Paulus under the Plautian law.[4] Finally, in order to conceal his designs or to clear himself, as though he had merely been the object of some private slander, he came

commons, *tresviri capitales* (lv. 1), etc. Here it is perhaps less inclusive.

[4] Passed in 89 B.C. by M. Plautius Silvanus, tribune of the commons, and directed against acts of violence and breaches of peace.

6 **foret, in** senatum venit. Tum M. Tullius consul,
sive praesentiam eius timens sive ira commotus,
orationem habuit luculentam atque utilem rei
7 publicae, quam postea scriptam edidit. Sed ubi ille
adsedit, Catilina, ut erat paratus ad dissimulanda
omnia, demisso voltu, voce supplici postulare a[1]
patribus coepit nequid de se temere crederent;
ea familia ortum, ita se ab adulescentia vitam in-
stituisse, ut omnia bona in spe haberet; ne existumarent sibi, patricio homini, cuius ipsius atque
maiorum pluruma beneficia in plebem Romanam
essent, perdita re publica opus esse, cum eam
servaret M. Tullius, inquilinus civis urbis Romae.
8 Ad hoc maledicta alia cum adderet, obstrepere
9 omnes, hostem atque parricidam vocare. Tum ille
furibundus "Quoniam quidem circumventus," inquit,
"ab inimicis praeceps agor, incendium meum ruina
restinguam."[2]

XXXII. Deinde se ex curia domum proripuit. Ibı
multa ipse secum volvens, quod neque insidiae consuli procedebant et ab incendio intellegebat urbem
vigiliis munitam, optumum factu credens exercitum
augere **ac** prius quam legiones scriberentur multa

---

[1] *mss. omit.*
[2] resting(u)am, *PNl²s*; restringam, *ACKl¹*; exsting(u)am,
BYnm.

---

[1] The First Oration against Catiline, delivered November 8,
63 B.C.
[2] This slur was unfair, for although Cicero was not born in
Rome, as a native of Arpinum he possessed full citizenship. .

into the senate. Then the consul Marcus Tullius, either fearing his presence or carried away by indignation, delivered a brilliant speech of great service to the state, which he later wrote out and published.[1] When he took his seat, Catiline, prepared as he was to deny everything, with downcast eyes and pleading accents began to beg the Fathers of the Senate not to believe any unfounded charge against him; he was sprung from such a family, he said, and had so ordered his life from youth up, that he had none save the best of prospects. They must not suppose that he, a patrician, who like his forefathers had rendered great service to the Roman people, would be benefited by the overthrow of the government, while its saviour was Marcus Tullius, a resident alien [2] in the city of Rome. When he would have added other insults, he was shouted down by the whole body, who called him traitor and assassin. Then in a transport of fury he cried : " Since I am brought to bay by my enemies and driven desperate, I will put out my [3] fire by general devastation."

XXXII. With this he rushed from the senate-house [4] and went home. There after thinking long upon the situation, since his designs upon the consul made no headway and he perceived that the city was protected against fires by watchmen, believing it best to increase the size of his army and secure many of the necessities of war before the legions were

---

[3] That is, "the fire which consumes me"; cf. Cic. pro Mur. 51, cum ille . . . respondisset, si quod esset in suas fortunas incendium excitatum, id se non aqua, sed ruina restincturum. He refers to the method of checking great fires by the demolition of buildings and the like. Valerius Maximus (9. 11. 3) has incendium ab ipso excitatum.

[4] On this occasion, the temple of Concord.

antecapere, quae bello usui forent, nocte intempesta
2 cum paucis in Manliana castra profectus est. Sed
Cethego atque Lentulo ceterisque, quorum cognoverat promptam audaciam, mandat quibus rebus
possent opes factionis confirment, insidias consuli
maturent, caedem, incendia, aliaque belli facinora
parent: sese prope diem cum magno exercitu ad
urbem accessurum.
3   Dum haec Romae geruntur, C. Manlius ex suo
numero legatos ad Marcium Regem mittit cum
mandatis huiuscemodi:

XXXIII. "Deos hominesque testamur, imperator,
nos arma neque contra patriam cepisse neque quo
periculum aliis faceremus, sed uti corpora nostra
ab iniuria tuta forent, qui miseri, egentes violentia
atque crudelitate faeneratorum plerique patriae [1]
sed omnes fama atque fortunis expertes sumus.
Neque cuiquam nostrum licuit more maiorum lege
uti neque amisso patrimonio liberum corpus habere;
tanta saevitia faeneratorum atque praetoris fuit.
2 Saepe maiores vostrum,[2] miseriti plebis Romanae,
decretis suis inopiae eius opitulati sunt, ac novissume
memoria nostra propter magnitudinem aeris alieni,
volentibus omnibus bonis, argentum aere solutum
3 est. Saepe ipsa plebes, aut dominandi studio
permota aut superbia magistratuum armata, a patri-

---

[1] patria, *VYmn*; *Ah*; patriae, *XNls*, *Or*; p. sedia,
Eussner.
[2] *See Gellius* 20. 6. 14; vestri, *VP²Al¹*; nostri, *P¹l²* *and*
the other mss.

---

[1] By the Valerian law of 86 B.C.; *cf.* Velleius Paterculus
2. 23. 2, who calls it a most shameful law (*lex turpissima*).
[2] Since the patricians allowed the plebeians no political
rights, the latter withdrew from the city and threatened to

enrolled, he left for the camp of Manlius with a few
followers in the dead of night. However, he instructed Cethegus, Lentulus, and the others whose
reckless daring he knew to be ready for anything,
to add to the strength of their cabal by whatever
means they could, to bring the plots against the
consul to a head, to make ready murder, arson, and
the other horrors of war; as for himself, he would
shortly be at the gates with a large army.

While this was going on at Rome, Gaius Manlius
sent a delegation from his army to Marcius Rex with
this message:

XXXIII. "We call gods and men to witness,
general, that we have taken up arms, not against
our fatherland nor to bring danger upon others, but
to protect our own persons from outrage; for we are
wretched and destitute, many of us have been driven
from our country by the violence and cruelty of the
moneylenders, while all have lost repute and fortune. None of us has been allowed, in accordance
with the usage of our forefathers, to enjoy the protection of the law and retain our personal liberty
after being stripped of our patrimony, such was the
inhumanity of the moneylenders and the praetor.
Your forefathers often took pity on the Roman commons and relieved their necessities by senatorial
decrees, and not long ago, within our own memory,
because of the great amount of their debt, silver
was paid in copper with the general consent of the
nobles.[1] Often the commons themselves, actuated
by a desire to rule or incensed at the arrogance of
the magistrates, have taken up arms and seceded[2]

form an independent community. Three such "secessions"
are recorded: to the Mons Sacer in 494, to the Aventine in
449, and to the Janiculum in 287 B.C.

4 bus secessit. At nos non imperium neque divitias
petimus, quarum rerum causa bella atque certamina
omnia inter mortalis sunt, sed libertatem, quam
5 nemo bonus nisi cum anima simul amittit. Te
atque senatum obtestamur, consulatis miseris civibus, legis praesidium, quod iniquitas praetoris
eripuit, restituatis, neve nobis eam necessitudinem
imponatis, ut quaeramus quonam modo maxume ulti
sanguinem nostrum pereamus."

XXXIV. Ad haec Q. Marcius respondit, si quid
ab senatu petere vellent, ab armis discedant,
Romam supplices proficiscantur; ea mansuetudine
atque misericordia senatum populi Romani semper
fuisse, ut nemo umquam ab eo frustra auxilium
petiverit.
2 At Catilina ex itinere plerisque consularibus,
praeterea optumo cuique litteras mittit: se falsis
criminibus circumventum, quoniam factioni inimicorum resistere nequiverit, fortunae cedere, Mas-
siliam in exsilium proficisci, non quo sibi tanti
sceleris conscius esset, sed uti res publica quieta
foret neve ex sua contentione seditio oreretur.[1]
3 Ab his longe divorsas litteras Q. Catulus in senatu
recitavit, quas sibi nomine Catilinae redditas dicebat.
Earum exemplum infra scriptum est.

XXXV. "L. Catilina Q. Catulo. Egregia tua
fides re cognita, grata mihi magnis in meis periculis,
2 fiduciam commendationi meae tribuit. Quam ob
rem defensionem in novo consilio non statui parare;

[1] *PN*[1]; *the other mss. have* oriretur.

---

[1] Catulus had defended Catiline from the charge relating
to Fabia, the vestal mentioned in chap. xv. 1.
[2] That is, in resorting to arms and going to Manlius instead of Massilia; for the force of *novo cf.* chap. li. 8.

from the patricians. But we ask neither for power nor for riches, the usual causes of wars and strife among mortals, but only for freedom, which no true man gives up except with his life. We implore you and the senate to take thought for your unhappy countrymen, to restore the bulwark of the law, of which the praetor's injustice has deprived us, and not to impose upon us the necessity of asking ourselves how we may sell our lives most dearly."

XXXIV. To this address Quintus Mucius made answer, that if they wished to ask anything of the senate, they must lay down their arms and come to Rome as suppliants; that the senate of the Roman people had always been so compassionate and merciful that no one had ever asked it for succour and been refused.

But on the way Catiline sent letters to many of the consulars and to the most prominent of the other nobles, saying that since he was beset by false accusations and unable to cope with the intrigues of his personal enemies, he bowed to fate and was on his way to exile at Massilia; not that he confessed to the dreadful crime with which he was charged, but in order that his country might be at peace and that no dissension might arise from a struggle on his part. A very different letter was read in the senate by Quintus Catulus, who said that it had been sent him in Catiline's name. The following is an exact copy of this letter:

XXXV. "Lucius Catilina to Quintus Catulus. Your eminent loyalty, known by experience [1] and grateful to me in my extreme peril, lends confidence to my plea. I have therefore resolved to make no defence of my unusual conduct; [2] that I offer an

satisfactionem ex nulla conscientia de culpa pro-
ponere decrevi, quam mediusfidius veram licet
3 cognoscas. Iniuriis contumeliisque concitatus, quod
fructu laboris industriaeque meae privatus statum
dignitatis non optinebam, publicam miserorum
causam pro mea consuetudine suscepi, non quia[1]
aes alienum meis nominibus ex possessionibus
solvere non possem[2] (et alienis nominibus liberalitas Orestillae suis filiaeque copiis persolveret);
sed quod non dignos homines honore honestatos
videbam meque falsa suspicione alienatum esse sen-
4 tiebam. Hoc nomine satis honestas pro meo casu
spes reliquae dignitatis conservandae sum secutus.
5 Plura cum scribere vellem, nuntiatum est vim mihi
6 parari. Nunc Orestillam commendo tuaeque fidei
trado. Eam ab iniuria defendas, per liberos tuos
rogatus. Haveto.''

XXXVI. Sed ipse paucos dies commoratus apud
C. Flaminium in agro Arretino,[3] dum vicinitatem
antea sollicitatam armis exornat, cum fascibus atque
aliis imperi insignibus in castra ad Manlium con-
2 tendit. Haec ubi Romae comperta sunt, senatus
Catilinam et Manlium hostis iudicat, ceterae multi-
tudini diem statuit ante quam sine fraude liceret
ab armis discedere, praeter rerum capitalium con-
3 demnatis. Praeterea decernit uti consules dilectum

---

[1] non quia, $B^2K^2HF^2ls$; non qui (n *erased*), N; non quin,
the other mss., *Ah, Or.*
[2] non possem, $VXNKls$, *Ah*; non *written above or omitted*,
$A\Gamma m$, *Or.*
[3] Arretino, A^1, *Ah, Or*; Reatinio, P; Reatino, *the other*
mss.

explanation is due to no feeling of guilt, and I am confident that you will be able to admit its justice. Maddened by wrongs and slights, since I had been robbed of the fruits of my toil and energy and was unable to attain to a position of honour, I followed my usual custom and took up the general cause of the unfortunate; not that I could not pay my personal debts from my own estate (and the liberality of Orestilla sufficed with her own and her daughter's resources to pay off even the obligations incurred through others), but because I saw the unworthy elevated to honours, and realized that I was an outcast because of baseless suspicion. It is for this reason that, in order to preserve what prestige I have left, I have adopted measures which are honourable enough considering my situation. When I would write more, word comes that I am threatened with violence. Now I commend Orestilla to you and entrust her to your loyalty. Protect her from insult, I beseech you in the name of your own children. Farewell."

XXXVI. Catiline himself, after spending a few days with Gaius Flaminius in the vicinity of Arretium, where he supplied arms to the populace, which had already been roused to revolt, hastened to join Manlius in his camp, taking with him the fasces[1] and the other emblems of authority. As soon as this became known at Rome, the senate pronounced Catiline and Manlius traitors and named a day before which the rest of the conspirators might lay down their arms and escape punishment, excepting those under sentence for capital offences. It was further voted that the consuls should hold a levy and that

[1] See note on chap. xviii. 5.

habeant, Antonius cum exercitu Catilinam persequi maturet, Cicero urbi praesidio sit.

4 Ea tempestate mihi imperium populi Romani multo maxume miserabile visum est. Cui cum ad occasum ab ortu solis omnia domita armis parerent, domi otium atque divitiae, quae prima mortales putant, adfluerent, fuere tamen cives qui seque remque publicam opstinatis animis perditum irent.

5 Namque duobus senati decretis ex tanta multitudine neque praemio inductus coniurationem patefecerat neque ex castris Catilinae quisquam omnium discesserat; tanta vis morbi aeque uti[1] tabes plerosque civium animos invaserat.

XXXVII. Neque solum illis aliena mens erat qui conscii coniurationis fuerant, sed omnino cuncta plebes novarum rerum studio Catilinae incepta 2 probabat. Id adeo more suo videbatur facere. 3 Nam semper in civitate quibus opes nullae sunt bonis invident, malos extollunt, vetera odere, nova exoptant, odio suarum rerum mutari omnia student; turba atque seditionibus sine cura aluntur, quoniam 4 egestas facile habetur sine damno. Sed urbana 5 plebes, ea vero praeceps erat de multis causis. Primum omnium, qui ubique probro atque petulantia maxume praestabant, item alii[2] per dedecora patrimoniis amissis, postremo omnes, quos flagitium aut

---

[1] aeque uti, *Mähly*; atque uti, *mss.*, *Ah, Or*; ac veluti, *Haupt*.

[2] alii per, *A*[1]*m, Sacerdos* vi. 446. 3 к, *Ah, Or*; *the other mss. have* alii qui per.

Antonius with an army should at once pursue Catiline, while Cicero defended the capital.

At no other time has the condition of imperial Rome, as it seems to me, been more pitiable. The whole world, from the rising of the sun to its setting, subdued by her arms, rendered obedience to her; at home there was peace and an abundance of wealth, which mortal men deem the chiefest of blessings. Yet there were citizens who from sheer perversity were bent upon their own ruin and that of their country. For in spite of the two decrees of the senate not one man of all that great number was led by the promised reward to betray the conspiracy, and not a single one deserted Catiline's camp; such was the potency of the malady which like a plague had infected the minds of many of our countrymen.

XXXVII. This insanity was not confined to those who were implicated in the plot, but the whole body of the commons through desire for change favoured the designs of Catiline. In this very particular they seemed to act as the populace usually does; for in every community those who have no means envy the good, exalt the base, hate what is old and established, long for something new, and from disgust with their own lot desire a general upheaval. Amid turmoil and rebellion they maintain themselves without difficulty, since poverty is easily provided for and can suffer no loss. But the city populace in particular acted with desperation for many reasons. To begin with, all who were especially conspicuous for their shamelessness and impudence, those too who had squandered their patrimony in riotous living, finally all whom disgrace or crime had forced to

facinus domo expulerat, ei Romam sicut in sentinam
6 confluxerant. Deinde multi memores Sullanae
victoriae, quod ex gregariis militibus alios senatores
videbant, alios ita divites ut regio victu atque cultu
aetatem agerent, sibi quisque, si in armis foret, ex
7 victoria talia sperabat. Praeterea iuventus, quae
in agris manuum mercede inopiam toleraverat,
privatis atque publicis largitionibus excita urbanum
otium ingrato labori praetulerat. Eos atque alios
8 omnis malum publicum alebat. Quo minus mirandum est homines egentis, malis moribus, maxuma
9 spe, rei publicae iuxta ac sibi consuluisse. Praeterea, quorum victoria Sullae parentes proscripti
bona erepta, ius libertatis imminutum erat, haud
10 sane alio animo belli eventum exspectabant. Ad
hoc, quicumque aliarum atque senatus partium
erant conturbari rem publicam quam minus valere
11 ipsi malebant. Id adeo malum multos post annos
in civitatem revorterat.

XXXVIII. Nam postquam Cn. Pompeio et M.
Crasso consulibus tribunicia potestas restituta est,
homines adulescentes, summam potestatem nacti,
quibus aetas animusque ferox erat, coepere senatum
criminando plebem exagitare, dein largiundo atque
pollicitando magis incendere, ita ipsi clari poten-
2 tesque fieri. Contra eos summa ope nitebatur pleraque nobilitas senatus specie pro sua magnitudine

---

[1] The actual time was eleven years, from the curtailment
of the rights of the tribunes by Sulla in 81 B.C. to their
restoration by Pompey in 70.   [2] 70 B.C.

leave home, had all flowed into Rome as into a cesspool. Many, too, who recalled Sulla's victory, when they saw common soldiers risen to the rank of senator, and others become so rich that they feasted and lived like kings, hoped each for himself for like fruits of victory, if he took the field. Besides this, the young men who had maintained a wretched existence by manual labour in the country, tempted by public and private doles had come to prefer idleness in the city to their hateful toil; these, like all the others, battened on the public ills. Therefore it is not surprising that men who were beggars and without character, with illimitable hopes, should respect their country as little as they did themselves. Moreover, those to whom Sulla's victory had meant the proscription of their parents, loss of property, and curtailment of their rights, looked forward in a similar spirit to the issue of a war. Finally, all who belonged to another party than that of the senate preferred to see the government overthrown rather than be out of power themselves. Such, then, was the evil which after many years [1] had returned upon the state.

XXXVIII. For after the tribunician power had been restored in the consulship of Gnaeus Pompeius and Marcus Crassus,[2] various young men, whose age and disposition made them aggressive, attained that high authority; they thereupon began to excite the commons by attacks upon the senate and then to inflame their passions still more by doles and promises, thus making themselves conspicuous and influential. Against these men the greater part of the nobles strove with might and main, ostensibly in behalf of the senate but really for their own

65

3 Namque, **uti** paucis verum absolvam, post illa tempora quicumque rem publicam agitavere honestis
nominibus, alii sicuti populi **iura** defenderent, pars
quo senatus auctoritas maxuma foret, bonum publicum simulantes pro sua quisque potentia certabant.

4 Neque illis modestia neque modus contentionis erat;
utrique victoriam crudeliter exercebant.

XXXIX. Sed postquam Cn. Pompeius ad bellum
maritumum atque Mithridaticum missus est, plebis

2 opes imminutae, paucorum potentia crevit.   Ei
magistratus, provincias, aliaque omnia tenere, ipsi
innoxii, florentes, sine metu aetatem agere ceterosque iudiciis terrere, quo plebem in magistratu

3 placidius tractarent.   Sed ubi primum dubiis rebus
novandi[1] spes oblata est, vetus certamen animos

4 eorum arrexit.   Quod si primo proelio Catilina
superior aut aequa manu discessisset, profecto magna
clades atque calamitas rem publicam oppressisset;
neque illis qui victoriam adepti forent diutius ea
uti licuisset, quin defessis et exsanguibus qui plus
posset imperium atque libertatem extorqueret.

5 Fuere tamen extra coniurationem complures qui

----

[1] novandi, *Gruter*; novandis, *mss.*

[1] Text and meaning are very uncertain. *Ceteros* seems to
refer to the other nobles with less political influence.
Having silenced these by threats of prosecution, the dominant
faction could assume a more conciliatory attitude towards
the people.

aggrandizement. For, to tell the truth in a few words, all who after that time assailed the government used specious pretexts, some maintaining that they were defending the rights of the commons, others that they were upholding the prestige of the senate; but under pretence of the public welfare each in reality was working for his own advancement. Such men showed neither self-restraint nor moderation in their strife, and both parties used their victory ruthlessly.

XXXIX. When, however, Gnaeus Pompeius had been dispatched to wage war against the pirates and against Mithridates, the power of the commons was lessened, while that of the few increased. These possessed the magistracies, the provinces and everything else; being themselves rich and secure against attack, they lived without fear and by resort to the courts terrified the others, in order that while they themselves were in office they might manage the people with less friction.[1] But as soon as the political situation became doubtful, and offered hope of a revolution, then the old controversy aroused their passions anew. If Catiline had been victor in the first battle, or had merely held his own, beyond a doubt great bloodshed and disaster would have fallen upon the state; nor would the victors have been allowed for long to enjoy their success, but when they had been worn out and exhausted, a more powerful adversary[2] would have wrested from them the supreme power and with it their freedom. Yet even as it was, there were many outside the ranks of the conspiracy

[2] Such a man as Crassus (see chap. xvii. 7) or Caesar, who, without taking part in the conspiracy, might have profited by a general disturbance.

ad Catilinam initio profecti sunt. In eis erat
Fulvius senatoris filius, quem retractum ex itinere
parens necari iussit.

6 Isdem temporibus Romae Lentulus, sicuti Catilina praeceperat, quoscumque moribus aut fortuna
novis rebus idoneos credebat aut per se aut per
alios sollicitabat, neque solum civis, sed cuiusque
modi genus hominum, quod modo bello usui foret.

XL. Igitur P. Umbreno cuidam negotium dat
uti legatos Allobrogum requirat eosque, si possit,
impellat ad societatem belli, existumans publice
privatimque aere alieno oppressos, praeterea quod
natura gens Gallica bellicosa esset, facile eos ad tale
2 consilium adduci posse. Umbrenus, quod in Gallia
negotiatus erat, plerisque principibus civitatium
notus erat atque eos noverat ; itaque sine mora, ubi
primum legatos in foro conspexit, percontatus pauca
de statu civitatis et quasi dolens eius casum, re-
quirere coepit quem exitum tantis malis sperarent.
3 Postquam illos videt queri de avaritia magistratuum,
accusare senatum quod in eo auxili nihil esset,
miseriis suis remedium mortem expectare, "At ego,"
inquit, " vobis, si modo viri esse voltis, rationem
ostendam qua tanta ista mala effugiatis."

---

[1] The *negotiatores* were engaged in money-lending, tax-
collecting, and public contracts of various kinds. *cf.* Cic.
Font. 11 : *referta Gallia negotiatorum est, plena civium
Romanorum ; nemo Gallorum sine cive Romano quidquam*

who, when hostilities began, went to join Catiline. Among them was Fulvius, a senator's son, who was brought back and put to death by order of his father.

All this time at Rome Lentulus, following Catiline's directions, was working, personally or through others, upon those whom he thought ripe for revolution by disposition or fortune—and not merely citizens, but all sorts and conditions of men, provided only that they could be of any service in war.

XL. Accordingly, he instructed one Publius Umbrenus to seek out the envoys of the Allobroges, and, if possible, entice them to an offensive alliance, thinking that they could readily be persuaded to such a course, since they were burdened with public and private debt; and besides the Gallic people is by nature prone to war. Umbrenus had carried on business with the Gauls[1] and was personally acquainted with many of the leading men of their states; therefore as soon as he caught sight of the envoys in the Forum, he at once asked them a few questions about the condition of their country, and pretending grief at its lot, began to inquire what remedy they hoped to find for such great troubles. On learning that they had complaints to make of the avarice of the magistrates, that they reproached the senate because it rendered no aid, and looked for death as the only remedy for their wretchedness, he said: "Why, I myself, if only you will show yourselves men, will disclose a plan which will enable you to escape the great evils from which you are suffering."

negotii gerit ; nummus in Gallia nullus sine civium Romanorum tabulis commovetur.

4 Haec ubi dixit, Allobroges in maxumam spem adducti Umbrenum orare ut sui misereretur : nihil tam asperum neque tam difficile esse, quod non cupidissume facturi essent, dum ea res civitatem aere alieno 5 liberaret. Ille eos in domum D. Bruti perducit, quod foro propinqua erat neque aliena consili propter Semproniam ; nam tum Brutus ab Roma[1] aberat. 6 Praeterea Gabinium arcessit, quo maior auctoritas sermoni inesset. Eo praesente coniurationem aperit, nominat socios, praeterea multos cuiusque generis innoxios, quo legatis animus amplior esset. Deinde eos pollicitos operam suam domum dimittit.

XLI. Sed Allobroges diu in incerto habuere quidnam 2 consili caperent. In altera parte erat aes alienum, studium belli, magna merces in spe victoriae, at in altera maiores opes, tuta consilia, pro 3 incerta spe certa praemia. Haec illis volventibus, 4 tandem vicit fortuna rei publicae. Itaque Q. Fabio Sangae cuius patrocinio civitas plurumum utebatur, 5 rem omnem uti cognoverant aperiunt. Cicero, per Sangam consilio cognito, legatis praecepit[2] ut studium coniurationis vehementer simulent, ceteros adeant, bene polliceantur, dentque operam uti eos quam maxume manifestos habeant.

[1] Romae, *P*; ab Roma, *the other mss.* (ab *superscribed in BD*), *Probus* iv. 150. 20, *Sergius* iv. 511. 13, *Prisc.* iii, 66, 15 K.   [2] praecipit, *Linker.*

[1] That is, he looked after their interests in Rome. Sanga had inherited this duty from his father, Quintus Fabius Maximus, who had won the surname Allobrogicus by reducing that people to submission.

When Umbrenus had said this, the Allobroges were filled with the greatest hope and begged him to take pity on them. They declared that nothing was so dangerous or difficult that they would not joyfully undertake it, provided it would relieve their country of debt. Thereupon he took them to the house of Decimus Brutus, which was not far from the Forum and not unsuitable for their plot because of the presence of Sempronia; Brutus, as it happened, was away from Rome at the time. He also sent for Gabinius, that what he was to say might have greater weight. When he arrived, Umbrenus disclosed the plot, named the participants, and, to give the envoys greater courage, included many guiltless men of all classes; then, after promising his assistance, he sent them home.

XLI. The Allobroges for a long time were in doubt what course to pursue. On the one hand was their debt, their love of war, and the hope of great booty in the event of victory; but on the other were the senate's greater resources, a course free from danger, and sure rewards in place of uncertain hopes. All these considerations they weighed, but in the end the fortune of the republic turned the scale. They accordingly divulged the whole affair, just as it had come to their ears, to Quintus Fabius Sanga, their nation's principal patron.[1] Cicero, on being informed of the plan[2] through Sanga, instructed the envoys to feign a strong interest in the conspiracy, approach the other members of it,[3] make liberal promises, and use every effort to show the guilt of the conspirators as clearly as possible.

[2] Namely, the conspirators' plan of enlisting the aid of the Allobroges. He already knew of the conspiracy.

[3] Other than Umbrenus and Gabinius.

XLII. Isdem fere temporibus in Gallia citeriore
atque ulteriore, item in agro Piceno, Bruttio, Apulia
2 motus erat. Namque illi, quos ante Catilina
dimiserat, inconsulte ac veluti per dementiam cuncta
simul agebant. Nocturnis consiliis, armorum atque
telorum portationibus, festinando, agitando omnia
3 plus timoris quam periculi effecerant. Ex eo
numero compluris Q. Metellus Celer praetor ex
senatus consulto, causa cognita, in vincula conie-
cerat; item in citeriore Gallia C. Murena, qui ei
provinciae legatus praeerat.

XLIII. At Romae Lentulus cum ceteris qui principes coniurationis erant, paratis ut videbatur magnis
copiis, constituerant uti, cum Catilina in agrum
Aefulanum[1] cum exercitu venisset, L. Bestia tribunus plebis contione habita quereretur de actionibus Ciceronis bellique gravissumi invidiam optumo
consuli imponeret; eo signo proxuma nocte cetera
multitudo coniurationis suum quisque[2] negotium
2 exsequeretur. Sed ea divisa hoc modo dicebantur:
Statilius et Gabinius uti cum magna manu duodecim
simul opportuna loca urbis incenderent, quo tumultu
facilior aditus ad consulem ceterosque quibus insidiae parabantur fieret; Cethegus Ciceronis ianuam

[1] Aefulanum, *Ah following Kunze, Berl. Phil. Woch.* 1912.
pp. 670 ff.; Faesulanum, *mss., Or.*
[2] quoque, *A*; que‖que, *N*; quaeque, *the other mss.*

XLII. At about this same time there were disturbances in both Hither and Farther Gaul, as well as in the Picene and Bruttian districts and in Apulia; for those whom Catiline had sent on ahead were doing everything at once, acting imprudently and almost insanely. By their meetings at night, by their transportation of arms and weapons, and by their bustle and general activity they caused more apprehension than actual danger. The praetor Quintus Metellus Celer had brought several of their number to trial by virtue of a decree of the senate, and had thrown them into prison; and in Hither Gaul[1] his example was followed by Gaius Murena, who was governing that province as a deputy.

XLIII. At Rome Lentulus and the other leaders of the conspiracy, having got together a great force as it appeared to them, had arranged that when Catiline arrived in the region of Faesulae with his army, Lucius Bestia, tribune of the commons, should convoke an assembly and denounce the conduct of Cicero, throwing upon that best of consuls the odium of a dangerous war. That was to be the signal for the rest of the band of conspirators to carry out their several enterprises on the following night. Now it is said that the parts assigned to them were the following: Statilius and Gabinius, with many followers, were to kindle fires at twelve important points in the city all at the same time, in order that in the ensuing confusion access might more easily be had to the consul and the others against whom their plots were directed. Cethegus was to beset Cicero's

---

[1] That Murena was in charge of Gallia Ulterior is clear from Cic. *Mur.* 41. Whether Sallust is in error, or the manuscripts, cannot be determined.

obsideret eumque vi aggrederetur, alius autem
alium; sed filii familiarum, quorum ex nobilitate
maxuma pars erat, parentis interficerent; simul
caede et incendio perculsis omnibus ad Catilinam
erumperent.

3 Inter haec parata atque decreta Cethegus semper
querebatur de ignavia sociorum : illos dubitando et
dies prolatando magnas opportunitates corrumpere;
facto, non consulto[1] in tali periculo opus esse, seque,
si pauci adiuvarent, languentibus aliis, impetum in

4 curiam facturum. Natura ferox, vehemens, manu
promptus erat; maximum bonum in celeritate
putabat.

XLIV. Sed Allobroges ex praecepto Ciceronis per
Gabinium ceteros conveniunt. Ab Lentulo, Cethego,
Statilio, item Cassio postulant ius iurandum, quod
signatum ad civis perferant; aliter haud facile eos

2 ad tantum negotium impelli posse. Ceteri nihil
suspicantes dant, Cassius semet eo brevi venturum
pollicetur, ac paulo ante legatos ex urbe proficis-

3 citur. Lentulus cum eis T. Volturcium quendam
Crotoniensem mittit, ut Allobroges prius quam
domum pergerent cum Catilina data atque accepta

4 fide societatem confirmarent. Ipse Volturcio litteras ad Catilinam dat, quarum exemplum infra

5 scriptum est : " Quis sim ex eo quem ad te misi
cognosces. Fac cogites in quanta calamitate sis,
et memineris te virum esse. Consideres quid tuae
rationes postulent. Auxilium petas ab omnibus,

[1] consultando, $PA^1N^1H^1D^1m$.

door and assault him, while to others were assigned
other victims. The eldest sons of several families,
the greater number of whom belonged to the nobility, were to slay their fathers. Then, when the
whole city was stunned by the bloodshed and the
fire, they were all to rush out and join Catiline.

During these preparations and arrangements Cethegus constantly complained of the inaction of his
associates, insisting that by indecision and delay they
were wasting great opportunities; that such a crisis
called for action, not deliberation, and that if a few
would aid him he would himself make an attack
upon the senate-house, even though the rest were
faint-hearted. Being naturally aggressive, violent,
and prompt to act, he set the highest value upon
dispatch.

XLIV. The Allobroges, as Cicero had recommended, were presented to the other conspirators by
Gabinius. They demanded of Lentulus, Cethegus,
Statilius, and also of Cassius an oath, which was to be
sealed and taken to their countrymen, saying that
otherwise they could not readily be induced to embark
upon so serious an enterprise. The others complied
without suspicion; Cassius, however, promised to
come to Gaul shortly, and then left the city just before the envoys. Lentulus sent with the Allobroges
a certain Titus Volturcius of Crotona, so that on their
way home they might confirm the alliance by exchanging pledges of fidelity with Catiline. He gave
Volturcius a letter for Catiline, of which the following is a copy: "Who I am you will learn from my
messenger. See to it that you bear in mind in what
peril you are, and remember that you are a man.
Consider what your plans demand; seek help from

6 etiam ab infimis." Ad hoc mandata verbis dat:
cum ab senatu hostis iudicatus sit, quo consilio
servitia repudiet? In urbe parata esse quae iusserit;
ne cunctetur ipse propius accedere.

XLV. His rebus ita actis, constituta nocte qua
proficiscerentur, Cicero per legatos cuncta edoctus
L. Valerio Flacco et C. Pomptino praetoribus imperat ut in ponte Mulvio per insidias Allobrogum
comitatus deprehendant. Rem omnem aperit cuius
gratia mittebantur, cetera, uti facto opus sit, ita
2 agant permittit. Illi, homines militares, sine
tumultu praesidiis collocatis, sicuti praeceptum erat,
3 occulte pontem obsidunt. Postquam ad id loci
legati cum Volturcio venerunt et simul utrimque
clamor exortus est, Galli cito cognito consilio sine
4 mora praetoribus se tradunt, Volturcius primo cohortatus ceteros gladio se a multitudine defendit,
deinde ubi a legatis desertus est, multa prius de
salute sua Pomptinum obtestatus, quod ei notus
erat, postremo timidus ac vitae diffidens velut
hostibus sese praetoribus dedit.

XLVI. Quibus rebus confectis omnia propere per
2 nuntios consuli declarantur. At illum ingens cura
atque laetitia simul occupavere. Nam laetabatur
intellegens coniuratione patefacta civitatem periculis
ereptam esse; porro autem anxius erat, dubitans in

all, even the lowest." He also sent him a verbal message, inquiring what his idea was in refusing the aid of slaves, when he had been declared a rebel by the senate. The preparations which he had ordered in the city had been made; he should not himself hesitate to come nearer the walls.

XLV. When arrangements had been thus perfected and the night for the departure appointed, Cicero, who had been informed of everything through the envoys, ordered the praetors Lucius Valerius Flaccus and Gaius Pomptinus to lie in wait for the Allobroges and their company at the Mulvian Bridge and arrest them. He fully explained why they were sent, but left the general course of action to their discretion. The praetors, who were soldiers, quietly posted their guards, according to their orders, and secretly invested the bridge. As soon as the envoys reached the spot with Volturcius and heard a shout on both sides of them at once, the Gauls quickly saw what was going on and immediately surrendered themselves to the praetors. Volturcius at first urged on his companions, and sword in hand defended himself against superior numbers; but when he was deserted by the envoys, he at first earnestly besought Pomptinus, with whom he was acquainted, to save him, but finally, being in fear and despairing of his life, surrendered to the praetors as if to enemies.

XLVI. When all was over, the details were quickly communicated to the consul by messengers; but he was beset at the same time by deep anxiety as well as by great joy. For while he rejoiced in the knowledge that by the disclosure of the plot his country was saved from peril, he was also troubled, and uncertain

maxumo scelere tantis civibus deprehensis, quid
facto opus esset; poenam illorum sibi oneri, impuni-
3 tatem perdundae rei publicae fore credebat. Igitur
confirmato animo vocari ad sese iubet Lentulum,
Cethegum, Statilium, Gabinium, itemque Caeparium
Tarracinensem, qui in Apuliam ad concitanda ser-
4 vitia proficisci parabat. Ceteri sine mora veniunt;
Caeparius, paulo ante domo egressus, cognito indicio
5 ex urbe profugerat. Consul Lentulum, quod
praetor erat, ipse manu tenens in senatum[1] perducit, reliquos cum custodibus in aedem Concordiae
6 venire iubet. Eo senatum advocat magnaque fre-
quentia eius ordinis Volturcium cum legatis introducit; Flaccum praetorem scrinium cum litteris,
quas a legatis acceperat, eodem adferre iubet.

XLVII. Volturcius interrogatus de itinere, de
litteris, postremo quid aut qua de causa consili habuisset, primo fingere alia, dissimulare de coniuratione; post ubi fide publica dicere iussus est, omnia
uti gesta erant aperit docetque se paucis ante diebus
a Gabinio et Caepario socium adscitum nihil amplius
scire quam legatos; tantum modo audire solitum ex
Gabinio P. Autronium, Ser. Sullam, L. Vargunteium,
2 multos praeterea in ea coniuratione esse. Eadem
Galli fatentur ac Lentulum dissimulantem coarguunt

---

[1] in senatum, *omitted by Cortius and others.*

---

[1] Where the meeting of the senate was held on this
occasion.

what ought to be done, when citizens of such standing were found guilty of a heinous crime. He realized that their punishment would be a load upon his own shoulders; their impunity the ruin of the state. He, therefore, steeling his resolution, ordered Lentulus, Cethegus, Statilius, and Gabinius to be brought before him, as well as a certain Caeparius of Terracina, who was making ready to go to Apulia and stir the slaves to revolt. The others came without delay; but Caeparius, who had left his home a short time before this, heard of the discovery of the plot and had made good his escape from the city. The consul himself took Lentulus by the hand, because he was praetor, and led him to the temple of Concord,[1] bidding the rest follow under guard. Thither he summoned the senate, and when it had assembled in full numbers he led in Volturcius and the envoys. He bade the praetor Flaccus bring to the same place the portfolio, together with the letters which he had taken from the Allobroges.

XLVII. When Volturcius was questioned about the journey and letters, and finally was asked what his design was and why he had entertained it, he at first invented another story and denied knowledge of the conspiracy. Afterwards, when invited to speak under a public pledge of pardon, he gave an exact account of the whole affair. He declared that he had been made a member of the cabal only a few days before by Gabinius and Caeparius, and knew no more than the envoys; except that he had often heard Gabinius mention Publius Autronius, Servius Sulla, Lucius Vargunteius, and many others as being in the plot. The Gauls gave the same testimony, and when Lentulus denied his guilt they confronted him not

praeter litteras sermonibus quos ille habere solitus
erat: ex libris Sibyllinis, regnum Romae tribus
Corneliis portendi; Cinnam atque Sullam antea, se
tertium esse, cui fatum foret urbis potiri. Praeterea
ab incenso Capitolio illum esse vigesumum annum,
quem saepe ex prodigiis haruspices respondissent
bello civili cruentum fore. Igitur perlectis litteris,
cum prius omnes signa sua cognovissent, senatus
decernit uti abdicato magistratu Lentulus itemque
3 ceteri in liberis custodiis habeantur. Itaque Lentulus P. Lentulo Spintheri, qui tum aedilis erat,
4 Cethegus Q. Cornificio, Statilius C. Caesari, Gabinius M. Crasso, Caeparius—nam is paulo ante
ex fuga retractus erat—Cn. Terentio senatori
traduntur.

XLVIII. Interea plebs, coniuratione patefacta,
quae primo cupida rerum novarum nimis bello
favebat, mutata mente Catilinae consilia exsecrari,
Ciceronem ad caelum tollere; veluti ex servitute
2 erepta gaudium atque laetitiam agitabat. Namque
alia belli facinora praedae magis quam detrimento
fore, incendium vero crudele, immoderatum, ac sibi
maxume calamitosum putabat, quippe cui omnes
copiae in usu cotidiano et cultu corporis erant.

---

¹ In such cases, which corresponded roughly to our release
on bail, each accused person was given into the charge of a
prominent citizen, who became responsible for his appearance
at his trial.

only with his letter, but also with statements which he was in the habit of making, to the effect that in the Sibylline books the rule of Rome by three Cornelii was foretold; that there had already been Cinna and Sulla, and that he was the third who was destined to be master of the city. Furthermore, that this was the twentieth year since the burning of the Capitol, a year which because of portents the soothsayers had often declared would be stained with the blood of a civil war. Accordingly, when the letters had been read through, each man having first acknowledged his own seal, the senate voted that after Lentulus had resigned his office he and the rest should be held in free custody.[1] As a result of this, Lentulus was delivered to Publius Lentulus Spinther, who at the time was an aedile, Cethegus to Quintus Cornificius, Statilius to Gaius Caesar, Gabinius to Marcus Crassus, and Caeparius (for he had just been caught and brought back) to a senator called Gnaeus Terentius.

XLVIII. Meanwhile, after the disclosure of the plot, the commons, who at first in their desire for a change of rulers had been only too eager for war, faced about and denounced the designs of Catiline, while they extolled Cicero to the skies, manifesting as much joy and exultation as if they had been rescued from slavery. For although they thought that other acts of war would lead to booty rather than to loss, they regarded a general conflagration as cruel, monstrous, and especially calamitous to themselves, since their sole possessions were their daily food[2] and clothing.

[2] cf. Liv. 4. 12. 10, *vendere quod usu menstruo superesset*; Tac. *Ann.* 4. 30. 2, *dandos vitae usus cui vita concederetur.*

3   Post eum diem quidam L. Tarquinius ad senatum
adductus erat, quem ad Catilinam proficiscentem ex
4 itinere retractum aiebant. Is cum se diceret indi-
caturum de coniuratione, si fides publica data esset,
iussus a consule quae sciret edicere, eadem fere
quae Volturcius de paratis incendiis, de caede bonorum, de itinere hostium senatum docet; praeterea
se missum a M. Crasso, qui Catilinae nuntiaret ne
eum Lentulus et Cethegus aliique ex coniuratione
deprehensi terrerent, eoque magis properaret ad
urbem accedere, quo et ceterorum animos reficeret
et illi facilius e periculo eriperentur.

5   Sed ubi Tarquinius Crassum nominavit, hominem
nobilem maxumis divitiis, summa potentia, alii rem
incredibilem rati, pars tametsi verum existumabant,
tamen quia in tali tempore tanta vis hominis magis
leniunda quam exagitanda videbatur, plerique Crasso
ex negotiis privatis obnoxii, conclamant indicem
falsum esse, deque ea re postulant uti referatur.
6 Itaque consulente Cicerone frequens senatus decernit, Tarquini indicium falsum videri, eumque in
vinculis retinendum, neque amplius potestatem faci-
undam, nisi de eo indicaret cuius consilio tantam
7 rem esset mentitus. Erant eo tempore qui existumarent indicium illud a P. Autronio machinatum,

82

On the following day one Lucius Tarquinius was brought before the senate, a man who was said to have been arrested and brought back as he was making his way to Catiline. When he said that he would give evidence about the conspiracy if the state would promise him a pardon, and when he had been invited by the consul to tell what he knew, he gave the senate practically the same testimony as Volturcius about the intended fires, the murder of loyal men, and the march of the rebels. He added that he had been sent by Marcus Crassus to advise Catiline not to be alarmed by the arrest of Lentulus, Cethegus, and the other conspirators, but to make the greater haste to come to the city, in order that he might thereby revive the spirits of the rest, and that they might the more easily be saved from their danger.

As soon, however, as Tarquinius named Crassus, a noble of great wealth and of the highest rank, some thought the charge incredible; others believed it to be true, but thought that in such a crisis so powerful a man ought to be propitiated rather than exasperated. There were many, too, who were under obligation to Crassus through private business relations. All these loudly insisted that the accusation was false, and demanded that the matter be laid before the senate. Accordingly, on the motion of Cicero, the senate in full session voted that the testimony of Tarquinius appeared to be false; that he should be kept under guard and given no further hearing until he revealed the name of the man at whose instigation he had lied about a matter of such moment. At the time some believed that this charge had been trumped up by Publius Autronius, in order

83

quo facilius appellato Crasso per societatem periculi
8 reliquos illius potentia tegeret. Alii Tarquinium
a Cicerone immissum aiebant, ne Crassus more suo
suscepto malorum patrocinio rem publicam conturba-
9 ret. Ipsum Crassum ego postea praedicantem
audivi tantam illam contumeliam sibi ab Cicerone
impositam.

XLIX. Sed isdem temporibus Q. Catulus et C.
Piso neque precibus neque gratia neque pretio[1]
Ciceronem impellere potuere[2] uti per Allobroges
aut alium indicem C. Caesar falso nominaretur.
2 Nam uterque cum illo gravis inimicitias exercebant;
Piso oppugnatus in iudicio pecuniarum repetundarum propter cuiusdam Transpadani supplicium
iniustum, Catulus ex petitione pontificatus odio
incensus, quod extrema aetate, maxumis honoribus
usus, ab adulescentulo Caesare victus discesserat.
3 Res autem opportuna videbatur, quod is privatim
egregia liberalitate, publice maxumis muneribus
4 grandem pecuniam debebat. Sed ubi consulem ad
tantum facinus impellere nequeunt, ipsi singillatim
circumeundo atque ementiundo quae se ex Volturcio
aut Allobrogibus audisse dicerent, magnam illi
invidiam conflaverant, usque eo ut non nulli equites

---

[1] neque precibus neque gratia neque pretio, *XNKMT*
(proemio *for* pretio) *lsn, Or*; n. pretio n. gratia, *Prisc.* ii.
539. 20 κ, *Ah.*

[2] impelli quivit, *Prisc.* ii. 539. 20 (*omitting* Ciceronem);
inlici quivit (Cicero), *Septimius, Belli Troiani* 1.18.

---

[1] Crassus gained popularity by acting as advocate for men
whom Pompey, Caesar and Cicero were unwilling to defend.
See Plutarch, *Crassus* iii. 2.

that by naming Crassus and involving him in the danger he might shield the rest behind his influence. Others declared that Tarquinius had been instigated by Cicero, to prevent Crassus from taking up the cause of the wicked, after his custom,[1] and embroiling the state. I heard Crassus himself assert afterwards that this grave insult was put upon him by Cicero.

XLIX. But at that very time Quintus Catulus and Gaius Piso tried in vain by entreaties, influence, and bribes to induce Cicero to have a false accusation brought against Gaius Caesar, either through the Allobroges or some other witness. For both these men were bitter personal enemies of Caesar, Piso because when he was on trial for extortion[2] Caesar had charged him with unjustly executing a native of Transpadine Gaul, while the hatred of Catulus arose from his candidacy for the pontificate, because after he had attained to a ripe old age and had held the highest offices, he had been defeated by Caesar, who was by comparison a mere youth.[3] Moreover, the opportunity for an attack upon Caesar seemed favourable, because he was heavily in debt on account of his eminent generosity in private life and lavish entertainments when in office. But when they could not persuade the consul to such an outrageous step, they took the matter into their own hands, and by circulating falsehoods which they pretended to have heard from Volturcius or the Allobroges, stirred up such hostility to Caesar that some Roman knights,

[2] The accusation of extortion was made by the Allobroges. Caesar, as patron of the province (see note on xli. 4), had made the additional charge. Piso was defended by Cicero and acquitted ; see Cic. *pro Flacco* 39. 98.

[3] Caesar was thirty-seven years old at the time.

Romani, qui praesidi causa cum telis erant circum
aedem Concordiae, seu periculi magnitudine seu
animi mobilitate impulsi, quo studium suum in rem
publicam clarius esset, ingredienti ex senatu Caesari
gladio minitarentur.

L. Dum haec in senatu aguntur et dum legatis
Allobrogum et T. Volturcio, comprobato eorum
indicio, praemia decernuntur, liberti et pauci ex
clientibus Lentuli divorsis itineribus opifices atque
servitia in vicis ad eum eripiundum sollicitabant,
partim exquirebant duces multitudinum, qui pretio
2 rem publicam vexare soliti erant. Cethegus autem
per nuntios familiam atque libertos suos, lectos et
exercitatos orabat in audaciam[1] ut grege facto cum
telis ad sese irrumperent.

3 Consul ubi ea parari cognovit, dispositis praesidiis
ut res atque tempus monebat, convocato senatu,
refert quid de eis fieri placeat qui in custodiam
traditi erant; sed eos paulo ante frequens senatus
4 iudicaverat contra rem publicam fecisse. Tum D.
Iunius Silanus, primus sententiam rogatus quod
eo tempore consul designatus erat, de eis qui in
custodiis tenebantur et praeterea de L. Cassio, P.
Furio, P. Umbreno, Q. Annio, si deprehensi forent,
supplicium sumundum decreverat; isque postea

[1] *Dietsch and others omit* in audaciam *with one inferior
codex; also Ahlberg without comment.*

who were stationed as an armed guard about the
temple of Concord, carried away either by the greatness of the danger or by their own excitability, drew
their swords upon Caesar as he was leaving the
senate, in order to make their loyalty to their
country more conspicuous.[1]

L. While all this was going on in the senate, and
rewards were being voted to the envoys of the Allobroges and to Titus Volturcius, when their information had been verified, the freedmen of Lentulus and
a few of his dependants were scouring the streets and
trying to rouse the artisans and slaves to rescue him,
while others were seeking out the leaders of
bands[2] who were wont to cause public disturbances
for hire. Cethegus, also, was sending messengers
to his slaves and freedmen, a picked and trained
body of men, entreating them to take a bold step,
get their band together, and force their way to him
with arms.

When the consul learned of these designs, station-
ing guards as the time and circumstances demanded
and convoking the senate, he put the question what
should be done with the men who had been delivered
into custody, the senate having shortly before this in
a full meeting resolved that they were guilty of
treason to their country. On the present occasion
Decimus Junius Silanus, who was consul-elect, and
hence the first to be called upon for his opinion regarding those who were held in custody, as well as
about Lucius Cassius, Publius Furius, Publius Umbrenus, and Titus Annius in case they should be
caught, had recommended that they be put to death;

---

[1] See Suetonius, *Jul.* 14, where the incident is referred to
the time of the debate about the punishment of the conspirators.   [2] Such as those of Clodius and Milo.

permotus oratione C. Caesaris pedibus in sententiam
Ti. Neronis iturum se dixerat, quod de ea re
5 praesidiis additis referundum censuerat. Sed Caesar,
ubi ad eum ventum est, rogatus sententiam a
consule huiuscemodi verba locutus est.

LI. "Omnis homines, patres conscripti, qui de
rebus dubiis consultant, ab odio, amicitia, ira atque
2 misericordia vacuos esse decet. Haud facile animus
verum providet, ubi illa officiunt, neque quisquam
3 omnium lubidini simul et usui paruit. Ubi in-
tenderis ingenium, valet; si lubido possidet, ea
4 dominatur, animus nihil valet. Magna mihi copia
est memorandi, patres conscripti, qui reges atque
populi ira aut misericordia impulsi male consulue-
rint. Sed ea malo dicere quae maiores nostri
contra lubidinem animi sui recte atque ordine
5 fecere. Bello Macedonico, quod cum rege Perse
gessimus, Rhodiorum civitas magna atque magnifica,
quae populi Romani opibus creverat, infida atque
advorsa nobis fuit. Sed postquam bello confecto
de Rhodiis consultum est, maiores nostri, ne quis
divitiarum magis quam iniuriae causa bellum in-
6 ceptum diceret, impunitos eos dimisere. Item

---

[1] After the members of the senate had expressed their
opinions, the supporters of a measure passed to one side of
the house (*pedibus ire in sententiam illius*) to be counted, the
opponents to the other.
[2] That is, the defences against the attempts of conspirators.
[3] Just before the battle of Pydna (168 B.C.) the Rhodians,
fearing the effect on their trade, threatened the Romans with
war unless they made peace with Perses. The elder Cato, in

later, profoundly influenced by the speech of Gaius Caesar, he said that, when a division was called for,[1] he would give his vote for the proposal of Tiberius Nero, who had advised merely that the guards be increased[2] and the question reopened. But Caesar, when his turn came and the consul asked him for his opinion, spoke in the following terms:

LI. "Fathers of the Senate, all men who deliberate upon difficult questions ought to be free from hatred and friendship, anger and pity. When these feelings stand in the way the mind cannot easily discern the truth, and no mortal man has ever served at the same time his passions and his best interests. When you apply your intellect, it prevails; if passion possesses you, it holds sway, and the mind is impotent. I might mention many occasions, Fathers of the Senate, when kings and peoples under the influence of wrath or pity have made errors of judgment; but I prefer to remind you of times when our forefathers, resisting the dictates of passion, have acted justly and in order. In the Macedonian war, which we waged with king Perses, the great and glorious community of the Rhodians, which owed its growth to the support of the Roman people, was unfaithful to us and hostile.[3] But after the war was over and the question of the Rhodians was under discussion, our ancestors let them go unpunished for fear that someone might say that the wealth of the Rhodians, rather than resentment for the wrong they had done, had led to the declaration of war. So, too, in all the Punic

a speech of which a part is preserved (Gell. 6. 3), persuaded the Romans not to retaliate. The Rhodians, however, were punished by the loss of their possessions in Lycia and Caria, which the Romans had given them as a reward for their help in the war with Antiochus.

bellis Punicis omnibus, cum saepe Carthaginienses
et in pace et per indutias multa nefaria facinora
fecissent, numquam ipsi per occasionem talia fecere ;
magis, quid se dignum foret, quam quid in illos
7 iure fieri posset quaerebant. Hoc item vobis providendum est, patres conscripti, ne plus apud vos
valeat P. Lentuli et ceterorum scelus quam vostra
dignitas, neu magis irae vostrae quam famae con-
8 sulatis. Nam si digna poena pro factis eorum
reperitur, novum consilium approbo ; sin magnitudo
sceleris omnium ingenia exsuperat, eis utendum
censeo quae legibus comparata sunt.

9   " Plerique eorum qui ante me sententias dixerunt
composite atque magnifice casum rei publicae mis-
erati sunt.   Quae belli saevitia esset, quae victis
acciderent, enumeravere ;   rapi virgines, pueros,
divelli liberos a parentum complexu, matres familiarum pati quae victoribus collubuissent,[1] fana atque
domos spoliari, caedem, incendia fieri, postremo
armis, cadaveribus, cruore atque luctu omnia com-
10 pleri. Sed, per deos immortalis, quo illa oratio
pertinuit ?   An uti vos infestos coniurationi faceret ?
Scilicet, quem res tanta et tam atrox non permovit,
11 eum oratio accendet.[2]   Non ita est, neque cuiquam
mortalium iniuriae suae parvae videntur ; multi eas
12 gravius aequo habuere. Sed alia aliis licentia est,
patres conscripti.   Qui demissi in obscuro vitam

[1] conlibuisset, *August. De Civ. Dei* i. 5.
[2] accendit, *VP²AMl.*

wars, although the Carthaginians both in time of peace and in the course of truces had often done many abominable deeds, the Romans never retaliated when they had the opportunity, but they inquired rather what conduct would be consistent with their dignity than how far the law would allow them to go in taking vengeance on their enemies. You likewise, Fathers of the Senate, must beware of letting the guilt of Publius Lentulus and the rest have more weight with you than your own dignity, and of taking more thought for your anger than for your good name. If a punishment commensurate with their crimes can be found, I favour a departure from precedent; but if the enormity of their guilt surpasses all men's imagination, I should advise limiting ourselves to such penalties as the law has established.

"The greater number of those who have expressed their opinions before me have deplored the lot of the commonwealth in finished and noble phrases; they have dwelt upon the horrors of war, the wretched fate of the conquered, the rape of maidens and boys, children torn from their parents' arms, matrons subjected to the will of the victors, temples and homes pillaged, bloodshed and fire; in short, arms and corpses everywhere, gore and grief. But, O ye immortal gods! what was the purpose of such speeches? Was it to make you detest the conspiracy? You think that a man who has not been affected by a crime so monstrous and so cruel will be fired by a speech! Nay, not so; no mortal man thinks his own wrongs unimportant; many, indeed, are wont to resent them more than is right. But not all men, Fathers of the Senate, are allowed the same freedom of action. If the humble, who pass their

habent siquid iracundia deliquere, pauci sciunt; fama atque fortuna eorum pares sunt : qui magno imperio praediti in excelso aetatem agunt, eorum facta
13 cuncti mortales novere. Ita in maxuma fortuna
14 minuma licentia est. Neque studere neque odisse, sed minume irasci decet. Quae apud alios iracundia dicitur, ea in imperio superbia atque crudelitas appellatur.

15 "Equidem ego sic existumo, patres conscripti, omnis cruciatus minores quam facinora illorum esse. Sed plerique mortales postrema meminere et in hominibus impiis sceleris eorum obliti de poena
16 disserunt, si ea paulo severior[1] fuit. D. Silanum, virum fortem atque strenuum, certo[2] scio quae dixerit studio rei publicae dixisse, neque illum in tanta re gratiam aut inimicitias exercere ; eos mores
17 eamque modestiam viri cognovi. Verum sententia eius mihi non crudelis—quid enim in talis homines crudele fieri potest ?—sed aliena a re publica nostra
18 videtur. Nam profecto aut metus aut iniuria te subegit, Silane, consulem designatum genus poenae
19 novum decernere. De timore supervacaneum[3] est disserere, cum praesertim diligentia clarissumi viri
20 consulis tanta praesidia sint in armis. De poena possum equidem dicere, id quod res habet, in luctu atque miseriis mortem aerumnarum requiem, non cruciatum esse, eam cuncta mortalium mala dissolvere, ultra neque curae neque gaudio locum esse.

---

[1] severior, *VACNT* ; sevior, *the other mss.*
[2] certo, *VXNnm* ; certe, *BYls.*
[3] supervacuaneum, *VPK, Ah.*

lives in obscurity, commit any offence through anger, it is known to few; their fame and fortune are alike. But the actions of those who hold great power, and pass their lives in a lofty station, are known to all the world. So it comes to pass that in the highest position there is the least freedom of action. There neither partiality nor dislike is in place, and anger least of all; for what in others is called wrath, this in a ruler is termed insolence and cruelty.

" For my own part, Fathers of the Senate, I consider no tortures sufficient for the crimes of these men; but most mortals remember only that which happens last, and in the case of godless men forget their guilt and descant upon the punishment they have received, if it is a little more severe than common. I have no doubt that Decimus Silanus, a gallant and brave man, was led by patriotism to say what he did say, and that in a matter of such moment he showed neither favour nor enmity; so well do I know the man's character and moderation. Yet his proposal seems to me, I will not say cruel (for what could be cruel in the case of such men?) but foreign to the customs of our country. For surely, Silanus, it was either fear or the gravity of the offence which impelled you, a consul elect, to favour a novel form of punishment. As regards fear it is needless to speak, especially since, thanks to the precautions of our distinguished consul, we have such strong guards under arms. So far as the penalty is concerned, I can say with truth that amid grief and wretchedness death is a relief from woes, not a punishment; that it puts an end to all mortal ills and leaves no room either for sorrow or for joy.

21 "Sed, per deos immortalis, quam ob rem in sententiam non addidisti, uti prius verberibus in eos
22 animadvorteretur? An quia lex Porcia vetat? At
aliae leges item condemnatis civibus non animam
23 eripi sed exsilium permitti iubent. An quia gravius
est verberari quam necari? Quid autem acerbum
aut nimis grave est in homines tanti facinoris
24 convictos? Sin quia levius est, qui convenit in
minore negotio legem timere, cum eam in maiore
25 neglegeris.[1] At enim quis reprehendet quod in
parricidas rei publicae decretum erit? Tempus,
dies, fortuna, cuius lubido gentibus moderatur.
26 Illis merito accidet quicquid evenerit; ceterum vos,
patres conscripti, quid in alios statuatis considerate.
27 Omnia mala exempla ex rebus bonis orta sunt; sed
ubi imperium ad ignaros eius[2] aut minus bonos
pervenit, novom illud exemplum ab dignis et idoneis
ad indignos et non idoneos transfertur.

28 "Lacedaemonii devictis Atheniensibus triginta
viros imposuere, qui rem publicam eorum tractarent.

---

[1] neglegeris, *P, Or*; neglexeris, *the other mss., Ah.*
[2] ignaros eius, *VPA¹NKlsm, Ah*; ignaros (ignavos) cives,
the other mss.; ignaros, *Or.*

---

[1] There were three laws of that name, the exact provisions
of which are unknown, but the scourging or putting to death
of a Roman citizen was forbidden.
[2] The Valerian laws and one of Gaius Gracchus.
[3] The proposal of Silanus to put Roman citizens to death

"But, in the name of Heaven! why did you not, Silanus, add the recommendation that they first be scourged? Was it because the Porcian law [1] forbids? Yes, but there are other laws [2] too which provide that Roman citizens, even when found guilty, shall not lose their lives, but shall be permitted to go into exile. Was it because it is more grievous to be scourged than to be killed? But what punishment is rigorous or too grievous for men convicted of so great a crime? If, however, it was because scourging is the lighter punishment, what consistency is there in respecting the law in the lesser point when you have disregarded it in the greater? [3] But, you may say, who will complain of a decree which is passed against traitors to their country? Time, I answer, the lapse of years, [4] and Fortune, whose caprice rules the nations. Whatever befalls these prisoners will be well deserved; but you, Fathers of the Senate, are called upon to consider how your action will affect other criminals. All bad precedents have originated in cases which were good; but when the control of the government falls into the hands of men who are incompetent or bad, your new precedent is transferred from those who well deserve and merit such punishment to the undeserving and blameless.

"The Lacedaemonians, after they had conquered the Athenians, set over them thirty men to carry

was a violation of the Porcian and other laws. If he omitted the scourging as too cruel, he minimized the guilt of the prisoners; but if he thought death the severer penalty, he violated the law in its more important part, especially since the prisoners had not been formally tried and condemned.

[4] *cf.* Verg. *Aen.* 5. 783, *quam* (= *Iunonem*), *nec longa dies pietas nec mitigat ulla* ; Liv. 2. 45. 2, *diem tempusque forsitan ipsum leniturum iras.*

SALLUST

29 Ei primo coepere pessumum quemque et omnibus
invisum indemnatum necare. Ea populus laetari et
30 merito dicere fieri. Post ubi paulatim licentia crevit,
iuxta bonos et malos lubidinose interficere, ceteros
31 metu terrere; ita civitas servitute oppressa stultae
32 laetitiae gravis poenas dedit. Nostra memoria victor
Sulla cum Damasippum et alios eiusmodi, qui malo
rei publicae creverant, iugulari iussit, quis non factum eius laudabat? Homines scelestos et factiosos,
qui seditionibus rem publicam exagitaverant, merito
33 necatos aiebant. Sed ea res magnae initium cladis
fuit; nam uti quisque domum aut villam, postremo
vas aut vestimentum alicuius concupiverat, dabat
34 operam ut is in proscriptorum numero esset. Ita
illi quibus Damasippi mors laetitiae fuerat paulo post
ipsi trahebantur, neque prius finis iugulandi fuit
quam Sulla omnis suos divitiis explevit.
35 "Atque ego haec[1] non in M. Tullio neque his
temporibus vereor; sed in magna civitate multa et
36 varia ingenia sunt. Potest alio tempore, alio consule, cui item exercitus in manu sit, falsum aliquid
pro vero credi; ubi hoc exemplo per senatus decretum consul gladium eduxerit, quis illi finem statuet
aut quis moderabitur?

haec ego, *V.*

---

[1] At the close of the Peloponnesian war (404 B.C.) the
Spartans attempted to maintain their hold upon the dependent
states by setting up in each a local governing board of

on their government.[1] These men began at first by putting to death without a trial the most wicked and generally hated citizens, whereat the people rejoiced greatly and declared that it was well done. But afterwards their licence gradually increased, and the tyrants slew good and bad alike at pleasure and intimidated the rest. Thus the nation was reduced to slavery and had to pay a heavy penalty for its foolish rejoicing. Within our own memory, when the conqueror Sulla ordered the execution of Damasippus and others of that kind, who had become prominent at the expense of the state, who did not commend his action? All declared that those criminal intriguers, who had vexed the country with their civil strife, deserved their fate. But that was the beginning of great bloodshed; for whenever anyone coveted a man's house in town or country, or at last even his goods or his garment, he contrived to have him enrolled among the proscribed. Thus those who had exulted in the death of Damasippus were themselves before long hurried off to execution, and the massacre did not end until Sulla glutted all his followers with riches.

"For my own part, I fear nothing of that kind for Marcus Tullius or for our times, but in a great commonwealth there are many different natures. It is possible that at another time, when someone else is consul and is likewise in command of an army, some falsehood may be believed to be true. When the consul, with this precedent before him, shall draw the sword in obedience to the senate's decree. who shall limit or restrain him?

aristocrats. The "Thirty Tyrants" at Athens were driven out after about eight months of excesses.

37 " Maiores nostri, patres conscripti, neque consili
neque audaciae umquam eguere, neque illis superbia
obstabat quo minus aliena instituta, si modo proba
38 erant, imitarentur.   Arma atque tela militaria ab
Samnitibus, insignia magistratuum ab Tuscis pleraque sumpserunt.   Postremo quod ubique apud socios
aut hostis idoneum videbatur, cum summo studio
domi exsequebantur; imitari quam invidere bonis
39 malebant.   Sed eodem illo tempore, Graeciae morem
imitati,[1] verberibus animadvortebant in civis, de con-
40 demnatis summum supplicium sumebant.   Postquam
res publica adolevit et multitudine civium factiones
valuere, circumveniri[2] innocentes, alia huiuscemodi
fieri coepere, tum lex Porcia aliaeque leges paratae
sunt, quibus legibus exsilium damnatis permissum
41 est.   Hanc ego[3] causam, patres conscripti, quo minus
novom consilium capiamus, in primis magnam puto.
42 Profecto virtus atque sapientia maior illis fuit, qui ex
parvis opibus tantum imperium fecere quam in nobis,
qui ea bene parta vix retinemus.
43   " Placet igitur eos dimitti et augeri exercitum
Catilinae ?   Minume.   Sed ita censeo, publicandas
eorum pecunias, ipsos in vinculis habendos per municipia quae maxume opibus valent, neu quis de eis
postea ad senatum referat neve cum populo agat;

----

[1] Graeciae morem imitati *put after* coepere tum (§ 40, l. 4)
by Döderlein.
[2] circumveniri, *V* ; *the other codices have* circumvenire.
[3] hanc ego, *PACNTm, Or* ; ego hanc, *VBHDFls, Ah* ;
hanc ergo, *KMn.*

----

[1] According to tradition, the laws of the Twelve Tables,
published in 449 B.C., were based upon those of Athens and

98

" Our ancestors, Fathers of the Senate, were never lacking either in wisdom or courage, and yet pride did not keep them from adopting foreign institutions, provided they were honourable. They took their offensive and defensive weapons from the Samnites, the badges of their magistrates for the most part from the Etruscans. In fine, whatever they found suitable among allies or foes, they put in practice at home with the greatest enthusiasm, preferring to imitate rather than envy the successful. But in that same age, following the usage of Greece,[1] they applied the scourge to citizens and inflicted the supreme penalty upon those found guilty. Afterwards, when the state reached maturity, and because of its large population factions prevailed; when the blameless began to be oppressed and other wrongs of that kind were perpetrated: then they devised the Porcian law[2] and other laws, which allowed the condemned the alternative of exile. This seems to me, Fathers of the Senate, a particularly cogent reason why we should not adopt a new policy. Surely there was greater merit and wisdom in those men, who from slight resources created this mighty empire, than in us, who can barely hold what they gloriously won.

" Do I then recommend that the prisoners be allowed to depart and swell Catiline's forces? By no means! This, rather, is my advice: that their goods be confiscated and that they themselves be kept imprisoned in the strongest of the free towns; further, that no one hereafter shall refer their case to the senate or bring it before the people, under

other Greek cities, to which a commission was sent from Rome for that purpose.　　　[2] See note on chap. li. 22.

qui aliter fecerit, senatum existumare eum contra
rem publicam et salutem omnium facturum."

LII. Postquam Caesar dicundi finem fecit, ceteri
verbo alius alii varie assentiebantur. At M. Porcius
Cato rogatus sententiam huiuscemodi orationem
habuit:

2 "Longe mihi alia mens est, patres conscripti, cum
res atque pericula nostra considero, et cum senten-
3 tias non nullorum ipse mecum reputo. Illi mihi
disseruisse videntur de poena eorum, qui patriae,
parentibus, aris atque focis suis bellum paravere.
Res autem monet cavere ab illis magis quam quid in
4 illos statuamus consultare. Nam cetera maleficia tum
persequare ubi facta sunt; hoc nisi provideris ne
accidat, ubi evenit frustra iudicia implores; capta
urbe nihil fit reliqui victis.

5 "Sed, per deos immortalis, vos ego appello, qui
semper domos, villas, signa, tabulas vostras pluris
quam rem publicam fecistis; si ista, cuiuscumque
modi sunt, quae amplexamini, retinere, si voluptatibus vostris otium praebere voltis, expergiscimini ali-
6 quando et capessite rem publicam. Non agitur de
vectigalibus neque de sociorum iniuriis; libertas et
7 anima nostra in dubio est. Saepe numero, patres
conscripti, multa verba in hoc ordine feci, saepe de

pain of being considered by the senate to have designs against the welfare of the state and the common safety."

LII. After Caesar had finished speaking, the rest briefly expressed their adherence to one or another of the various proposals. But Marcus Porcius Cato, when called upon for his opinion, spoke to the following purport:

"My feelings are very different, Fathers of the Senate, when I turn my mind to the plot and the danger we are in, and when I reflect upon the recommendations of some of our number. The speakers appear to me to have dwelt upon the punishment of these men who have plotted warfare upon their country, parents, altars, and hearths; but the situation warns us rather to take precautions against them than to argue about what we are to do with them. For in the case of other offences you may proceed against them after they have been committed; with this, unless you take measures to forestall it, in vain will you appeal to the laws when once it has been consummated. Once a city has been taken nothing is left to the vanquished.

"Nay, in the name of the immortal gods I call upon you, who have always valued your houses, villas, statues, and paintings more highly than your country; if you wish to retain the treasures to which you cling, of whatsoever kind they may be, if you even wish to provide peace for the enjoyment of your pleasures, wake up at last and lay hold of the reins of the state. Here is no question of revenues or the wrongs of our allies; our lives and liberties are at stake. Oftentimes, Fathers of the Senate, I have spoken at great length before this body; I have

luxuria atque avaritia nostrorum civium questus sum,
8 multosque mortalis ea causa advorsos habeo. Qui
mihi atque animo meo nullius umquam delicti gratiam fecissem, haud facile alterius lubidini male
9 facta condonabam. Sed ea tametsi vos parvi pen-
debatis, tamen res publica firma erat, opulentia
neglegentiam tolerabat.

10   "Nunc vero non id agitur, bonisne an malis moribus vivamus, neque quantum aut quam magnificum
imperium populi Romani sit, sed haec, cuiuscumque
modi videntur, nostra an nobiscum una hostium
11 futura sint. Hic mihi quisquam mansuetudinem et
misericordiam nominat. Iam pridem equidem nos
vera vocabula rerum amisimus. Quia bona aliena
largiri liberalitas, malarum rerum audacia fortitudo
12 vocatur, eo res publica in extremo sita est. Sint
sane, quoniam ita se mores habent, liberales ex
sociorum fortunis, sint misericordes in furibus aerari;
ne illi sanguinem nostrum largiantur et, dum paucis
sceleratis parcunt, bonos omnis perditum eant.

13   "Bene et composite C. Caesar paulo ante in hoc
ordine de vita et morte disseruit, credo falsa existumans ea quae de inferis memorantur, divorso itinere
malos a bonis loca taetra, inculta, foeda atque formi-
14 dulosa habere. Itaque censuit pecunias eorum publicandas, ipsos per municipia in custodiis habendos,

---

[1] That is, because of his scepticism about future punishment.

often deplored the extravagance and greed of our citizens, and in that way I have made many men my enemies. I, who had never granted to myself or to my impulses indulgence for any transgression, could not readily condone misdeeds prompted by another's passion. But although you were wont to give little weight to my words, yet the state was unshaken; its prosperity made good your neglect.

"Now, however, the question before us is not whether our morals are good or bad, nor how great or glorious the empire of the Roman people is, but whether all that we have, however we regard it, is to be ours, or with ourselves is to belong to the enemy. At this point (save the mark!) someone hints at gentleness and long-suffering! But in very truth we have long since lost the true names for things. It is precisely because squandering the goods of others is called generosity, and recklessness in wrong doing is called courage, that the republic is reduced to extremities. Let these men by all means, since such is the fashion of the time, be liberal at the expense of our allies, let them be merciful to plunderers of the treasury; but let them not be prodigal of our blood, and in sparing a few scoundrels bring ruin upon all good men.

"In fine and finished phrases did Gaius Caesar a moment ago before this body speak of life and death, regarding as false, I presume, the tales which are told of the Lower World, where they say that the wicked take a different path from the good, and dwell in regions that are gloomy, desolate, unsightly, and full of fears. Therefore[1] he recommended that the goods of the prisoners be confiscated, and that they themselves be imprisoned in the free towns, doubtless

videlicet timens ne, si Romae sint, aut a popularibus
coniurationis aut a multitudine conducta per vim
15 eripiantur. Quasi vero mali atque scelesti tantum
modo in urbe et non per totam Italiam sint, aut non
ibi plus possit audacia, ubi ad defendundum opes
16 minores sunt. Quare vanum equidem hoc consilium
est, si periculum ex illis metuit; sin in tanto omnium
metu solus non timet, eo magis refert me mihi atque
17 vobis timere. Quare cum de P. Lentulo ceterisque
statuetis, pro certo habetote vos simul de exercitu
18 Catilinae et de omnibus coniuratis decernere. Quanto
vos attentius ea agetis, tanto illis animus infirmior
erit; si paululum modo vos languere viderint, iam
19 omnes feroces aderunt. Nolite existumare maiores
nostros armis rem publicam ex parva magnam fecisse.
20 Si ita res esset, multo pulcherrumam eam nos habe-
remus, quippe sociorum atque civium, praeterea armorum atque equorum maior copia nobis quam illis
21 est. Sed alia fuere quae illos magnos fecere, quae
nobis nulla sunt; domi industria, foris iustum imperium, animus in consulundo liber neque delicto
22 neque lubidini obnoxius. Pro his nos habemus luxu-
riam atque avaritiam, publice egestatem, privatim
opulentiam. Laudamus divitias, sequimur inertiam.
Inter bonos et malos discrimen nullum, omnia virtutis
23 praemia ambitio possidet. Neque mirum; ubi vos
separatim sibi quisque consilium capitis, ubi domi
voluptatibus, hic pecuniae aut gratiae servitis, eo fit
ut impetus fiat in vacuam rem publicam.

through fear that if they remained in Rome the adherents of the plot or a hired mob would rescue them by force. As if, indeed, there were base and criminal men only in our city and not all over Italy, or as if audacity had not greatest strength where the power to resist it is weakest! Therefore, this advice is utterly futile if Caesar fears danger from the conspirators; but if amid such general fear he alone has none, I have the more reason to fear for you and for myself. Be assured, then, that when you decide the fate of Publius Lentulus and the rest, you will at the same time be passing judgment on Catiline's army and all the conspirators. The more vigorous your action, the less will be their courage; but if they detect the slightest weakness on your part, they will all be here immediately, filled with reckless daring. Do not suppose that it was by arms that our forefathers raised our country from obscurity to greatness. If that were so, we should have a much fairer state than theirs, since we have a greater number of citizens and allies than they possessed, to say nothing of arms and horses. But there were other qualities which made them great, which we do not possess at all: efficiency at home, a just rule abroad, in counsel an independent spirit free from guilt or passion. In place of these we have extravagance and greed, public poverty and private opulence. We extol wealth and foster idleness. We make no distinction between good men and bad, and ambition appropriates all the prizes of merit. And no wonder! When each of you schemes for his own private interests, when you are slaves to pleasure in your homes and to money or influence here, the natural result is an attack upon the defenceless republic.

24 " Sed ego haec omitto. Coniuravere nobilissumi
cives patriam incendere, Gallorum gentem infestis-
sumam nomini Romano ad bellum arcessunt. Dux
25 hostium cum exercitu supra caput est. Vos cunctamini etiam nunc et dubitatis quid intra moenia
26 deprensis hostibus faciatis? Misereamini censeo—
deliquere homines adulescentuli per ambitionem—
27 atque etiam armatos dimittatis. Ne ista vobis man-
suetudo et misericordia, si illi arma ceperint, in
28 miseriam convortat. Scilicet res ipsa aspera est, sed
vos non timetis eam. Immo vero maxume; sed
inertia et mollitia animi alius alium exspectantes
cunctamini, videlicet dis immortalibus confisi, qui
hanc rem publicam saepe in maxumis periculis ser-
29 vavere. Non votis neque suppliciis muliebribus
auxilia deorum parantur; vigilando, agundo, bene
consulundo prospera omnia cedunt. Ubi socordiae
te atque ignaviae tradideris, nequiquam deos implores; irati infestique sunt.
30 " Apud maiores nostros A. Manlius Torquatus
bello Gallico filium suum, quod is contra imperium
31 in hostem pugnaverat, necari iussit, atque ille egregius adulescens immoderatae fortitudinis morte poe-
32 nas dedit. Vos de crudelissumis parricidis quid
statuatis cunctamini? Videlicet cetera vita eorum
33 huic sceleri obstat. Verum[1] parcite dignitati Lentuli,
si ipse pudicitiae, si famae suae, si dis aut hominibus

---

[1] vero, *VPA*[1]*l.*

---

[1] An error for Titus.

"But I let that pass. Citizens of the highest rank have conspired to fire their native city, they stir up to war the Gauls, bitterest enemies of the Roman people. The leader of the enemy with his army is upon us. Do you even now hesitate and doubtfully ask yourselves what is to be done with foemen taken within your walls? Have compassion upon them, I conjure you (they are but young men, led astray by ambition), and even let them go, taking their arms with them! Of a truth, if they should resort to war, that gentleness and long-suffering of yours would result in suffering. No doubt the situation is a terrible one, you say, but you are not afraid of it. Nay, but you do fear it exceedingly, though from slothfulness and weakness of spirit you hesitate, waiting one for the other, doubtless trusting to the immortal gods, who have often saved our country in moments of extreme danger. Not by vows nor womanish entreaties is the help of the gods secured; it is always through watchfulness, vigorous action, and wisdom in counsel that success comes. When you abandon yourself to cowardice and baseness, it is vain to call upon the gods; they are offended and hostile.

"In the days of our forefathers Aulus[1] Manlius Torquatus, while warring with the Gauls, ordered the execution of his own son, because he had fought against the enemy contrary to orders, and the gallant young man paid the penalty for too great valour with his life. Do you hesitate what punishment to inflict upon the most ruthless traitors? No doubt their past lives have been such as to palliate this crime! By all means spare Lentulus because of his rank, if he ever spared his own chastity, his good name, or

umquam ullis pepercit. Ignoscite Cethegi adules-
34 centiae, nisi iterum patriae bellum fecit. Nam quid
ego de Gabinio, Statilio, Caepario loquar? Quibus
si quicquam umquam pensi fuisset, non ea consilia
de re publica habuissent.

35 "Postremo, patres conscripti, si mehercule pec-
cato locus esset, facile paterer vos ipsa re corrigi,
quoniam verba contemnitis. Sed undique circumventi sumus. Catilina cum exercitu faucibus[1] urget;
alii intra moenia atque in sinu urbis sunt hostes;
neque parari neque consuli quicquam potest occulte;
36 quo magis properandum est. Quare ego ita censeo:
cum nefario consilio sceleratorum civium res publica
in maxuma pericula venerit, eique indicio T. Volturci
et legatorum Allobrogum convicti confessique sint
caedem, incendia aliaque se foeda atque crudelia
facinora in civis patriamque paravisse, de confessis,
sicuti de manufestis rerum capitalium, more maiorum
supplicium sumundum."

LIII. Postquam Cato assedit, consulares omnes
itemque senatus magna pars sententiam eius lau-

---

[1] in faucibus Etruriae agit, *Linker.*

---

[1] That is, if there were time to correct an error once made.
[2] Although the conspirators had only planned these crimes
and had been prevented from committing them, because of
their confession they should be punished as if they had been
caught in the act of perpetrating them.

anyone, god or man. Pardon the youth of Cethegus, if this is not the second time that he has made war upon his country. And what shall I say of Gabinius, Statilius, and Caeparius, who would never have formed such designs against the republic if they had ever respected anything?

"Finally, Fathers of the Senate, if (Heaven help us!) there were any room for error[1] I should be quite willing to let you learn wisdom by experience, since you scorn my advice. But as it is, we are beset on every side. Catiline with his army is at our throats; other foes are within our walls, aye, in the very heart of Rome. Neither preparations nor plans can be kept secret; therefore the more need of haste. This, then, is my recommendation: whereas our country has been subjected to the greatest peril through the abominable plot of wicked citizens, and whereas they have been proven guilty by the testimony of Titus Volturcius and the envoys of the Allobroges, and have confessed that they have planned murder, arson, and other fearful and cruel crimes against their fellow citizens and their country, let those who have confessed be treated as though they had been caught red-handed in capital offences,[2] and be punished after the manner of our forefathers."[3]

LIII. As soon as Cato had taken his seat, all the ex-consuls, as well as a great part of the other senators, praised his proposal and lauded his courage to

---

[3] The meaning apparently is that they be not allowed the choice of exile. Some have thought that Cato recommended the specific *supplicium de more maiorum* described in Suetonius, *Nero* 49, but there are many reasons for rejecting this view. See Oldfather in *Trans. Amer. Phil. Assoc.* xxxix. 49 ff.

dant, virtutem animi ad caelum ferunt, alii alios increpantes timidos vocant. Cato clarus atque magnus habetur; senati decretum fit sicuti ille censuerat.

2 Sed mihi multa legenti multa audienti quae populus Romanus domi militiaeque, mari atque terra, praeclara facinora fecit, forte lubuit attendere quae

3 res maxume tanta negotia sustinuisset. Sciebam saepe numero parva manu cum magnis legionibus hostium contendisse; cognoveram parvis copiis bella gesta cum opulentis regibus, ad hoc saepe fortunae violentiam toleravisse; facundia Graecos, gloria belli

4 Gallos ante Romanos fuisse. Ac mihi multa agitanti constabat paucorum civium egregiam virtutem cuncta patravisse eoque factum uti divitias paupertas, mul-

5 titudinem paucitas superaret. Sed postquam luxu atque desidia civitas corrupta est, rursus res publica magnitudine sua imperatorum atque magistratuum vitia sustentabat ac, sicuti effeta parentum vi,[1] multis tempestatibus haud sane quisquam Romae virtute

6 magnus fuit. Sed memoria mea ingenti virtute, divorsis moribus fuere viri duo, M. Cato et C. Caesar; quos quoniam res obtulerat, silentio praeterire non fuit consilium, quin utriusque naturam et mores, quantum ingenio possum,[2] aperirem.

LIV. Igitur eis genus, aetas, eloquentia prope

---

[1] effeta parentum, *mss.*; effeta vi parentum, *Ritschl*; effeta parentum vi, *Ah, Or.*

[2] possum, *PDl s*; possem, *the other mss., Ah, Or.*

the skies, while they taxed one another with timorousness. Cato was hailed as great and noble, and a decree of the senate was passed in accordance with his recommendation.

For my own part, as I read and heard of the many illustrious deeds of the Roman people at home and abroad, on land and sea, it chanced that I was seized by a strong desire of finding out what quality in particular had been the foundation of so great exploits. I knew that often with a handful of men they had encountered great armies of the enemy; I was aware that with small resources they had waged wars with mighty kings; also that they had often experienced the cruelty of Fortune; that the Romans had been surpassed by the Greeks in eloquence and by the Gauls in warlike glory. After long reflection I became convinced that it had all been accomplished by the eminent merit of a few citizens; that it was due to them that poverty had triumphed over riches, and a few over a multitude. But after the state had become demoralized by extravagance and sloth, it was the commonwealth in its turn that was enabled by its greatness to sustain the shortcomings of its generals and magistrates, and for a long time, as when mothers are exhausted by child-bearing, no one at all was produced at Rome who was great in merit. But within my own memory there have appeared two men of towering merit, though of diverse character, Marcus Cato and Gaius Caesar. As regards these men, since the occasion has presented itself, it is not my intention to pass them by in silence, or fail to give, to the best of my ability, an account of their disposition and character.

LIV. In birth then, in years and in eloquence,

aequalia fuere, magnitudo animi par, item gloria, sed
2 alia alii. Caesar beneficiis ac munificentia magnus
habebatur, integritate vitae Cato. Ille mansuetudine et misericordia clarus factus, huic severitas
3 dignitatem addiderat. Caesar dando, sublevando,
ignoscundo, Cato nihil largiundo gloriam adeptus
est. In altero miseris perfugium erat, in altero
malis pernicies. Illius facilitas, huius constantia
4 laudabatur. Postremo Caesar in animum induxerat
laborare, vigilare; negotiis amicorum intentus sua
neglegere, nihil denegare quod dono dignum esset;
sibi magnum imperium, exercitum, bellum novom
5 exoptabat, ubi virtus enitescere posset. At Catoni
studium modestiae, decoris, sed maxume severitatis
6 erat. Non divitiis cum divite neque factione cum
factioso, sed cum strenuo virtute, cum modesto pudore, cum innocente abstinentia certabat; esse quam
videri bonus malebat; ita quo minus petebat gloriam,
eo magis illum sequebatur.

LV. Postquam, ut dixi, senatus in Catonis sententiam discessit, consul optumum factu ratus noctem
quae instabat antecapere, ne quid eo spatio novaretur,
triumviros quae ad supplicium postulabantur[1] parare

---

[1] postulabantur, *Ah* (*Or*); postulabat (·bant, *A*), *mss.*

---

[1] But see Suetonius, *Jul.* 19. 1, where Cato is said to have
connived at bribery in order to secure the election of Bibulus.
[2] One for which he had the entire responsibility (*cf.* Livy
9. 42. 3 and 31. 8. 6). Perhaps said in disparagement of
Pompey, who finished wars begun by other men.

they were about equal; in greatness of soul they were evenly matched, and likewise in renown, although the renown of each was different. Caesar was held great because of his benefactions and lavish generosity, Cato for the uprightness of his life. The former became famous for his gentleness and compassion, the austerity of the latter had brought him prestige. Caesar gained glory by giving, helping, and forgiving; Cato by never stooping to bribery.[1] One was a refuge for the unfortunate, the other a scourge for the wicked. The good nature of the one was applauded, the steadfastness of the other. Finally, Caesar had schooled himself to work hard and sleep little, to devote himself to the welfare of his friends and neglect his own, to refuse nothing which was worth the giving. He longed for great power, an army, a new[2] war to give scope for his brilliant merit. Cato, on the contrary, cultivated self-control, propriety, but above all austerity. He did not vie with the rich in riches nor in intrigue with the intriguer, but with the active in good works, with the self-restrained in moderation, with the blameless in integrity. He preferred to be, rather than to seem, virtuous;[3] hence the less he sought fame, the more it pursued him.

LV. After the senate had adopted the recommendation of Cato, as I have said, the consul thought it best to forestall any new movement during the approaching night. He therefore ordered the triumvirs[4] to make the necessary preparations for the

---

[3] cf. Aeschylus, Seven against Thebes, 589: οὐ γὰρ δοκεῖν ἄριστος, ἀλλ᾽ εἶναι θέλει.

[4] The tresviri capitales were minor magistrates who had charge of prisons and executions and performed certain police duties.

2 iubet, ipse praesidiis dispositis Lentulum in carcerem
deducit ; idem fit ceteris per praetores.

3   Est in carcere locus, quod Tullianum appellatur,
ubi paululum ascenderis [1] ad laevam, circiter duode-
4 cim pedes humi depressus. Eum muniunt undique
parietes atque insuper camera lapideis fornicibus
iuncta : sed incultu, tenebris, odore foeda atque
5 terribilis eius facies est. In eum locum postquam
demissus est Lentulus, vindices rerum capitalium,
6 quibus praeceptum erat, laqueo gulam fregere. Ita
ille patricius ex gente clarissuma Corneliorum, qui
consulare imperium Romae habuerat, dignum moribus factisque suis exitium [2] vitae invenit. De Cethego,
Statilio, Gabinio, Caepario, eodem modo supplicium
sumptum est.

   LVI. Dum ea Romae geruntur, Catilina ex omni
copia quam et ipse adduxerat et Manlius habuerat
2 duas legiones instituit, cohortis pro numero militum
complet ; deinde, ut quisque voluntarius aut ex sociis
in castra venerat, aequaliter distribuerat, ac brevi
spatio legiones numero hominum expleverat, cum
3 initio non amplius duobus milibus habuisset. Sed
ex omni copia circiter pars quarta erat militaribus

   [1] descenderis, *n.*
   [2] exitum, *Treb. Poll. Claud.* 5. 3 ; *Aug. Epist.* 43. 2,
perhaps rightly (Ah).

---

   [1] This statement can hardly be reconciled with the
existing remains ; the rest of the description is clear and
applies to the Carcer, the so-called "Mamertine Prison,"
near the north-western corner of the Roman Forum.
   [2] It was probably an old spring-house and derived its name
from an early Latin word *tullius,* meaning "spring," although

execution. After setting guards, he personally led Lentulus to the dungeon, while the praetors performed the same office for the others.

In the prison, when you have gone up a little way towards the left,[1] there is a place called the Tullianum,[2] about twelve feet below the surface of the ground. It is enclosed on all sides by walls, and above it is a chamber with a vaulted roof of stone. Neglect, darkness, and stench make it hideous and fearsome to behold. Into this place Lentulus was let down, and then the executioners[3] carried out their orders and strangled him. Thus that patrician, of the illustrious stock of the Cornelii, who had held consular authority at Rome, ended his life in a manner befitting his character and his crimes. Cethegus, Statilius, Gabinius, and Caeparius suffered the same punishment.

LVI. While this was taking place in Rome, Catiline combined the forces which he had brought with him with those which Manlius already had, and formed two legions, filling up the cohorts so far as the number of his soldiers permitted.[4] Then distributing among them equally such volunteers or conspirators as came to the camp, he soon completed the full quota of the legions, although in the beginning he had no more than two thousand men. But only about a fourth part of the entire force was

the Romans themselves connected it with **Servius Tullius**. See Platner, *Topography of Rome*, pp. 251 f.

[3] The *carnifices*, servants of the *tresviri*, or perhaps those officials themselves ; see Cic. *de Leg.* 3. 3. 6.

[4] That is, he made two legions of ten cohorts each, but the number in each cohort was below the normal one until he filled it up from the volunteers and conspirators that came into his camp. At first he had two thousand men ; at last, two full legions.

armis instructa, ceteri, ut quemque casus armaverat, sparos aut lanceas, alii praeacutas sudis portabant.

4 Sed postquam Antonius cum exercitu adventabat, Catilina per montis iter facere, modo ad urbem modo Galliam [1] vorsus castra movere, hostibus occasionem pugnandi non dare; sperabat prope diem magnas copias sese habiturum, si Romae socii incepta patra-

5 vissent. Interea servitia repudiabat, cuius initio ad eum magnae copiae concurrebant, opibus coniurationis fretus, simul alienum suis rationibus existumans videri causam civium cum servis fugitivis communicavisse.

LVII. Sed postquam in castra nuntius pervenit, Romae coniurationem patefactam, de Lentulo et Cethego ceterisque quos supra memoravi supplicium sumptum, plerique, quos ad bellum spes rapinarum aut novarum rerum studium illexerat, dilabuntur, reliquos Catilina per montis asperos magnis itineribus in agrum Pistoriensem abducit eo consilio, uti per tramites occulte perfugeret in Galliam Trans-

2 alpinam. At Q. Metellus Celer cum tribus legionibus in agro Piceno praesidebat, ex difficultate rerum eadem illa existumans quae supra diximus Catilinam

3 agitare. Igitur ubi iter eius ex perfugis cognovit, castra propere movit ac sub ipsis radicibus montium consedit, qua illi descensus erat in Galliam prope-

---

[1] in G. vorsus, *Or, Prisc.* ii. 514, 22 κ; in G., *NKmn*; ad G., *F*; G. vorsus, *the other mss., Ah.*

---

[1] The *gladius* (sword), *pilum* (pike), *scutum* (shield), *lorica* (coat of mail), *cassis* (helmet), and *ocreae* (greaves).

provided with regular arms.[1] The others carried whatever weapons chance had given them; namely, javelins or lances, or in some cases pointed stakes.

When Antonius was drawing near with his army, Catiline marched through the mountains, moved his camp now towards the city and now in the direction of Gaul, and gave the enemy no opportunity for battle, hoping shortly to have a large force if the conspirators at Rome succeeded in carrying out their plans. Meanwhile he refused to enroll slaves, a great number of whom flocked to him at first, because he had confidence in the strength of the conspiracy and at the same time thought it inconsistent with his designs to appear to have given runaway slaves a share in a citizens' cause.[2]

LVII. But when news reached the camp that the plot had been discovered at Rome, and that Lentulus, Cethegus, and the others whom I mentioned had been done to death, very many of those whom the hope of pillage or desire for revolution had led to take up arms began to desert. The remainder Catiline led by forced marches over rugged mountains to the neighbourhood of Pistoria, intending to escape secretly by cross-roads into Transalpine Gaul. But Quintus Metellus Celer, with three legions, was on the watch in the Picene district, inferring from the difficulty of the enemy's position that he would take the very course which I have mentioned. Accordingly, when he learned through deserters in what direction Catiline was going, he quickly moved his camp and took up a position at the foot of the very mountains from which the conspirator would have to

[2] On the attitude towards the military service of slaves and freedmen, see Suetonius, *Aug.* 25.

4 ranti. Neque tamen Antonius procul aberat, utpote qui magno exercitu locis aequioribus expedito in 5 fuga[1] sequeretur. Sed Catilina, postquam videt montibus atque copiis hostium sese clausum, in urbe res advorsas, neque fugae neque praesidi ullam spem, optumum factu ratus in tali re fortunam belli temptare, statuit cum Antonio quam primum confligere. Itaque contione advocata huiuscemodi orationem habuit.

LVIII. "Compertum ego habeo, milites, verba virtutem non addere, neque ex ignavo strenuum neque fortem ex timido exercitum oratione impera-2 toris fieri. Quanta cuiusque animo audacia natura aut moribus inest, tanta in bello patere solet. Quem neque gloria neque pericula excitant, nequiquam 3 hortere; timor animi auribus officit. Sed ego vos, quo pauca monerem, advocavi, simul uti causam mei consili aperirem.

4 "Scitis equidem, milites, socordia atque ignavia Lentuli quantam ipsi nobisque cladem attulerit quoque modo, dum ex urbe praesidia opperior, in Gal-5 liam proficisci nequiverim. Nunc vero quo loco res 6 nostrae sint, iuxta mecum omnes intellegitis. Exercitus hostium duo, unus ab urbe alter a Gallia obstant. Diutius in his locis esse, si maxume animus ferat, frumenti atque aliarum rerum egestas pro-

---

[1] expedito, *Wirz*; expeditos in fuga (fugam), *mss., Prisc.* iii. 343. 20 κ; expeditus in fuga, *Ah, Or.* "*Fortasse cum Dietschio scribendum* expeditus impeditos," *Ah.*

descend in his flight into Gaul. Antonius also was
not far distant, since he was following the fleeing
rebels over more level ground with an army which,
though large, was lightly equipped.[1] Now, when
Catiline perceived that he was shut in between the
mountains and the forces of his enemies, that his
plans in the city had failed, and that he had hope
neither of escape nor reinforcements, thinking it best
in such a crisis to try the fortune of battle, he decided
to engage Antonius as soon as possible. Accordingly
he assembled his troops and addressed them in a
speech of the following purport:

LVIII. "I am well aware, soldiers, that words do
not supply valour, and that a spiritless army is not
made vigorous, or a timid one stout-hearted, by a
speech from its commander. Only that degree of
courage which is in each man's heart either by disposition or by habit, is wont to be revealed in battle.
It is vain to exhort one who is roused neither by
glory nor by dangers; the fear he feels in his heart
closes his ears. I have, however, called you together
to offer a few words of advice, and at the same time
to explain the reason for my resolution.

"You know perfectly well, soldiers, how great is
the disaster that the incapacity and cowardice of
Lentulus have brought upon himself and us, and
how, waiting for reinforcements from the city, I
could not march into Gaul. At this present time,
moreover, you understand as well as I do in what
condition our affairs stand. Two hostile armies,
one towards Rome, the other towards Gaul, block
our way. We cannot remain longer where we
are, however much we may desire it, because of

[1] Text and meaning are uncertain; see the critical note.

7 hibet. Quocumque ire placet, ferro iter aperiundum
8 est. Qua propter vos moneo uti forti atque parato
animo sitis et, cum proelium inibitis, memineritis
vos divitias, decus, gloriam, praeterea libertatem
9 atque patriam in dextris vostris portare. Si vinci-
mus, omnia nobis tuta erunt, commeatus abunde,
municipia atque coloniae patebunt; si[1] metu cesseri-
10 mus, eadem illa advorsa fient, neque locus neque
amicus quisquam teget quem arma non texerint.
11 Praeterea, milites, non eadem nobis et illis necessitudo impendet; nos pro patria, pro libertate, pro
vita certamus, illis supervacuaneum est pro potentia
12 paucorum pugnare. Quo audacius aggrediamini,[2]
memores pristinae virtutis.
13 "Licuit vobis[3] cum summa turpitudine in exsilio
aetatem agere, potuistis non nulli Romae, amissis
14 bonis, alienas opes expectare; quia illa foeda atque
intoleranda viris videbantur, haec sequi decrevistis.
15 Si haec relinquere voltis, audacia opus est; nemo
16 nisi victor pace bellum mutavit. Nam in fuga salutem sperare, cum arma, quibus corpus tegitur, ab
17 hostibus avorteris, ea vero dementia est. Semper in
proelio eis maxumum est periculum qui maxume
timent, audacia pro muro habetur.
18 "Cum vos considero, milites, et cum facta vostra
19 aestumo, magna me spes victoriae tenet. Animus,
aetas, virtus vostra me hortantur, praeterea necessi-
20 tudo, quae etiam timidos fortis facit. Nam multitudo hostium ne circumvenire queat, prohibent

---

[1] sin, *Kritz.* [2] aggredimini, *VC l, Ah, Or.*
[3] vobis, *VP²C²D n* ; nobis, *the other mss.*

lack of grain and other necessities. Wherever we decide to go, we must hew a path with the sword. Therefore I counsel you to be brave and ready of spirit, and when you enter the battle to remember that you carry in your own right hands riches, honour, glory; yea, even freedom and your native land. If we win, complete security will be ours, supplies will abound, free towns and colonies will open their gates; but if we yield to fear, the very reverse will be true: no place and no friend will guard the man whom arms could not protect. Moreover, soldiers, we and our opponents are not facing the same exigency. We are battling for country, for freedom, for life; theirs is a futile contest, to uphold the power of a few men. March on, therefore, with the greater courage, mindful of your former valour.

"You might have passed your life in exile and in utter infamy, at Rome some of you might look to others for aid after losing your estates; but since such conditions seemed base and intolerable to true men, you decided upon this course. If you wish to forsake it, you have need of boldness; none save the victor exchanges war for peace. To hope for safety in flight when you have turned away from the enemy the arms which should protect your body, is surely the height of madness. In battle the greatest danger always threatens those who show the greatest fear; boldness is a bulwark.

"When I think on you, my soldiers, and weigh your deeds, I have high hopes of victory. Your spirit, youth, and valour give me heart, not to mention necessity, which makes even the timid brave. In this narrow defile the superior numbers of the

21 angustiae loci.[1] Quod si virtuti vostrae fortuna in-
viderit, cavete inulti animam amittatis, neu capti
potius sicuti pecora trucidemini quam virorum more
pugnantes cruentam atque luctuosam victoriam
hostibus relinquatis."

LIX. Haec ubi dixit, paululum commoratus signa
canere iubet atque instructos ordines in locum
aequum deducit. Dein remotis omnium equis, quo
militibus exaequato periculo animus amplior esset,
ipse pedes exercitum pro loco atque copiis instruit.
2 Nam uti planities erat inter sinistros montis et ab
dextra rupe aspera, octo cohortis in fronte consti-
3 tuit, reliquarum signa in subsidio artius collocat. Ab
eis centuriones, omnis lectos et evocatos, praeterea
ex gregariis militibus optumum quemque armatum
in primam aciem subducit. C. Manlium in dextra,
Faesulanum quendam in sinistra parte curare iubet.
Ipse cum libertis et calonibus[2] propter aquilam ad-
sistit, quam bello Cimbrico C. Marius in exercitu
habuisse dicebatur.
4 At ex altera parte C. Antonius, pedibus aeger,
quod proelio adesse nequibat M. Petreio legato
5 exercitum permittit. Ille cohortis veteranas, quas
tumultus causa conscripserat, in fronte, post eas
ceterum exercitum in subsidiis locat; ipse equo cir-

---

[1] colonibus, *PA[1]Nl* ; colonis, *C[2]HΓs m, Ah, Or* ; coloniis,
A[2]C[1]BKn.

---

[1] *cf.* Caesar, *B.G.* 1. 25.
[2] The *evocati* were veterans who after their discharge had
been induced to enlist again, usually with the rank of

enemy cannot surround us. But if Fortune frowns
upon your bravery, take care not to die unavenged.
Do not be captured and slaughtered like cattle, but,
fighting like heroes, leave the enemy a bloody and
tearful victory."

LIX. When he had thus spoken, after a brief pause
he ordered the trumpets to sound and led his army
in order of battle down into the plain. Then, after
sending away all the horses,[1] in order to make the
danger equal for all and thus to increase the soldiers'
courage, himself on foot like the rest he drew up his
army as the situation and his numbers demanded.
Since, namely, the plain was shut in on the left by
mountains and on the right by rough, rocky ground, en-
posted eight cohorts in front and held the rest in reserve in closer order. From these he took the centurions, all picked men and reservists,[2] as well as the
best armed of the ordinary soldiers, and placed them
in the front rank. He gave the charge of the right
wing to Gaius Manlius, and that of the left to a man
of Faesulae. He himself with his freedmen and
the camp-servants took his place beside the eagle,
which, it was said, had been in the army of Gaius
Marius during the war with the Cimbri.

On the other side Gaius Antonius, who was ill
with the gout[3] and unable to enter the battle, he
trusted his army to Marcus Petreius, his lieutenant.
Petreius placed in the van the veteran cohorts which
he had enrolled because of the outbreak, and behind
them the rest of his army in reserve. Riding up

centurion. In this case many of them were probably old
soldiers of Sulla.

[3] Cassius Dio, 37. 39, asserts that Antonius feigned
illness, so as not to take the field against his old associate.

cumiens unum quemque nominans appellat, hortatur,
rogat ut meminerint se contra latrones inermis[1] pro
patria, pro liberis, pro aris atque focis suis certare.
6 Homo militaris, quod amplius annos triginta tribunus
aut praefectus aut legatus aut praetor cum magna
gloria in exercitu fuerat, plerosque ipsos factaque
eorum fortia noverat; ea commemorando militum
animos accendebat.

LX. Sed ubi, omnibus rebus exploratis, Petreius
tuba signum dat, cohortis paulatim incedere iubet.
2 Idem facit hostium exercitus. Postquam eo ventum
est unde a[2] ferentariis proelium committi posset,[3]
maxumo clamore cum infestis signis concurrunt;
3 pila omittunt, gladiis res geritur. Veterani, pristinae
virtutis memores, comminus acriter instare, illi haud
4 timidi resistunt; maxuma vi certatur. Interea Catilina cum expeditis in prima acie vorsari, laborantibus
succurrere, integros pro sauciis arcessere, omnia providere, multum ipse pugnare, saepe hostem ferire;
strenui militis et boni imperatoris officia simul exse-
quebatur.
5 Petreius ubi videt Catilinam, contra ac ratus erat,

[1] inhermos, *P.*
[2] a *omitted in* X, *superscribed in* A *l.*
[3] possit, *P¹A C¹.*

---

[1] That is, without regular arms; see chap. lvi. 3.

and down upon his horse, he addressed each of his men by name, exhorted him, and begged him to remember that he was fighting against unarmed[1] highwaymen in defence of his country, his children, his altars, and his hearth. Being a man of military experience, who had served in the army with high distinction for more than thirty years as tribune, prefect, lieutenant, or commander, he personally knew the greater number of his soldiers and their valorous deeds of arms, and by mentioning these he fired the spirits of his men.

LX. When Petreius, after making all his preparations, gave the signal with the trumpet, he ordered his cohorts to advance slowly; the army of the enemy followed their example. After they had reached a point where battle could be joined by the skirmishers,[2] the hostile armies rushed upon each other with loud shouts, then threw down their pikes and took to the sword. The veterans, recalling their old-time prowess, advanced bravely to close quarters; the enemy, not lacking in courage, stood their ground, and there was a terrific struggle. Meanwhile Catiline, with his light-armed troops, was busy in the van, aided those who were hard pressed, summoned fresh troops to replace the wounded, had an eye to everything, and at the same time fought hard himself, often striking down the foe—thus performing at once the duties of a valiant soldier and of a skilful leader.

When Petreius saw that Catiline was making so

---

[2] The *ferentarii* were light-armed infantry stationed on the wings, who hurled their javelins and then retired behind the battle line.

magna vi tendere, cohortem praetoriam in medios
hostis inducit eosque perturbatos atque alios alibi
resistentis interficit. Deinde utrimque ex lateribus
6 ceteros aggreditur. Manlius et Faesulanus in primis
7 pugnantes cadunt. Catilina postquam fusas copias
seque cum paucis relictum videt, memor generis
atque pristinae suae dignitatis in confertissumos
hostis incurrit ibique pugnans confoditur.

LXI. Sed confecto proelio tum vero cerneres
quanta audacia quantaque animi vis fuisset in exer-
2 citu Catilinae. Nam fere quem quisque vivos pugnando locum ceperat, eum amissa anima corpore
3 tegebat. Pauci autem, quos medios cohors praetoria
disiecerat, paulo divorsius sed omnes tamen advorsis
4 volneribus conciderant. Catilina vero longe a suis
inter hostium cadavera repertus est, paululum etiam
spirans ferociamque animi, quam habuerat vivos, in
5 voltu retinens. Postremo ex omni copia neque in
proelio neque in fuga quisquam civis ingenuus captus
6 est; ita cuncti suae hostiumque vitae iuxta perper-
cerant.

7 Neque tamen exercitus populi Romani laetam aut
incruentam victoriam adeptus erat. Nam strenuis-
sumus quisque aut occiderat in proelio aut graviter

---

[1] The praetorian cohort was the general's bodyguard, made
up of selected infantry and cavalry. Thus Caesar (*B. G.* 1. 40)

much stronger a fight than he had expected, he led his praetorian cohort[1] against the enemy's centre, threw them into confusion, and slew those who resisted in various parts of the field; then he attacked the rest on both flanks at once. Manlius and the man from Faesulae were among the first to fall, sword in hand. When Catiline saw that his army was routed and that he was left with a mere handful of men, mindful of his birth and former rank he plunged into the thickest of the enemy and there fell fighting, his body pierced through and through.

LXI. When the battle was ended it became evident what boldness and resolution had pervaded Catiline's army. For almost every man covered with his body, when life was gone, the position which he had taken when alive at the beginning of the conflict. A few, indeed, in the centre, whom the praetorian cohort had scattered, lay a little apart from the rest, but the wounds even of these were in front. But Catiline was found far in advance of his men amid a heap of slain foemen, still breathing slightly, and showing in his face the indomitable spirit which had animated him when alive. Finally, out of the whole army not a single citizen of free birth was taken during the battle or in flight, showing that all had valued their own lives no more highly than those of their enemies.

But the army of the Roman people gained no joyful nor bloodless victory, for all the most valiant had either fallen in the fight or come off with severe

proposes to give that honour to the Tenth legion. Under the empire the praetorian guard gradually acquired great importance and political power.

8 volneratus discesserat. Multi autem, qui e castris visundi aut spoliandi gratia processerant, volventes hostilia cadavera amicum alii pars hospitem aut cognatum reperiebant; fuere item qui inimicos suos 9 cognoscerent. Ita varie per omnem exercitum laetitia, maeror, luctus atque gaudia agitabantur.

wounds. Many, too, who had gone from the camp to visit the field or to pillage, on turning over the bodies of the rebels found now a friend, now a guest or kinsman; some also recognized their personal enemies. Thus the whole army was variously affected with sorrow and grief, rejoicing and lamentation.

THE WAR WITH JUGURTHA

BELLUM IUGURTHINUM

I. Falso queritur de natura sua genus humanum,
quod imbecilla atque aevi brevis forte potius quam
2 virtute regatur.   Nam contra reputando neque
maius aliud neque praestabilius invenias magisque
naturae industriam hominum quam vim aut tempus
3 deesse.   Sed dux atque imperator vitae mortalium
animus est.   Qui ubi ad gloriam virtutis via gras-
satur, abunde pollens potensque et clarus est neque
fortuna eget, quippe[1] probitatem, industriam, aliasque artis bonas neque dare neque eripere cuiquam
4 potest.   Sin captus pravis cupidinibus ad inertiam
et voluptates corporis pessum datus est, perniciosa
lubidine paulisper usus, ubi per socordiam vires,
tempus, ingenium diffluxere, naturae infirmitas ac-
cusatur; suam quisque culpam auctores[2] ad negotia
transferunt.
5   Quodsi hominibus bonarum rerum tanta cura
esset, quanto studio aliena ac nihil profutura multaque etiam periculosa petunt, neque regerentur magis
quam regerent casus et eo magnitudinis procederent,
ubi pro mortalibus gloria aeterni fierent.

[1] quippe quae, *NK¹H²MD n m, Donat. Ter. Eun.* 241,
Ah, Or.
[2] auctores, *BH¹T¹*; *the other mss. have* actores.

132

THE WAR WITH JUGURTHA

I. WITHOUT reason do mankind complain of their nature, on the ground that it is weak and of short duration and ruled rather by chance than by virtue. For reflection would show on the contrary that nothing is greater or more excellent, and that nature has more often found diligence lacking in men than strength or endurance in itself. But the leader and ruler of man's life is the mind, and when this advances to glory by the path of virtue, it has power and potency in abundance, as well as fame; and it needs not fortune, since fortune can neither give to any man honesty, diligence, and other good qualities, nor can she take them away. But if through the lure of base desires the mind has sunk into sloth and the pleasures of the body, when it has enjoyed ruinous indulgence for a season, when strength, time, and talents have been wasted through indolence, the weakness of human nature is accused, and the guilty shift their own blame to circumstances.

But if men had as great regard for honourable enterprises as they have ardour in pursuing what is foreign to their interests, and bound to be unprofitable and often even dangerous, they would control fate rather than be controlled by it, and would attain to that height of greatness where from mortals their glory would make them immortal.

II. Nam uti genus hominum compositum ex corpore et anima est, ita res cunctae studiaque omnia nostra corporis alia, alia animi naturam 2 secuntur. Igitur praeclara facies, magnae divitiae, ad hoc vis corporis et alia omnia huiuscemodi brevi dilabuntur, at ingeni egregia facinora sicuti anima immortalia sunt.

3 Postremo corporis et fortunae bonorum ut initium sic finis est, omniaque orta occidunt et aucta senescunt; animus incorruptus, aeternus, rector humani generis agit atque habet cuncta neque ipse 4 habetur. Quo magis pravitas eorum admiranda est, qui dediti corporis gaudiis per luxum et ignaviam aetatem agunt, ceterum ingenium, quo neque melius neque amplius aliud in natura mortalium est, incultu atque socordia torpescere sinunt, cum praesertim tam multae variaeque sint artes animi, quibus summa claritudo paratur.

III. Verum ex eis magistratus et imperia, postremo omnis cura rerum publicarum minume mihi hac tempestate cupiunda videntur, quoniam neque virtuti honos datur, neque illi quibus per fraudem 2 ius[1] fuit, tuti aut eo magis honesti sunt. Nam vi quidem regere patriam aut parentes, quamquam et possis et delicta corrigas, tamen importunum est, cum praesertim omnes rerum mutationes caedem, 3 fugam, aliaque hostilia portendant. Frustra autem

---

[1] is, n^2; iis, PNK^2l.

II. For just as mankind is made up of body and soul, so all our acts and pursuits partake of the nature either of the body or of the mind. Therefore notable beauty and great riches, as well as bodily strength and all other gifts of that kind, soon pass away, but the splendid achievements of the intellect, like the soul, are everlasting.

In short, the goods of the body and of fortune have an end as well as a beginning, and they all rise and fall, wax and wane; but the mind, incorruptible, eternal, ruler of mankind, animates and controls all things, yet is itself not controlled. Therefore we can but marvel the more at the perversity of those who pass their life in riotous living and idleness, given over to the pleasures of the body, but allow the mind, which is better and greater than anything else in man's nature, to grow dull from neglect and inaction; especially when there are so many and so varied intellectual pursuits by which the highest distinction may be won.

III. But among these pursuits, in my opinion, magistracies and military commands, in short all public offices, are least desirable in these times, since honour is not bestowed upon merit, while those who have gained it wrongfully are neither safe nor the more honourable because of it.[1] For to rule one's country or subjects[2] by force, although you both have the power to correct abuses, and do correct them, is nevertheless tyrannical; especially since all attempts at change foreshadow bloodshed, exile, and other horrors of war. Moreover, to struggle in

---

[1] Sallust was writing in the troublous times which followed the assassination of Caesar.

[2] For this meaning cf. cii. 7, *parentes abunde habemus.*

niti neque aliud se fatigando nisi odium quaerere,
extremae dementiae est, nisi forte quem inhonesta
et perniciosa lubido tenet potentiae paucorum decus
atque libertatem suam gratificari.

IV. Ceterum ex aliis negotiis quae ingenio exer-
centur, in primis magno usui est memoria rerum
2 gestarum. Cuius de virtute quia multi dixere,
praetereundum puto, simul ne per insolentiam quis
existumet memet studium meum laudando extollere.
3 Atque ego credo fore qui, quia decrevi procul a re
publica aetatem agere, tanto tamque utili labori
meo nomen inertiae imponant, certe quibus maxuma
industria videtur salutare plebem et conviviis gra-
4 tiam quaerere. Qui si reputaverint, et quibus ego
temporibus magistratus adeptus sim et quales viri
idem adsequi nequiverint et postea quae genera
hominum in senatum pervenerint, profecto existu-
mabunt me magis merito quam ignavia iudicium
animi mei mutavisse maiusque commodum ex otio
meo quam ex aliorum negotiis rei publicae venturum.
5 Nam saepe ego audivi Q. Maxumum, P. Scipionem,
praeterea civitatis nostrae praeclaros viros solitos ita
dicere, cum maiorum imagines intuerentur, vehem-

---

[1] *Nisi forte* is strongly ironical, introducing an incredible
motive for holding office; *cf. Cat.* xx. 17 ; before *nisi forte*
we must supply " But one must be either a tyrant or a fool."
[2] Sallust contrasts the time when he held office with the
time when he was writing; see note on iii. 1 and the
Introduction.

vain and after wearisome exertion to gain nothing
but hatred, is the height of folly, unless haply one
is possessed by a dishonourable and pernicious
passion for sacrificing one's personal honour and
liberty to the power of a few men.[1]

IV. But among intellectual pursuits, the recording
of the events of the past is especially serviceable;
but of that it becomes me to say nothing, both because many men have already spoken of its value,
and in order that no one may suppose that I am led
by vanity to eulogize my own favourite occupation.
I suppose, too, that since I have resolved to pass my
life aloof from public affairs, some will apply to this
arduous and useful employment of mine the name
of idleness, certainly those who regard courting the
people and currying favour by banquets as the height
of industriousness. But if such men will only bear
in mind in what times I was elected to office,[2] what
men of merit were unable to attain the same honour[3]
and what sort of men have since come into the
senate,[4] they will surely be convinced that it is rather
from justifiable motives than from indolence that I
have changed my opinion, and that greater profit will
accrue to our country from my inactivity than from
others' activity.

I have often heard that Quintus Maximus, Publius
Scipio, and other eminent men of our country, were
in the habit of declaring that their hearts were set
mightily aflame for the pursuit of virtue whenever

---

[3] Such as Cato, who was an unsuccessful candidate for the
praetorship in 55 B.C.

[4] Referring both to the Gauls admitted by Julius Caesar
and to the "orcini," so called from *Orcus* apparently, because Mark Antony pretended that they had been designated
as senators in Caesar's will ; see Suetonius, *Jul.* 80 ; *Aug.* 35.

6 entissume sibi animum ad virtutem accendi. Scilicet
non ceram illam neque figuram tantam vim in sese
habere, sed memoria rerum gestarum eam flammam
egregiis viris in pectore crescere neque prius sedari,
quam virtus eorum famam atque gloriam adaequa-
verit.

7   At contra quis est omnium his moribus, quin
divitiis et sumptibus, non probitate neque industria
cum maioribus suis contendat? Etiam homines
novi, qui antea per virtutem soliti erant nobilitatem
antevenire, furtim et per latrocinia potius quam
bonis artibus ad imperia et honores nituntur;
8 proinde quasi praetura et consulatus atque alia
omnia huiuscemodi per se ipsa clara et magnifica
sint, ac non perinde habeantur ut eorum qui ea
9 sustinent virtus est. Verum ego liberius altiusque
processi, dum me civitatis morum piget taedetque.
Nunc ad inceptum redeo.

  V. Bellum scripturus sum quod populus Romanus
cum Iugurtha rege Numidarum gessit, primum quia
magnum et atrox variaque victoria fuit, dehinc quia
tunc primum superbiae nobilitatis obviam itum est.
2 Quae contentio divina et humana cuncta permiscuit
eoque vecordiae processit, ut studiis civilibus bellum
3 atque vastitas Italiae finem faceret. Sed priusquam

---

  [1] A Roman had the right to make waxen masks of those of
his ancestors who had held a curule office (consul, praetor,
censor, or curule aedile) and keep them in the atrium of his

they gazed upon the masks[1] of their ancestors. Of course they did not mean to imply that the wax or the effigy had any such power over them, but rather that it is the memory of great deeds that kindles in the breasts of noble men this flame that cannot be quelled until they by their own prowess have equalled the fame and glory of their forefathers.

But in these degenerate days, on the contrary, who is there that does not vie with his ancestors in riches and extravagance rather than in uprightness and diligence? Even the "new men,"[2] who in former times always relied upon worth to outdo the nobles, now make their way to power and distinction by intrigue and open fraud rather than by noble practices; just as if a praetorship, a consulship, or anything else of the kind were distinguished and illustrious in and of itself and were not valued according to the merit of those who live up to it. But in giving expression to my sorrow and indignation at the morals of our country I have spoken too freely and wandered too far from my subject. To this I now return.

V. I propose to write of the war which the people of Rome waged with Jugurtha, king of the Numidians: first, because it was long, sanguinary and of varying fortune; and secondly, because then for the first time resistance was offered to the insolence of the nobles—the beginning of a struggle which threw everything, human and divine, into confusion, and rose to such a pitch of frenzy that civil discord ended in war and the devastation of Italy. But before

house. They were worn in funerals of members of the family by actors who impersonated the dead, and were exhibited on other solemn occasions.

[2] See note on *Cat.* xxiii. 6.

huiuscemodi rei initium expedio, pauca supra re-
petam, quo ad cognoscundum omnia illustria magis
magisque in aperto sint.

4   Bello Punico secundo, quo dux Carthaginiensium
Hannibal post magnitudinem nominis Romani Italiae
opes maxume attriverat, Masinissa rex Numidarum
in amicitiam receptus a P. Scipione, cui postea
Africano cognomen ex virtute fuit, multa et praeclara rei militaris facinora fecerat. Ob quae victis
Carthaginiensibus et capto Syphace, cuius in Africa
magnum atque late imperium valuit, populus
Romanus quascumque urbis et agros manu ceperat
5 regi dono dedit. Igitur amicitia Masinissae bona
atque honesta nobis permansit. Sed imperi vitaeque
6 eius finis idem fuit. Dein Micipsa filius regnum
solus obtinuit, Mastanabale et Gulussa fratribus
7 morbo absumptis. Is Adherbalem et Hiempsalem
ex sese genuit Iugurthamque filium Mastanabalis
fratris, quem Masinissa, quod ortus ex concubina
erat, privatum dereliquerat, eodem cultu quo liberos
suos domi habuit.

VI. Qui ubi primum adolevit, pollens viribus,
decora facie, sed multo maxume ingenio validus, non
se luxu [1] neque inertiae corrumpendum dedit, sed,
uti mos gentis illius est, equitare, iaculari, cursu
cum aequalibus certare, et cum omnis gloria anteiret,
omnibus tamen carus esse ; ad hoc pleraque tempora

[1] luxu, *Ym, Fronto, p.* 108 *Naber* ; *Diomedes*, i. 341. 6 к;
luxui, *XNTlsn* ; luxuriae, *Macrob.* v. 624, 24 к.

actually beginning such a narrative, let me recall a few earlier events, in order that everything may be placed in a better light for our understanding and may be the more clearly revealed.

During the second Punic war, when Hannibal, leader of the Carthaginians, had dealt Italy's power the heaviest blow since the Roman nation attained its full stature, Masinissa, king of Numidia, had become the friend of Publius Scipio, afterwards surnamed Africanus because of his prowess, and performed many illustrious deeds of arms. In return for this, after the defeat of the Carthaginians and the capture of Syphax, whose dominion in Africa was great and extensive, the Roman people gave Masinissa as a free gift all the cities and territories that he[1] had taken in war. Consequently Masinissa was ever our true and loyal friend. But his reign and his 148 B.C. life ended together. His son Micipsa then became sole ruler, since his brothers Mastanabal and Gulussa had fallen ill and died. Micipsa begot Adherbal and Hiempsal, and brought up in the palace, in the same manner as his own children, a son of his brother Mastanabal called Jugurtha, whom Masinissa in his will had allowed to remain a commoner because he was the offspring of a concubine.

VI. As soon as Jugurtha grew up, endowed as he was with physical strength, a handsome person, but above all with a vigorous intellect, he did not allow himself to be spoiled by luxury or idleness, but following the custom of that nation, he rode, he hurled the javelin, he contended with his fellows in foot-races; and although he surpassed them all in renown, he nevertheless won the love of all. Besides this, he devoted much time to the chase, he was

[1] Or perhaps "they," *i.e. populus Romanus.*

in venando agere, leonem atque alias feras primus
aut in primis ferire, plurumum facere et minumum
ipse de se loqui.

2   Quibus rebus Micipsa tametsi initio laetus fuerat,
existumans virtutem Iugurthae regno suo gloriae
fore, tamen postquam hominem adulescentem exacta
sua aetate et parvis liberis magis magisque crescere
intellegit, vehementer eo negotio permotus, multa
3 cum animo suo volvebat. Terrebat eum natura
mortalium avida imperi et praeceps ad explendam
animi cupidinem, praeterea opportunitas suae liberorumque aetatis, quae etiam mediocris viros spe
praedae transvorsos agit; ad hoc studia Numidarum
in Iugurtham accensa, ex quibus, si talem virum
dolis interfecisset, ne qua seditio aut bellum oriretur
anxius erat.

    VII. His difficultatibus circumventus ubi videt
neque per vim neque insidiis opprimi posse hominem
tam acceptum popularibus, quod erat Iugurtha manu
promptus et appetens gloriae militaris, statuit eum
obiectare periculis et eo modo fortunam temptare.
2 Igitur bello Numantino Micipsa cum populo Romano
equitum atque peditum auxilia mitteret, sperans vel
ostentando virtutem vel hostium saevitia facile eum
occasurum, praefecit Numidis quos in Hispaniam
mittebat.

3   Sed ea res longe aliter ac ratus erat evenit.
4 Nam Iugurtha, ut erat impigro atque acri ingenio,

the first or among the first to strike down the lion and other wild beasts, he distinguished himself greatly, but spoke little of his own exploits.

At first Micipsa was delighted with this conduct, believing that the prowess of Jugurtha would contribute to the glory of his kingdom; but when he realized that the man was young and constantly growing in power, while he himself was advanced in years and his children were small, he was seriously troubled by the situation and gave it constant thought. He dreaded the natural disposition of mankind, which is greedy for power and eager to gratify its heart's desire, while his own years and the youthfulness of his sons offered that opportunity which through the hope of gain leads astray even men of moderate ambition. He observed too the devotion which Jugurtha had inspired in the Numidians, and was apprehensive of some rebellion or war from that source, if by treachery he should cause the death of such a man.

VII. Embarrassed by these problems, and seeing that one so dear to the people could not be put out of the way by violence or by stratagem, he resolved, inasmuch as Jugurtha was full of energy and eager for military glory, to expose him to dangers and thus put fortune to the proof. Accordingly, when Micipsa sent cavalry and infantry to aid the Romans in the war with Numantia, he gave Jugurtha command of the Numidians whom he sent to Spain, hoping that 134 B.C he would easily fall a victim either to a desire to display his valour or to the ruthless foe.

But the result was not at all what he had expected; for Jugurtha, who had an active and keen intellect, soon became acquainted with the character of Publius

143

ubi naturam P. Scipionis, qui tum Romanis imperator erat, et morem hostium cognovit, multo labore
multaque cura, praeterea modestissume parendo et
saepe obviam eundo periculis in tantam claritudinem
brevi pervenerat, ut nostris vehementer carus,
5 Numantinis maxumo terrori esset. Ac sane, quod
difficillumum in primis est, et proelio strenuus erat
et bonus consilio, quorum alterum ex providentia
timorem, alterum ex audacia temeritatem afferre
6 plerumque solet. Igitur imperator omnis fere res
asperas per Iugurtham agere, in amicis habere,
magis magisque eum in dies amplecti, quippe cuius
neque consilium neque inceptum ullum frustra erat.
7 Huc accedebat munificentia animi et ingeni soller-
tia, quis rebus sibi multos ex Romanis familiari
amicitia coniunxerat.

VIII. Ea tempestate in exercitu nostro fuere
complures novi atque nobiles, quibus divitiae bono
honestoque potiores erant, factiosi domi, potentes
apud socios, clari magis quam honesti, qui Iugurthae
non mediocrem animum pollicitando accendebant, si
Micipsa rex occidisset, fore uti solus imperi Numidiae
potiretur: in ipso maxumam virtutem, Romae omnia
venalia esse.

2 Sed postquam Numantia deleta P. Scipio dimittere
auxilia et ipse revorti domum decrevit, donatum
atque laudatum magnifice pro contione Iugurtham
in praetorium abduxit ibique secreto monuit ut
potius **publice** quam privatim amicitiam populi

Scipio, who then commanded the Romans, and with the tactics of the enemy. Then by hard labour and attention to duty, at the same time by showing strict obedience and often courting dangers, he shortly acquired such a reputation that he became very popular with our soldiers and a great terror to the Numantians. In fact, he was both valiant in war and wise in counsel, a thing most difficult to achieve, for most often wisdom through caution leads to timorousness and valour through boldness to rashness. Therefore Scipio relied upon Jugurtha for almost all difficult undertakings, treated him as a friend, and grew more and more attached to him every day, since the young Numidian failed neither in judgment nor in any enterprise. He had, besides, a generous nature and a ready wit, qualities by which he had bound many Romans to him in intimate friendship.

VIII. At that time there were a great many in our army, both new men and nobles, who cared more for riches than for virtue and self-respect; they were intriguers at home, influential with our allies, rather notorious than respected. These men fired Jugurtha's ambitious spirit by holding out hopes that if king Micipsa should die, he might gain the sole power in Numidia, since he himself stood first in merit,[1] while at Rome anything could be bought.

Now when Numantia had been destroyed and 133 B.C. Publius Scipio determined to disband his auxiliary troops and return to Rome himself, after giving Jugurtha gifts and commending him in the highest terms before the assembled soldiers, he took him into his tent. There he privately advised the young man

---

[1] As compared with Hiempsal and Adherbal, the sons of Micipsa.

Romani coleret neu quibus largiri insuesceret; periculose a paucis emi, quod multorum esset. Si permanere vellet in suis artibus, ultro illi et gloriam et regnum venturum, sin properantius pergeret, suamet ipsum pecunia praecipitem casurum.

IX. Sic locutus cum litteris eum, quas Micipsae redderet, dimisit. Earum sententia haec erat:
2 "Iugurthae tui bello Numantino longe maxuma virtus fuit, quam rem tibi certo scio gaudio esse. Nobis ob merita sua carus est; ut idem senatui et populo Romano sit, summa ope nitemur. Tibi quidem pro nostra amicitia gratulor. En habes virum dignum te atque avo suo Masinissa."
3 Igitur rex ubi ea quae fama acceperat ex litteris imperatoris ita esse cognovit, cum virtute tum gratia viri permotus flexit animum suum et Iugurtham beneficiis vincere aggressus est, statimque eum adoptavit et testamento pariter cum filiis heredem
4 instituit. Sed ipse paucos post annos morbo atque aetate confectus cum sibi finem vitae adesse intellegeret, coram amicis et cognatis itemque Adherbale et Hiempsale filiis dicitur huiuscemodi verba cum Iugurtha habuisse.

X. "Parvom ego, Iugurtha, te amisso patre sine spe sine opibus in regnum meum accepi, existumans

---

[1] But in xi. 6 *tribus proximis annis* must mean some time between 121 and 118 B.C., since Micipsa died in 118. Sallust is loose in his chronology.

to cultivate the friendship of the Roman people at large rather than that of individual Roman citizens, and not to form the habit of bribery. It was dangerous, he said, to buy from a few what belonged to the many. If Jugurtha would continue as he had begun, fame and a throne would come to him unsought; but if he acted too hastily, he would bring about his ruin by means of his own money.

IX. After speaking in this way, Scipio dismissed the young man with a letter to be delivered to Micipsa, the purport of which was this: "The valour of your Jugurtha in the Numantine war was most conspicuous, as I am sure you will be glad to learn. To us he is dear because of his services, and we shall use our best efforts to make him beloved also by the senate and people of Rome. As your friend I congratulate you; in him you have a hero worthy of yourself and of his grandfather Masinissa."

Then the king, upon learning from the general's letter that the reports which had come to his ears were true, was led both by Jugurtha's merits and by his influential position to change his plans and attempt to win the young man by kindness. He adopted him at once [1] and in his will named him joint heir with his sons. But a few years later and upon his own motion the king, then enfeebled by years and illness and realizing that the end of his life was near, is said to have talked with Jugurtha in the presence of his friends and kinsfolk, including his sons Adherbal and Hiempsal, in some such terms as the following.

X. "When you were a small boy, Jugurtha, an orphan without prospects or means, I took you into the royal household, believing that because of my

non minus me tibi, quam[1] si genuissem, ob beneficia
2 carum fore. Neque ea res falsum me habuit. Nam,
ut alia magna et egregia tua omittam, novissume
rediens Numantia meque regnumque meum gloria
honoravisti tuaque virtute nobis Romanos ex amicis
amicissumos fecisti; in Hispania nomen familiae
renovatum est. Postremo, quod difficillumum inter
3 mortalis est, gloria invidiam vicisti. Nunc, quoniam
mihi natura finem vitae facit, per hanc dexteram,
per regni fidem moneo obtestorque te, uti hos, qui
tibi genere propinqui, beneficio meo fratres sunt,
caros habeas neu malis alienos adiungere quam
4 sanguine coniunctos retinere. Non exercitus neque
thesauri praesidia regni sunt, verum amici, quos
neque armis cogere neque auro parare queas; officio
5 et fide pariuntur. Quis autem amicior quam frater
fratri aut quem alienum fidum invenies, si tuis hostis
6 fueris? Equidem ego vobis regnum trado firmum,
si boni eritis, sin mali, imbecillum. Nam concordia
parvae res crescunt, discordia maxumae dilabuntur.
7 Ceterum ante hos te, Iugurtha, qui aetate et
sapientia prior es, ne aliter quid eveniat providere
decet. Nam in omni certamine qui opulentior est,
etiam si accipit iniuriam, tamen, quia plus potest,
8 facere videtur. Vos autem, Adherbal et Hiempsal,

---

[1] quam liberis, *mss.*, *Ah*, *Or.*

kindness you would love me as if you were my own child. And I was not mistaken; for, to say nothing of your other great and noble actions, of late on your return from Numantia you have conferred honour upon me and my realm by your glory, and by your prowess have made the Romans still more friendly to Numidia than before; while in Spain the name of our family has been given new life.[1] Finally, by the glory you have won you have overcome envy, a most difficult feat for mortal man. Now, since nature is bringing my life to its close, I conjure and implore you by this right hand, by the loyalty due to the kingdom,[2] hold dear these youths who are your kinsmen by birth and through my favour are your brothers; and do not desire to make new friends among strangers in preference to keeping the love of those who are bound to you by ties of blood. Neither armies nor treasure form the bulwarks of a throne, but friends; these you can neither acquire by force of arms nor buy with gold; it is by devotion and loyalty that they are won. But who is more bound by ties of friendship than brother to brother, or what stranger will you find loyal, if you become the enemy of your kindred? I deliver to you three a realm that is strong if you prove virtuous, but weak if you do ill; for harmony makes small states great, while discord undermines the mightiest empires. As for the rest, it devolves upon you, Jugurtha, rather than upon these children, since you are older and wiser than they, to see to it that my hopes are not disappointed. For in all strife the stronger, even though he suffer wrong, is looked upon as the aggressor because of his superior power. As for you, Adherbal and Hiempsal,

---

[1] Referring to the exploits of Masinissa.
[2] cf. xxiv. 10, *fides amicitiae.*

colite, observate talem hunc virum, imitamini virtutem et enitimini ne ego meliores liberos sumpsisse videar quam genuisse."

XI. Ad ea Iugurtha, tametsi regem ficta locutum intellegebat et ipse longe aliter animo agitabat, 2 tamen pro tempore benigne respondit. Micipsa paucis post diebus moritur. Postquam illi more regio iusta magnifice fecerant, reguli in unum convenerunt, ut inter se de cunctis negotiis discep- 3 tarent. Sed Hiempsal, qui minumus ex illis erat, natura ferox et iam antea ignobilitatem Iugurthae, quia materno genere impar erat, despiciens, dextra Adherbalem assedit, ne medius ex tribus, quod apud 4 Numidas honori ducitur, Iugurtha foret. Dein tamen ut aetati concederet fatigatus a fratre, vix in partem alteram transductus est.

5 Ibi cum multa de administrando imperio dissererent, Iugurtha inter alias res iacit, oportere quinquenni consulta et decreta omnia rescindi; nam per ea tempora confectum annis Micipsam parum 6 animo valuisse. Tum idem Hiempsal placere sibi respondit; nam ipsum illum tribus proxumis annis 7 adoptatione in regnum pervenisse. Quod verbum in pectus Iugurthae altius quam quisquam ratus erat 8 descendit. Itaque ex eo tempore ira et metu anxius moliri, parare atque ea modo cum animo habere,

love and respect this great man, emulate his virtues, and strive to show that I did not adopt better children than I begat."

XI. Although Jugurtha knew that the king spoke insincerely, and though he had very different designs in his own mind, yet he returned a gracious answer, suited to the occasion. A few days later Micipsa died. After the princes had performed his obsequies with regal splendour, they met together for a general discussion of their affairs. Then Hiempsal, the youngest of the three, who was naturally haughty and even before this had shown his contempt for Jugurtha's inferior birth because he was not his equal on the maternal side, sat down on the right of Adherbal, in order to prevent Jugurtha from taking his place between the two, a position which is regarded as an honour among the Numidians. Afterwards, however, when his brother begged him to show respect to greater years, he was reluctantly induced to move to the other side.

At this meeting, in the course of a long discussion about the government of the kingdom, Jugurtha suggested, among other measures, that they ought to annul all laws and decrees passed within the past five years, on the ground that during that time Micipsa was far gone in years and hardly of sound mind. Thereupon Hiempsal again spoke up and declared that he approved the suggestion; for it was within the last three years, he said, that Jugurtha himself had been adopted and thus given a share in the kingdom. This remark sank more deeply into Jugurtha's mind than anyone would have supposed. So, from that moment he was a prey to resentment and fear, planned and schemed, and thought of

9 quibus Hiempsal per dolum caperetur. Quae ubi tardius procedunt neque lenitur animus ferox, statuit quovis modo inceptum perficere.

XII. Primo conventu, quem ab regulis factum supra memoravi, propter dissensionem placuerat dividi thesauros finisque imperi singulis constitui. 2 Itaque tempus ad utramque rem decernitur, sed maturius ad pecuniam distribuendam. Reguli interea in loca propinqua thesauris alius alio con- 3 cessere. Sed Hiempsal in oppido Thirmida forte eius domo utebatur qui, proxumus lictor Iugurthae, carus acceptusque ei semper fuerat. Quem ille casu ministrum oblatum promissis onerat impellitque uti tamquam suam visens domum eat, portarum clavis adulterinas paret—nam verae ad Hiempsalem referebantur—, ceterum, ubi res postularet, se ipsum cum 4 magna manu venturum. Numida mandata brevi conficit, atque, uti doctus erat, noctu Iugurthae 5 milites introducit. Qui postquam in aedis irrupere, divorsi regem quaerere, dormientis alios, alios occursantis interficere, scrutari loca abdita, clausa effringere, strepitu et tumultu omnia miscere ; cum interim Hiempsal reperitur occultans se tugurio mulieris ancillae, quo initio pavidus et ignarus loci perfugerat. Numidae caput eius, uti iussi erant, ad Iugurtham referunt.

---

[1] The term *lictor* is transferred from Roman usage. It is not probable that the Numidians had adopted the Roman custom.

nothing except some means by which he might outwit and ensnare Hiempsal. But since his plans moved too slowly and his proud spirit retained its anger, he resolved to effect his design in any possible way.

XII. At the first meeting of the princes, which I have already mentioned, they failed to agree and therefore determined to divide the treasures and partition the kingdom among the three. Accordingly, they set a time for both events, that for the division of the money being the earlier, and meanwhile came by different routes to a place near the treasury. Now it chanced that Hiempsal was occupying a house in the town of Thirmida which belonged to Jugurtha's most confidential attendant,[1] who had always been his master's dear and beloved friend. This man, whom chance threw in his way as an agent, Jugurtha loaded with promises, and induced him to go to his house on the pretext of inspecting it and to have false keys made for the doors; for the true ones used to be delivered to Hiempsal.[2] As to the rest, Jugurtha himself promised to be at hand at the proper time with a strong force. The Numidian promptly carried out his instructions, and, as he had been directed, let in Jugurtha's soldiers by night. They rushed into the house, scattered in search of the king, slew some of the household in their sleep and others as they offered resistance, ransacked all hiding-places, broke down doors, and filled the whole place with noise and confusion. Meanwhile, Hiempsal was found hiding in the cell of a maid-servant, where in his first terror, unacquainted as he was with the premises, he had taken refuge. The Numidians did as they were ordered, and brought his head to Jugurtha.

[2] That is, every evening.

XIII. Ceterum fama tanti facinoris per omnem Africam brevi divolgatur. Adherbalem omnisque qui sub imperio Micipsae fuerant metus invadit. In duas partis discedunt Numidae; plures Adherbalem 2 secuntur, sed illum alterum bello meliores. Igitur Iugurtha quam maxumas potest copias armat, urbis partim vi alias voluntate imperio suo adiungit, 3 omni Numidiae imperare parat. Adherbal tametsi Romam legatos miserat, qui senatum docerent de caede fratris et fortunis suis, tamen fretus multitu- 4 dine militum parabat armis contendere. Sed ubi res ad certamen venit, victus ex proelio profugit in provinciam ac deinde Romam contendit.

5 Tum Iugurtha patratis consiliis, postquam omnis Numidiae potiebatur, in otio facinus suum cum animo reputans timere populum Romanum neque advorsus iram eius usquam nisi in avaritia nobilitatis et pe- 6 cunia sua spem habere. Itaque paucis diebus cum auro et argento multo Romam legatos mittit, quis praecipit,[1] primum uti veteres amicos muneribus ex- pleant, deinde novos adquirant, postremo quaecum- que possint largiundo parare ne cunctentur.

7 Sed ubi Romam legati venere et ex praecepto regis hospitibus aliisque quorum ea tempestate in senatu auctoritas pollebat magna munera misere, tanta commutatio incessit, ut ex maxuma invidia in gratiam et favorem nobilitatis Iugurtha veniret. 8 Quorum pars spe, alii praemio inducti, singulos ex

---

[1] praecipit, $A^2CBN\,l\,n$; *the other mss. have* praecepit.

---

[1] The Roman province of Africa, consisting of the territory possessed by Carthage in 146 B.C. ; *cf. fines quos novissime habuerant*, xix. 7.

XIII. Now, in a short time the news of this awful crime spread over all Africa. Fear seized Adherbal and all the former subjects of Micipsa. The Numidians were divided into two parties, the greater number siding with Adherbal, but the better soldiers with his rival. Jugurtha then armed the largest possible number of troops, brought some cities under his sway by force and others with their consent, and prepared to make himself ruler of all Numidia. Although Adherbal had at once dispatched envoys to Rome, to inform the senate of his brother's murder and his own position, yet he prepared to take the field, relying upon the superior number of his troops. But he was defeated in the very first engagement, fled to our province,[1] and thence made his way to Rome.

Then Jugurtha, when he had carried out his plans and was in possession of all Numidia, having leisure to think over what he had done, began to be afraid of the Roman people and to despair of escaping their anger except through the avarice of the Roman nobles and his own wealth. Accordingly, a few days later, he sent envoys to Rome with a great amount of gold and silver, directing them first to load his old friends with presents, and then to win new ones— in short, to make haste to accomplish by largess whatever they could.

But when the envoys arrived at Rome, and, as the king had commanded, sent magnificent presents to his friends and to others of the senate whose influence at the time was powerful, such a change of sentiment ensued that in place of the pronounced hostility of the nobles Jugurtha gained their favour and support. Induced in some cases by hope, in others by bribery, they went about to

senatu ambiundo nitebantur ne gravius in eum con-
9 suleretur. Igitur ubi legati satis confidunt, die
constituto senatus utrisque datur. Tum Adherbalem
hoc modo locutum accepimus:

XIV. "Patres conscripti, Micipsa pater meus
moriens mihi praecepit, ut regni Numidiae tantum
modo procurationem existumarem meam, ceterum
ius et imperium eius penes vos esse; simul eniterer
domi militiaeque quam maxumo usui esse populo
Romano, vos mihi cognatorum, vos adfinium loco[1]
ducerem : si ea fecissem, in vostra amicitia exercitum, divitias, munimenta regni me habiturum.
2 Quae cum praecepta parentis mei agitarem, Iugurtha, homo omnium quos terra sustinet sceleratis-
sumus, contempto imperio vostro, Masinissae me
nepotem et iam ab stirpe socium atque amicum
populi Romani regno fortunisque omnibus expulit.

3   "Atque ego, patres conscripti, quoniam eo miseriarum venturus eram, vellem potius ob mea quam ob
maiorum meorum benificia posse me[2] a vobis auxilium
petere, ac maxume deberi mihi beneficia a populo
Romano, quibus non egerem; secundum ea, si
4 desideranda erant, uti debitis uterer. Sed quoniam
parum tuta per se ipsa probitas est neque mihi in
manu fuit Iugurtha qualis foret, ad vos confugi,

---

[1] adfinium loco, VM^2m^1, Ah, Or; adfinium locum, A^1C^1;
in adf. loco, MFm^2; in adf. locum, *the other mss.*

[2] posse a, Vm^1; possem ea, A^1N; posse me, *the other mss.*,
Ah, Or.

individual members of the senate and urged them not to take too severe measures against Jugurtha. When, because of this, the envoys came to feel sufficient confidence, a time was appointed for the appearance of both parties before the senate. Thereupon Adherbal is said to have spoken in the following terms:

XIV. "Fathers of the Senate, my sire Micipsa admonished me on his death-bed to consider that I was only a steward of the kingdom of Numidia,[1] but that the right and authority were in your hands; at the same time he bade me strive to be as helpful as possible to the Roman people in peace and in war and to regard you as my kindred and relatives. He declared that if I did this, I should find in your friendship an army, and wealth, and bulwarks for my kingdom. As I was following these injunctions of my father, Jugurtha, wickedest of all men on the face of the earth, in despite of your power robbed me, the grandson of Masinissa and hereditary friend and ally of the Roman people, of my throne and all my fortunes.

"And for myself, Fathers of the Senate, since I was doomed to such a depth of wretchedness, I could wish that I might ask your help rather because of my own services than those of my ancestors; I could wish above all that favours were due to me from the Roman people which I did not need; and failing this, that if they were needed I might accept them as my due. But since virtue alone is not its own protection, and since it was not in my power to mould the character of Jugurtha, I

[1] cf. Liv. 45. 13. 15, *Masinissam . . . usu regni contentum scire dominium et ius eorum qui dederint esse.*

patres conscripti, quibus, quod mihi miserrumum
5 est, cogor prius oneri quam usui esse. Ceteri reges
aut bello victi in amicitiam a vobis recepti sunt
aut in suis dubiis rebus societatem vostram appeti-
verunt. Familia nostra cum populo Romano bello
Carthaginiensi amicitiam instituit, quo tempore
6 magis fides eius quam fortuna petunda erat. Quorum
progeniem vos, patres conscripti, nolite pati me
nepotem Masinissae frustra a vobis auxilium petere.

7   "Si ad impetrandum nihil causae haberem praeter
miserandam fortunam, quod paulo ante rex genere,
fama atque copiis potens, nunc deformatus aerumnis,
inops, alienas opes expecto, tamen erat maiestatis
populi Romani prohibere iniuriam neque pati cuius-
8 quam regnum per scelus crescere. Verum ego eis
finibus eiectus sum quos maioribus meis populus
Romanus dedit, unde pater et avos meus una vobiscum expulere Syphacem et Carthaginiensis. Vostra
beneficia mihi erepta sunt, patres conscripti, vos in
9 mea iniuria despecti estis. Eheu me miserum! hucine,
Micipsa pater, beneficia tua evasere ut, quem tu parem
cum liberis tuis regnique participem fecisti, is potissumum stirpis tuae extinctor sit?

    "Numquamne ergo familia nostra quieta erit?
10 Semperne in sanguine, ferro, fuga vorsabitur? Dum
Carthaginienses incolumes fuere, iure omnia saeva

---

[1] That is, the alliance with Rome offered more hope for
the future than aid in the immediate present.

have had recourse to you, Fathers of the Senate, to whom (and this is the greatest part of my wretchedness) I am compelled to be a burden before I have been an aid. All other kings have been admitted to your friendship when they were vanquished in war, or have sought your alliance in their time of peril; our family established friendly relations with Rome during the war with Carthage, at a time when the plighted word of Rome was a greater inducement to us than her fortune.[1] Therefore do not allow me, their descendant and the grandson of Masinissa, to implore your aid in vain.

"If I had no other reason for asking the favour than my pitiable lot—of late a king, mighty in family, fame and fortune; now broken by woes, destitute and appealing to others for help—it would nevertheless be becoming to the majesty of the Roman people to defend me against wrong and not to allow any man's power to grow great through crime. But in fact I am driven from the lands which the people of Rome gave to my forefathers and from which my father and grandfather helped you to drive Syphax and the Carthaginians. It is your gift, Fathers of the Senate, which has been wrested from me, and in the wrong done to me you have been scorned. Woe's me! O my father Micipsa, has this been the effect of your kindness, that the man whom you put on an equality with your own children, whom you made a partner in your kingdom, should of all men be the destroyer of your house?

"Shall my family then never find rest? Shall we always dwell amid blood, arms and exile? While the Carthaginians were unconquered, we naturally

patiebamur; hostes ab latere, vos amici procul, spes
omnis in armis erat. Postquam illa pestis ex Africa
eiecta est, laeti pacem agitabamus, quippe quis
hostis nullus erat, nisi forte quem vos iussissetis.

11 Ecce autem ex improviso Iugurtha, intoleranda
audacia, scelere atque superbia sese[1] ecferens, fratre
meo atque eodem propinquo suo interfecto, primum
regnum eius sceleris sui praedam fecit; post, ubi me
eisdem dolis nequit[2] capere, nihil minus quam vim
aut bellum expectantem in imperio vostro, sicut
videtis extorrem patria, domo, inopem et coopertum
miseriis effecit, ut ubivis tutius quam in meo regno
essem.

12 "Ego sic existumabam, patres conscripti, uti praedicantem audiveram patrem meum, qui vostram
amicitiam diligenter colerent, eos multum laborem
suscipere, ceterum ex omnibus maxume tutos esse.

13 Quod in familia nostra fuit, praestitit uti in omnibus
bellis adesset vobis; nos uti per otium tuti simus, in

14 vostra manu est, patres conscripti. Pater nos duos
fratres reliquit, tertium Iugurtham beneficiis suis
ratus est coniunctum nobis fore. Alter eorum
necatus est, alterius ipse ego manus impias vix effugi.

15 Quid agam? Aut quo potissumum infelix accedam?
Generis praesidia omnia extincta sunt. Pater, uti
necesse erat, naturae concessit. Fratri, quem
minume decuit, propincus per scelus vitam eripuit.
Adfinis, amicos, propinquos ceteros meos alium alia

[1] se, V; P omits.
[2] non quit, V, P^2.

suffered all kinds of hardship; the enemy were upon our flank, you, our friends, were far away; all our hope was in our arms. After Africa had been freed from that pestilence, we enjoyed the delights of peace, since we had no enemy, unless haply at your command.[1] But lo! on a sudden, Jugurtha, carried away by intolerable audacity, wickedness and arrogance, after killing my brother, who was also his kinsman, first made Hiempsal's realm the spoil of his crime; then, when he had failed to outwit me by the same wiles, and when under your sovereignty I was looking for anything rather than violence or war, he has made me, as you see, an exile from home and country, a prey to want and wretchedness, and safer anywhere than in my own kingdom.

"I always used to think, Fathers of the Senate, as I had heard my father maintain, that those who diligently cultivated your friendship undertook an arduous duty, indeed, but were safe beyond all others. Our family has done its best to aid you in all your wars; that we may enjoy peace and safety, Fathers of the Senate, is in your power. Our father left two of us brothers; a third,[2] Jugurtha, he hoped to add to our number by his favours. One of the three has been slain; I myself have barely escaped the sacrilegious hands of the other. What shall I do, or to what special protection shall I appeal in my troubles? All the defences of my house are destroyed. My father, as was inevitable, has paid the debt of nature. My brother has lost his life through the crime of a kinsman, the last man who ought to have raised a hand against him. Relatives, friends, and others who were near to me have fallen by one blow

---

[1] Those enemies, namely, which their alliance with Rome forced upon them.   [2] cf. x. 3, *beneficio meo fratres.*

clades oppressit; capti ab Iugurtha pars in crucem
acti, pars bestiis obiecti sunt, pauci, quibus relicta
est anima, clausi in tenebris cum maerore et[1] luctu
16 morte graviorem vitam exigunt. Si omnia quae aut
amisi aut ex necessariis advorsa facta sunt in-
columia manerent, tamen, siquid ex improviso mali
accidisset, vos implorarem, patres conscripti, quibus
pro magnitudine imperi ius et iniurias omnis curae
17 esse decet. Nunc vero exul patria, domo, solus
atque omnium honestarum rerum egens, quo accedam
aut quos appellem? Nationesne an reges? Qui
omnes familiae nostrae ob vostram amicitiam infesti
sunt? An quoquam mihi adire licet, ubi non maiorum,
meorum hostilia monumenta pluruma sint? Aut
quisquam nostri misereri potest, qui aliquando vobis
18 hostis fuit? Postremo Masinissa nos ita instituit
patres conscripti, nequem coleremus nisi populum
Romanum, ne societates, ne[2] foedera nova acci-
peremus: abunde magna praesidia nobis in vostra
amicitia fore; si huic imperio fortuna mutaretur, una
occidundum nobis esse.

19 "Virtute ac dis volentibus magni estis et opulenti,
omnia secunda et oboedientia sunt; quo facilius
20 sociorum iniurias curare licet. Tantum illud vereor,
nequos privata amicitia Iugurthae parum cognita
transvorsos agat, quos ego audio maxuma ope niti,
ambire, fatigare vos singulos, nequid de absente

[1] atque, V.
[2] neu, V.

or another. Of those taken by Jugurtha some have been crucified, others thrown to wild beasts; a few, whose lives were spared, in gloomy dungeons amid sorrow and lamentation drag out an existence worse than death. But if all that I have lost, or all that has turned from affection to hostility, remained untouched, even then, if any unexpected misfortune had befallen me, I should appeal to you, Fathers of the Senate, whom it befits, because of the extent of your dominion, to take under your care all matters of right and wrong everywhere. As it is, however, an exile from home and country, alone, and stripped of all that becomes my station, where shall I take refuge or to whom shall I appeal? To nations or kings, all of whom are hostile to our family because of our friendship for you? To what land can I turn and not find there many a record of my ancestors' acts of hostility? Can anyone feel compassion for us who was ever your enemy? Finally, Fathers of the Senate, Masinissa instructed us to attach ourselves to none save the Roman people and to contract no new leagues and alliances; he declared that in your friendship there would be for us all an ample protection, and that, if the fortune of your empire should change, we must fall with it.

"Through valour and the favour of the gods you are mighty and powerful, all things are favourable and yield obedience to you; hence you may the more readily have regard to the wrongs of your allies. My only fear is lest private friendship for Jugurtha, the true character of which is not evident, may lead some of your number astray; for I hear that his partisans are using every effort, and are soliciting and entreating each of you separately not to pass any judgment upon him in his absence without

incognita causa statuatis: fingere me verba et fugam
21 simulare, cui licuerit in regno manere. Quod utinam
illum, cuius[1] impio facinore in has miserias proiectus
sum, eadem haec simulantem videam et aliquando
aut apud vos aut apud deos immortalis rerum humanarum cura oriatur; ne ille, qui nunc sceleribus
suis ferox atque praeclarus est, omnibus malis excru-
ciatus impietatis in parentem nostrum, fratris mei
necis mearumque miseriarum gravis poenas reddat.

22 " Iam iam frater, animo meo carissume, quamquam
tibi immaturo et unde minume decuit vita erepta est,
tamen laetandum magis quam dolendum puto casum
23 tuum. Non enim regnum sed fugam, exsilium,
egestatem et omnis has quae me premunt aerumnas,
cum anima simul amisisti. At ego infelix, in tanta
mala praecipitatus ex patrio regno, rerum humanarum spectaculum praebeo, incertus quid agam,
tuasne iniurias persequar ipse auxili egens an regno
consulam, cuius vitae necisque potestas ex opibus
24 alienis pendet. Utinam emori fortunis meis hones-
tus exitus esset, neu iure[2] contemptus viderer si
defessus malis iniuriae concessissem. Nunc neque
vivere lubet neque mori licet sine dedecore.

25 " Patres conscripti, per vos, per liberos atque
parentes vostros, per maiestatem populi Romani,

[1] quoius, *Ah* ; cuius, *Or.*
[2] neu iure, *VP²A l, Ah, Or*; ne iure, *B¹*; ne vivere, *the other mss.*

a hearing. They declare that I am speaking falsely and feigning the necessity for flight, when I might have remained in my own kingdom. As to that, I hope that I may yet see the man through whose impious crime I have been subjected to these woes making the same pretence, and that at last either you or the immortal gods may begin to take thought for human affairs! Then of a truth that wretch, who now exults and glories in his crimes, will be tortured by ills of every kind and pay a heavy penalty for his treachery to our father, for the murder of my brother, and for my unhappiness.

"At last, brother dearest to my heart, although life has been taken from you untimely by the last hand that should have been raised against you, yet your fate seems to me a cause for joy rather than for sorrow. For when you lost your life it was not your throne you lost, but it was flight, exile, want and all these woes which weigh me down. While I, poor wretch, hurled from my father's throne into this sea of troubles, present a tragedy of human vicissitude, being at a loss what course to take, whether to try to avenge your wrongs when I myself am in need of aid, or to take thought for my throne when the very question of my life or death hangs upon the help of others. Would that death were an honourable means of escape for one of my estate! Would that, worn out by affliction, I could succumb to oppression without appearing justly contemptible! As it is, life has no charms for me, but death is impossible without shame.

"Fathers of the Senate, I beseech you in your own name, by your children and parents, and by the majesty of the Roman people, aid me in my distress,

subvenite mihi misero, ite obviam iniuriae, nolite
pati regnum Numidiae, quod vostrum est, per scelus
et sanguinem familiae nostrae tabescere."

XV. Postquam rex finem loquendi fecit, legati
Iugurthae, largitione magis quam causa freti, paucis
respondent. Hiempsalem ob saevitiam suam ab
Numidis interfectum, Adherbalem ultro bellum
inferentem, postquam superatus sit, queri quod
iniuriam facere nequivisset ; Iugurtham ab senatu
petere ne se alium putarent ac Numantiae cognitus
esset, neu verba inimici ante facta sua ponerent.

2 Deinde utrique curia egrediuntur. Senatus statim
consulitur. Fautores legatorum, praeterea senatus
magna pars gratia depravata Adherbalis dicta con-
temnere, Iugurthae virtutem extollere laudibus; gratia, voce, denique omnibus modis pro alieno scelere
3 et flagitio sua quasi pro gloria nitebantur. At contra pauci, quibus bonum et aequom divitiis carius
erat, subveniundum Adherbali et Hiempsalis mortem
4 severe vindicandam censebant; sed ex omnibus
maxume Aemilius Scaurus, homo nobilis, impiger,
factiosus, avidus potentiae, honoris, divitiarum, ce-
5 terum vitia sua callide occultans. Is postquam videt
regis largitionem famosam impudentemque, veritus,
quod in tali re solet, ne polluta licentia invidiam
accenderet, animum a consueta lubidine continuit.

set your faces against injustice, do not permit the kingdom of Numidia, which belongs to you, to be ruined by villainy and the blood-guiltiness of our family."

XV. After the king had finished speaking, the envoys of Jugurtha, who relied rather upon bribery than upon the justice of their cause, replied briefly. They declared that Hiempsal had been slain by the Numidians because of his savage cruelty; that Adherbal after making war without provocation and suffering defeat, was complaining because he had been prevented from inflicting injury. Jugurtha, they said, begged the senate not to think him other than he had shown himself at Numantia, or let the words of an enemy outweigh his own actions.

Then both parties left the House and the matter was at once laid before the senate. The partisans of the envoys, and a large number of other senators who had been corrupted by their influence, derided the words of Adherbal and lauded the virtues of Jugurtha; exerting their influence, their eloquence, in short every possible means, they laboured as diligently in defence of the shameful crime of a foreigner as though they were striving to win honour. A few, on the other hand, to whom right and justice were more precious than riches, recommended that aid be given to Adherbal and that the death of Hiempsal be severely punished. Conspicuous among these was Aemilius Scaurus, a noble full of energy, a partisan, greedy for power, fame, and riches, but clever in concealing his faults. As soon as this man saw the king's bribery, so notorious and so brazen, fearing the usual result in such cases, namely, that such gross corruption would arouse popular resentment, he curbed his habitual cupidity.

XVI. Vicit tamen in senatu pars illa, quae vero
2 pretium aut gratiam anteferebat. Decretum fit uti
decem legati regnum, quod Micipsa optinuerat, inter
Iugurtham et Adherbalem dividerent. Cuius lega-
tionis princeps fuit L. Opimius, homo clarus et tum
in senatu potens, quia consul[1] C. Graccho et M. Fulvio
Flacco interfectis acerrume victoriam nobilitatis in
3 plebem exercuerat. Eum Iugurtha tametsi Romae
in inimicis[2] habuerat, tamen accuratissume recepit,
dando et pollicendo multa perfecit, uti fama, fide,
postremo omnibus suis rebus commodum regis ante-
4 ferret. Reliquos legatos eadem via aggressus pleros-
5 que capit, paucis carior fides quam pecunia fuit. In
divisione quae pars Numidiae Mauretaniam attingit,
agro virisque opulentior, Iugurthae traditur, illam
alteram specie quam usu potiorem, quae portuosior
et aedificiis magis exornata erat, Adherbal pos-
sedit.

XVII. Res postulare videtur Africae situm paucis
exponere et eas gentis, quibuscum nobis bellum aut
2 amicitia fuit, attingere. Sed quae loca et nationes
ob calorem aut asperitatem, item solitudines minus

---

[1] consuls, *P* ; consulibus, *H²Γl n.*
[2] in inimicis, *editors* ; in amicis, *mss.*

---

[1] In 121 B.C. He led the attack against the Aventine,
where Gaius Gracchus and his followers had taken refuge, and

XVI. In spite of all, that faction of the senate prevailed which rated money and favour higher than justice. It was voted that ten commissioners should divide Micipsa's former kingdom between Jugurtha and Adherbal. The head of this commission was Lucius Opimius, a distinguished man, who was influential in the senate at that time because in his consulship,[1] after bringing about the death of Gaius Gracchus and Marcus Fulvius Flaccus, he had made cruel use of the victory of the nobles over the people. Although at Rome Opimius had been one of Jugurtha's opponents, the king received him with the greatest respect, and soon induced him, by many gifts and promises, to consider Jugurtha's advantage of more consequence than his own fair fame, his honour, and in short, than all personal considerations. Then adopting the same tactics with the other envoys, Jugurtha won over the greater number of them; only a few held their honour dearer than gold. When the division was made, the part of Numidia adjoining Mauretania, which was the more fertile and thickly populated, was assigned to Jugurtha; the other part, preferable in appearance rather than in reality, having more harbours and being provided with more buildings, fell to Adherbal.

XVII. My subject seems to call for a brief account of the geography of Africa and some description of the nations there with which the people of Rome has had wars or alliances. Of those regions and peoples, however, which are seldom visited because of the heat, the difficulty of access, or the stretches of

offered for the heads of the rebels their weight in gold. It is said that three thousand men were slain in the streets of Rome or in the proscriptions which followed.

frequentata sunt, de eis haud facile compertum
narraverim. Cetera quam paucissumis absolvam.

3 In divisione orbis terrae plerique in parte tertia
Africam posuere, pauci tantum modo Asiam et
4 Europam esse, sed Africam in Europa. Ea finis
habet ab occidente fretum nostri maris et Oceani,
ab ortu solis declivem latitudinem, quem locum
5 Catabathmon incolae appellant. Mare saevom, in-
portuosum, ager frugum fertilis, bonus pecori,
arbori[1] infecundus, caelo terraque penuria aquarum.
6 Genus hominum salubri corpore, velox, patiens
laborum. Plerosque[2] senectus dissolvit, nisi qui ferro
aut bestiis interiere ; nam morbus haud saepe quemquam superat. Ad hoc malifici generis pluruma
animalia.

7 Sed qui mortales initio Africam habuerint, quique
postea accesserint, aut quo modo inter se permixti
sint, quamquam ab ea fama quae plerosque optinet
divorsum est, tamen uti ex libris Punicis, qui regis
Hiempsalis dicebantur, interpretatum nobis est, utique rem sese habere cultores eius terrae putant,
quam paucissumis dicam. Ceterum fides eius rei
penes auctores erit.

XVIII. Africam initio habuere Gaetuli et Libyes,
asperi incultique, quis cibus erat caro ferina atque

[1] arbori, mss., Ah ; arbore, Arus. vi. 473. 18 к, Or.
[2] ac plerosque, Fronto, p. 109 N, Ah.

---

[1] Herodotus (2. 16) criticises the threefold division of the
Ionian geographers, which is accepted by Strabo, 17. 3. 1 ;
Varro (Ling. Lat. 5. 31) adopts the twofold division.

desert, I could not easily give an account based upon certain information. The rest I shall dispatch in the fewest possible words.

In their division of the earth's surface geographers commonly regard Africa as a third part, a few recognize only Asia and Europe, including Africa in the latter.[1] Africa is bounded on the west by the strait between our sea and the Ocean, on the east by a broad sloping tract which the natives call Catabathmos.[2] The sea is rough and without harbours, the soil fertile in grain, and favourable to flocks and herds but unproductive of trees; heaven and earth are niggardly of water.[3] The natives are healthy, swift of foot, and of great endurance. They commonly die of old age, unless they fall victims to the steel or to wild beasts; for disease seldom gets the better of any of them. Moreover the country abounds in dangerous wild animals.

What men inhabited Africa originally, and who came later, or how the races mingled, I shall tell as briefly as possible. Although my account varies from the prevailing tradition, I give it as it was translated to me from the Punic books said to have been written by king Hiempsal,[4] and in accordance with what the dwellers in that land believe. But the responsibility for its truth will rest with my authorities.

XVIII. In the beginning Africa was inhabited by the Gaetulians and Libyans, rude and uncivilized folk, who fed like beasts on the flesh of wild

---

[2] "The Descent"; it lay between the Cyrenaica and Egypt, and was regarded by Sallust and others as a part of Asia.

[3] That is, there is little rainfall and few lakes and streams.

[4] Not the brother of Adherbal, but a second king of the same name, father of Pompey's ally Juba.

2 humi pabulum uti pecoribus. Ei neque moribus
neque lege aut imperio cuiusquam regebantur; vagi,
palantes, quas nox coegerat sedes habebant.

3 Sed postquam in Hispania Hercules, sicuti Afri
putant, interiit, exercitus eius, compositus ex variis
gentibus, amisso duce ac passim multis sibi quisque
4 imperium petentibus, brevi dilabitur. Ex eo numero
Medi, Persae et Armenii, navibus in Africam trans-
5 vecti, proxumos nostro mari locos occupavere, sed
Persae intra Oceanum magis; eique alveos navium
invorsos pro tuguriis habuere, quia neque materia in
agris neque ab Hispanis emundi aut mutandi copia
6 erat; mare magnum et ignara lingua commercio
7 prohibebant. Ei paulatim per conubia Gaetulos
secum [1] miscuere, et, quia saepe temptantes agros
alia deinde alia loca petiverant, semet ipsi Nomadas
8 appellavere. Ceterum adhuc aedificia Numidarum
agrestium, quae mapalia illi vocant, oblonga incurvis
lateribus tecta quasi navium carinae sunt.

9 Medis autem et Armeniis accessere Libyes—nam
ei propius mare Africum agitabant, Gaetuli sub sole
magis, haud procul ab ardoribus—eique mature oppida habuere; nam freto divisi ab Hispania mutare

[1] *Omitted by P l.*

---

[1] *cf. Cat.* vi. 1.
[2] That is, outside of the strait connecting the Atlantic
with the Mediterranean.
[3] Nomades, "wanderers," and *Numidae,* "Numidians,"
are identical. The Greek word νομάδες probably came to
Africa by way of Sicily.

animals and the fruits of the earth. They were governed neither by institutions [1] nor law, nor were they subject to anyone's rule. A restless, roving people, they had their abodes wherever night compelled a halt.

But when Hercules died in Spain, as the Africans believe, the men of divers nationalities who formed his army, now that their leader was gone and since there were many on every hand who aspired to succeed him, soon dispersed. Of those who made up the army, the Medes, Persians and Armenians crossed by ships into Africa and settled in the regions nearest to our sea, the Persians closer to the Ocean; [2] and these used as huts the inverted hulls of their ships; for there was no timber in the land, and there was no opportunity to obtain it from the Spaniards by purchase or barter, since the wide expanse of sea and ignorance of the language were a bar to intercourse. The Persians intermarried with the Gaetulians and were gradually merged with them, and because they often moved from place to place trying the soil, they called themselves Nomads. [3] It is an interesting fact, that even to the present day the dwellings of the rustic Numidians, which they call *mapalia*, are oblong and have roofs with curved sides, like the hulls of ships.

But the Medes and the Armenians had the Libyans as their nearest neighbours; for that people lived closer to the Afric sea, [4] while the Gaetulians were farther to the south, not far from the regions of heat. These three peoples [5] soon had towns; for being separated from the Spaniards only by the strait,

[4] The western part of the Mediterranean.
[5] The Medes, Armenians and Libyans.

10 res inter se instituerant. Nomen eorum paulatim Libyes corrupere, barbara lingua Mauros pro Medis appellantes.

11 Sed res Persarum brevi adolevit ac postea nomine Numidae propter multitudinem a parentibus digressi possedere ea loca, quae proxume[1] Carthagine[2]

12 Numidia appellatur. Deinde utrique alteris freti finitumos armis aut metu sub imperium suum coegere, nomen gloriamque sibi addidere, magis ei, qui ad nostrum mare processerant, quia Libyes quam Gaetuli minus bellicosi. Denique Africae pars inferior pleraque ab Numidis possessa est, victi omnes in gentem nomenque imperantium concessere.

XIX. Postea Phoenices, alii multitudinis domi minuendae gratia, pars imperi cupidine sollicitata plebe et aliis novarum rerum avidis, Hipponem, Hadrumetum, Lepcim aliasque urbis in ora marituma condidere eaeque brevi multum auctae, pars

2 originibus suis praesidio, aliae decori fuere. Nam de Carthagine silere melius puto quam parum dicere, quoniam alio properare tempus monet.

<hr/>

¹ proxima, *Arusianus* vii. 498. 17 κ, *Ah*; proxime *mss.* ("*fortasse recte,*" *Ah*), *Or.*
² Carthagine, *Arus. l.c., Ah, Or*; Carthaginem, *mss.*

<hr/>

¹ The derivation of Mauri from Medi is of course impossible. The Moors seem to have been of Aethiopian origin.
² That is, the Persians and Gaetulians.

they began to exchange wares with them. The Libyans gradually altered the name of the Medes, calling them in their barbarian tongue *Mauri* (Moors).[1]

Now the commonwealth of the Persians[2] soon increased and finally the younger generation, under the name of Numidians, separated from their parents because of the excess of population and took possession of the region next to Carthage, which is called Numidia. Then both peoples,[3] relying upon each other's aid, brought their neighbours under their sway by arms or by fear and acquired renown and glory, especially those who had come near to our sea, because the Libyans are less warlike than the Gaetulians. Finally, the greater part of northern Africa fell into the hands of the Numidians, and all the vanquished were merged in the race and name of their rulers.

XIX. Later the Phoenicians, sometimes for the sake of ridding themselves of the superfluous population at home, sometimes from desire for dominion tempting away the commons and others who were desirous of a change, founded Hippo,[4] Hadrumetum, Lepcis,[5] and other cities on the coast. These soon became very powerful and were in some cases a defence and in others a glory to the mother city. As to Carthage, I think it better to be silent rather than say too little, since time warns me to hasten on to other topics.

[3] The older Numidians (Persians) and Gaetulians near the Ocean and those who had settled near Carthage.

[4] Probably Hippo Diarrhytus, near Utica, rather than Hippo Regius, which was farther to the west.

[5] Lepcis Minor is meant. On the spelling Lepcis (*Ah*) see *Berl. Phil. Woch.* 1916, p. 511; also *cf.* van Baren, *Amer. Journal of Archaeology* XXXII, p. 398.

3 Igitur ad Catabathmon, qui locus Aegyptum ab Africa dividit, secundo mari prima Cyrene est, colonia Theraeon, ac deinceps duae Syrtes interque eas Lepcis; deinde Philaenon arae, quem locum Aegyptum vorsus finem imperi habuere Carthagini-
4 enses; post aliae Punicae urbes. Cetera loca usque ad Mauretaniam Numidae tenent, proximi[1] Hispania[2]
5 Mauri sunt. Super Numidiam Gaetulos accepimus partim in tuguriis, alios incultius vagos agitare, post
6 eos Aethiopas esse, dehinc loca exusta solis ardoribus.
7 Igitur bello Iugurthino pleraque ex Punicis op-pida et finis Carthaginiensium, quos novissume habuerant, populus Romanus per magistratus ad-ministrabat; Gaetulorum magna pars et Numidae usque ad flumen Muluccham sub Iugurtha erant; Mauris omnibus rex Bocchus imperitabat, praeter nomen cetera ignarus populi Romani itemque nobis neque bello neque pace antea cognitus.
8 De Africa et eius incolis ad necessitudinem rei satis dictum.

XX. Postquam diviso regno legati Africa deces-sere et Iugurtha contra timorem animi praemia

[1] proximi, *P l, Arusianus* vii. 498. 18 κ, *Ah, Or*; proxime, *the other mss.*
[2] Hispania, *Arus., Ah, Or*; Hispanias, *P l*; Hispaniam, *the other mss.*

---

[1] To the westward, setting out from the Catabathmos.
[2] Founded in 631 B.C. in obedience to a Delphic oracle by Battus, the first of the famous Battiadae, who ruled for eight generations; see Herodotus 4. 150.

In the neighbourhood, then, of the Catabathmos, the region which separates Egypt from Africa, the first city as you follow the coast[1] is Cyrene,[2] a colony of Thera, and then come the two Syrtes[3] with Lepcis[4] between them. Next we come to the altars of the Philaeni, the point which the Carthaginians regarded as marking the boundary between their empire and Egypt; then other Punic cities. The rest of the region as far as Mauretania is held by the Numidians, while the people nearest Spain are the Moors. South of Numidia, so we are told, are the Gaetulians, some of whom live in huts, while others lead a less civilized nomadic life. Still farther to the south are the Aethiopians, and then come the regions parched by the sun's heat.

Now at the time of the war with Jugurtha the Romans were governing through their officials nearly all the Punic cities, as well as the territory which in their latter days[5] had belonged to the Carthaginians. The greater number of the Gaetulians, and Numidia as far as the river Muluccha, were subject to Jugurtha. All the Moors were ruled by king Bocchus, who knew nothing of the Roman people save their name and was in turn unknown to us before that time either in peace or in war.

This account of Africa and its peoples is enough for my purpose.

XX. As soon as the deputies left Africa, after dividing the kingdom, and Jugurtha found, in spite of his secret fears, that he had gained the price of his

---

[3] Sallust's brevity makes him unclear. The order is: Greater Syrtis, Philaenae Arae, Leptis Magna, Lesser Syrtis.

[4] Leptis Magna is here referred to, not Leptis Minor, as in xix. 1.

[5] In 146 B.C. See note on xiii. 4.

sceleris adeptum sese videt, certum esse ratus, quod
ex amicis apud Numantiam acceperat, omnia Romae
venalia esse, simul et illorum pollicitationibus accensus quos paulo ante muneribus expleverat, in
2 regnum Adherbalis animum intendit.   Ipse acer,
bellicosus, at is quem petebat quietus, imbellis,
placido ingenio, opportunus iniuriae, metuens magis
3 quam metuendus.   Igitur ex improviso finis eius
cum magna manu invadit, multos mortalis cum
pecore atque alia praeda capit, aedificia incendit,
pleraque loca hostiliter cum equitatu accedit; deinde
4 cum omni multitudine in regnum suum convortit,
existumans Adherbalem dolore permotum iniurias
suas manu vindicaturum eamque rem belli causam
5 fore.   At ille, quod neque se parem armis existumabat et amicitia populi Romani magis quam Numidis fretus erat, legatos ad Iugurtham de iniuriis
questum misit.   Qui tametsi contumeliosa dicta ret-
tulerant, prius tamen omnia pati decrevit quam
bellum sumere, quia temptatum antea secus cesserat.
6 Neque eo magis cupido Iugurthae minuebatur,
quippe qui totum eius regnum animo iam invaserat.
7 Itaque non uti antea cum praedatoria manu, sed
magno exercitu comparato bellum gerere coepit et
8 aperte totius Numidiae imperium petere.   Ceterum
qua pergebat urbis, agros vastare, praedas agere,
suis animum hostibus terrorem augere.

---

[1] See chap. viii. 1.

crime, he felt convinced of the truth of what he had heard from his friends at Numantia, that at Rome anything could be bought.[1] Accordingly, he began to covet Adherbal's kingdom, spurred on besides by the promises of those whom he had shortly before loaded with presents. He himself was active and warlike, while his intended victim was quiet, peaceful, of a tranquil disposition, open to attack and rather inclined to fear than an object of fear. Therefore when Jugurtha suddenly invaded Adherbal's territory with a large force, he took many prisoners, as well as cattle and other plunder, set fire to buildings, and raided several places with his cavalry. He then withdrew with his entire force into his own kingdom, supposing that Adherbal would be led by resentment to resort to force in order to avenge the wrongs which had been done him, and that this would furnish a pretext for war. Adherbal, however, realizing that in arms he was no match for his rival and putting more trust in the friendship of the Roman people than in the Numidians, sent envoys to Jugurtha to protest against the outrages; and although they brought back an insulting answer, he resolved to put up with anything rather than resort to war, which he had already tried with so little success. This, however, did not diminish the ardour of Jugurtha, who in his mind's eye had already seized all Adherbal's realm. He therefore began to wage war, not as before with a predatory band, but with a great army which he had got together, and to lay claim openly to the sovereignty of all Numidia. Wherever he went he laid waste cities and fields and drove off booty, thus inspiring his own followers with confidence and striking the enemy with fear.

XXI. Adherbal ubi intellegit eo processum, uti regnum aut relinquendum esset aut armis retinendum, necessario copias parat et Iugurthae obvius procedit. 2 Interim haud longe a mari prope Cirtam oppidum utriusque exercitus consedit et quia diei extremum erat proelium non inceptum. Sed ubi plerumque noctis processit, obscuro etiam tum lumine, milites Iugurthini signo dato castra hostium invadunt, semisomnos partim, alios arma sumentis fugant funduntque. Adherbal cum paucis equitibus Cirtam profugit et ni multitudo togatorum fuisset, quae Numidas insequentis moenibus prohibuit, uno die inter duos reges coeptum atque patratum bellum 3 foret. Igitur Iugurtha oppidum circumsedit, vineis turribusque et machinis omnium generum expugnare aggreditur, maxume festinans tempus legatorum ante-capere, quos ante proelium factum ab Adherbale Romam missos audiverat.

4 Sed postquam senatus de bello eorum accepit, tres adulescentes in Africam legantur, qui ambos reges adeant, senatus populique Romani verbis nun-tient velle et censere eos ab armis discedere, de controvorsiis suis iure potius quam bello disceptare;[1] ita seque illisque dignum esse.

XXII. Legati in Africam maturantes veniunt, eo magis quod Romae, dum proficisci parant, de proelio

---

[1] *The phrase* de controversiis . . . disceptare *is omitted by all the best mss., but is found in a few integri.*

XXI. When Adherbal perceived that matters
had gone so far that he must either give up his
kingdom or retain it by force of arms, he yielded to
necessity, mustered an army, and went to meet
Jugurtha. At first the two armies encamped not far
from the sea near the town of Cirta, but because it
was late in the day they did not join battle. When the
greater part of the night had passed but while it was
still dark, the soldiers of Jugurtha on a given signal
attacked the camp of the enemy, surprised them
either half asleep or just taking up arms, and routed
them. Adherbal with a few horsemen fled to Cirta,
and if it had not been for a throng of Roman
civilians, who held off the pursuing Numidians from
the walls, the war between the two kings would have
begun and ended on the selfsame day. Jugurtha
thereupon invested the town and attempted to carry
it by mantlets,[1] towers and engines of all kinds,
making all haste to anticipate the coming of the
envoys, who, as he had heard, had been sent to
Rome by Adherbal before the battle was fought.

Now after the senate heard that they were at war,
three young men were despatched to Africa, with
instructions to approach both kings and announce in
the name of the Roman senate and people that it
was their desire and command that the combatants
should lay down their arms and settle their disagree-
ment by law rather than by war; that this was due
both to the Romans and to themselves.

XXII. The envoys soon arrived in Africa, making
the more haste because, as they were preparing to
leave Rome, word came that the battle had taken

---

[1] Movable sheds with sloping roofs used as a shelter for
soldiers working the artillery or trying to undermine the
wall.

facto et oppugnatione Cirtae audiebatur; sed is
2 rumor clemens erat. Quorum Iugurtha accepta
oratione respondit sibi neque maius quicquam neque
carius auctoritate senatus esse; ab adulescentia ita
se enisum ut ab optumo quoque probaretur; virtute,
non malitia P. Scipioni summo viro placuisse; ob
easdem artis a Micipsa, non penuria liberorum in
3 regnum adoptatum esse. Ceterum quo plura bene
atque strenue fecisset, eo animum suum iniuriam
4 minus tolerare. Adherbalem dolis vitae suae insidia-
tum; quod ubi comperisset, sceleri eius obviam isse.
Populum Romanum neque recte neque pro bono
facturum, si ab iure gentium sese prohibuerit. Postremo de omnibus rebus legatos Romam brevi
5 missurum. Ita utrique digrediuntur. Adherbalis
appellandi copia non fuit.

XXIII. Iugurtha ubi eos Africa decessisse ratus
est, neque propter loci naturam Cirtam armis expugnare potest, vallo atque fossa moenia circumdat,
turris extruit easque praesidiis firmat, praeterea dies
noctisque aut per vim aut dolis temptare, defensori-
bus moenium praemia modo, modo formidinem
ostentare, suos hortando ad virtutem arrigere,[1]
prorsus intentus cuncta parare.

2 Adherbal ubi intellegit omnis suas fortunas in
extremo sitas, hostem infestum, auxili spem nullam,

---

[1] arrigere, *X l s*; erigere, *Y n m*.

---

[1] *Pro bono=bene*; *cf.* Suet. *Tib.* vii.; Caes. *B.G.* 5. 7. 7,
etc.

place and that Cirta was besieged; but the rumour failed to do justice to the reality. When Jugurtha heard their message, he rejoined that nothing had more weight and nothing was more precious to him than the will of the senate; from youth up he had striven to win the approval of all good men; it was by merit, not by baseness, that he had found favour with the great Publius Scipio, and it was for the same qualities that Micipsa had made him heir to a part of his kingdom, not because the king lacked children. But, he said, the more numerous his acts of virtue and courage had been, the less his spirit was able to brook wrongs. Adherbal had treacherously plotted against his life, and he had discovered and resisted the criminal attempt. The people of Rome would act neither justly nor rightly,[1] if they denied him the privileges of the law of nations. In conclusion, he said that he would soon send envoys to Rome to explain the whole affair. Thereupon both parties separated; no opportunity was allowed of addressing Adherbal.

XXIII. Jugurtha waited until he thought that the envoys had left Africa, and then, finding himself unable to take Cirta by storm because of its natural strength, surrounded its wall with a rampart and a ditch. He built towers and filled them with armed men, attacked besides day and night either with force or craft, now offering bribes to the defenders and now threats, rousing his own men to courage by exhortations and displaying the greatest vigour in all his efforts.

When Adherbal saw that all his fortunes were in jeopardy, that his enemy was implacable, that there was no hope of succour, and that because of lack of

penuria rerum necessariarum bellum trahi non posse,
ex eis qui una Cirtam profugerant duos maxume
impigros delegit. Eos multa pollicendo ac miserando
casum suum confirmat uti per hostium munitiones
noctu ad proxumum mare, dein Romam pergerent.

XXIV. Numidae paucis diebus iussa efficiunt.
Litterae Adherbalis in senatu recitatae, quarum
sententia haec fuit:

2   "Non mea culpa saepe ad vos oratum mitto, patres
conscripti, sed vis Iugurthae subigit, quem tanta
lubido extinguendi me invasit, ut neque vos neque
deos immortalis in animo habeat, sanguinem meum
3 quam omnia malit. Itaque quintum iam mensem
socius et amicus populi Romani armis obsessus
teneor, neque mihi Micipsae patris mei benificia
neque vostra decreta auxiliantur; ferro an fame
4 acrius urgear incertus sum. Plura de Iugurtha
scribere dehortatur me fortuna mea. Etiam antea
5 expertus sum parum fidei miseris esse. Nisi tamen
intellego illum supra quam ego sum petere neque
simul amicitiam vostram et regnum meum sperare.
Utrum gravius existumet, nemini occultum est.
6 Nam initio occidit Hiempsalem fratrem meum,
deinde patrio regno me expulit. Quae sane fuerint
7 nostrae iniuriae, nihil ad vos. Verum nunc vostrum
regnum armis tenet, me, quem vos imperatorem

184

the necessities of life he could not endure a protracted war, he selected two of the boldest of the soldiers who had fled with him to Cirta. These he induced by many promises, and by dwelling upon his desperate plight, to make their way through the enemy's lines by night to the nearest sea-coast, and from there to Rome.

XXIV. Within a few days these Numidians had carried out Adherbal's instructions, and a letter of his was read in the senate, of which the substance was as follows:

"It is no fault of mine, Fathers of the Senate, that I often address an appeal to you; on the contrary, I am constrained by the violence of Jugurtha, who is possessed with such a desire for my destruction that he regards neither you nor the immortal Gods, but above everything thirsts for my blood. Hence it is that I, though an ally and friend of the Roman people, have now for more than four months been held in a state of siege, and that neither the services of my father Micipsa nor your decrees avail me; whether sword or famine press harder on me I know not. My condition would dissuade me from writing more about Jugurtha; for I have already learned that little confidence is bestowed upon the unfortunate. Except that I feel sure that he is aiming at a higher mark than myself, and that he does not hope at the same time for your friendship and my kingdom. Which of these two he values the more highly is evident to everyone; for he first slew Hiempsal, my brother, and then drove me from my father's kingdom. With my personal wrongs you have no concern, but it is your realm that he now holds by force of arms, and it is I, whom you made

185

Numidis posuistis, clausum obsidet; legatorum verba
8 quanti fecerit, pericula mea declarant. Quid est
9 reliquom nisi vis vostra, quo moveri possit? Nam
ego quidem vellem et haec quae scribo et illa quae
antea in senatu questus sum vana forent potius quam
10 miseria mea fidem verbis faceret. Sed quoniam eo
natus sum, ut Iugurthae scelerum ostentui essem,
non iam mortem neque aerumnas, tantum modo
inimici imperium et cruciatus corporis deprecor.
Regno Numidiae, quod vostrum est, uti lubet
consulite; me manibus impiis eripite, per maiestatem
imperi, per amicitiae fidem, si ulla apud vos memoria
remanet avi mei Masinissae."

XXV. His litteris recitatis fuere qui exercitum
in Africam mittundum censerent et quam primum
Adherbali subveniundum; de Iugurtha interim uti
2 consuleretur, quoniam legatis non paruisset. Sed
ab eisdem illis regis fautoribus summa ope enisum
3 est ne tale decretum fieret. Ita bonum publicum,
ut in plerisque negotiis solet, privata gratia devictum.
4 Legantur tamen in Africam maiores natu nobiles,
amplis honoribus usi. In quis fuit M. Scaurus de
quo supra memoravimus, consularis et tum senatus
princeps.
5 Ei, quod res in invidia erat, simul et ab Numidis
obsecrati, triduo navem ascendere. Dein brevi

ruler of Numidia, that he is besieging. How much regard he has for the commands of your envoys is shown by my perilous state. What is there left but your might which can influence him? For my own part, I could wish that these words which I am now writing, and the complaints which I have already made in the senate, were false, rather than that they should be proved true by my own wretchedness. But since I was created merely to be a monument to Jugurtha's crimes, I no longer pray to be spared death or unhappiness, but only that I may escape the tyranny of an enemy and bodily torment. As to Numidia, which is yours, take any action you choose, but save me from impious hands, I implore you by the majesty of your empire and by the loyalty of your friendship, if you retain any memory at all of my grandfather Masinissa."

XXV. Upon the reading of this letter some were for sending an army to Africa and rendering aid to Adherbal as soon as possible, recommending that in the meantime the senate should take cognizance of Jugurtha's failure to obey the envoys. But those same partisans of the king to whom I have already referred used every effort to prevent the passing of such a decree. Thus, as happens in many instances, the public welfare was sacrificed to private interests. Nevertheless men of years and rank, who had held the highest offices of state, were sent to Africa, among them Marcus Scaurus, of whom I have already spoken, an ex-consul and at the time the leader of the senate.

These men, influenced by the public indignation and also by the prayers of the Numidians, embarked within three days. Landing shortly afterward at

Uticam appulsi litteras ad Iugurtham mittunt:
quam ocissume ad provinciam accedat seque ad eum
6 ab senatu missos. Ille ubi accepit homines claros,
quorum auctoritatem Romae pollere audiverat, contra
inceptum suum venisse, primo commotus metu atque
7 lubidine divorsus agitabatur. Timebat iram senatus,
ni paruisset legatis; porro animus cupidine caecus
8 ad inceptum scelus rapiebatur. Vicit tamen in avido
9 ingenio pravom consilium. Igitur exercitu circumdato summa vi Cirtam irrumpere nititur, maxume
sperans diducta[1] manu hostium aut vi aut dolis sese
10 casum victoriae inventurum. Quod ubi secus procedit
neque quod intenderat efficere potest, ut prius quam
legatos conveniret Adherbalis potiretur, ne amplius
morando Scaurum, quem plurumum metuebat, in-
cenderet, cum paucis equitibus in provinciam venit.
11 Ac tametsi senati verbis graves minae nuntiabantur,
quod ab oppugnatione non desisteret, multa tamen
oratione consumpta legati frustra discessere.

XXVI. Ea postquam Cirtae audita sunt, Italici,
quorum virtute moenia defensabantur, confisi deditione facta propter magnitudinem populi Romani
inviolatos sese fore, Adherbali suadent uti seque et
2 oppidum Iugurthae tradat, tantum ab eo vitam
paciscatur, de ceteris senatui curae fore. At ille,
tametsi omnia potiora fide Iugurthae rebatur, tamen

---

[1] diducta, *NTDFs n m*; deducta, *Hm*; ducta, *X l*.

[1] See xxi. 2.

Utica, they sent a letter to Jugurtha, directing him to come as speedily as possible to the Roman province, adding that they had been sent to him by the senate. When Jugurtha learned that men of distinction, whose influence at Rome was said to be powerful, had come to oppose his attempt, he was at first greatly disturbed and began to waver between fear and greed. He dreaded the senate's wrath in case he disobeyed the envoys; at the same time his spirit, blinded by cupidity, urged him to consummate his crime. But in his greedy soul the worst counsel prevailed. Accordingly he surrounded Cirta with his army, and made a supreme effort to carry the town, having great hopes that by extending the enemy's line of defence he might find an opportunity for victory either in force or in stratagem. But when he was disappointed in this and thwarted in his purpose of getting Adherbal into his power before meeting the envoys, he was unwilling by further delay to exasperate Scaurus, whom he particularly feared; he therefore came into our province with a few horsemen. But although terrible threats were made in the name of the senate because he did not abandon the siege, the envoys went away unsuccessful after wasting a deal of oratory.

XXVI. When this was reported at Cirta, the Italiotes,[1] on whose valour the defence of the town depended, were confident that in the event of surrender they would escape injury because of the prestige of Rome. They therefore advised Adherbal to deliver himself and the town to Jugurtha, stipulating merely that his life should be spared and leaving the rest to the senate. But Adherbal, though he thought that anything was better than trusting to

quia penes eosdem, si advorsaretur, cogundi potestas erat, ita uti censuerant Italici deditionem facit. 3 Iugurtha in primis Adherbalem excruciatum necat, deinde omnis puberes Numidas atque negotiatores promiscue, uti quisque armatus[1] obvius fuerat, interficit.

XXVII. Quod postquam Romae cognitum est et res in senatu agitari coepta, idem illi ministri regis interpellando ac saepe gratia, interdum iurgiis tra- 2 hundo tempus, atrocitatem facti leniebant. Ac ni C. Memmius tribunus plebis designatus, vir acer et infestus potentiae nobilitatis, populum Romanum edocuisset id agi ut per paucos factiosos Iugurthae scelus condonaretur, profecto omnis invidia prolatandis consultationibus dilapsa foret; tanta vis gratiae 3 atque pecuniae regis erat. Sed ubi senatus delicti conscientia populum timet, lege Sempronia provinciae futuris consulibus Numidia atque Italia decretae, 4 consules declarati P. Scipio Nasica, L. Bestia; Cal- 5 purnio Numidia, Scipioni Italia obvenit. Deinde exercitus qui in Africam portaretur scribitur, stipendium aliaque quae bello usui forent decernuntur.

XXVIII. At Iugurtha, contra spem nuntio accepto, quippe cui Romae omnia venire[2] in animo haeserat, filium et cum eo duos familiaris ad senatum legatos

---

[1] armatus, $X\,l\,n$; armatis, A^1 *and the other mss.*
[2] venum ire, $C\,B\,H\,s.$

---

[1] See note on p. 44.

Jugurtha, yet because the Italiotes were in a position to use compulsion if he opposed them, surrendered on the terms which they had advised. Thereupon Jugurtha first tortured Adherbal to death and then made an indiscriminate massacre of all the adult Numidians and of traders whom he found with arms in their hands.

XXVII. When this outrage became known at Rome and the matter was brought up for discussion in the senate, those same tools of the king, by interrupting the discussions and wasting time, often through their personal influence, often by wrangling, tried to disguise the atrocity of the deed. And had not Gaius Memmius, tribune of the commons elect, a man of spirit who was hostile to the domination of the nobles, made it clear to the populace of Rome that the motive of these tactics was to condone Jugurtha's crime through the influence of a few of his partisans, the deliberations would undoubtedly have been protracted until all indignation had evaporated : so great was the power of the king's influence and money. But when the senate from consciousness of guilt began to fear the people, Numidia and Italy, as the Sempronian law[1] required, were assigned to the consuls who should next be elected. The consuls in question were Publius Scipio Nasica and Lucius Calpurnius Bestia ; Numidia fell to Bestia, Italy to Scipio. An army was then enrolled to be transported to Africa, the soldiers' pay and other necessaries of war were voted.

XXVIII. When Jugurtha heard this unexpected news (for he had a firm conviction that at Rome anything could be bought) he sent his son, and with him two friends, as envoys to the senate, giving them the

mittit eisque, uti illis quos Hiempsale interfecto
miserat, praecipit omnis mortalis pecunia aggredian-
2 tur. Qui postquam Romam adventabant, senatus
a Bestia consultus est placeretne legatos Iugurthae
recipi moenibus, eique decrevere, nisi regnum
ipsumque deditum venissent, uti in diebus proxumis
3 decem Italia decederent. Consul Numidis ex senatus
decreto nuntiari iubet; ita infectis rebus illi domum
discedunt.

4   Interim Calpurnius, parato exercitu, legat sibi
homines nobilis, factiosos, quorum auctoritate quae
deliquisset munita fore sperabat. In quis fuit Scaurus,
5 cuius de natura et habitu supra memoravimus. Nam
in consule nostro multae bonaeque artes animi et
corporis erant, quas omnis avaritia praepediebat;
patiens laborum, acri ingenio, satis providens, belli
haud ignarus, firmissumus contra pericula et insidias.
6 Sed legiones per Italiam Regium atque inde Siciliam,
7 porro ex Sicilia in Africam transvectae. Igitur Calpurnius initio, paratis commeatibus, acriter Numidiam
ingressus est multosque mortalis et urbis aliquot pugnando cepit.

XXIX. Sed ubi Iugurtha per legatos pecunia
temptare bellique quod administrabat asperitatem
ostendere coepit, animus aeger avaritia facile convor-
2 sus est. Ceterum socius et administer omnium

----

same directions that he had given those whom he sent after murdering Hiempsal, namely, to try the power of money on everybody. As this deputation drew near the city, Bestia referred to the senate the question whether they would consent to receive Jugurtha's envoys within the walls. The members thereupon decreed that unless the envoys had come to surrender the king and his kingdom, they must leave Italy within the next ten days. The consul gave orders that the Numidians should be notified of the senate's action; they therefore went home without fulfilling their mission.

Meanwhile Calpurnius, having levied his army, chose as his lieutenants men of noble rank and strong party spirit, by whose influence he hoped that any misdeeds of his would be upheld. Among these was Scaurus, whose character and conduct I described a short time ago.[1] For though our consul possessed many excellent qualities of mind and body, they were all nullified by avarice. He had great endurance, a keen intellect, no little foresight, considerable military experience, and a stout heart in the face of dangers and plots. Now the legions were transported across Italy to Rhegium, from there to Sicily, from Sicily to Africa. Then Calpurnius, having provided himself with supplies, began by making a vigorous attack on the Numidians, taking many prisoners and storming several of their towns.

XXIX. But when Jugurtha through his emissaries began to try the power of money upon Calpurnius and to point out the difficulty of the war which he was conducting, the consul's mind, demoralized as it was by avarice, was easily turned from its purpose. Moreover, he took Scaurus as an accomplice and tool

consiliorum adsumitur Scaurus, qui tametsi a principio, plerisque ex factione eius corruptis, acerrume
regem impugnaverat, tamen magnitudine pecuniae a
3 bono honestoque in pravom abstractus est. Sed
Iugurtha primum tantum modo belli moram redime-
bat, existumans sese aliquid interim Romae pretio
aut gratia effecturum. Postea vero quam participem
negoti Scaurum accepit, in maxumam spem adductus
recuperandae pacis, statuit cum eis de omnibus
pactionibus praesens agere.

4   Ceterum interea fidei causa mittitur a consule
Sextius quaestor in oppidum Iugurthae Vagam.[1]
Cuius rei species erat acceptio frumenti, quod Calpurnius palam legatis imperaverat quoniam deditionis
5 mora indutiae agitabantur. Igitur rex, uti constituerat,
in castra venit ac pauca praesenti consilio locutus de
invidia facti sui atque uti in deditionem acciperetur,
reliqua cum Bestia et Scauro secreta transigit. Dein
postero die, quasi per saturam sententiis exquisitis, in
6 deditionem accipitur. Sed uti pro consilio imperatum
erat, elephanti triginta, pecus atque equi multi cum
7 parvo argenti pondere quaestori traduntur. Calpur-

---

[1] *The form given by some good mss. as well as in inscrr. and
the Greek writers ; P and some other good mss. have* Vaccam *or*
Vacam ; *see Ah. Proleg.* p. 59.

---

[1] A council of war, called to consider the terms of
surrender. Such a council commonly consisted of the *legati*,
tribunes, and chief centurions.

in all his designs; for although at first, even after
many of his own party had been seduced, Scaurus
had vigorously opposed the king, a huge bribe had
turned him from honour and virtue to criminality.
At first, however, Jugurtha merely purchased a delay in hostilities, thinking that he could meanwhile
effect something at Rome by bribery or by his
personal interest. But as soon as he learned that
Scaurus was implicated, he conceived a strong hope
of gaining peace, and decided to discuss all the
conditions in person with the envoys.

But meanwhile, as a token of good faith, the consul
sent his quaestor Sextius to Vaga, a town of Jugurtha's, ostensibly to receive the grain which Calpurnius
had publicly demanded of the envoys in return for
observing an armistice until a surrender should be
arranged. Thereupon the king, as he had agreed,
came to the camp and after he had spoken a few
words in the presence of the council[1] in justifica-
tion of his conduct and had asked to be received in surrender, he arranged the rest privately with Bestia and
Scaurus. Then on the next day an irregular vote[2]
was taken and the surrender accepted. As had been
ordered before the council, thirty elephants, many
cattle and horses, with a small amount of silver[3] were
handed over to the quaestor. Calpurnius went to Rome

---

[2] That is, all the questions involved were voted on together
in a confused and irregular manner. Festus, *s.v. satura*, says:
*satura est cibi genus ex variis rebus conditum et lex multis
rebus conferta* (an "omnibus" bill). He adds: *Itaque in
sanctione legum adscribitur: neve per saturam abrogato aut
derogato; i.e.* no existing law is to be abrogated by a vote
of that kind.

[3] This payment to the state was apart from the private
arrangement with Scaurus and Bestia.

195

nius Romam ad magistratus rogandos proficiscitur
In Numidia et exercitu nostro pax agitabatur.

XXX. Postquam res in Africa gestas quoque modo
actae forent fama divolgavit, Romae per omnis locos
et conventus de facto consulis agitari. Apud plebem
gravis invidia, patres solliciti erant: probarentne
tantum flagitium an decretum consulis subvorterent
2 parum constabat. Ac maxume eos potentia Scauri,
quod is auctor et socius Bestiae ferebatur, a vero
3 bonoque impediebat. At C. Memmius, cuius de
libertate ingeni et odio potentiae nobilitatis supra
diximus, inter dubitationem et moras senatus contionibus populum ad vindicandum hortari, monere
ne rem publicam, ne[1] libertatem suam desererent,
multa superba et crudelia facinora nobilitatis ostendere; prorsus intentus omni modo plebis animum
4 incendebat. Sed quoniam ea tempestate Romae
Memmi facundia clara pollensque fuit, decere existu-
mavi unam ex tam multis orationem eius perscribere
ac potissumum ea[2] dicam, quae[3] in contione post
reditum Bestiae huiuscemodi verbis disseruit.

XXXI. "Multa me dehortantur a vobis, Quirites,
ni studium rei publicae omnia superet: opes factionis,
vostra patientia, ius nullum, ac maxume quod inno-
2 centiae plus periculi quam honoris est. Nam illa

---

[1] m. ne rem p. ne lib., N^1m, Ah; m. rem p. (p. Rom. corr.)
ne lib., A; m. P. R. ne lib., PB (movere) $l s n$, Or; m. ne p.
Rom. ne lib., C; m. p. R. ne remp. ne lib., *the other mss.*
[2] eam, PA^2CBMT.　　[3] quam, P^2CB^2MT.

to preside at the elections. In Numidia and in our army peace reigned.

XXX. When the news was circulated at Rome of what had happened in Africa, and how it was brought about, the consul's conduct was discussed wherever men gathered together. The commons were highly indignant, while the senators were in suspense and unable to make up their minds whether to condone such an outrage or to set aside the consul's decree. In particular the power of Scaurus, who was reported to be Bestia's abettor and accomplice, deterred them from acting justly and honourably. But while the senate delayed and hesitated, Gaius Memmius, of whose independence and hatred of the power of the nobles I have already spoken,[1] urged the assembled people to vengeance, warned them not to prove false to their country and their own liberties, pointed out the many arrogant and cruel deeds of the nobles: in short, did his utmost in every way to inflame the minds of the commons. And since the eloquence of Memmius was famous and potent in Rome at that time,[2] I have thought it worth while to reproduce one of his numerous speeches, and I shall select the one which he delivered before the people after the return of Bestia. It ran as follows:

XXXI. "Were not devotion to our country paramount, I should be deterred, fellow citizens, from addressing you by many considerations : the power of the dominant faction, your spirit of submission, the absence of justice, and especially because more danger than honour awaits integrity. Some things,

---

[1] See xxvii. 2.
[2] Cicero, however (*Brutus*, 136), speaks of Memmius and his brother as *oratores mediocres*.

quidem piget dicere, his annis quindecim quam ludibrio fueritis superbiae paucorum, quam foede quam-
que inulti perierint vostri defensores, ut vobis animus
3 ab ignavia atque socordia corruptus sit, qui ne nunc
quidem, obnoxiis inimicis, exsurgitis atque etiam nunc
4 timetis eos quibus decet terrori esse. Sed quamquam
haec talia sunt, tamen obviam ire factionis potentiae
5 animus subigit. Certe ego libertatem, quae mihi a
parente meo tradita est, experiar. Verum id frustra
an ob rem faciam, in vostra manu situm est, Quirites.
6 Neque ego vos hortor, quod saepe maiores vestri
fecere, uti contra iniurias armati eatis; nihil vi,
nihil secessione opus est. Necesse est suomet ipsi
7 more praecipites eant. Occiso Ti. Graccho, quem
regnum parare aiebant, in plebem Romanam quaestiones habitae sunt. Post C. Gracchi et M. Fulvi
caedem item vostri ordinis multi mortales in carcere
necati sunt. Utriusque cladis non lex verum lubido
eorum finem fecit.

8   " Sed sane fuerit regni paratio plebi sua restituere.
Quidquid sine sanguine civium ulcisci nequitur, iure
9 factum sit. Superioribus annis taciti indignabamini
aerarium expilari, reges et populos liberos paucis
nobilibus vectigal pendere, penes eosdem et summam
gloriam ut maxumas divitias esse. Tamen haec talia
facinora impune suscepisse parum habuere itaque

---

[1] That is, through their own vices and crimes.
[2] Before a special tribunal formed to try the supporters of
Tiberius Gracchus for treason.

indeed, I am ashamed to speak of: how during the past fifteen years you have been the sport of a few men's insolence; how shamefully your defenders have perished unavenged; how your own spirits have been so demoralized because of weakness and cowardice that you do not rise even now, when your enemies are in your power, but still fear those in whom you ought to inspire fear. But although conditions are such, yet my spirit prompts me to brave the power of this faction. At least, I shall make use of the freedom of speech which is my inheritance from my father; but whether I shall do so in vain or to good purpose lies in your hands, my countrymen. I do not urge you to take up arms against your oppressors, as your fathers often did; there is no need of violence, none of secession. They must go to ruin their own way.[1] After the murder of Tiberius Gracchus, whom they accused of trying to make himself king, prosecutions were instituted against the Roman commons.[2] Again, after Gaius Gracchus and Marcus Fulvius were slain, many men of your order suffered death in the dungeon.[3] In both cases bloodshed was ended, not by law, but by the caprice of the victors.

"But let us admit that to restore their rights to the commons was the same thing as to aspire to royal power, and that whatever cannot be avenged without shedding the blood of citizens was justly done. In former years you were silently indignant that the treasury was pillaged, that kings and free peoples paid tribute to a few nobles, that those nobles possessed supreme glory and vast wealth. Yet they were not satisfied with having committed with impunity these

[3] See note on xvi. 2.

postremo leges, maiestas vostra, divina et humana
10 omnia hostibus tradita sunt. Neque eos, qui ea
fecere, pudet aut paenitet, sed incedunt per ora
vostra magnifici, sacerdotia et consulatus, pars triumphos suos ostentantes; proinde quasi ea honori non
praedae habeant.

11 "Servi aere parati iniusta imperia dominorum non
perferunt; vos, Quirites, in imperio nati, aequo animo
12 servitutem toleratis? At qui sunt ei, qui rem publicam occupavere? Homines sceleratissumi, cruentis
manibus, immani avaritia, nocentissumi et eidem
superbissumi, quibus fides, decus, pietas, postremo
13 honesta atque inhonesta omnia quaestui sunt. Pars
eorum occidisse tribunos plebis, alii quaestiones
iniustas, plerique caedem in vos fecisse pro muni-
14 mento habent. Ita quam quisque pessume fecit tam
maxume tutus est. Metum ab scelere suo ad ignaviam
vostram transtulere, quos omnis eadem cupere,
15 eadem odisse, eadem metuere in unum coegit. Sed
haec inter bonos amicitia, inter malos factio est.
16 Quodsi tam vos libertatis curam haberetis quam illi
ad dominationem accensi sunt, profecto neque res
publica, sicuti nunc, vastaretur et benificia vostra
17 penes optumos non audacissumos forent. Maiores
vostri parandi iuris et maiestatis constituendae gratia
bis per secessionem armati Aventinum occupavere.

---

[1] That is, "they ought to feel fear because of their crimes
but you feel it instead because of your cowardice."

great crimes, and so at last the laws, your sovereignty, and all things human and divine have been delivered to your enemies. And they who have done these things are neither ashamed nor sorry, but they walk in grandeur before your eyes, some flaunting their priesthoods and consulships, others their triumphs, just as if these were honours and not stolen goods.

"Slaves bought with a price do not put up with unjust treatment from their masters; will you, Roman citizens born to power, endure slavery with patience? But who are they who have seized upon our country? Men stained with crime, with gory hands, of monstrous greed, guilty, yet at the same time full of pride, who have made honour, reputation, loyalty, in short everything honourable and dishonourable, a source of gain. Some of them are safeguarded by having slain tribunes of the commons, others by unjust prosecutions, many by having shed your blood. Thus the more atrocious the conduct, the greater the safety. They have shifted fear from their crimes to your cowardice,[1] united as they are by the same desires, the same hatred, the same fears. This among good men constitutes friendship; among the wicked it is faction. But if your love of freedom were as great as the thirst for tyranny which spurs them on, surely our country would not be torn asunder as it now is, and your favours would be bestowed on the most virtuous, not on the most reckless. Your forefathers, to assert their legal rights and establish their sovereignty, twice seceded and took armed possession of the Aventine;[2] will you

---

[2] There was only one secession to the Aventine, in 449 B.C. Other secessions were to the Mons Sacer in 494 and to the Janiculum in 287.

Vos pro libertate, quam ab illis accepistis, nonne summa ope nitemini? Atque eo vehementius, quo maius dedecus est parta amittere quam omnino non paravisse.

18   "Dicet aliquis 'Quid igitur censes?' Vindicandum in eos qui hosti prodidere rem publicam. Non manu neque vi, quod magis vos fecisse quam illis accidisse indignum est, verum quaestionibus et indicio ipsius

19 Iugurthae. Qui si dediticius est, profecto iussis vostris oboediens erit, sin ea contemnit, scilicet existumabitis, qualis illa pax aut deditio sit, ex qua ad Iugurtham scelerum impunitas, ad paucos potentis maxumae divitiae, ad rem publicam damna atque dedecora

20 pervenerint. Nisi forte nondum etiam vos dominationis eorum satietas tenet et illa quam haec tempora magis placent, cum regna, provinciae, leges, iura, iudicia, bella atque paces, postremo divina et humana omnia penes paucos erant, vos autem, hoc est populus Romanus, invicti ab hostibus, imperatores omnium gentium, satis habebatis animam retinere; nam servitutem quidem quis vostrum recusare audebat?

21   "Atque ego, tametsi viro[1] flagitiosissumum existumo impune iniuriam accepisse, tamen vos hominibus sceleratissumis ignoscere, quoniam cives sunt, aequo animo paterer, ni misericordia in perniciem casura

22 esset. Nam et illis, quantum importunitatis habent,

[1] viro, *VPMm*; virs, *F*; viros, *A¹N¹s*; virum, *A²N²* and the other mss.

not exert yourselves to the utmost in order to retain
the liberty which they bequeathed to you? And
will you not show the greater ardour, because it is
more shameful to lose what has been won than never
to have won it?

"I seem to hear someone say, 'What then do you
advise?' I reply, 'Let those who have betrayed their
country to the enemy be punished, not by arms or
violence, which it is less becoming for you to inflict
than for them to suffer, but by the courts and
Jugurtha's own testimony. If he is a prisoner of
war, he will surely be obedient to your commands;
but if he scorns them, you may well ask yourselves
what kind of peace or surrender that is from which
Jugurtha has gained impunity for his crimes and a few
powerful men immense wealth, while our country
suffers damage and disgrace. Unless haply you are not
even yet sated with their domination, unless these
times[1] please you less than the days when kingdoms,
provinces, statutes, laws, courts, war and peace, in
short all things human and divine, were in the hands
of a few; and when you, that is to say the Roman
people, unconquered by your enemies, rulers of all
nations, were content to retain the mere breath of
life. For which of you dared to refuse slavery?

"For my own part, although I consider it most
shameful for a true man to suffer wrong without
taking vengeance, yet I could willingly allow you to
pardon those most criminal of men, since they are
your fellow citizens, were it not that mercy would
end in destruction. For such is their insolence that
they are not satisfied to have done evil with impunity,

---

[1] "The contrast lies between the recent period of oppression and the chance which is now presented of punishing the guilty rulers" (Capes).

parum est impune male fecisse, nisi deinde faciundi
licentia eripitur, et vobis aeterna[1] sollicitudo re-
manebit, cum intellegetis aut serviundum esse aut
per manus libertatem retinendam.

23 "Nam fidei quidem aut concordiae quae spes est?
Dominari illi volunt, vos liberi esse; facere illi
iniurias, vos prohibere; postremo sociis nostris veluti
24 hostibus, hostibus[2] pro sociis utuntur. Potestne in
25 tam divorsis mentibus pax aut amicitia esse? Qua
re moneo hortorque vos ne tantum scelus impunitum
omittatis. Non peculatus aerari factus est neque per
vim sociis ereptae pecuniae, quae quamquam gravia
sunt, tamen consuetudine iam pro nihilo habentur.
Hosti acerrumo prodita senatus auctoritas, proditum
imperium vostrum est; domi militiaeque res publica
26 venalis fuit. Quae nisi quaesita erunt, nisi vindicatum in noxios, quid erit relicum, nisi ut illis, qui ea
fecere, oboedientes vivamus? Nam impune quae
27 lubet facere, id est regem esse. Neque ego vos,
Quirites, hortor ut malitis civis vostros perperam
quam recte fecisse, sed ne ignoscundo malis bonos
28 perditum eatis. Ad hoc in re publica multo praestat
benifici quam malifici immemorem esse. Bonus tantum modo segnior fit, ubi neglegas, at malus improbior.
29 Ad hoc si iniuriae non sint, haud saepe auxili egeas."

[1] alterna, *VXD l n.*

[2] hostibus, hostibus, *P¹l n; the other mss. have only* hostibus
(*once*).

---

[1] The meaning appears to be that the people would not
need to bestow favours in return for protection, or to secure

unless the opportunity for further wrong-doing be wrung from you; and you will be left in eternal anxiety, because of the consciousness that you must either submit to slavery or use force to maintain your freedom.

"Pray, what hope have you of mutual confidence or harmony? They wish to be tyrants, you to be free; they desire to inflict injury, you to prevent it; finally, they treat our allies as enemies and our enemies as allies. Are peace and friendship compatible with sentiments so unlike? They are not, and therefore I warn and implore you not to let such wickedness go unscathed. It is not a matter of plundering the treasury or of extorting money from our allies— serious crimes, it is true, but so common now-a-days as to be disregarded. Nay, the senate's dignity has been prostituted to a ruthless enemy, your sovereignty has been betrayed, your country has been offered for sale at home and abroad. Unless cognizance is taken of these outrages, unless the guilty are punished, what will remain except to pass our lives in submission to those who are guilty of these acts? For to do with impunity whatever one fancies is to be a king. I am not urging you, Romans, to rejoice rather in the guilt than in the innocence of your fellow citizens; but you should not insist upon ruining the good by pardoning the wicked. More- over, in a republic it is far better to forget a kindness than an injury. The good man merely becomes less active in well doing when you neglect him, but the bad man grows more wicked. Finally, if there should be no wrongs, you would not often need help."[1]

protection in the future, and hence would be more indepen- dent.

XXXII. Haec atque alia huiuscemodi saepe dicundo[1] Memmius populo persuadet uti L. Cassius, qui tum praetor erat, ad Iugurtham mitteretur eumque interposita fide publica Romam duceret, quo facilius indicio regis Scauri et reliquorum, quos pecuniae captae arcessebat, delicta patefierent.

2 Dum haec Romae geruntur, qui in Numidia relicti a Bestia exercitui praeerant, secuti morem imperatoris 3 sui, pluruma et flagitiosissuma facinora fecere. Fuere qui auro corrupti elephantos Iugurthae traderent, alii perfugas vendere,[2] pars ex pacatis praedas agebant; 4 tanta vis avaritiae in animos eorum veluti tabes in- 5 vaserat. At Cassius praetor, perlata rogatione a C. Memmio ac perculsa omni nobilitate, ad Iugurtham proficiscitur eique timido et ex conscientia diffidenti rebus suis persuadet, quoniam se populo Romano dedisset, ne vim quam misericordiam eius experiri mallet. Privatim praeterea fidem suam interponit, quam ille non minoris quam publicam ducebat; talis ea tempestate fama de Cassio erat.

XXXIII. Igitur Iugurtha contra decus regium cultu quam maxume miserabili cum Cassio Romam 2 venit. Ac tametsi in ipso magna vis animi erat, confirmatus ab omnibus quorum potentia aut scelere cuncta ea gesserat, quae supra diximus, C. Baebium

---

[1] indicendo, *mss.*; in . . . dicendo, *Jordan, who suggests that* contione *has fallen out*; *Ah deletes* in *and suggests* contionibus; inducendo, *Or.*

[2] venderent, *mss., corr. by Kortte.*

XXXII. By repeating these and similar sentiments Memmius induced the people to send Lucius Cassius, who was praetor at the time, to Jugurtha. Cassius was instructed to bring the king to Rome under pledge of public protection, in order that through his testimony the offences of Scaurus and the rest who were accused of taking bribes might the more readily be disclosed.

While all this was going on at Rome, those who had been left by Bestia in command of the army in Numidia, following their general's example, were guilty of many shameless misdeeds. Some were induced by bribes to return his elephants to Jugurtha, others sold him his deserters, and a part plundered those who were at peace with us: so strong was the love of money which had attacked their minds like a pestilence. But when, to the consternation of all the nobility, the bill of Gaius Memmius was passed, the praetor Cassius went to Jugurtha and, in spite of the king's fears and the distrust due to his guilty conscience, persuaded him that since he had surrendered himself to the Roman people, it would be better to experience their mercy than their force. He also gave Jugurtha his personal pledge of safety, which the king rated no less highly than that of the state; such was the repute which Cassius enjoyed at that time.

XXXIII. Accordingly Jugurtha, exchanging the pomp of a king for a garb especially designed to excite pity, came to Rome with Cassius; and although personally he possessed great assurance, yet with the encouragement of all those through whose power or guilt he had committed the numerous crimes that I have mentioned he won over Gaius Baebius,[1]

---

[1] That is, although Jugurtha had plenty of assurance, he nevertheless took the advice of his friends and did not rely upon his impudence alone, but added the support of Baebius.

tribunum plebis magna mercede parat, cuius impudentia contra ius et iniurias omnis munitus foret.
3 At C. Memmius advocata contione, quamquam regi infesta plebes erat et pars in vincula duci iubebat, pars, nisi socios sceleris sui aperiret, more maiorum de hoste supplicium sumi, dignitati quam irae magis consulens sedare motus et animos eorum mollire, postremo confirmare, fidem publicam per sese invio-
4 latam fore. Post, ubi silentium coepit, producto Iugurtha verba facit, Romae Numidiaeque facinora eius memorat, scelera in patrem fratresque ostendit. Quibus iuvantibus quibusque ministris ea egerit quamquam intellegat populus Romanus, tamen velle manifesta magis ex illo habere. Si verum aperiat, in fide et clementia populi Romani magnam spem illi sitam, sin reticeat, non sociis saluti fore sed se suasque spes corrupturum.

XXXIV. Deinde ubi Memmius dicundi finem fecit et Iugurtha respondere iussus est, C. Baebius tribunus plebis quem pecunia corruptum supra diximus, regem tacere iubet; ac tametsi multitudo, quae in contione aderat, vehementer accensa terrebat eum clamore, voltu, saepe impetu atque aliis omnibus quae ira fieri
2 amat, vicit tamen impudentia. Ita populus ludibrio

---

[1] See note on p. 109.

tribune of the commons, by a heavy bribe, that through this officer's effrontery he might be protected against the strong arm of the law and against all personal violence. But when Gaius Memmius had called an assembly of the people, the commons were so exasperated at the king that some demanded that he should be imprisoned, others that if he did not reveal the accomplices in his guilt, he should be punished as an enemy after the usage of our forefathers.[1] But Memmius, taking counsel of propriety rather than of resentment, quieted their excitement and soothed their spirits, finally declaring that, so far as it was in his power to prevent it, the public pledge should not be broken. Afterwards, when silence followed and Jugurtha was brought out, Memmius made an address, recalled the king's actions at Rome and in Numidia, and described his crimes against his father and brothers. He said to him that although the Roman people were aware through whose encouragement and help the king had done these things, yet they wished clearer testimony from his own lips. If he would reveal the truth, he had much to hope for from the good faith and mercy of the Roman people, but if he kept silence, he could not save his accomplices and would ruin himself and his hopes.

XXXIV. When Memmius had finished and Jugurtha was bidden to reply, Gaius Baebius, the tribune of the commons who, as I just said, had been bribed, thereupon bade the king hold his peace. And although the populace, who were gathered in assembly, were greatly excited and tried to intimidate the tribune by shouting, by angry looks, often by threatening gestures and all the other means which anger prompts, yet his impudence triumphed. Hence

habitus ex contione discedit, Iugurthae Bestiaeque et ceteris quos illa quaestio exagitabat, animi augescunt.

XXXV. Erat ea tempestate Romae Numida quidam nomine Massiva, Gulussae filius, Masinissae nepos, qui quia in dissensione regum Iugurthae advorsus fuerat, dedita Cirta et Adherbale interfecto profugus 2 ex patria abierat. Huic Sp. Albinus, qui proxumo anno post Bestiam cum Q. Minucio Rufo consulatum gerebat, persuadet, quoniam ex stirpe Masinissae sit Iugurthamque ob scelera invidia cum metu urgeat, 3 regnum Numidiae ab senatu petat. Avidus consul belli gerundi movere quam senescere omnia malebat. 4 Ipsi provincia Numidia, Minucio Macedonia evenerat. Quae postquam Massiva agitare coepit neque Iugurthae in amicis satis praesidi est, quod eorum alium conscientia alium mala fama et timor impediebat, Bomilcari proxumo ac maxume fido sibi imperat, pretio, sicuti multa confecerat, insidiatores Massivae paret, ac maxume occulte; sin id parum procedat, quovis modo Numidam interficiat. 5 Bomilcar mature regis mandata exsequitur et per homines talis negoti artifices itinera egressusque eius, postremo loca atque tempora cuncta explorat. Deinde, 6 ubi res postulabat, insidias tendit. Igitur unus ex eo numero qui ad caedem parati erant paulo inconsultius Massivam aggreditur; illum obtruncat, sed

---

¹ 110 B.C.   ² See note on p. 44.

the people left the assembly after being made ridic-
ulous, while Jugurtha, Bestia, and the others who
were fearful of conviction, recovered their assurance.

XXXV. There was in Rome at that time a Numidian named Massiva, a son of Gulussa and grandson of Masinissa, who had taken sides against
Jugurtha in the quarrel of the kings and had fled from
Africa after the capture of Cirta and the death of
Adherbal. This man was persuaded by Spurius
Albinus, who was holding the consulship with Quintus Minucius Rufus[1] the year after Bestia, to ask
the senate for the throne of Numidia, since he was
descended from Masinissa and since Jugurtha was
feared and hated for his crimes. For the consul was
eager to make war, and preferred a state of general
confusion to inactivity. He had drawn[2] Numidia as
his province, while Minucius had Macedonia. When
Massiva began to push these designs, Jugurtha
found little support in his friends, some of whom
were hampered by a bad conscience, others by ill
repute and fear. He therefore directed Bomilcar, his
nearest and most trusted attendant, to bring about
Massiva's assassination by the use of money, through
which the king had already accomplished so much.
He asked him to do this secretly, if possible; but if
secrecy were not possible, to slay the Numidian in any
way he could.

Bomilcar hastened to carry out the king's orders
and through men who were adepts in such business
he kept track of Massiva's comings and goings; in
short, found out where he was at all times. Finally,
when the opportunity came, he set his trap. Thereupon one of those who had been hired to do the
murder attacked Massiva somewhat incautiously; he

ipse deprehensus, multis hortantibus et in primis
7 Albino consule, indicium profitetur. Fit reus magis
ex aequo bonoque quam ex iure gentium Bomilcar,
comes eius qui Romam fide publica venerat.

8 At Iugurtha manufestus tanti sceleris non prius
omisit contra verum niti, quam animadvortit supra
gratiam atque pecuniam suam invidiam facti esse.
9 Igitur quamquam in priore actione ex amicis quinquaginta vades dederat, regno magis quam vadibus
consulens clam in Numidiam Bomilcarem dimittit,
veritus ne reliquos popularis metus invaderet parendi
sibi, si de illo supplicium sumptum foret. Et ipse
paucis diebus eodem profectus est, iussus a senatu
10 Italia decedere. Sed postquam Roma egressus est,
fertur saepe eo tacitus respiciens postremo dixisse,
" Urbem[1] venalem et mature perituram, si emptorem
invenerit ! "

XXXVI. Interim Albinus renovato bello commeatum, stipendium aliaque, quae militibus usui forent,
maturat in Africam portare ; ac statim ipse profectus,
uti ante comitia, quod tempus haud longe aberat,
armis aut deditione aut quovis modo bellum conficeret.
2 At contra Iugurtha trahere omnia et alias deinde
alias morae causas facere, polliceri deditionem ac
deinde metum simulare, cedere instanti et paulo

---

[1] O urbem, *AH²M²*, *Livy*, *Per.* 64, *Aug. Ep.* 138. 16, *Oros.
Hist.* v. 15. 16, *Ah, Or.*

---

[1] When the accused was admitted to bail.

slew his victim, but was himself caught, and at the solicitation of many, in particular of Albinus the consul, he made a full confession. Bomilcar was brought to trial rather from the demands of equity and justice than in accordance with the law of nations, inasmuch as he was in the company of one who had come to Rome under pledge of public protection.

Jugurtha, however, although he was clearly responsible for so flagrant a crime, did not cease to resist the evidence, until he realized that the indignation at the deed was too strong even for his influence and his money. Therefore, although in the first stage of the trial[1] he had given fifty of his friends as sureties,[2] yet having an eye rather to his throne than to the sureties, he sent Bomilcar secretly to Numidia, fearing that if he paid the penalty, the rest of his subjects would fear to obey his orders. A few days later he himself returned home, being ordered by the senate to leave Italy. After going out of the gates, it is said that he often looked back at Rome in silence and finally said, " A city for sale and doomed to speedy destruction if it finds a purchaser ! "

XXXVI. Albinus meanwhile renewed hostilities and hastened to transport to Africa provisions, money for paying the soldiers, and other apparatus of war. He himself set out at once, desiring by arms, by surrender, or in any possible way to bring the war to an end before the elections, the time of which was not far off. Jugurtha, on the contrary, tried in every way to gain time, inventing one pretext for delay after another. He promised a surrender and then feigned fear, gave way to the consul's attack and then, that

---

[2] For Bomilcar's appearance.

post, ne sui diffiderent, instare; ita belli modo, modo pacis mora consulem ludificare.

3 Ac fuere qui tum Albinum haud ignarum consili regis existumarent, neque ex tanta properantia tam facile tractum bellum socordia magis quam dolo 4 crederent. Sed postquam dilapso tempore comitiorum dies adventabat, Albinus Aulo fratre in castris pro praetore relicto Romam decessit.

XXXVII. Ea tempestate Romae seditionibus tri-2 buniciis atrociter res publica agitabatur. P. Lucullus et L. Annius tribuni plebis resistentibus collegis continuare magistratum nitebantur, quae dissensio 3 totius anni comitia impediebat. Ea mora in spem adductus Aulus, quem pro praetore in castris relictum supra diximus, aut conficiundi belli aut terrore exercitus ab rege pecuniae capiundae, milites mense Ianuario ex hibernis in expeditionem evocat magnisque itineribus hieme aspera pervenit ad oppidum 4 Suthul, ubi regis thesauri erant. Quod quamquam et saevitia temporis et opportunitate loci neque capi neque obsideri poterat—nam circum murum situm in praerupti montis extremo planities limosa hiemalibus aquis paludem fecerat—tamen aut simulandi gratia, quo regi formidinem adderet, aut cupidine

---

[1] By using their veto to forbid the holding of elections.

[2] Up to Dec. 9, when the election of tribunes was held.

[3] 109 B.C. The defeat of Aulus probably occurred before January, 109, since Metellus and Silanus are called *consules designati* after his defeat; see xliii. 1.

his followers might not lose courage, attacked in his turn; thus baffling the consul now by the delays of war and now by those of peace.

There were some who thought that even then Albinus was not unaware of the king's design, and who found it impossible to believe that the ease with which the king protracted a war begun with such urgency was not due rather to guile than to incompetence. Now when in the course of time the day of the elections drew near, Albinus sailed for Rome, leaving his brother Aulus in charge of the camp.

XXXVII. At that time the Roman commonwealth was cruelly racked by the dissensions of the tribunes. Two of their number, Publius Lucullus and Lucius Annius, were trying to prolong their term of office, in spite of the opposition of their colleagues;[1] and this strife blocked the elections of the whole year.[2] Because of this delay Aulus, who, as I just said, had been left in charge of the camp, was inspired with the hope of either finishing the war or forcing a bribe from the king through fear of his army. He therefore summoned his soldiers in the month of January[3] from their winter quarters for active duty in the field, and making forced marches in spite of the severity of the winter season, reached the town of Suthul, where the king's treasure was kept. He was unable either to take the town or lay siege to it because of the inclemency of the weather and the strength of its position; for all about the walls, which were built along the edge of a steep cliff, was a muddy plain, of which the winter rains had made a marshy pool. Yet either with the idea of making a feint, in order to frighten the king, or because he was blinded by a desire to possess the town

caecus ob thesauros oppidi potiundi, vineas agere, aggerem iacere, aliaque quae incepto usui forent properare.

XXXVIII. At Iugurtha, cognita vanitate atque imperitia legati, subdole eius augere amentiam, missitare supplicantis legatos, ipse quasi vitabundus per
2 saltuosa loca et tramites exercitum ductare. Denique Aulum spe pactionis perpulit, uti relicto Suthule in abditas regiones sese veluti cedentem insequeretur;
3 ita delicta occultiora fore.[1] Interea per homines callidos diu[2] noctuque exercitum temptabat, centuriones ducesque turmarum partim[3] uti transfugerent corrumpere, alii signo dato locum uti desererent.

4 Quae postquam ex sententia instruit, intempesta nocte de improviso multitudine Numidarum Auli
5 castra circumvenit. Milites Romani perculsi tumultu insolito arma capere alii, alii se abdere, pars territos confirmare, trepidare omnibus locis. Vis magna hostium, caelum nocte atque nubibus obscuratum, periculum anceps, postremo fugere an manere tutius
6 foret, in incerto erat. Sed ex eo numero, quos paulo ante corruptos diximus, cohors una Ligurum cum duabus turmis Thracum et paucis gregariis militibus transiere ad regem, et centurio primi pili tertiae

---

[1] fuere (fuit), *mss.*, *Ah, Or.* *Dietsch and others regarded* ita fuere *as a gloss.*

[2] diu, *PNA (corr.)*; *the other mss. have* die.

[3] partim, *T D² Fs n m* ; partium, *the other mss.* (s. duces *written above in A*).

---

[1] That is, any bargain which Aulus made with Jugurtha would be less likely to attract the attention of the senate.

for the sake of its treasure, he brought up the mantlets, constructed a mound, and hastily made the other
preparations for an assault.

XXXVIII. Jugurtha, however, well aware of the
presumption and incapacity of the acting commander,
craftily added to his infatuation and constantly sent
him suppliant envoys, while he himself, as if trying
to avoid an encounter, led his army through woody
places and by-paths. Finally, by holding out hope
of an agreement, he induced Aulus to leave Suthul
and follow him in a pretended retreat into remote
regions; thus, he suggested, any misconduct of the
Roman's [1] would be less obvious. Meanwhile through
clever emissaries the king was working upon the
Roman army day and night, bribing the centurions
and commanders of cavalry squadrons either to desert
or to abandon their posts at a given signal.

After he had arranged these matters to his satisfaction, in the dead of night he suddenly surrounded
the camp of Aulus with a throng of Numidians.
The Roman soldiers were alarmed by the unusual
disturbance; some seized their arms, others hid
themselves, a part encouraged the fearful; consternation reigned. The hostile force was large, night
and clouds darkened the heavens, there was danger
whichever course they took [2]: in short, whether it was
safer to stand or flee was uncertain. Then from the
number of those who had been bribed, as I just said,
one cohort of Ligurians with two squadrons of Thrac-
ians and a few privates went over to the king, while
the chief centurion of the Third legion gave the

---

[2] Namely, within the camp because of the panic, and
without because of the difficulty of making their escape; the
following sentence repeats the idea in a more definite form.

legionis per munitionem, quam uti defenderet acceperat, locum hostibus introeundi dedit eaque
7 Numidae cuncti irrupere. Nostri foeda fuga, plerique
8 abiectis armis, proxumum collem occupaverunt. Nox
atque praeda castrorum hostis quo minus victoria
9 uterentur remorata sunt. Deinde Iugurtha postero
die cum Aulo in colloquio verba facit. Tametsi ipsum
cum exercitu fame et ferro clausum teneret,[1] tamen
se memorem humanarum rerum, si secum foedus
faceret, incolumis omnis sub iugum missurum. Prae-
10 terea uti diebus decem Numidia decederet. Quae
quamquam gravia et flagiti plena erant, tamen quia
mortis metu mutabantur, sicuti regi lubuerat pax
convenit.

XXXIX. Sed ubi ea Romae comperta sunt, metus
atque maeror civitatem invasere. Pars dolere pro
gloria imperi, pars insolita rerum bellicarum timere
libertati, Aulo omnes infesti, ac maxume qui bello
saepe praeclari fuerant,[2] quod armatus dedecore
2 potius quam manu salutem quaesiverat. Ob ea
consul Albinus, ex delicto fratris invidiam ac deinde
periculum timens, senatum de foedere consulebat et
tamen interim exercitui supplementum scribere, ab
sociis et nomine Latino auxilia arcessere, denique
omnibus modis festinare.

3 Senatus, ita uti par fuerat, decernit suo atque

---

[1] tenet, *mss.*
[2] fuerint, $PAN^1K^1T^2Dln.$

enemy an opportunity of entering the part of the fortification which he had been appointed to guard, and there all the Numidians burst in. Our men in shameful flight, in most cases throwing away their arms, took refuge on a neighbouring hill. Night and the pillaging of the camp delayed the enemy and prevented them from following up their victory. Then on the following day, Jugurtha held a conference with Aulus. He said that he had the general and his army at the mercy of starvation or the sword; yet in view of the uncertainty of human affairs, if Aulus would make a treaty with him, he would let them all go free after passing under the yoke, provided Aulus would leave Numidia within ten days. Although the conditions were hard and shameful, yet because they were offered in exchange for the fear of death,[1] peace was accepted on the king's terms.

XXXIX. Now, when the news of this disaster reached Rome, fear and grief seized upon the community. Some grieved for the glory of the empire, others, who were unused to matters of war, feared for their freedom. All men, especially those who had often gained renown in war, were incensed at Aulus, because with arms in his hands he had sought safety by disgrace rather than by combat. Therefore the consul Albinus, fearing odium and consequent danger as the result of his brother's misconduct, laid the question of the treaty before the senate; but in the meantime he enrolled reinforcements, summoned aid from the allies and the Latin peoples; in short, bestirred himself in every way.

The senate decided that no treaty could be binding

---

[1] That is, the Romans had to accept the terms or die.

4 populi iniussu nullum potuisse foedus fieri. Consul,
impeditus a tribunis plebis ne quas paraverat copias
secum portaret, paucis diebus in Africam proficiscitur;
nam omnis exercitus, uti convenerat, Numidia deduc-
5 tus in provincia hiemabat. Postquam eo venit, quamquam persequi Iugurtham et mederi fraternae invidiae animo ardebat, cognitis militibus, quos praeter
fugam soluto imperio licentia atque lascivia corruperat,
ex copia rerum statuit sibi nihil agitandum.

XL. Interim Romae C. Mamilius Limetanus tribunus plebis rogationem ad populum promulgat, uti
quaereretur in eos quorum consilio Iugurtha senati
decreta neglegisset,[1] quique ab eo in legationibus
aut imperiis pecunias accepissent, qui elephantos
quique perfugas tradidissent, item qui de pace aut
2 bello cum hostibus pactiones fecissent. Huic rogati-
oni partim conscii sibi, alii ex partium invidia pericula
metuentes, quoniam aperte resistere non poterant,
quin illa et alia talia placere sibi faterentur, occulte
per amicos ac maxume per homines nominis Latini
3 et socios Italicos impedimenta parabant. Sed plebes
incredibile memoratu est quam intenta fuerit quantaque vi rogationem iusserit, magis odio nobilitatis,
cui mala illa parabantur, quam cura rei publicae;
tanta lubido in partibus erat.

---

[1] neglegisset, *B, Or*; neglexisset, *the other mss., Ah.*

without its order and that of the people; as indeed was to have been expected. The consul was prevented by the tribunes of the commons from taking with him the forces which he had raised, but within a few days left for Africa; for the whole army had withdrawn from Numidia according to the agreement and was wintering in that province. But although Albinus on his arrival was eager to pursue Jugurtha and atone for his brother's disgrace, yet knowing his soldiers, who were demoralized not only by their rout but by the licence and debauchery consequent upon lax discipline, he decided that he was in no condition to make any move.

XL. Meanwhile, at Rome, Gaius Mamilius Limetanus, tribune of the commons, proposed to the people a bill, in which it was provided that legal proceedings should be begun against those at whose advice Jugurtha had disregarded decrees of the senate; against those who had accepted money from him while serving as envoys or commanders; against those who had handed back the elephants and deserters; and against those who had made terms of peace and war with the enemy. Preparations for obstructing this bill were made both by all who were conscious of guilt and also by others who feared the dangers arising from factional hatred; but since they could not openly oppose it without admitting their approval of these and similar acts, they did so secretly through their friends, and especially through men of the Latin cities and the Italian allies. But the commons passed the bill with incredible eagerness and enthusiasm, rather from hatred of the nobles, for whom it boded trouble, than from love of country: so high did party passion run.

4 Igitur, ceteris metu perculsis, M. Scaurus, quem
legatum Bestiae fuisse supra docuimus, inter laetitiam
plebis et suorum fugam, trepida etiam tum civitate,
cum ex Mamilia rogatione tres quaesitores rogaren-
5 tur, effecerat uti ipse in eo numero crearetur. Sed
quaestio exercita aspere violenterque ex rumore
et lubidine plebis. Ut saepe nobilitatem, sic ea
tempestate plebem ex secundis rebus insolentia
ceperat.

XLI. Ceterum mos partium[1] et factionum[2] ac
deinde omnium malarum artium paucis ante annis
Romae ortus est otio atque abundantia earum rerum,
2 quae prima mortales ducunt. Nam ante Carthaginem
deletam populus et senatus Romanus placide mo-
desteque inter se rem publicam tractabant, neque
gloriae neque dominationis certamen inter civis erat;
metus hostilis in bonis artibus civitatem retinebat.
3 Sed ubi illa formido mentibus decessit, scilicet ea
quae res secundae amant, lascivia atque superbia
4 incessere. Ita quod in advorsis rebus optaverant
otium postquam adepti sunt, asperius acerbiusque
5 fuit. Namque coepere nobilitas dignitatem, populus libertatem in lubidinem vortere, sibi quisque
ducere, trahere, rapere. Ita omnia in duas partis
abstracta sunt, res publica, quae media fuerat,
dilacerata.

---

[1] partium, *m*[1]; partium popularium, *the other mss.*
[2] factionum, *N*[1]*m*[1]; senatus f., *C B n, m.* 2 *of A N K T*;
senatores f., *the other mss.*

Upon this the rest were panic stricken; but in the midst of the exultation of the people and the rout of his party, Marcus Scaurus, who, as I have already said, had been Bestia's lieutenant, took advantage of the political confusion to have himself named as one of the three commissioners[1] authorized by the bill of Mamilius. Nevertheless[2] the investigation was conducted with harshness and violence, on hearsay evidence and at the caprice of the commons; for then the commons, as so often the nobles, had been made insolent by success.

XLI. Now the institution of parties and factions, with all their attendant evils, originated at Rome a few years before this as the result of peace and of an abundance of everything that mortals prize most highly. For before the destruction of Carthage the people and senate of Rome together governed the republic peacefully and with moderation. There was no strife among the citizens either for glory or for power; fear of the enemy preserved the good morals of the state. But when the minds of the people were relieved of that dread, wantonness and arrogance naturally arose, vices which are fostered by prosperity. Thus the peace for which they had longed in time of adversity, after they had gained it proved to be more cruel and bitter than adversity itself. For the nobles began to abuse their position and the people their liberty, and every man for himself robbed, pillaged, and plundered. Thus the community was split into two parties, and between these the state was torn to pieces.

[1] These *quaesitores* were doubtless to preside over three separate courts, in order to dispose more promptly of the great number of cases.

[2] In spite of what Scaurus could effect.

6 Ceterum nobilitas factione magis pollebat, plebis
vis soluta atque dispersa in multitudine minus
7 poterat. Paucorum arbitrio belli domique agitabatur, penes eosdem aerarium, provinciae, magistratus,
gloriae triumphique erant; populus militia atque
inopia urgebatur, praedas bellicas imperatores cum
8 paucis diripiebant. Interea parentes aut parvi
liberi militum, uti quisque potentiori confinis erat,
9 sedibus pellebantur. Ita cum potentia avaritia sine
modo modestiaque invadere, polluere et vastare
omnia, nihil pensi neque sancti habere, quoad semet
10 ipsa[1] praecipitavit. Nam ubi primum ex nobilitate
reperti sunt qui veram gloriam iniustae potentiae
anteponerent, moveri civitas et dissensio civilis
quasi permixtio terrae oriri coepit.

XLII. Nam postquam Ti. et C. Gracchus, quorum
maiores Punico atque aliis bellis multum rei publicae
addiderant, vindicare plebem in libertatem et paucorum scelera patefacere coepere, nobilitas noxia
atque eo perculsa, modo per socios ac nomen
Latinum, interdum per equites Romanos, quos spes
societatis a plebe dimoverat, Gracchorum actionibus
obviam ierat, et primo Tiberium, dein paucos post
annos eadem ingredientem Gaium, tribunum alte-

---

[1] ipsa, AN^1m, *Arus.* vii. 505. 2 κ; ipsam, *the other mss.*

---

[1] The number is due to the influence of the other plurals;
or *gloriae* may mean "opportunities for winning glory."
Bernays suggested *laureae* (*loriae*) and Bergk *adoreae*.

But the nobles had the more powerful organization, while the strength of the commons was less effective because it was incompact and divided among many. Affairs at home and in the field were managed according to the will of a few men, in whose hands were the treasury, the provinces, public offices, glory[1] and triumphs. The people were burdened with military service and poverty. The generals divided the spoils of war with a few friends. Meanwhile the parents or little children of the soldiers, if they had a powerful neighbour, were driven from their homes. Thus, by the side of power, greed arose, unlimited and unrestrained, violated and devastated everything, respected nothing, and held nothing sacred, until it finally brought about its own downfall. For as soon as nobles were found who preferred true glory to unjust power, the state began to be disturbed and civil dissension to arise like an upheaval of the earth.

XLII. For example, when Tiberius and Gaius Gracchus, whose forefathers[2] had added greatly to the power of the republic in the Punic and other wars, began to assert the freedom of the commons and expose the crimes of the oligarchs, the nobility, who were guilty, were therefore panic stricken. They accordingly opposed the acts of the Gracchi, now through the allies and the Latin cities and again through the knights, whom the hope of an alliance[3] with the senate had estranged from the commons. And first Tiberius, then a few years later Gaius, who had followed in his brother's footsteps, were slain with the sword, although one was a tribune and the

[1] The Gracchi were grandsons on their mother's side of the elder Scipio Africanus ; their father had served with distinction in Spain and Sardinia.

[2] That is, a share in their privileges.

rum, alterum [1] triumvirum coloniis deducundis, cum

2 M. Fulvio Flacco ferro necaverat. Et sane Gracchis cupidine victoriae haud satis moderatus animus fuit.

3 Sed bono vinci satius est quam malo more iniuriam vincere.

4 Igitur ea victoria nobilitas ex lubidine sua usa multos mortalis ferro aut fuga exstinxit plusque in relicum sibi timoris quam potentiae addidit. Quae res plerumque magnas civitatis pessum dedit, dum alteri alteros vincere quovis modo et victos acerbius

5 ulcisci volunt. Sed de studiis partium et omnis civitatis moribus si singillatim aut pro magnitudine parem disserere, tempus quam res maturius me deseret. Quam ob rem ad inceptum redeo.

XLIII. Post Auli foedus exercitusque nostri foedam fugam Metellus et Silanus consules designati provincias inter se partiverant Metelloque Numidia evenerat, acri viro et quamquam adverso populi

2 partium, fama tamen aequabili et inviolata. Is ubi primum magistratum ingressus est, alia omnia sibi cum collega ratus, ad bellum quod gesturus erat

3 animum intendit. Igitur diffidens veteri exercitui milites scribere,[2] praesidia undique arcessere, arma,

---

[1] *All the mss. except n have only one* alterum.
[2] scribere, *NMm, Ah, Or*; eligere, *D*; eligere scr., *XKHls n*; scr. elig., *F*; e. praesidia s., *T*.

---

[1] The connection of thought is not quite clear. The meaning apparently is that the excesses of the Gracchi did not justify the unconstitutional acts of the nobles.
[2] Sallust's word-play is on *foedus*, "treaty," and *foeda fuga*, "foul flight."   [3] For 109 B.C.; see note on xxxvii. 3.

other a commissioner for founding colonies; and with them fell Marcus Fulvius Flaccus. It must be admitted that the Gracchi were so eager for victory that they had not shown a sufficiently moderate spirit; but a good man would prefer to be defeated rather than to triumph over injustice by establishing a bad precedent.[1]

The nobles then abused their victory to gratify their passions; they put many men out of the way by the sword or by banishment, and thus rendered themselves for the future rather dreaded than powerful. It is this spirit which has commonly ruined great nations, when one party desires to triumph over another by any and every means and to avenge itself on the vanquished with excessive cruelty. But if I should attempt to speak of the strife of parties and of the general character of the state in detail or according to the importance of the theme, time would fail me sooner than material. Therefore I return to my subject.

XLIII. After the foul pact of Aulus and the foul flight [2] of our army the consuls elect,[3] Metellus and Silanus, had shared the provinces between them; Numidia had fallen to Metellus, a man of spirit, and, although he was an opponent of the popular party, of a consistently unblemished reputation. When he first entered upon his term of office, thinking that his colleague shared with him all the other business [4] he devoted his attention to the war which he was going to conduct. Accordingly, being distrustful of the old army, he enrolled soldiers, summoned auxiliaries from every hand, got together arms, weapons,

---

[4] But not the war, which was his special charge; he could leave to Silanus the chief responsibility in other matters.

tela, equos et cetera instrumenta militiae parare, ad
hoc commeatum affatim, denique omnia, quae in
bello vario et multarum rerum egenti usui esse
4 solent. Ceterum ad ea patranda senatus auctoritate,
socii nomenque Latinum et reges ultro auxilia
mittundo, postremo omnis civitas summo studio
5 adnitebatur. Itaque ex sententia omnibus rebus
paratis compositisque in Numidiam proficiscitur,
magna spe civium, cum propter artis bonas tum
maxume quod advorsum divitias invictum animum
gerebat; et avaritia magistratuum ante id tempus in
Numidia nostrae opes contusae hostiumque auctae
erant.

XLIV. Sed ubi in Africam venit, exercitus ei
traditur a Sp. Albino proconsule iners, imbellis,
neque periculi neque laboris patiens, lingua quam
manu promptior, praedator ex sociis et ipse praeda
2 hostium, sine imperio et modestia habitus. Ita
imperatori novo plus ex malis moribus sollicitudinis
quam ex copia militum auxili aut spei bonae ac-
3 cedebat. Statuit tamen Metellus, quamquam et
aestivorum tempus comitiorum mora imminuerat et
expectatione eventus civium animos intentos putabat, non prius bellum attingere quam maiorum
4 disciplina milites laborare coegisset. Nam Albinus
Auli fratris exercitusque clade perculsus, postquam
decreverat non egredi provincia, quantum temporis

---

horses, and other munitions of war, as well as an abundance of supplies; in short, he provided everything which commonly proves useful in a war of varied character and demanding large resources. Furthermore, in making these preparations the senate aided him by its sanction, allies, Latin cities, and kings by the voluntary contribution of auxiliaries; in short, the whole state showed the greatest enthusiasm. Therefore, after everything was prepared and arranged to his satisfaction, Metellus left for Numidia, bearing with him the high hopes of the citizens, which were inspired not only by his good qualities in general, but especially because he possessed a mind superior to riches; for it had been the avarice of the magistrates that before this time had blighted our prospects in Numidia and advanced those of the enemy.

XLIV. But when Metellus reached Africa, the proconsul Spurius Albinus handed over to him an army that was weak, cowardly, and incapable of facing either danger or hardship, readier of tongue than of hand, a plunderer of our allies and itself a prey to the enemy, subject to no discipline or restraint. Hence their new commander gained more anxiety from the bad habits of his soldiers than security or hope from their numbers. Although the postponement of the elections had trenched upon the summer season and Metellus knew that the citizens were eagerly anticipating his success, yet, notwithstanding this, he resolved not to take the field until he had forced the soldiers to undergo the old-time drill and training. For Albinus, utterly overcome by the disaster to his brother Aulus and the army, had decided not to leave the province;[1] and during that part of the summer

229

SALLUST

aestivorum in imperio fuit, plerumque milites stativis
castris habebat, nisi cum odor[1] aut pabuli egestas
5 locum mutare subegerat. Sed neque muniebantur[2]
ea neque more militari vigiliae deducebantur; uti
cuique lubebat ab signis aberat. Lixae permixti
cum militibus diu noctuque vagabantur et palantes
agros vastare, villas expugnare, pecoris et manci-
piorum praedas certantes agere eaque mutare cum
mercatoribus vino advecticio et aliis talibus, praeterea
frumentum publice datum vendere, panem in dies
mercari; postremo quaecumque dici aut fingi queunt
ignaviae luxuriaeque probra[3] in illo exercitu cuncta
fuere et alia amplius.

XLV. Sed in ea difficultate Metellum non minus
quam in rebus hostilibus magnum et sapientem
virum fuisse comperior; tanta temperantia inter am-
2 bitionem saevitiamque moderatum. Namque edicto
primum adiumenta ignaviae sustulisse, ne quisquam
in castris panem aut quem alium coctum cibum
venderet, ne lixae exercitum sequerentur, ne miles
gregarius in castris neve in agmine servum aut
iumentum haberet; ceteris arte modum statuisse.
Praeterea transvorsis itineribus cotidie castra movere,
iuxta ac si hostes adessent vallo atque fossa munire,
vigilias crebras ponere et eas ipse cum legatis circumire, item in agmine in primis modo, modo in
postremis, saepe in medio adesse, ne quispiam ordine

---

[1] *Fronto, ad Anton.* 2. 6 *has* odos.
[2] muniebantur, *Fronto, l.c., Ah, who adds*: "*fortasse scribendum* mun. ea, *ut in integro cod. Paris.* 6087"; mun. ea,
mss., Or.   [3] probra ea, *Fronto, Ah, Or.*

when he retained the command he had kept the soldiers for the most part in a permanent camp, except when the stench or the need of fodder had compelled him to change his position. But his camps were not fortified, nor was watch kept in military fashion; men absented themselves from duty whenever they pleased. Camp followers and soldiers ranged about in company day and night, and in their forays laid waste the country, stormed farmhouses, and vied with one another in amassing booty in the form of cattle and slaves, which they bartered with the traders for foreign wine and other luxuries. They even sold the grain which was allotted them by the state and bought bread from day to day. In short, whatever disgraceful excesses resulting from idleness and wantonness can be mentioned or imagined were all to be found in that army and others besides.

XLV. But in dealing with these difficulties, as well as in waging war, I find that Metellus showed himself a great and prudent man, so skilful a course did he steer between indulgence and severity. For in the first place he is said to have removed the incentives to indolence by an edict that no one should sell bread or any other cooked food within the camp, that sutlers should not attend the army, and that no private soldier should have a slave or a pack animal in camp or on the march; and he set a strict limit on other practices of the kind. Moreover he broke camp every day for cross-country marches, fortified it with a palisade and moat just as if the enemy were near, and set guards at short intervals and inspected them in person attended by his lieutenants. On the march too he was now with those in the van, now in the rear, often in the middle of the line, to see that no one

egrederetur, ut cum signis frequentes incederent,
3 miles cibum et arma portaret. Ita prohibendo a
delictis magis quam vindicando exercitum brevi
confirmavit.

XLVI. Interea Iugurtha, ubi quae Metellus agebat ex nuntiis accepit, simul de innocentia eius
certior Roma[1] factus, diffidere suis rebus ac tum
2 demum veram deditionem facere conatus est. Igitur
legatos ad consulem cum suppliciis mittit, qui tantum modo ipsi liberisque vitam peterent, alia omnia
3 dederent populo Romano. Sed Metello iam antea
experimentis cognitum erat genus Numidarum infidum, ingenio mobili, novarum rerum avidum esse.
4 Itaque legatos alium ab alio divorsos aggreditur ac
paulatim temptando, postquam opportunos sibi
cognovit, multa pollicendo persuadet, uti Iugurtham
maxume vivom, sin id parum procedat, necatum sibi
traderent. Ceterum palam quae ex voluntate forent
regi nuntiari[2] iubet.

5 Deinde ipse paucis diebus intento atque infesto
exercitu in Numidiam procedit, ubi contra belli
faciem tuguria plena hominum, pecora cultoresque
in agris erant. Ex oppidis et mapalibus praefecti
regis obvii procedebant parati frumentum dare,
commeatum portare, postremo omnia quae imperar-

---

[1] Romae, *mss.* ; Roma, *Fronto*, p. 110 *N* ; *Non.* p. 325. 31.
[2] nuntiari, *ACBNKs n* ; nuntiare, *the other mss.*

---

[1] Branches of laurel or olive, indicating that they came to
sue for peace.

left the ranks, that they advanced in a body about the standards, and that the soldiers carried food and arms. In this way, rather by keeping them from doing wrong than by punishing them, he soon restored the temper of his army.

XLVI. Jugurtha meanwhile learned through messengers what Metellus was about, and at the same time received word from Rome that his opponent was incorruptible. He therefore began to lose heart in his cause and for the first time attempted to arrange a genuine surrender. Accordingly, he sent envoys to the consul with tokens of submission,[1] merely asking that his own life and those of his children be spared and leaving all else to the discretion of the Roman people. But Metellus had already learned from experience that the Numidians were a treacherous race, of fickle disposition, and fond of a change. He therefore separated the envoys and approached them one by one. When by gradually sounding them he found that they could be used for his design, he induced them by lavish promises to deliver Jugurtha into his hands, alive if possible; or dead, if he could not be taken alive. But publicly he bade them take back a reply in accordance with the king's wishes.

A few days later the consul with his army alert and ready for battle invaded Numidia, where he found nothing to indicate a state of war; the huts were full of men, and cattle and farmers were to be seen in the fields. The king's officers came out to meet him from the towns and villages,[2] offering to furnish grain, transport provisions—in short, to do

---

[2] *Mapalia* (see chap. xviii.) is here used collectively of a collection of huts; we may compare the various uses of *vicus* (οἶκος) in Latin.

6 entur facere. Neque Metellus idcirco minus, sed pariter ac si hostes adessent, munito agmine incedere, late explorare omnia, illa deditionis signa 7 ostentui credere et insidiis locum temptari. Itaque ipse cum expeditis cohortibus, item funditorum et sagittariorum delecta manu apud primos erat, in postremo C. Marius legatus cum equitibus curabat, in utrumque latus auxiliarios equites tribunis legionum et praefectis cohortium dispertiverat, ut cum eis permixti velites, quocumque accederent equi- 8 tatus hostium, propulsarent. Nam in Iugurtha tantus dolus tantaque peritia locorum et militiae erat, ut absens an praesens, pacem an[1] bellum gerens perniciosior esset, in[2] incerto haberetur.

XLVII. Erat haud longe ab eo itinere, quo Metellus pergebat, oppidum Numidarum nomine Vaga, forum rerum venalium totius regni maxume celebratum, ubi et incolere et mercari consueverant 2 Italici generis multi mortales. Huc consul simul temptandi gratia si paterentur, et ob opportunitates[3] loci praesidium imposuit. Praeterea imperavit frumentum et alia quae bello usui forent comportare,

[1] an, *X l n* ; et, *K* ; aut *or* vel, *the other mss.*
[2] in incerto, *KT²F²s m* ; incerto, *XNl n m²*; incertum, *HΓ.*
[3] si paterentur et ob opportunitates, *Schmalz, Ah* ; et si paterentur opportunitates, *mss., Or.*

---

[1] This title was peculiar to the allied contingent of the Roman army, which was divided into two *alae* of ten cohorts

234

everything that they were ordered. None the less, exactly as if the enemy were close at hand, Metellus advanced with his line protected on all sides, and reconnoitred the country far and wide, believing that these indications of submission were a pretence and that the enemy were seeking an opportunity for treachery. Accordingly, he himself led the van with the light-armed cohorts as well as a picked body of slingers and archers, his lieutenant Gaius Marius with the cavalry had charge of the rear, while on both flanks he had apportioned the cavalry of the auxiliaries to the tribunes of the legions and the prefects[1] of the cohorts. With these the light-armed troops were mingled,[2] whose duty it was to repel the attacks of the enemy's horsemen, wherever they might be made. For Jugurtha was so crafty, so well acquainted with the region and so versed in military science, that it was not certain whether he was more dangerous when absent or when present, at peace or making war.

XLVII. Not far from the route which Metellus was taking lay a town of the Numidians called Vaga, the most frequented emporium of the entire kingdom, where many men of Italic race traded and made their homes. Here the consul stationed a garrison, both to see whether the inhabitants would accept his overtures and because of the advantages of the situation.[3] He gave orders too that grain and other necessaries of war should be brought together there,

---

each; each cohort was made up of men of the same nationality under the command of a native *praefectus*.

[2] Between their ranks; see Livy 26. 4. 9, *institutum ut velites in legionibus essent. Auctorem peditum equiti immiscendorum centurionem Q. Navium ferunt.*

[3] Text and meaning are somewhat uncertain.

235

ratus, id quod res monebat, frequentiam negotiatorum et commeatu iuvaturam[1] exercitum et iam paratis rebus munimento fore.

3 Inter haec negotia Iugurtha impensius modo legatos supplices mittere, pacem orare, praeter suam liberorumque vitam omnia Metello dedere. Quos item uti priores consul illectos ad proditionem domum dimittebat, regi pacem quam postulabat neque abnuere neque polliceri, et inter eas moras promissa legatorum expectare.

XLVIII. Iugurtha ubi Metelli dicta cum factis composuit ac se suis artibus temptari animadvortit, quippe cui verbis pax nuntiabatur, ceterum re bellum asperrumum erat, urbs maxuma alienata, ager hostibus cognitus, animi popularium temptati, coactus
2 rerum necessitudine statuit armis certare. Igitur explorato hostium itinere, in spem victoriae adductus ex opportunitate loci, quam maxumas potest copias omnium generum parat ac per tramites occultos exercitum Metelli antevenit.

3 Erat in ea parte Numidiae quam Adherbal in divisione possederat, flumen oriens a meridie nomine Muthul, a quo aberat mons ferme milia passuum viginti tractu pari, vastus ab natura et humano cultu. Sed ex eo medio quasi collis oriebatur in immensum

---

[1] commeatu iuvaturam, *Ursinus* ; commeatum iuvaturum, *mss.*

---

[1] The meaning is not clear. Apparently Metellus counted upon the traders to furnish him with supplies and to protect those which he had ordered to be sent to the town. Capes,

believing, as the circumstances suggested, that the large number of traders would aid his army in getting supplies and serve as a protection to those which he had already prepared.[1]

While this was going on, Jugurtha with even greater insistence sent suppliant envoys, begged for peace, and offered Metellus everything except his life and that of his children. These envoys too, like the former ones, the consul persuaded to turn traitors and sent home, neither refusing nor promising the king the peace for which he asked and meanwhile waiting for the envoys to fulfil their promises.

XLVIII. When Jugurtha came to compare the words of Metellus with his actions, he realized that he was being attacked with his own weapons; for ostensibly peace was offered him but in reality the bitterest warfare was on foot. His principal city had been taken from him, the country was now familiar to the enemy, the loyalty of his subjects was being undermined. He was therefore compelled to try the fortune of battle. Accordingly, having reconnoitred the enemy's march, he was led to hope for victory from the nature of the country, and after assembling the greatest possible forces of all kinds, he got in advance of Metellus' army by obscure by-paths.

In that part of Numidia which the partition had given to Adherbal there was a river flowing from the south called the Muthul, and about twenty miles from it was a naturally desolate and uncultivated range of hills running parallel with the river. From about the middle of this range an elevation branched

however, takes *rebus paratis* of the preparations made by the inhabitants " for a revolt against Jugurtha."

pertingens, **vestitus** oleastro **ac** murtetis aliisque
generibus arborum quae humi arido atque harenoso
4 gignuntur.[1] Media autem planities deserta penuria
aquae praeter flumini propinqua loca ; ea consita
arbustis pecore atque cultoribus frequentabantur.

XLIX. Igitur in eo colle, quem transvorso itinere
porrectum docuimus, Iugurtha extenuata suorum
acie consedit, elephantis et parti copiarum pedestrium Bomilcarem praefecit eumque edocet quae
ageret.   Ipse propior montem cum omni equitatu et
2 peditibus delectis suos conlocat.   Dein singulas
turmas et manipulos circumiens monet atque obtestatur uti memores pristinae virtutis et victoriae sese
regnumque suum ab Romanorum avaritia defendant ;
cum eis certamen fore, quos antea victos sub iugum
miserint ; ducem illis, non animum mutatum ; qua**e**
ab imperatore decuerint omnia suis provisa, locum
superiorem, ut prudentes cum imperitis, ne pauciores
cum pluribus aut rudes cum belli [2] melioribus manum
3 consererent ; proinde parati intentique essent signo
dato Romanos invadere ; illum diem aut omnis

---

[1] nascuntur, *Arus.* vii. 477. 32 к.
[2] belli, *PA l, Arus.* vii. 492. 3 к. *The other mss. have* bello.

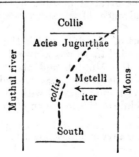

off and extended for a long distance, clothed with wild olive, myrtles, and other varieties of trees which grow in a dry and sandy soil. The intervening plain [1] was uninhabited from lack of water except the parts along the river, which were covered with shrubs and frequented by cattle and farmers.

XLIX. On this hill then, which flanked the Romans' line of march,[2] as I have said, Jugurtha took his position with his line greatly extended. He gave the command of the elephants and a part of the infantry to Bomilcar and told him what his plan was. He placed his own men nearer the mountain with all the cavalry and the flower of his infantry. Then going about to the various squads and companies, he admonished and besought them to be mindful of their old time valour and victories, and to defend themselves and their country from the greed of the Romans. They were to fight, he said, with men whom they had already vanquished and sent under the yoke; their leader was changed but not their spirit. For his own part, he had provided for his men everything that a leader ought: that on higher ground and prepared for action they might fight against men taken by surprise; that they might not have to fight few against many nor untrained against better soldiers. Therefore they must be ready and eager to attack the Romans when the signal was given, for that day

---

[1] That is, between the range of hills and the Muthul.

[2] *Transverso itinere* is taken by some to mean simply "cross-wise"; that is, at right angles to the river and the mountains (*mons*), as in the diagram on the opposite page, exclusive of the dotted line. Others take it as "across the line of march." The *collis* would then be represented by the dotted line.

labores et victorias confirmaturum aut maxumarum
4 aerumnarum initium fore. Ad hoc viritim, uti
quemque ob militare facinus pecunia aut honore
extulerat, commonefacere benifici sui et eum ipsum
aliis ostentare, postremo pro [1] cuiusque ingenio
pollicendo, minitando, obtestando, alium alio modo
excitare ; cum interim Metellus, ignarus hostium,
monte degrediens cum exercitu conspicatur.[2] Primo
5 dubius quidnam insolita facies ostenderet—nam inter
virgulta equi Numidaeque consederant, neque plane
occultati humilitate arborum et tamen incerti quidnam esset, cum natura loci tum dolo ipsi atque
signa militaria obscurati—dein brevi cognitis insidiis
6 paulisper agmen constituit. Ibi commutatis ordinibus in dextro [3] latere, quod proxumum hostis erat,
triplicibus subsidiis aciem instruxit ; inter manipulos
funditores et sagittarios dispertit, equitatum omnem
in cornibus locat ac pauca pro tempore milites hortatus aciem, sicuti instruxerat, transvorsis principiis
in planum deducit.

L. Sed ubi Numidas quietos neque colle degredi
animadvortit, veritus ex anni tempore et inopia

---

[1] pro, *omitted by the mss.*
[2] conspicatur, *Donat. in Ter. Eun.* 383, *Prisc.* ii. 436. 4 κ ;
conspicitur, *mss.*   [3] dextero, *P, Or.*

---

[1] He made the marching column face to the right (towards
the enemy), and placed the cavalry on what were the wings
as long as the army faced in that direction ; he then
wheeled towards the river and continued his march with
those who had formed the front rank (of the battle line)

would either crown all their toil and victories, or would be the beginning of the utmost wretchedness. He also addressed them individually and recalled his favours to the mind of every soldier whom he had ever rewarded with money or honour for any deed of arms, and pointed out the recipient to his comrades. Finally, by promises, threats or entreaties he incited one man after another, each in a different way according to his disposition, when meanwhile Metellus, unaware of the enemy and coming down the mountain with his army, caught sight of them. At first the Roman wondered what the unusual appearance of things meant, for the Numidians with their horses had taken their places amid the woods, and while because of the lowness of the trees they were not entirely covered, yet it was difficult to make out just what they were, since the men and their standards were concealed both by the nature of the place and by disguise. But the consul soon detected the ambuscade, halted his army for a space, and then made a change in its formation, His right flank, which was nearest the enemy, he strengthened with three lines of reserves. Between the maniples he placed the slingers and archers, while on the wings he stationed all the cavalry. Then after exhorting the soldiers briefly, as the time demanded, he led his army down into the plain, just as he had drawn it up, with those who had been in the van now forming the flank.[1]

L. When Metellus saw that the Numidians remained quiet and did not come down from the hill, he feared that at that season of the year and because

---

sideways to the enemy: *i.e.*, forming the flank of his marching column. In other words, those who had faced the enemy now had them on the right hand.

aquae, ne siti conficeretur exercitus, Rutilium legatum cum expeditis cohortibus et parte equitum
praemisit ad flumen, uti locum castris antecaperet,
existumans hostis crebro impetu et transvorsis proeliis iter suum remoraturos, et quoniam armis diffiderent, lassitudinem et sitim militum temptaturos.
2 Deinde ipse pro re atque loco, sicuti monte descenderat paulatim procedere, Marium post principia
habere, ipse cum sinistrae alae equitibus esse, qui in
agmine principes facti erant.

3   At Iugurtha, ubi extremum agmen Metelli primos
suos praetergressum[1] videt, praesidio quasi duum
milium peditum montem occupat, qua Metellus
descenderat, ne forte cedentibus advorsariis receptui
ac post munimento foret.   Dein repente signo dato
4 hostis invadit.   Numidae alii postremos caedere,
pars a sinistra ac dextra temptare, infensi adesse
atque instare, omnibus locis Romanorum ordines
conturbare, quorum etiam qui firmioribus animis
obvii hostibus fuerant, ludificati incerto proelio ipsi
modo eminus sauciabantur neque contra feriundi
5 aut conserundi manum copia erat; ante iam docti
ab Iugurtha equites, ubi Romanorum turma insequi
coeperat, non confertim neque in unum sese recipie-

---

[1] praetergressos, *mss.*; praetergressum, *editors.*

---

[1] That is, they would form the van if the army wheeled
about to face the Numidians.
[2] Those nearest to the mountain from which Metellus had
come.

of the scarcity of water his army might be exhausted
by thirst. He therefore sent his lieutenant Rutilius
with the light-armed cohorts and a part of the cavalry
towards the river, with instructions to occupy in advance a position for the camp; for he thought that
the enemy would try to delay his progress by frequent
assaults on the flank, and since they put little trust
in their arms, that they would try the effect of fatigue
and thirst upon his soldiers. Then, as the circumstances and situation demanded, he advanced slowly
in the same order in which he had come down from
the mountain, keeping Marius behind what had been
the front line,[1] while he himself was with the cavalry
on the left wing, which had now become the van.

As soon as Jugurtha saw that Metellus' rear had
passed by the first of his own men,[2] he stationed a
force of about two thousand infantry on the mountain at the point from which the Romans had just
come, so that if his opponents should give ground,
they might not have this refuge and protection in
their rear. Then he suddenly gave the signal
and launched his attack. Some of the Numidians
cut down the hindermost Romans, while a part
attacked them on the right and left, pressing on
with vigour and energy and throwing the ranks
into general confusion. For even those who had
withstood the charge with a stout heart were baffled
by this irregular manner of fighting, in which they
were only wounded from a distance, without having
the opportunity of striking back or of joining in
hand to hand conflict. Jugurtha's horsemen, following the instructions given them beforehand, whenever
a squadron of the Roman cavalry began to attack
them, gave way; not, however, in a body or in one

6 bant, sed alius alio quam maxume divorsi. Ita
numero priores, si ab persequendo hostis deterrere
nequiverant, disiectos ab tergo aut lateribus circum-
veniebant; sin opportunior fugae collis quam campi
fuerat, ea vero consueti Numidarum equi facile inter
virgulta evadere, nostros asperitas et insolentia loci
retinebat.

LI. Ceterum facies totius negoti varia, incerta,
foeda atque miserabilis. Dispersi a suis pars cedere,
alii insequi, neque signa neque ordines observare,
ubi quemque periculum ceperat ibi resistere ac pro-
pulsare, arma tela, equi viri, hostes atque cives permixti, nihil consilio neque imperio agi, fors omnia
regere.

2 Itaque multum diei processerat, cum etiam tum
3 eventus in incerto erat. Denique, omnibus labore et
aestu languidis, Metellus, ubi videt Numidas minus
instare, paulatim milites in unum conducit, ordines
restituit et cohortis legionarias quattuor advorsum
pedites hostium collocat. Eorum magna pars su-
4 perioribus locis fessa consederat. Simul orare et
hortari milites, ne deficerent neu paterentur hostis
fugientis vincere; neque illis castra esse neque
munimentum ullum, quo cedentes tenderent; in
5 armis omnia sita. Sed ne Iugurtha quidem interea

direction, but dispersing as widely as possible. Thus even if they had been unable to check the enemy's pursuit, with their superior numbers they cut off the stragglers in the rear or on the flanks. If the hill proved to be more favourable for their flight than the plains, there too the horses of the Numidians, being acquainted with the ground, easily made their escape amid the thickets, while the steep and unfamiliar ground proved a hindrance to our men.

LI. Thus the aspect of the whole affair was confused, uncertain, horrible and lamentable. Separated from their comrades, some of our men gave way, others attacked. They could neither follow the standards nor keep their ranks; but wherever each man had been overtaken by danger, there he stood his ground and defended himself. Arms and weapons, men and horses, Numidians and Romans were mingled in confusion. There was no opportunity for advice nor command; chance held sway everywhere.

In this way a considerable part of the day had passed and the outcome of the battle was still uncertain. Finally, when all the Romans were growing wearied from their exertions and the heat, Metellus noticed that the Numidians also were attacking with less vigour. He therefore gradually united his soldiers, reformed the ranks, and opposed four legionary cohorts to the enemy's infantry, the greater part of which through fatigue had taken refuge on the higher ground. At the same time he begged and implored his men not to weaken or allow a fleeing enemy to win the victory; he pointed out that the Romans had no camp or fortress as a refuge, but must rely wholly upon their arms. Meanwhile Jugurtha in his turn was not quiet, went about and

quietus erat; circumire, hortari, renovare proelium
et ipse cum delectis temptare omnia, subvenire suis,
hostibus dubiis instare, quos firmos cognoverat eminus
pugnando retinere.

LII. Eo modo inter se duo imperatores summi
viri certabant, ipsi pares, ceterum opibus disparibus.
2 Nam Metello virtus militum erat, locus advorsus,
Iugurthae alia omnia praeter milites opportuna.
3 Denique Romani, ubi intellegunt neque sibi perfugium esse neque ab hoste copiam pugnandi fieri—
et iam die[1] vesper erat—advorso colle, sicuti prae-
4 ceptum fuerat, evadunt. Amisso loco Numidae fusi
fugatique. Pauci interiere, plerosque[2] velocitas et
regio hostibus ignara tutata sunt.
5 Interea Bomilcar, quem elephantis et parti copiarum pedestrium praefectum ab Iugurtha supra
diximus, ubi eum Rutilius praetergressus est, paulatim suos in aequom locum deducit ac dum legatus
ad flumen, quo praemissus erat, festinans pergit,
quietus, uti res postulabat, aciem exornat neque
6 remittit quid ubique hostis ageret explorare. Post
quam Rutilium consedisse iam et animo vacuom
accepit simulque ex Iugurthae proelio clamorem
augeri, veritus ne legatus cognita re laborantibus
suis auxilio foret, aciem quam diffidens virtuti mili-

[1] diei, $CBK^2H^2Fl\ s\ m^2$.
[2] plerosque, A^1Ys^2m; *the other mss. have* pluresque.

---

[1] That is, unaware of the danger; *cf.* Tacitus, *Ann.* 2. 46,
tres vacuas legiones et ducis fraudis ignarum.

encouraged his men, and endeavoured to renew the battle; in person with the flower of his troops he tried every device, aided his men, charged the enemy where they wavered, and by attacks at long range held at bay those whom he had found to be unshaken.

LII. Thus did these two men, both great commanders, struggle with each other; personally they were on an equality but they were ill matched in their resources; for Metellus had valiant soldiers but an unfavourable position, while Jugurtha had the advantage in all except his men. At last the Romans, realizing that they had no place of refuge and that the foe gave them no opportunity for fighting (and it was already evening), charged up the hill as they had been ordered and broke through. Losing that position, the Numidians gave way and fled. A few were killed; the greater number were saved by their quickness and the Romans' lack of familiarity with the country.

In the meantime Bomilcar, who had been put in command of the elephants and a part of the infantry by Jugurtha, as I have already said, when Rutilius had passed him, slowly led his forces down into the plain; and while the lieutenant was hastily making his way to the river, to which he had been sent on, Bomilcar drew up his line quietly, as the circumstances demanded, continuing to keep an eye on the enemy's movements in all parts of the field. When he found that Rutilius had encamped and was now easy in mind,[1] while the din from Jugurtha's battle increased, he feared that the lieutenant, if he knew the critical condition of his countrymen, might go to their aid. Accordingly, wishing to intercept the

tum arte statuerat, quo hostium itineri officeret,
latius porrigit eoque modo ad Rutili castra procedit.

LIII. Romani ex improviso pulveris vim magnam
animadvortunt; nam prospectum ager arbustis con-
situs prohibebat. Et primo rati humum aridam
vento agitari, post ubi aequabilem manere, et sicuti
acies movebatur, magis magisque appropinquare
vident, cognita re properantes arma capiunt ac pro
2 castris, sicuti imperabatur, consistunt. Deinde, ubi
propius ventum est, utrimque magno clamore con-
3 curritur. Numidae tantum modo remorati, dum in
elephantis auxilium putant, postquam eos impeditos
ramis arborum atque ita disiectos circumveniri vident, fugam faciunt ac plerique abiectis armis collis
aut noctis, quae iam aderat, auxilio integri abeunt.
4 Elephanti quattuor capti, reliqui omnes numero
5 quadraginta interfecti. At Romani, quamquam
itinere atque opere castrorum et proelio fessi[1] erant,
tamen, quod Metellus amplius opinione morabatur,
6 instructi intentique obviam procedunt. Nam dolus
Numidarum nihil languidi neque remissi patiebatur.
7 Ac primo obscura nocte, postquam haud procul inter
se erant, strepitu velut hostes adventare,[2] alteri
apud alteros formidinem simul et tumultum facere
et paene imprudentia admissum facinus miserabile,
ni utrimque praemissi equites rem exploravissent.

[1] fessi laetique, *mss.*, *Ah, Or*; *Ah compares Livy* xxii. 60. 9,
but suggests confecti *or* lacerati ; *Jordan deleted* laetique.
[2] adventarent, *D*; *Korrte deleted* adventare.

enemy's march, he extended his line, which he had drawn up in close order through distrust of his soldiers' courage, and in that formation approached Rutilius's camp.

LIII. The Romans on a sudden became aware of a great cloud of dust, for the bushes which covered the ground cut off their view. At first they thought that the wind was blowing up the dry soil; but later, as they saw that the cloud remained unchanged and came nearer and nearer as the line advanced, they realized the truth, and hastily catching up their arms, took their places before the camp, as they were ordered. Then, when they were at close quarters, both sides charged with loud shouts. The Numidians stood their ground only so long as they thought the elephants could protect them; but when they saw that the brutes became entangled in the branches of the trees and were thus separated and surrounded, they took to flight. The greater number, after throwing away their arms, escaped unhurt, thanks to the hill and the night, which was now close at hand. Four elephants were taken, and all the rest to the number of forty were killed. But although the Romans were wearied by their march, by the work on the camp, and by the battle, yet because Metellus was later than they expected, they went to meet him in order of battle on the alert; for the craft of the Numidians admitted of no relaxation or carelessness. It was now dark night, and at first, when the armies were not far apart, the sound, as of a hostile force approaching, caused fear and confusion on both sides; and the mistake might have led to a deplorable catastrophe, had not the horsemen who were sent out by both sides to reconnoitre discovered what the

249

8 Igitur pro metu repente gaudium exortum,[1] milites
alius alium laeti appellant, acta edocent atque
audiunt, sua quisque fortia facta ad caelum fert.
Quippe res humanae ita sese habent: in victoria
vel ignavis gloriari licet, advorsae res etiam bonos
detrectant.

LIV. Metellus in eisdem castris quatriduo[2] moratus saucios cum cura reficit, meritos in proeliis more
militiae donat, univorsos in contione laudat atque
agit gratias, hortatur ad cetera, quae levia sunt,
parem animum gerant; pro victoria satis iam pug-
2 natum, reliquos labores pro praeda fore. Tamen
interim transfugas et alios opportunos, Iugurtha ubi
gentium aut quid agitaret, cum paucisne esset an
exercitum haberet, ut sese victus gereret exploratum
3 misit. At ille sese in loca saltuosa et natura munita
receperat ibique cogebat exercitum numero hominum ampliorem sed hebetem infirmumque, agri ac
4 pecoris magis quam belli cultorem. Id ea gratia
eveniebat, quod praeter regios equites nemo omnium
Numida ex fuga regem sequitur; quo cuiusque
animus fert, eo discedunt neque id flagitium militiae
ducitur. Ita se mores habent.

5 Igitur Metellus ubi videt regis etiam tum animum
ferocem esse, bellum renovari, quod nisi ex illius
lubidine geri non posset, praeterea iniquum[3] certa-

---

[1] exortum, *mss.*; mutatur, *Prisc.* iii. 296. 6 к, *Ah, Or.*
[2] quatriduom, *Ah.*
[3] iniquum (iniquom, inicum), *editors*; inimicum, *mss.*

situation was. Thereupon in place of fear a sudden joy arose. The exultant soldiers called out to one another, told of their exploits and heard the tales of others. Each man praised his own valiant deeds to the skies. For so it is with human affairs; in time of victory the very cowards may brag, while defeat discredits even the brave.

LIV. Metellus remained in the same camp for four days, giving careful attention to the wounded, rewarding good service in the battles with military prizes,[1] and praising and thanking all the troops in a body. He urged them to have like courage for the easy tasks which remained; their fight for victory was at an end, the rest of their efforts would be for booty. Meanwhile, however, he sent deserters and other available spies to find out where in the world Jugurtha was and what he was about, whether he had but few followers or an army, how he conducted himself in defeat. As a matter of fact, the king had retreated to a wooded district of natural strength and was there recruiting an army which in numbers was larger than before, but inefficient and weak, being more familiar with farming and grazing than with war. The reason for this was, that except for the horsemen of his bodyguard not a single Numidian follows his king after a defeat, but all disperse whithersoever they choose, and this is not considered shameful for soldiers. Such are their customs.

Accordingly, when Metellus saw that the king was still full of confidence, and that a war was being renewed which could be carried on only as his opponent chose, he realized that his struggle with

---

[1] Some of these are enumerated in lxxxv. 29.

men sibi cum hostibus, minore detrimento illos vinci quam suos vincere, statuit non proeliis neque in acie 6 sed alio more bellum gerundum. Itaque in loca Numidiae opulentissuma pergit, agros vastat, multa castella et oppida temere munita aut sine praesidio capit incenditque, puberes interfici[1] iubet, alia omnia militum praedam esse. Ea formidine multi mortales Romanis dediti obsides, frumentum et alia quae usui forent affatim praebita, ubicumque res postulabat praesidium impositum.

7 Quae negotia multo magis quam proelium male 8 pugnatum ab suis regem terrebant, quippe cuius spes omnis in fuga sita erat, sequi cogebatur, et qui sua loca defendere nequiverat, in alienis bellum gerere. 9 Tamen ex copia quod optumum videbatur consilium capit, exercitum plerumque in eisdem locis opperiri iubet, ipse cum delectis equitibus Metellum sequitur, nocturnis et aviis itineribus ignoratus Romanos pa- 10 lantis repente aggreditur. Eorum plerique inermes cadunt, multi capiuntur, nemo omnium intactus profugit, et Numidae, prius quam ex castris subveniretur, sicuti iussi erant, in proxumos collis discedunt.

LV. Interim Romae gaudium ingens ortum cognitis Metelli rebus, ut seque et exercitum more

---

[1] interfici, *A T²*, *Serv. Aen.* v. 546, *Or* ; interfecit, *Probus* iv. 16. 23 κ ; *the other mss. and Ah have* interficit.

the enemy was an unequal one, since defeat cost
them less than victory did his own men. He accordingly decided that he must conduct the campaign, not
by pitched battles, but in another fashion. He therefore marched into the most fertile parts of Numidia,
laid waste the country, captured and burned many
strongholds and towns which had been hurriedly
fortified or left without defenders, ordered the death
of all the adults and gave everything else to his soldiers
as booty. In this way he caused such terror that
many men were given to the Romans as hostages,
grain and other necessities were furnished in abundance, and garrisons were admitted wherever Metellus
thought it advisable.

These proceedings alarmed the king much more
than the defeat which his men had suffered; for
while all his hopes depended upon flight, he was
forced to pursue, and when he had been unable to
defend favourable positions, he was obliged to fight
in those which were unfavourable. However, he
adopted the plan which seemed best under the circumstances and ordered the greater part of the
army to remain where it was, while he himself
followed Metellus with a select body of cavalry.
Making his way at night and through by-paths he
suddenly fell upon the Roman stragglers when they
least expected it; the greater number of them were
killed before they could arm themselves, many were
taken, not one escaped unscathed. Before aid could
be sent from the camp, the Numidians, as they had
been ordered, scattered to the nearest hills.

LV. Meanwhile, great joy had arisen at Rome from
the news of Metellus' exploits, when it was learned
that he conducted himself and treated his army after

maiorum gereret, in advorso loco victor tamen virtute fuisset, hostium agro potiretur, Iugurtham magnificum ex Albini socordia spem salutis in solitudine 2 aut fuga coegisset habere. Itaque senatus ob ea feliciter acta dis immortalibus supplicia decernere, civitas trepida antea et sollicita de belli eventu laeta 3 agere, de Metello fama praeclara esse. Igitur eo intentior ad victoriam niti, omnibus modis festinare, cavere tamen necubi hosti opportunus fieret, memi- 4 nisse post gloriam invidiam sequi. Ita quo clarior erat, eo magis anxius erat, neque post insidias Iugurthae effuso exercitu praedari; ubi frumento aut pabulo opus erat, cohortes cum omni equitatu praesidium agitabant; exercitus partem ipse, reliquos 5 Marius ducebat. Sed igni magis quam praeda ager 6 vastabatur. Duobus locis haud longe inter se castra 7 faciebant. Ubi vi opus erat, cuncti aderant. Ceterum, quo fuga atque formido latius cresceret, divorsi agebant.

8 Eo tempore Iugurtha per collis sequi, tempus aut locum pugnae quaerere, qua venturum hostem audierat, pabulum et aquarum fontis, quorum penuria erat, corrumpere, modo se Metello, interdum Mario ostendere, postremos in agmine temptare ac statim

the fashion of old, that he, though caught in an unfavourable position, had nevertheless won the victory by his valour, was holding possession of the enemy's territory, and had compelled Jugurtha, who had been made insolent by Albinus' incapacity, to rest his hopes of safety on the desert or on flight. The senate accordingly voted a thanksgiving to the immortal gods because of these successes, while the community, which before this had been in fear and anxiety as to the outcome of the war, gave itself up to rejoicing. Metellus' fame was brilliant. He therefore strove the harder for victory, hastened matters in every way, yet was careful not to give the enemy an opening anywhere, remembering that envy follows hard upon glory. Hence the greater his fame, the more caution he showed; after Jugurtha's ambuscade he no longer ravaged the country with his army in disorder; when he required grain or fodder, a number of cohorts stood on guard along with all the cavalry; he led part of the army himself and Marius the rest. But fire did more than plundering to devastate the land. The consul and his lieutenant used to encamp in two places not far apart. When necessity demanded the use of strength, they joined forces; otherwise they acted separately, in order that the enemy's terror and flight might be more widespread.

Meanwhile Jugurtha would follow along the hills, watching for a suitable time or place for battle : he spoiled the fodder and contaminated the springs, which were very few, in the places to which he had heard that the enemy were coming; showed himself now to Metellus, again to Marius; made an attempt on the hindermost in the line and at once retreated

in collis regredi, rursus aliis, post aliis minitari, neque proelium facere neque otium pati, tantum modo hostem ab incepto retinere.

LVI. Romanus imperator ubi se dolis fatigari videt neque ab hoste copiam pugnandi fieri, urbem magnam et in ea parte qua sita erat arcem regni nomine Zamam statuit oppugnare, ratus, id quod negotium poscebat, Iugurtham laborantibus suis auxilio venturum ibique proelium fore. 2 At ille quae parabantur a perfugis edoctus, magnis itineribus Metellum antevenit. Oppidanos hortatur moenia defendant, additis auxilio perfugis, quod genus ex copiis regis, quia fallere nequibat, firmissumum erat. Praeterea pollicetur 3 in tempore semet cum exercitu adfore. Ita compositis rebus, in loca quam maxume occulta discedit, ac post paulo cognoscit Marium ex itinere frumentatum cum paucis cohortibus Siccam missum, quod oppidum primum omnium post malam pugnam 4 ab rege defecerat. Eo cum delectis equitibus noctu pergit et iam egredientibus Romanis in porta pugnam facit, simul magna voce Siccenses hortatur uti cohortis ab tergo circumveniant; fortunam illis praeclari facinoris casum dare. Si id fecerint, postea sese in regno, illos in libertate sine metu aetatem 5 acturos. Ac ni Marius signa inferre atque evadere

---

[1] The Romans punished deserters with great severity. They were sometimes crucified or thrown to wild beasts; see Valerius Maximus 2. 7.

to the hills; again threatened others and afterwards others, neither gave battle nor let the enemy rest, but merely prevented them from carrying out their plans.

LVI. When the Roman general began to realize that he was being exhausted by the strategy of his opponent, who gave him no chance for battle, he decided to lay siege to a large city called Zama, the citadel of the part of the kingdom in which it was situated. He thought that as a matter of course Jugurtha would come to the aid of his subjects in distress and that a battle would be fought in that place. But Jugurtha, learning from deserters what was on foot, by forced marches outstripped Metellus; he encouraged the townspeople to defend their walls, and gave them the help of a band of deserters, who formed the strongest part of the king's forces because they dared not be treacherous.[1] He promised too that he would come himself in due season with an army. Having made these arrangements, the king withdrew to places as secluded as possible, and presently learned that Marius had been ordered to leave the line of march and go with a few cohorts to forage at Sicca, which was the very first town to revolt from the king after his defeat. Thither Jugurtha hastened by night with the best of his cavalry and engaged the Romans at the gate just as they were coming out. At the same time, in a loud voice he urged the people of Sicca to surround the cohorts in the rear; fortune, he said, gave them the chance for a brilliant exploit. If they took advantage of it, he would be restored to his kingdom and they would live for the future in freedom and without fear. And had not Marius hastened to advance and leave the town, surely the

oppido properavisset, profecto cuncti aut magna pars
Siccensium fidem mutavissent; tanta mobilitate sese
6 Numidae gerunt. Sed milites Iugurthini paulisper
ab rege sustentati, postquam maiore vi hostes urgent,
paucis amissis profugi discedunt.

LVII. Marius ad Zamam pervenit. Id oppidum
in campo situm magis opere quam natura munitum
erat, nullius idoneae rei egens, armis virisque opu-
2 lentum. Igitur Metellus pro tempore atque loco
paratis rebus cuncta moenia exercitu circumvenit,
3 legatis imperat ubi quisque curaret. Deinde signo
dato undique simul clamor ingens oritur neque ea
res Numidas terret; infensi intentique sine tumultu
4 manent, proelium incipitur. Romani pro ingenio
quisque pars eminus glande aut lapidibus pugnare,
alii succedere ac murum modo subfodere modo scalis
5 aggredi, cupere proelium in manibus facere. Contra
ea oppidani in proxumos[1] saxa volvere, sudes, pila,
praeterea picem sulphure mixtam et taeda ardentia[2]
6 mittere. Sed ne illos quidem, qui procul manserant,
timor animi satis muniverat. Nam plerosque iacula
tormentis aut manu emissa volnerabant parique periculo sed fama impari boni atque ignavi erant.

LVIII. Dum apud Zamam sic certatur, Iugurtha
ex improviso castra hostium cum magna manu invadit,
remissis qui in praesidio erant et omnia magis quam

---

[1] proximis, *PA²CBKl*.
[2] picem . . . ardentia, *scripsi*, p. s. et t. m. ardentia
(ardenti, *A²KΓs*, ardentem, *m*), *mss.*, *Ah*, *Or*.

greater part of the townspeople, if not all of them, would have changed their allegiance; such is the fickleness with which the Numidians act. Jugurtha's soldiers were held firm for a time by the king, but when the enemy attacked with greater force they fled in disorder after suffering slight losses.

LVII. Marius went on to Zama. That town, situated in an open plain and fortified rather by art than by nature, lacked no essential, and was well supplied with arms and men. Therefore Metellus, making his preparations to suit the circumstances and the locality, completely invested the walls with his army, assigning to each of his lieutenants his special point of attack. Then, upon a given signal, a mighty shout arose from all sides at once, but without in the least frightening the Numidians; ready and eager for action they awaited the fray without disorder and the battle began. The Romans acted each according to his own quality: some fought at long range with slings or stones, others advanced and undermined the wall or applied scaling-ladders, striving to get at grips with the foe. The townsmen met their attacks by rolling down stones upon the foremost and hurling at them beams, pikes, burning pitch mixed with sulphur, and firebrands. Not even those of our men who had remained at a distance were wholly protected by their timidity, for very many of them were wounded by javelins hurled from engines or by hand. Thus the valiant and the craven were in like danger but of unlike repute.

LVIII. While this struggle was going on at Zama, Jugurtha unexpectedly fell upon the Roman camp with a large force, and through the carelessness of the guards, who were looking for anything rather than

2 proelium **expectantibus** portam irrumpit. **At** nostri
repentino metu perculsi sibi quisque pro moribus
consulunt; alii fugere, alii arma capere, magna pars
3 volnerati aut occisi. Ceterum ex omni multitudine
non amplius quadraginta memores nominis Romani,
grege facto, locum cepere paulo quam alii editiorem
neque inde maxuma vi depelli quiverunt, sed tela
eminus missa remittere, pauci in pluribus minus
frustrari;[1] sin Numidae propius accessissent, ibi vero
virtutem ostendere et eos maxuma vi caedere, fundere atque fugare.

4 Interim Metellus cum acerrume rem gereret, clamorem ut tumultum[2] hostilem a tergo accepit, dein
convorso equo animadvortit fugam ad se vorsum
5 fieri; quae res indicabat popularis esse. Igitur equitatum omnem ad castra propere misit ac statim
C. Marium cum cohortibus sociorum, eumque lacrumans per amicitiam perque rem publicam obsecrat
nequam contumeliam remanere in exercitu victore
neve hostis inultos abire sinat. Ille brevi mandata
6 efficit. At Iugurtha munimento castrorum impeditus,
cum alii super vallum praecipitarentur, alii in angus-
tiis ipsi sibi properantes officerent, multis amissis in
7 loca munita sese recepit. Metellus infecto negotio,
postquam nox aderat, in castra cum exercitu revor-
titur.

[1] frustrari, *XTm*; frustrati, *A²C²Ylsn*; frustrabantur
Schol. Stat. Theb. ii. 594.
[2] clamorem, *M¹D F, Ah, Or*; o. vel tumultum, *the other mss.*

a battle, forced one of the gates. Our men were struck with a sudden panic and sought safety each according to his temperament; some fled, others armed themselves, nearly all were killed or wounded. But out of the entire number forty or less remembered that they were Romans. These gathered together and took a position a little higher than the rest, from which they could not be dislodged by the greatest efforts of the enemy, but they threw back the weapons which were thrown at them from a distance, and few against many could hardly miss. But if the Numidians came nearer, they then showed their real quality, charging them with the greatest fury, routing and scattering them.

Meanwhile, Metellus, who was vigorously pressing the attack on the town, heard shouts like the melley of a hostile force behind him; then, wheeling his horse about, he saw that the fugitives were coming his way, which indicated that they were his countrymen. He therefore sent all the cavalry to the camp in haste and ordered Gaius Marius to follow at once with the cohorts of allies, begging him with tears in the name of their friendship and their common country not to allow any disgrace to stain their victorious army, and not to suffer the enemy to escape unpunished. Marius promptly did as he was ordered. As for Jugurtha, he was hampered by the fortifications of the camp, since some of his men were tumbling over the ramparts and others, endeavouring to make haste in the crowded spaces, were getting in each other's way; he therefore, after considerable losses, withdrew to a place of safety. Metellus was prevented by the coming of night from following up his victory and returned to camp with his army.

LIX. Igitur postero die, prius quam ad oppugnandum egrederetur, equitatum omnem in ea parte, qua regis adventus erat, pro castris agitare iubet, portas et proxuma loca tribunis dispertit, deinde ipse pergit ad oppidum atque uti superiore die 2 murum aggreditur. Interim Iugurtha ex occulto repente nostros invadit. Qui in proxumo locati fuerant, paulisper territi perturbantur, reliqui cito 3 subveniunt. Neque diutius Numidae resistere quivissent, ni pedites cum equitibus permixti magnam cladem in congressu facerent. Quibus illi freti non, uti equestri proelio solet, sequi, dein cedere, sed advorsis equis[1] concurrere, implicare ac perturbare aciem; ita expeditis peditibus suis hostis paene victos dare.

LX. Eodem tempore apud Zamam magna vi certabatur. Ubi quisque legatus aut tribunus curabat, eo acerrume niti, neque alius in alio magis quam in sese[2] spem habere, pariterque oppidani agere; oppugnare aut parare omnibus locis, avidius alteri alteros 2 sauciare quam semet tegere, clamor permixtus hortatione, laetitia, gemitu, item strepitus armorum ad

[1] adversis equi(s), $P^2K^2T^2l^2$; adversi sequi, *mss.*
[2] sese, $XK^2Ts\,n$; se, *the other mss.*

---

[1] *Victos dare* is equivalent to *vincere*: cf. Livy, 8. 6. 6, *stratas legiones Latinorum dabo.*
[2] In this sentence *eo* is said to be used in the unusual sense of *eo loco = ubi*; cf. Tac. *Ann.* 15. 74: (*decernitur*) *ut templum Saluti extrueretur eo loci ... ex quo Scevinus*

LIX. Accordingly, the next day, before going out to attack the town, Metellus ordered all the cavalry to ride up and down before that part of the camp where the king was likely to attack, assigned to the several tribunes the defence of the gates and their neighbourhood, and then himself proceeded to the town and assailed the wall as on the day before. Meanwhile Jugurtha suddenly rushed upon our men from ambush. Those who were stationed nearest the point of attack were terrified and thrown into confusion for a time, but the rest quickly came to their help. And the Numidians would not have been able to make a long resistance, had not their combination of infantry and cavalry done great execution in the melley; for the Numidian horsemen, trusting to this infantry, did not alternately advance and retreat, as is usual in a cavalry skirmish, but charged at full speed, rushing into and breaking up our line of battle; thus with their light-armed infantry they all but conquered their enemy.[1]

LX. At the same time the contest at Zama continued with great fury. Wherever each of the lieutenants or tribunes was in charge, there[2] was the bitterest strife and no one relied more on another than on himself. The townspeople showed equal courage; men were fighting or making preparations at all points, and both sides were more eager to wound one another than to protect themselves. There was a din of mingled encouragement, exultation, and groans; the clash of arms also rose to

ferrum prompserat, where the addition of loci makes the construction less bold than here. It may, however, be taken (with Summers) as "against that part of the wall."

3 caelum ferri, tela utrimque volare. Sed illi qui
moenia defensabant, ubi hostes paulum modo pugnam remiserant, intenti proelium equestre prospec-
4 tabant. Eos, uti quaeque Iugurthae res erant, laetos
modo, modo pavidos animadvorteres, ac sicuti audiri
a suis aut cerni possent, monere alii, alii hortari aut
manu significare aut niti corporibus et ea huc et
illuc, quasi vitabundi aut iacientes tela, agitare.
5 Quod ubi Mario cognitum est—nam is in ea parte
curabat—consulto lenius agere ac diffidentiam rei
simulare, pati Numidas sine tumultu regis proelium
6 visere. Ita illis studio suorum adstrictis repente
magna vi murum aggreditur. Et iam scalis egressi
milites prope summa ceperant, cum oppidani concurrunt, lapides, ignem, alia praeterea tela ingerunt.
7 Nostri primo resistere, deinde, ubi unae atque alterae
scalae comminutae, qui supersteterant afflicti sunt,
ceteri quoquo modo potuere, pauci integri, magna
8 pars volneribus confecti abeunt. Denique utrimque
proelium nox diremit.

LXI. Metellus postquam videt frustra inceptum,
neque oppidum capi neque Iugurtham nisi[1] ex insidiis aut suo loco pugnam facere et iam aestatem
exactam esse, ab Zama discedit et in eis urbibus
quae ad se[2] defecerant satisque munitae loco aut

---

[1] nisi, *M and m.* 2 *of AKHl*; ni, *F*; niti, *PA¹NK¹H¹Dl¹ m*;
niti nisi, *CBsn.*
[2] ad se, *P²N²HT¹, Arus.* vii. 466. 20 к; ab se, *the other mss.*

heaven, and a shower of missiles fell on both sides.
But whenever the besiegers relaxed their assault ever
so little, the defenders of the walls became interested
spectators of the cavalry battle. As Jugurtha's fortunes shifted, you might see them now joyful, now
alarmed; acting as if their countrymen could see
or hear them, some shouted warnings, others urged
them on; they gesticulated or swayed their bodies,
moving them this way and that as if dodging or hurling weapons.[1]

When Marius perceived all this (for he was in
charge at that point) he purposely slackened his
efforts and feigned discouragement, allowing the Numidians to witness their king's battle undisturbed.
When their attention was thus riveted upon their
countrymen, he suddenly assaulted the wall with the
utmost violence. Our soldiers, mounting on scaling-
ladders, had almost reached the top of the wall, when
the townsmen rushed to the spot and met them with
a rain of stones, firebrands, and other missiles besides.
At first our men resisted; then, as ladder after ladder
was shattered and those who stood upon them were
dashed to the ground, the rest made off as best they
could, some few unharmed but the greater number
badly wounded. At last night ended the combat on
both sides.

LXI. After Metellus saw that his attempt was
vain, that the town was no nearer being taken,
that Jugurtha would not fight except from ambush
or on his own ground, and that the summer was
now at an end, he left Zama and placed garrisons
in such of the towns which had gone over to him

[1] This description is an obvious imitation of Thucydides'
account of the Athenians at Syracuse (7. 71) watching the
naval battle in the harbour.

2 moenibus erant praesidia imponit. Ceterum exercitum in provinciam, quae proxuma est Numidiae,
3 hiemandi gratia collocat. Neque id tempus ex aliorum more quieti aut luxuriae concedit, sed quoniam armis bellum parum procedebat, insidias regi per amicos tendere et eorum perfidia pro armis uti parat.

4 Igitur Bomilcarem, qui Romae cum Iugurtha fuerat et inde vadibus datis de Massivae nece iudicium fugerat, quod ei per maxumam amicitiam maxuma copia
5 fallundi erat, multis pollicitationibus aggreditur. Ac primo efficit uti ad se colloquendi gratia occultus veniat, deinde fide data, si Iugurtham vivom aut necatum sibi tradidisset, fore ut illi senatus impunitatem et sua omnia concederet, facile Numidae persuadet cum ingenio infido tum metuenti ne, si[1] pax cum Romanis fieret, ipse per condiciones ad supplicium traderetur.

LXII. Is, ubi primum opportunum fuit, Iugurtham anxium ac miserantem fortunas suas accedit. Monet atque lacrumans obtestatur uti aliquando sibi liberisque et genti Numidarum optume meritae provideat: omnibus proeliis sese victos, agrum vastatum, multos mortalis captos, occisos, regni opes comminutas esse;

[1] nisi, $PAK^1T^2D^2l$; si (ne *om.*) $A^2HT^1D^1F$; ne (si *om.*) $Mn.$

---

[1] Of Africa.   [2] See xxxv. 4 ff.

as were strongly enough fortified by their situation
or by walls. The rest of his army he stationed in
the part of our province[1] which lies nearest to
Numidia, that they might pass the winter there.
But he did not devote that season, as others commonly do, to rest or dissipation, but since the war
was making little progress through arms, he prepared to lay snares for the king through his friends
and to make their treachery his weapons.

Now Bomilcar had been at Rome with Jugurtha,[2]
and then, after being released on bail, had fled to
escape trial for the murder of Massiva. Since this
man's special intimacy with the king gave him special
opportunities for deceiving him, Metellus tried to win
his co-operation by many promises. First, he contrived
that the Numidian should come to him secretly for a
conference; then after he had pledged his honour
that if Bomilcar would deliver Jugurtha into his
hands alive or dead, the senate would grant him impunity and restore all his property, he persuaded him
without difficulty; for he was treacherous by nature
and besides feared that if peace should ever be made
with the Romans, one condition would be his own
surrender and execution.

LXII. As soon as an opportune time came, when Jugurtha was worried and lamenting his fate, Bomilcar
approached him. He warned the king and begged
him with tears that he should at last take thought
for himself, his children, and the people of Numidia
who had served him so faithfully. He reminded
him that they had been worsted in every battle,
that his country had been ravaged, many of his subjects killed or taken prisoners, and the resources of the
kingdom drained. He had now made sufficient trial

satis saepe iam et virtutem militum et fortunam
temptatam; caveat ne illo cunctante Numidae sibi
2 consulant. His atque talibus aliis ad deditionem
3 regis animum impellit. Mittuntur ad imperatorem
legati, qui Iugurtham imperata facturum dicerent ac
sine ulla pactione sese regnumque suum in illius
4 fidem tradere. Metellus propere cunctos senatorii
ordinis ex hibernis accersi iubet, eorum et aliorum
5 quos idoneos ducebat consilium habet. Ita more
maiorum ex consili decreto per legatos Iugurthae
imperat argenti pondo ducenta milia, elephantos
6 omnis, equorum et armorum aliquantum. Quae
postquam sine mora facta sunt, iubet omnis perfugas
7 vinctos adduci. Eorum magna pars uti iussum erat
adducti, pauci, cum primum deditio coepit, ad regem
Bocchum in Mauretaniam abierant.
8   Igitur Iugurtha, ubi armis virisque et pecunia
spoliatus est, cum[1] ipse ad imperandum Tisidium
vocaretur, rursus coepit flectere animum suum et ex
9 mala conscientia digna timere. Denique, multis
diebus per dubitationem consumptis, cum modo
taedio rerum advorsarum omnia bello potiora duceret, interdum secum ipse reputaret quam gravis
casus in servitium ex regno foret, multis magnisque
praesidiis nequiquam perditis, de integro bellum
10 sumit. Et Romae senatus de provinciis consultus
Numidiam Metello decreverat.

[1] cum, *AYm, Or* (quom, *Ah*); quom . . . vocaretur,
Serv. Ecl. viii. 71; *the other mss. have* dum.

---

[1] *More maiorum* modifies *ex concili decreto*. There was no
private arrangement with Jugurtha; cf. xxix. 5.

both of his soldiers' courage and of the will of fortune, and must take heed, lest while he hesitated the Numidians should take measures for their own safety. By these and other similar arguments he reconciled the king to the thought of a surrender. Envoys were sent to the Roman general to say that Jugurtha would submit to his orders and entrusted himself and his kingdom unconditionally to his honour. Metellus at once gave orders that all men of senatorial rank should be summoned from the winter quarters; with them and with such others as he considered suitable he held a council. He obeyed the decree of the council—thus conforming to the usage of our forefathers[1]—and sent envoys to demand of Jugurtha two hundred thousand pounds' weight of silver, all his elephants, and a considerable quantity of horses and arms. When these conditions had promptly been met, he ordered all the deserters to be brought to him in fetters. The greater part of them were brought as ordered, but a few had taken refuge with King Bocchus in Mauretania as soon as the negotiations for surrender began.

Now, when Jugurtha, after being stripped of arms, men and money, was himself summoned to Tisidium to receive his orders, he began once more to waver in his purpose, and prompted by a guilty conscience, to dread the punishment due to his crimes. At last, after spending many days in hesitation, at one time so weary of adversity as to think anything better than war, and anon reflecting how great a fall it was from a throne to slavery, after having lost to no purpose many great resources, he renewed the war. Meanwhile at Rome, when the question of the provinces came up, the senate had assigned Numidia to Metellus.

LXIII. Per idem tempus Uticae forte C. Mario per
hostias dis supplicanti magna atque mirabilia portendi
haruspex dixerat; proinde, quae animo agitabat fretus dis ageret,[1] fortunam quam saepissume experire-
2 tur, cuncta prospere eventura. At illum iam antea
consulatus ingens cupido exagitabat, ad quem capiun-
dum praeter vetustatem familiae alia omnia abunde
erant : industria, probitas, militiae magna scientia,
animus belli ingens, domi modicus, lubidinis et divi-
3 tiarum victor, tantum modo gloriae avidus. Sed is
natus et omnem pueritiam Arpini altus, ubi primum
aetas militiae patiens fuit, stipendiis faciundis, non
Graeca facundia neque urbanis munditiis sese exercuit; ita inter artis bonas integrum ingenium brevi
4 adolevit. Ergo ubi primum tribunatum militarem a
populo petit, plerisque faciem eius ignorantibus,
5 factis[2] notus per omnis tribus declaratur. Deinde ab
eo magistratu alium post alium sibi peperit semperque in potestatibus eo modo agitabat, ut ampliore
6 quam gerebat dignus haberetur. Tamen is ad id
locorum talis vir—nam postea ambitione praeceps
datus est—consulatum[3] appetere non audebat. Etiam
tum alios magistratus plebs, consulatum nobilitas

---

[1] ageret, $B^2K^2T^2D^2$; agere, *the other mss.*
[2] factis, *Palmer* ; facile, *mss., Or.*
[3] *Omitted by almost all mss.*

---

[1] *cf.* lxxxv. 1.
[2] *cf. Cat.* xxv. 4 ; xxxi. 9 ; *Jug.* viii. 2.

LXIII. At about that same time it chanced that when Gaius Marius was offering victims to the gods at Utica a soothsayer declared that a great and marvellous career awaited him; the seer accordingly advised him, trusting in the gods, to carry out what he had in mind and put his fortune to the test as often as possible, predicting that all his undertakings would have a happy issue. Even before this Marius had been possessed with a mighty longing for the consulship, for which he had in abundance every qualification except an ancient lineage : namely, diligence, honesty, great military skill, and a spirit that was mighty in war, unambitious [1] in peace, which rose superior to passion and the lure of riches, and was greedy only for glory. Nay more, having been born and reared at Arpinum, where he had spent all his boyhood, he had no sooner reached the age for military life than he had given himself the training of active service, not of Grecian eloquence or the elegance of the city. Thus engrossed in wholesome pursuits his unspoiled nature soon matured. The result was that when he first sought the office of military tribune from the people, the greater number did not know him by sight; yet his deeds were familiar and he was elected by the vote of all the tribes. Then, after that success, he won office after office, always so conducting himself in each of them as to be regarded worthy of a higher position than that which he was holding. Nevertheless, although he had up to that time shown himself so admirable a man (for afterwards he was driven headlong [2] by ambition), he did not venture to aspire to the consulship; for even as late as that time, although the commons could bestow the other magistracies, the

7 inter se per manus tradebat. Novus nemo tam
clarus neque tam egregiis factis erat, quin indignus
illo honore et is[1] quasi pollutus haberetur.

LXIV. Igitur ubi Marius haruspicis[2] dicta eodem
intendere videt, quo cupido animi hortabatur, ab
Metello petundi gratia missionem rogat. Cui quamquam virtus, gloria atque alia optanda bonis supera-
bant, tamen inerat contemptor animus et superbia,
2 commune nobilitatis malum. Itaque primum commotus insolita re mirari eius consilium et quasi per
amicitiam monere ne tam prava inciperet neu super
fortunam animum gereret: non omnia omnibus
cupiunda esse, debere illi res suas satis placere;
postremo caveret id petere a populo Romano, quod illi
iure negaretur.

3 Postquam haec atque alia talia dixit neque animus
Mari flectitur, respondit, ubi primum potuisset per
4 negotia publica, facturum sese quae peteret. Ac
postea saepius eadem postulanti fertur dixisse, ne
festinaret abire, satis mature illum cum filio suo consulatum petiturum. Is eo tempore contubernio patris
ibidem militabat, annos natus circiter viginti. Quae

---

[1] quin is (quin, P^1F^1; qui nisi, l) indignus honore et quasi
pollutus, *mss.*, *Or*; *order changed by Eussner, followed by Ah.*
[2] cum haruspicis, $PA^1NK^1H^1$.

---

[1] If *is* is retained before *indignus*, we must translate
" unworthy of the honour and, as it were, unclean."
[2] The earliest age at which the consulship could legally
be held was forty-three; Marius was forty-nine.

nobles passed the consulate from hand to hand
within their own order. No "new man" was so
famous or so illustrious for his deeds, that he was
not considered unworthy of that honour, and the
office, so to speak, sullied by such an incumbency.[1]

LXIV. Now when Marius perceived that the words
of the soothsayer pointed to the goal towards which
his heart's desire was urging him, he asked Metellus
for a furlough, in order to become a candidate. Now,
although Metellus possessed in abundance valour,
renown, and other qualities to be desired by good
men, yet he had a disdainful and arrogant spirit, a
common defect in the nobles. At first then he was
astonished at the unusual request, expressed his surprise at Marius' design, and with feigned friendship
advised him not to enter upon so mad a course or to
entertain thoughts above his station. All men, he
said, should not covet all things; Marius should be
content with his own lot; and finally, he must
beware of making a request of the Roman people
which they would be justified in denying.

After Metellus had made this and other similar
remarks without shaking Marius' resolution, he at
last replied that as soon as the business of the state
allowed he would do what he asked. Later, when
Marius often repeated the same request, Metellus is
said to have rejoined: "Don't be in a hurry to go to
Rome; it will be soon enough for you to be a candidate when my son becomes one." That young man
at the time was about twenty years old[2] and was
serving in Numidia on his father's personal staff;[3]

---

[3] In this way young nobles commonly gained their first
military experience; *cf.* Suetonius, *Jul.* 2: *stipendia prima
in Asia (Caesar) fecit M. Thermi praetoris contubernio.*

res Marium cum pro honore quem affectabat tum
5 contra Metellum vehementer accenderat. Ita cupidine atque ira, pessumis consultoribus, grassari neque
facto ullo neque dicto abstinere, quod modo ambitio-
sum foret, milites quibus in hibernis praeerat laxi-
ore imperio quam antea habere, apud negotiatores,
quorum magna multitudo Uticae erat, criminose
simul et magnifice de bello loqui: dimidia pars
exercitus si sibi permitteretur, paucis diebus Iugurtham in catenis habiturum; ab imperatore consulto
trahi, quod homo inanis et regiae superbiae imperio
6 nimis gauderet. Quae omnia illis eo firmiora videbantur, quia diuturnitate belli res familiaris corrup-
erant et animo cupienti nihil satis festinatur.

LXV. Erat praeterea in exercitu nostro Numida
quidam nomine Gauda, Mastanabalis filius, Masinissae
nepos, quem Micipsa testamento secundum heredem
scripserat, morbis confectus et ob eam causam mente
2 paulum imminuta. Cui Metellus petenti more regum
ut sellam iuxta poneret, item postea custodiae causa
turmam equitum Romanorum, utrumque negaverat;
honorem, quod eorum more foret, quos populus
Romanus reges appellavisset, praesidium, quod contu-

---

[1] They inherited only in case of the disability of the heirs
in the first degree (*primi heredes*).

hence the taunt resulted in inflaming Marius not
only with greater desire for the honour to which
he aspired, but also with a deep hatred of Metellus.
Accordingly, he allowed himself to be swayed by the
worst of counsellors, ambition and resentment; he
hesitated at no act or word, provided only it could
win him popularity; he was less strict than before in
maintaining discipline among the soldiers under his
command in the winter quarters, and talked about
the war to the traders, of whom there were a great
number in Utica, at the same time disparagingly and
boastfully. He declared that if but half the army
were put in his charge, he would have Jugurtha in
fetters within a few days. His commander, he said,
was purposely protracting the war, because he was a
man of extravagant and tyrannical pride, and enjoyed too much the exercise of power. And all this
talk appealed the more strongly to the traders, because they had suffered pecuniary loss from the long
duration of the war, and for greedy spirits nothing
moves fast enough.

LXV. Furthermore, there was in our army a
Numidian named Gauda, a son of Mastanabal and
grandson of Masinissa, whom Micipsa had made
one of his heirs in the second degree;[1] he was
enfeebled by ill-health and was consequently of a
somewhat weak mind. This man had petitioned
Metellus that he might be given the privilege ac-
corded to royalty and allowed to sit beside him,
and afterwards also requested a squadron of Roman
knights as a bodyguard. Metellus denied both re-
quests: the honour, because it belonged only to
those on whom the Romans had formally conferred
the title of king; the guard, because it would have

meliosum in eos foret, si equites Romani satellites
3 Numidae traderentur. Hunc Marius anxium aggreditur atque hortatur ut contumeliarum in imperatorem cum suo auxilio poenas petat; hominem ob
morbos animo parum valido secunda oratione extollit: illum regem, ingentem virum, Masinissae
nepotem esse; si Iugurtha captus aut occisus foret,
imperium Numidiae sine mora habiturum; id adeo
mature posse evenire, si ipse consul ad id bellum
missus foret.

4   Itaque et illum et equites Romanos, milites et
negotiatores, alios ipse, plerosque pacis spes impellit
uti Romam ad suos necessarios aspere in Metellum
5 de bello scribant, Marium imperatorem poscant. Sic
illi a multis mortalibus honestissuma suffragatione
consulatus petebatur. Simul ea tempestate plebs,
nobilitate fusa per legem Mamiliam, novos extolle-
bat. Ita Mario cuncta procedere.

LXVI. Interim Iugurtha postquam omissa deditione bellum incipit, cum magna cura parare omnia,
festinare, cogere exercitum, civitatis quae ab se
defecerant formidine aut ostentando praemia affec-
tare, communire suos locos; arma, tela aliaque quae
spe pacis amiserat reficere aut commercari, servitia
Romanorum allicere et eos ipsos qui in praesidiis

---

¹ Their support was a high compliment to Marius because
it was the result, not of bribery, but of his merits.
² See chap. xl.

been an insult to Roman knights to make them the attendants of a Numidian. While Gauda was brooding over this refusal, he was approached by Marius, who urged him to avenge himself on the general for his affronts and offered him his help. In flattering terms he lauded this man whose mind was weakened by illness, declaring that he was a king, a mighty hero, the grandson of Masinissa; that if Jugurtha should be taken or killed, he would without delay be made ruler of Numidia; and Marius asserted that this would very soon come to pass, if only he were made consul and sent to the war.

In this way Marius induced Gauda and the Roman knights, both those who were in the army and those who were doing business in the town, some by his personal influence, the most by the hope of peace, to write to their friends in Rome in criticism of Metellus' conduct of the war and to call for Marius as a commander. As a result many men supported Marius' canvass for the consulship in a highly flattering fashion;[1] moreover, just at that time the nobles had been given a check by the bill of Mamilius[2] and the commons were striving to advance "new men." Thus everything favoured Marius.

LXVI. Meanwhile Jugurtha, having abandoned the idea of surrender and having resumed hostilities, was making all his preparations with great care and despatch. He was levying a new army, trying either by intimidation or by offering rewards to win back the cities which had revolted from him, and fortifying advantageous positions. He was making or buying arms, weapons and other things which he had sacrificed to his hope of peace, tempting the Roman slaves to revolt, and trying to bribe even those who

erant, pecunia temptare; prorsus nihil intactum
neque quietum pati, cuncta agitare. Igitur Vagenses,
quo Metellus initio Iugurtha pacificante praesidium
imposuerat, fatigati regis suppliciis neque antea
voluntate alienati, principes civitatis inter se con-
iurant. Nam volgus, uti plerumque solet et maxume
Numidarum, ingenio mobili seditiosum atque discord-
iosum erat, cupidum novarum rerum, quieti et otio
advorsum. Dein compositis inter se rebus in diem
tertium constituunt, quod is festus celebratusque per
omnem Africam ludum et lasciviam magis quam
3 formidinem ostentabat. Sed ubi tempus fuit, centuriones tribunosque militaris et ipsum praefectum
oppidi T. Turpilium Silanum alius alium domos suas
invitant. Eos omnis praeter Turpilium inter epulas
obtruncant. Postea milites palantis inermos, quippe
4 in tali die ac sine imperio, aggrediuntur. Idem
plebes facit, pars edocti ab nobilitate, alii studio
talium rerum incitati, quis acta consiliumque ignorantibus tumultus ipse et res novae satis placebant.

LXVII. Romani milites, improviso metu incerti
ignarique quid potissumum facerent, trepidare. Arce[1]
oppidi, ubi signa et scuta erant, praesidium hostium,

[1] ad arcem, Γ (except D); arce, the other mss.; arcem . . .
pr. h. obsidebat, Dietsch, Ah; ad arcem . . . pr. h.;
fuga, Or.

[1] His title may refer to his command of the city garrison;
but it is also possible that he was the Latin praefectus cohortis
(see note on xlvi. 7). Plutarch (Marius, 8) says that he was
praefectus fabrum.

formed the Roman garrisons. In short, he left absolutely nothing untried or undisturbed, but kept everything in commotion. As a result of his efforts the Vagenses, in whose town Metellus had placed a garrison at first, at the time when Jugurtha was suing for peace, yielded to the entreaties of the king, towards whom they had always been well disposed, and the leading men of the town entered into a conspiracy. As to the commons, they were of a fickle disposition, as is usually the case and as is particularly true of the Numidians, prone to rebellion and disorder, fond of change and opposed to peace and quiet. Then, after arranging matters among themselves, they appointed the third day from that time, because it was observed as a holiday all over Africa and promised entertainment and festivity rather than danger. However, when the appointed time arrived, they invited the centurions and military tribunes and even the prefect[1] of the town himself, Titus Turpilius Silanus by name, to their several homes. There all except Turpilius were slain while feasting. The conspirators then fell upon the common soldiers, who were strolling about unarmed, as was natural on such a day, when they were off duty. The commons joined in the massacre, some at the instigation of the nobles, others inspired by a natural fondness for such conduct; for although they knew neither what was being done nor its purpose, they found sufficient incentive in mere revolution and disorder.

LXVII. The Roman soldiers, being bewildered by this unexpected peril and not knowing what to do first, were thrown into disorder. They were cut off from the citadel of the town, where their standards and shields were, by a hostile force, and from flight

portae ante clausae fugam prohibebant.[1] Ad hoc
mulieres puerique pro tectis aedificiorum saxa et alia
2 quae locus praebebat certatim mittere. Ita neque
caveri anceps malum neque a fortissimis infirmis-
sumo generi resisti posse ; iuxta boni malique, strenui
et imbelles inulti obtruncari.

3 In ea tanta asperitate, saevissumis Numidis et
oppido undique clauso, Turpilius praefectus unus ex
omnibus Italicis intactus profugit. Id misericordiane
hospitis an pactione aut casu[2] ita evenerit, parum
comperimus ; nisi, quia illi in tanto malo turpis vita
integra fama potior fuit, improbus intestabilisque
videtur.

LXVIII. Metellus postquam de rebus Vagae
actis comperit, paulisper maestus ex conspectu abit.
Deinde ubi ira et aegritudo permixta sunt, cum
2 maxuma cura ultum ire iniurias festinat. Legionem,
cum qua hiemabat, et quam plurumos potest Numidas
equites pariter cum occasu solis expeditos educit et
postera die circiter hora tertia pervenit in quandam
3 planitiem locis paulo superioribus circumventam. Ibi
milites, fessos itineris magnitudine et iam abnuentis
omnia, docet oppidum Vagam non amplius mille
passuum abesse : decere illos relicum laborem aequo
animo pati, dum pro civibus suis, viris fortissumis

---

[1] fuga prohibebant, *Jordan* ; fuga prohibebat, *PA*[1] ; fugam
prohibebant, *the other mss.*
[2] aut casu, *XNl s n* ; an casu, *the other mss.*

by the gates, closed beforehand. Moreover, women
and boys from the roofs of the houses were busily
pelting them with stones and whatever else they
could lay hands on. It was quite impossible to
guard against the double danger[1] and brave men
were helpless before the feeblest of opponents.
Side by side valiant and cowardly, strong and weak,
fell without striking a blow.

During this merciless slaughter, although the Numidians were in a frenzy and the town was completely
closed, Turpilius the commander, alone of all the
Italians, escaped unscathed. Whether he owed this
to the mercy of his host, to connivance, or to chance
I have been unable to learn; at any rate, since in
such a disaster he chose to live disgraced rather than
die with an unsullied reputation, he seems to me a
wretch utterly detestable.

LXVIII. When Metellus learned what had happened at Vaga, for a time his grief was such that he
would see no one. Then, when anger was mingled
with his sorrow, he devoted all his thoughts to
prompt vengeance for the outrage. No sooner had
the sun set than he led out the legion with which he
was wintering, and as many Numidian horse as he
could muster, all lightly equipped; and on the following day at about the third hour he arrived at a
plain, which was surrounded on all sides by somewhat higher ground. At that point, finding that his
soldiers were worn out by the long march and were
on the point of mutiny, he told them that the town
of Vaga was only a mile away. They ought, he said,
patiently to endure what toil remained, for the sake

---

[1] From the armed force, on the one hand, between them
and the citadel, and, on the other, the women and boys on
the housetops.

atque miserrumis, poenas caperent. Praeterea prae-
4 dam benigne ostentat. Sic animis eorum arrectis,
equites in primo late,[1] pedites quam artissume ire et
signa occultare iubet.

LXIX. Vagenses ubi animum advortere ad se
vorsum exercitum pergere, primo, uti erat res,
Metellum esse rati portas clausere; deinde, ubi neque
agros vastari et eos qui primi aderant Numidas
equites vident, rursum Iugurtham arbitrati cum
2 magno gaudio obvii procedunt. Equites peditesque
repente signo dato alii volgum effusum oppido
caedere, alii ad portas festinare, pars turris capere;
ira[2] atque praedae spes amplius quam lassitudo posse
3 Ita Vagenses biduom modo ex perfidia laetati.
4 Civitas magna et opulens cuncta poenae aut praedae
fuit. Turpilius, quem praefectum oppidi unum ex
omnibus profugisse supra ostendimus, iussus a Metello causam dicere, postquam sese parum expurgat,
condemnatus verberatusque capite poenas solvit;
nam is civis ex Latio[3] erat.

LXX. Per idem tempus Bomilcar, cuius impulsu
Iugurtha deditionem, quam metu deseruit, inceperat,
suspectus regi et ipse eum suspiciens novas res

[1] late, *Mm*; *the other mss. have* latere.
[2] irae, *PANHl*.
[3] Latio, *A¹K²HD²s*; collatio, *the other mss.*

---

[1] Neither of these punishments might be inflicted upon
a Roman citizen; see note, p. 94. According to Plutarch

of avenging the unhappy fate of their brave fellow-citizens. He also made generous promises about the booty. When he had thus roused their spirits, he ordered the cavalry to take the lead in open order, while the infantry followed in the closest possible formation and with their standards hidden.

LXIX. When the people of Vaga perceived that an army was coming their way, at first they closed their gates, thinking that it was Metellus, as in fact it was. Later, seeing that the fields were not being laid waste and that the horsemen in the van were Numidians, they changed their minds, and taking the newcomers for Jugurtha, went out full of joy to meet him. Then on a sudden the signal sounded and some of the cavalry and infantry began to cut down the crowd which was pouring from the town; others hurried to the gates, while a part took possession of the towers; anger and desire for booty triumphed over their weariness.

Thus it was only two days that the people of Vaga exulted in their treachery; then their rich and populous city in its entirety fell a victim to vengeance and plunder. Turpilius, the commandant of the town, who, as I have already said, had been the only one to escape, was summoned by Metellus before a court martial, and being unable to justify himself was condemned to be scourged and put to death; for he was only a Latin citizen.[1]

LXX. At this same time Bomilcar, who had induced Jugurtha to begin the negotiations for surrender which he later discontinued through fear, being an object of suspicion to Jugurtha and himself looking

(*Marius*, 8), Turpilius was innocent, but was condemned through the efforts of Marius.

cupere, ad perniciem eius dolum quaerere, die
2 noctuque fatigare animum ; denique omnia temptando socium sibi adiungit Nabdalsam, hominem
nobilem, magnis opibus, clarum [1] acceptumque
popularibus suis, qui plerumque seorsum ab rege
exercitum ductare et omnis res exequi solitus erat,
quae Iugurthae fesso aut maioribus adstricto super-
3 averant. Ex quo illi gloria opesque inventae. Igitur
4 utriusque consilio dies insidiis statuitur. Cetera, uti
res posceret, ex tempore parari placuit. Nabdalsa
ad exercitum profectus, quem inter hiberna Romanorum iussus habebat, ne ager inultis hostibus vasta-
5 retur. Is postquam magnitudine facinoris perculsus
ad tempus non venit metusque rem impediebat,
Bomilcar simul cupidus incepta patrandi et timore
soci anxius, ne omisso vetere consilio novom quae-
reret, litteras ad eum per homines fidelis mittit, in
quis mollitiam socordiamque viri accusare, testari
deos per quos iuravisset, monere ne praemia Metelli
in pestem convorteret. Iugurthae exitium adesse,
ceterum suane an Metelli virtute periret, id modo
agitari ; proinde reputaret cum animo suo, praemia
an cruciatum mallet.

---

[1] clarum, *mss.*; carum, *Colerus.*

---

[1] That is, he kept it moving about between the various
points where the Romans were encamped for the winter.
[2] *converteret* means " allow to turn."

on the king with suspicion, was desirous of a change
of rulers; he therefore began to cast about for a stratagem by which to effect the ruin of Jugurtha, and
racked his brains day and night. Finally, while trying
every device, he won the support of Nabdalsa, a man
of rank, wealth and distinction, who was very popular with his countrymen. This man was in the habit
of exercising a command independently of the king
and of attending to all business which Jugurtha
could not transact in person when he was weary or
engaged in more important duties; in this way he
had gained fame and power. He and Bomilcar accordingly took counsel together and chose a time for
their plot, deciding to arrange the details on the spot
according to circumstances. Nabdalsa then went to
the army, which by the royal command he kept between the winter quarters of the Romans,[1] for the
purpose of preventing the enemy from ravaging the
country with impunity. There, however, he took
fright at the enormity of the proposed crime, and
since he did not appear at the appointed hour, his
fears thwarted the attempt. Therefore Bomilcar,
being at once eager to carry out his design and also
fearing that the timidity of his accomplice might lead
him to abandon their former plan and look for a
new one, sent a letter to him by trusty messengers.
In this he upbraided the man for his weakness and
cowardice, called to witness the gods by whom he
had sworn, and warned him not to exchange[2] ruin
for the rewards offered by Metellus. Jugurtha's
end, he said, was at hand; the only question was
whether he should succumb to their valour or to
that of Metellus. Nabdalsa must therefore consider
whether he preferred rewards or torture.

285

LXXI. Sed cum eae litterae allatae, forte Nab-
2 dalsa exercito corpore fessus in lecto quiescebat, ubi
cognitis Bomilcaris verbis primo cura, deinde, uti
3 aegrum animum solet, somnus cepit. Erat ei Numida
quidam negotiorum curator, fidus acceptusque et
4 omnium consiliorum nisi novissumi particeps. Qui
postquam allatas litteras audivit et ex consuetudine
ratus opera aut ingenio suo opus esse, in taberna-
culum introiit, dormiente illo epistulam super caput
in pulvino temere positam sumit ac perlegit, dein
propere cognitis insidiis ad regem pergit.
5 Nabdalsa paulo post experrectus ubi neque epistulam repperit et rem omnem uti acta erat[1] cognovit,
primo indicem persequi conatus, postquam id frustra
fuit, Iugurtham placandi gratia accedit; dicit quae
ipse paravisset facere perfidia clientis sui praeventa;
lacrumans obtestatur per amicitiam perque sua
antea fideliter acta, ne super tali scelere suspectum
sese haberet.
LXXII. Ad ea rex aliter atque animo gerebat
placide respondit. Bomilcare aliisque multis, quos
socios insidiarum cognoverat, interfectis iram oppres-
2 serat, nequa ex eo negotio seditio oreretur.[2] Neque
post id locorum Iugurthae dies aut nox ulla quieta
fuit; neque loco neque mortali cuiquam aut tempori
satis credere, civis hostisque iuxta metuere, circum-
spectare omnia et omni strepitu pavescere, alio atque

---

[1] ex servis *before* cognovit, *A*; expertus, *N*; ex perfugis, *the other mss.* *The phrase was omitted by Kritz, Ah, Or.*
[2] *PA¹N¹*; *the other mss. have* oriretur.

LXXI. Now when this letter arrived, it chanced that Nabdalsa, fatigued by bodily exercise, was resting on his couch. On reading Bomilcar's message, he was at first troubled, and then, as is usual with a wearied mind, sleep overcame him. He had as his secretary a Numidian whom he trusted and loved, a man whom he had made acquainted with all his designs except this last one. When this man heard that a letter had arrived, he thought that as usual his services or advice would be needed. He therefore entered the tent where his master was sleeping, took the letter, which Nabdalsa had carelessly left on the pillow above his head, and read it; then perceiving the plot, he went in haste to the king.

When Nabdalsa woke up a little later and did not find the letter, realizing exactly what had happened, he first made an attempt to overtake the informer, and failing in that went to Jugurtha in order to pacify him. He declared that he had been anticipated by his faithless dependant in doing what he himself had intended. Bursting into tears, he begged the king by his friendship and his own faithful service of old not to suspect him of such a crime.

LXXII. To these words the king made a courteous reply, disguising his real feelings. After putting to death Bomilcar and many others whom he knew to be implicated in the plot, he restrained his anger, for fear that the affair might cause a rebellion. But from that time forward Jugurtha never passed a quiet day or night; he put little trust in any place, person, or time; feared his countrymen and the enemy alike; was always on the watch; started at every sound; and spent his nights in different places, many of

alio loco saepe contra decus regium noctu requies-
cere, interdum somno excitus[1] arreptis armis tumultum facere, ita formidine quasi vecordia exagitari.

LXXIII. Igitur Metellus, ubi de casu Bomilcaris
et indicio patefacto ex perfugis cognovit, rursus tamquam ad integrum bellum cuncta parat festinatque.
2 Marium, fatigantem de profectione, simul et invitum
et offensum sibi parum idoneum ratus, domum
3 dimittit. Et Romae plebes, litteris quae de Metello
ac Mario missae erant cognitis, volenti animo de
4 ambobus acceperant. Imperatori nobilitas, quae
antea decori fuit, invidiae esse, at illi alteri generis
humilitas favorem addiderat. Ceterum in utroque
magis studia partium quam bona aut mala sua
5 moderata. Praeterea seditiosi magistratus volgum
exagitare, Metellum omnibus contionibus capitis
6 arcessere, Mari virtutem in maius celebrare. Denique
plebes sic accensa uti opifices agrestesque omnes,
quorum res fidesque in manibus sitae erant, relictis
operibus frequentarent Marium et sua necessaria
7 post illius honorem ducerent. Ita perculsa nobilitate, post multas tempestates novo homini consulatus mandatur. Et postea populus a tribuno plebis
T. Manlio Mancino rogatus quem vellet cum Iugurtha
bellum gerere, frequens Marium iussit. Sed paulo

[1] exercitus, *PN*; excitatus, *M*; experrectus, *Diom*. i.
376. 15 к.

---

[1] Referring to the tribunes of the commons ; see *Cat.*
xxxviii. 1.

which were ill suited to the dignity of a king. Sometimes on being roused from sleep he would utter outcries and seize his arms; he was hounded by a fear that was all but madness.

LXXIII. Now when Metellus learned from deserters of the fate of Bomilcar and the discovery of the plot, he again hastened to make all his preparations, as if for a new war. Since Marius constantly asked for a furlough, he sent him home, thinking that a man who was at once both discontented and at odds with his commander, would be of little service. At Rome, too, the commons, on hearing the letters which had been written about Metellus and Marius, had readily accepted what was said in them about both men. The general's noble rank, which before this had been an honour to him, became a source of unpopularity, while to Marius his humble origin lent increased favour; but in the case of both men their own good or bad qualities had less influence than party spirit. More than this, seditious[1] magistrates were working upon the feelings of the populace, in every assembly charging Metellus with treason and exaggerating the merits of Marius. At length the commons were so excited that all the artisans and farmers, whose prosperity and credit depended upon the labour of their own hands, left their work and attended Marius, regarding their own necessities as less important than his success. The result was that the nobles were worsted and after the lapse of many years the consulship was given to a "new man." Afterwards, when the tribune Titus Manlius Mancinus asked the people whom they wished to have as leader of the war with Jugurtha, they chose Marius by a large majority. It is true that the senate had

ante senatus Metello Numidiam decreverat[1] ; ea res frustra fuit.

LXXIV. Eodem tempore Iugurtha amissis amicis —quorum plerosque ipse necaverat, ceteri formidine pars ad Romanos, alii ad regem Bocchum profugerant—cum neque bellum geri sine administris posset et novorum fidem in tanta perfidia veterum experiri periculosum duceret, varius incertusque agitabat. Neque illi res neque consilium aut quisquam hominum satis placebat. Itinera praefectosque in dies mutare, modo advorsum hostis, interdum in solitudines pergere, saepe in fuga ac post paulo in armis spem habere, dubitare virtuti an fidei popularium minus crederet ; ita quocumque intenderat res advorsae erant.

2 Sed inter eas moras repente sese Metellus cum exercitu ostendit. Numidae ab Iugurtha pro tempore 3 parati instructique, dein proelium incipitur. Qua in parte rex pugnae affuit, ibi aliquamdiu certatum, ceteri eius omnes milites primo congressu pulsi fugatique. Romani signorum et armorum aliquanto numero, hostium paucorum potiti ; nam ferme Numidis in omnibus proeliis magis pedes quam arma tuta[2] sunt.

LXXV. Ea fuga Iugurtha impensius modo rebus suis diffidens, cum perfugis et parte equitatus in

---

[1] sed paulo (paulum, *n*) decreverat, *XNDlnm, Ah, Or* ; sed senatus p. decio decreverat (decr. decio, *H*), *the other mss. Ah suggests* ante senatus aliam provinciam Mario.

[2] tutata, *CBHT²F²l²m* ; tutati, *n* ; tutarant, *MT¹*.

shortly before this voted Numidia to Metellus, but their action was to no purpose.

LXXIV. By this time Jugurtha had lost all his friends, having himself slain the greater part of them, while others through fear had taken refuge either with the Romans or with King Bocchus. Therefore, since he could not carry on the war without officers, and at the same time considered it dangerous to trust to the fidelity of new friends when old friends had proved so treacherous, he lived in doubt and uncertainty. There was no measure, there was neither plan nor man that he could fully approve. He changed his routes and his officials from day to day, now went forth to meet the enemy, now took to the desert; often placed hope in flight and shortly afterwards in arms; was in doubt whether to trust less to the courage or to the good faith of his countrymen : thus, wherever he turned, he faced adversity.

While the king was thus procrastinating, Metellus unexpectedly appeared with his army; whereupon Jugurtha made ready and drew up his Numidians as well as time allowed. Then the battle began. Wherever the king was present in person, there was some show of resistance ; everywhere else his soldiers broke and fled at the first charge. The Romans captured a considerable number of standards and arms, but few prisoners ; for in almost all their battles the Numidians depend more upon speed of foot than on arms.

LXXV. Reduced to even deeper despair by this defeat, Jugurtha took refuge with the fugitives and a part of the cavalry in the desert, and then made his

solitudines, dein Thalam pervenit, in oppidum magnum atque opulentum, ubi plerique thesauri filiorum-
2 que eius multus pueritiae cultus erat. Quae postquam Metello comperta sunt, quamquam inter Thalam
flumenque proxumum in spatio milium quinquaginta
loca arida atque vasta esse cognoverat, tamen spe
patrandi belli, si eius oppidi potitus foret, omnis
asperitates supervadere ac naturam etiam vincere
3 aggreditur. Igitur omnia iumenta sarcinis levari
iubet nisi frumento dierum decem, ceterum utris
4 modo et alia aquae idonea portari. Praeterea conquirit ex agris quam plurumum potest domiti pecoris.
Eo imponit vasa cuiusque modi, sed pleraque lignea,
5 collecta ex tuguriis Numidarum. Ad hoc finitumis
imperat, qui se post regis fugam Metello dederant,
quam plurumum quisque aquae portaret; diem
6 locumque, ubi praesto fuerint,[1] praedicit. Ipse ex
flumine, quam proxumam oppido aquam esse supra
diximus, iumenta onerat; eo modo instructus ad
7 Thalam proficiscitur. Deinde ubi ad id loci ventum
quo Numidis praeceperat et castra posita munitaque
sunt, tanta repente caelo missa vis aquae dicitur, ut
8 ea modo exercitui satis superque foret. Praeterea
commeatus spe amplior, quia Numidae, sicuti pleri-

---

[1] fuerit, *mss.* (fuerat, *N*; fuit *M*); forent, *Kritz*; fuerint,
Ah; futuri sint, *Or.*

---

[1] The meaning seems to be that a large establishment was
kept there for the maintenance of the royal children in a
manner befitting their station.

way to Thala, a large and wealthy town in which the greater part of his treasure was kept, and his children were being brought up in grand style.[1] As soon as Metellus learned of this, although he knew that between Thala and the nearest river lay fifty miles of dry and desolate country, yet in hope of ending the war by getting possession of so important a town he undertook to surmount all the difficulties and even to defeat Nature herself. Accordingly, he gave orders that every pack animal should be relieved of all burdens except a ten days' allowance of grain, and that in addition to this only skins and other vessels for carrying water should be taken. Moreover, he scoured the fields to find as many domestic animals as possible and upon them he loaded utensils of every kind, but especially wooden ones, which he obtained from the huts of the Numidians. Besides this, he ordered all the people who dwelt near by (they had surrendered to Metellus after the flight of the king), to bring each as much water as he could, naming the day and the place where they were to appear. He himself loaded his animals from the river which, as I have already said, was the nearest water to the town, and with this supply began his march for Thala. When Metellus had reached the place which he had appointed with the Numidians and had pitched and fortified his camp, suddenly such an abundance of rain is said to have fallen from heaven that this alone furnished the army with water enough and to spare. The amount also which was brought to him[2] was greater than he anticipated, since the Numidians, as is common just after a

---

[2] By the neighbouring people; see lxxv. 5 above.

9 que in nova deditione, officia intenderant. Ceterum
milites religione pluvia magis usi, eaque res multum
animis eorum addidit. Nam rati sese dis immortalibus curae esse.

Deinde postero die contra opinionem Iugurthae ad
10 Thalam perveniunt. Oppidani, qui se locorum
asperitate munitos crediderant, magna atque insolita
re perculsi, nihilo segnius bellum parare; idem nostri
facere.

LXXVI. Sed rex nihil iam infectum Metello credens—quippe qui omnia, arma, tela, locos, tempora,
denique naturam ipsam ceteris imperitantem industria vicerat—cum liberis et magna parte pecuniae
ex oppido noctu profugit, neque postea in ullo loco
amplius uno die aut una nocte moratus, simulabat
sese negoti gratia properare. Ceterum proditionem
timebat, quam vitare posse celeritate putabat; nam
talia consilia per otium et ex opportunitate capi.

2 At Metellus ubi oppidanos proelio intentos, simul
oppidum et operibus et loco munitum videt, vallo
3 fossaque moenia circumvenit. Dein duobus locis ex
copia maxume idoneis vineas agere, aggerem iacere [1]
et super aggerem impositis turribus opus et adminis-
4 tros tutari. Contra haec oppidani festinare, parare;

---

[1] vineas agere superque eas aggerem iacere, *mss.*; superque
eas *deleted by Korrte.*

---

[1] That is, they had done more than was required, they had
strained their services.

surrender, had more than done their duty.[1] But religious motives led the soldiers to prefer the rain water and its fall added greatly to their spirits; for they thought that they enjoyed the favour of the immortal gods.

The next day, contrary to Jugurtha's expectation, the Romans arrived at Thala. The townspeople had supposed themselves protected by their inaccessible situation; but although they were amazed at this great and unexpected feat, they none the less made diligent preparations for battle. Our men did the same.

LXXVI. But the king now believed that there was nothing which Metellus could not accomplish, since his energy had triumphed over all obstacles: arms, weapons, places, seasons, even Nature herself, to whom all others bowed. He therefore fled from the town by night with his children and the greater part of his treasure. And after that he never lingered in any place for more than one day or one night, pretending that his haste was due to important affairs; but as a matter of fact he feared treachery and thought that he could escape it by rapid movements, since such designs require leisure and opportunity.

But when Metellus saw that the inhabitants were eager for battle and also that the town was fortified both by its position and by defensive works, he encompassed the walls with a stockade and a moat Then in the two most suitable places that he could find he brought up the mantlets, built a mound, and upon it placed turrets to protect the besiegers and their work. The townsmen for their part hastened their preparations; indeed, nothing was left undone by

5 prorsus ab utrisque nihil relicum fieri. Denique
Romani multo ante labore proeliisque fatigati, post
dies quadraginta quam eo ventum erat, oppido modo
6 potiti, praeda omnis ab perfugis corrupta. Ei postquam murum arietibus feriri resque suas afflictas
vident, aurum atque argentum et alia quae prima
ducuntur domum regiam comportant. Ibi vino et
epulis onerati illaque et domum et semet igni cor-
rumpunt et quas victi ab hostibus poenas metuerant,
eas ipsi volentes pependere.

LXXVII. Sed pariter cum capta Thala legati ex
oppido Lepci ad Metellum venerant, orantes uti
praesidium praefectumque eo mitteret : Hamil-
carem quendam, hominem nobilem, factiosum, novis
rebus studere, advorsum quem neque imperia magistratuum neque leges valerent. Ni id festinaret, in
summo periculo suam salutem, illorum socios fore.
2 Nam Lepcitani iam inde a principio belli Iugurthini
ad Bestiam consulem et postea Romam miserant
3 amicitiam societatemque rogatum. Deinde, ubi ea
impetrata, semper boni fidelesque mansere et cuncta
a Bestia, Albino Metelloque imperata nave fecerant.
4 Itaque ab imperatore facile quae petebant adepti.
Emissae eo cohortes Ligurum quattuor et C. Annius
praefectus.

LXXVIII. Id oppidum ab Sidoniis conditum est,
quos accepimus profugos ob discordias civilis navibus

---

[1] Sallust's brevity makes his meaning obscure. The safety
of the Lepcitani would be jeopardized, and the Romans

either side. At last, after much exhausting toil and many battles, the Romans, forty days after their arrival, got possession of the town only, all the booty having been destroyed by the deserters. For when these men saw the wall battered by the rams and realized that all was lost, they carried the gold, silver, and other valuables to the palace. There, gorged with food and wine, they burned the treasure, the palace and themselves, thus voluntarily paying the penalty which they feared they would suffer at the hands of a victorious enemy.

LXXVII. Now simultaneously with the capture of Thala envoys had come to Metellus from the town of Lepcis, begging him to send them a garrison and a commandant. They declared that one Hamilcar, a man of rank and given to intrigue, was plotting a revolution and could be restrained neither by the commands of the magistrates nor by the laws: unless Metellus acted promptly, they would be in extreme peril of their lives; the Romans, of losing their allies.[1] And in fact the citizens of Lepcis at the very beginning of the war with Jugurtha had sent messengers to Bestia the consul and later to Rome, asking for friendship and an alliance. After their request was granted, they had always remained true and loyal, and had diligently executed all the commands of Bestia, Albinus and Metellus. Therefore Metellus willingly granted their petition, and four cohorts of Ligurians were sent to their aid under the command of Gaius Annius.

LXXVIII. The town of Lepcis was founded by Sidonians, who are reported to have left their homes

would run the risk of losing the Lepcitani as allies, owing to the intrigues of Hamilcar.

297

in eos locos venisse; ceterum situm inter duas Syrtis,
2 quibus nomen ex re inditum. Nam duo sunt sinus
prope in extrema Africa impares magnitudine, pari
natura. Quorum proxuma terrae praealta sunt,
cetera, uti fors tulit, alta,[1] alia in tempestate[2] vadosa.
3 Nam ubi mare magnum esse et saevire ventis coepit,
limum harenamque et saxa ingentia fluctus trahunt :
ita facies locorum cum ventis simul mutatur, Syrtes
ab tractu nominatae.

4   Eius civitatis lingua modo convorsa conubio Numidarum ; legum cultusque pleraque Sidonica, quae eo
facilius retinebant, quod procul ab imperio regis
5 aetatem agebant. Inter illos et frequentem Numidiam multi vastique loci erant.

   LXXIX. Sed quoniam in eas regiones per Lepci-
tanorum negotia venimus, non indignum videtur
egregium atque mirabile facinus duorum Carthaginiensium memorare ; eam rem nos locus admonuit.
2 Qua tempestate Carthaginienses pleraque Africa[3]
imperitabant, Cyrenenses quoque magni atque
3 opulenti fuere. Ager in medio harenosus, una specie;
neque flumen neque mons erat, qui finis eorum dis-
cerneret. Quae res eos in magno diuturnoque bello
inter se habuit.

4   Postquam utrimque legiones item classes saepe
fusae fugataeque, et alteri alteros aliquantum

   [1] alta alia alia, *A* ; alta alia, *the other mss.*
   [2] in t. *deleted by Kunze, Ah.*
   [3] pleraque Africa, *A n, Arus.* vii. 481. 22; pleraeque
Africae, *the other mss.*

because of civil discord and come to that region in ships. It lies between the two Syrtes, which derive their name from their nature; for they are two bays situated almost at the extreme end of Africa,[1] of unequal size but alike in character. Near the shore the water is very deep, elsewere it is sometimes deep and sometimes shoal, just as it happens[2]; for when the breeze causes the sea to swell and rage, the waves sweep along mud, sand, and great rocks, so that the aspect of the place changes with the winds. From this "sweeping"[3] the Syrtes get their name.

Only the speech of this city has been affected by intermarriage with the Numidians; its laws and customs are for the most part Sidonian, and these the inhabitants retained the more easily because they passed their life at a distance from the Numidian capital. For between them and the thickly settled part of Numidia lay an extensive desert.

LXXIX. Since the affairs of the people of Lepcis have brought us to this region, it seems fitting to relate the noble and memorable act of two Carthaginians; the place calls the event to mind. At the time when the Carthaginians ruled in the greater part of Africa, the people of Cyrene were also strong and prosperous. Between that city and Carthage lay a sandy plain of monotonous aspect. There was neither river nor hill to mark the frontiers, a circumstance which involved the two peoples in bitter and lasting strife.

After many armies and fleets had been beaten and put to flight on both sides, and the long struggle

---

[1] That is, close to the Egyptian frontier. Sallust seems to have confused Leptis Minor with the later city of Leptis Magna.   [2] That is, according to the wind and weather.
[3] From the Greek σύρω, to sweep.

attriverant, veriti ne mox victos victoresque defessos
alius aggrederetur, per indutias sponsionem faciunt,
uti certo die legati domo proficiscerentur; quo in
loco inter se obvii fuissent, is communis utriusque
5 populi finis haberetur. Igitur Carthagine duo fratres
missi, quibus nomen Philaenis erat, maturavere iter
pergere. Cyrenenses tardius iere. Id socordiane an
6 casu acciderit parum cognovi. Ceterum solet in illis
locis tempestas haud secus atque in mari retinere.
Nam ubi per loca aequalia et nuda gignentium ventus
coortus harenam humo excitavit, ea magna vi agitata
ora oculosque implere solet; ita prospectu impedito
7 morari iter. Postquam Cyrenenses aliquanto poste-
riores se esse vident et ob rem corruptam domi
poenas metuunt, criminari Carthaginiensis ante
tempus domo digressos, conturbare rem, denique
8 omnia malle quam victi abire. Sed cum Poeni aliam
condicionem, tantum modo aequam, peterent, Graeci
optionem Carthaginiensium faciunt, ut vel illi, quos
finis populo suo peterent, ibi vivi obruerentur, vel
eadem condicione sese quem in locum vellent pro-
9 cessuros. Philaeni condicione probata seque vitam-
que suam rei publicae condonavere: ita vivi obruti.
10 Carthaginienses in eo loco Philaenis fratribus aras
consecravere aliique illis domi honores instituti.
Nunc ad rem redeo.

---

[1] *nuda gignentium,* "bare of vegetation." *Gignentium* is
the n.pl. used as a substantive with an active sense ("growing things"). It is gen. with *nuda* in place of the usual
abl. *Cf. frugum vacuos,* xc. 1.

had somewhat wearied them both, they began to
fear that presently a third party might attack victors
and vanquished in their weak state. They therefore
called a truce and agreed that on a given day envoys
should set out from each city and that the place
where they met should be regarded as the common
frontier of the two peoples. Accordingly, two
brothers were sent from Carthage, called Philaeni,
and these made haste to complete their journey.
Those from Cyrene went more deliberately. Whether
this was due to sloth or chance I cannot say, but
in those lands a storm often causes no less delay
than on the sea; for when the wind rises on those
level and barren[1] plains, it sweeps up the sand from
the ground and drives it with such violence as to fill
the mouth and eyes. Thus one is halted because one
cannot see. Now when the men of Cyrene realized
that they were somewhat belated and feared punishment for their failure when they returned, they
accused the Carthaginians of having left home ahead
of time and refused to abide by the agreement; in
fact they were willing to do anything rather than
go home defeated. But when the Carthaginians demanded other terms, provided they were fair, the
Greeks gave them the choice, either of being buried
alive in the place which they claimed as the boundary
of their country, or of allowing the Greeks on the
same condition to advance as far as they wished.
The Philaeni accepted the terms and gave up their
lives for their country; so they were buried alive.
The Carthaginians consecrated altars on that spot to
the Philaeni brothers, and other honours were established for them at home. I now return to my
subject.

LXXX. Iugurtha postquam amissa Thala nihil satis firmum contra Metellum putat, per magnas solitudines cum paucis profectus, pervenit ad Gaetulos, genus hominum ferum incultumque et eo tempore
2 ignarum nominis Romani. Eorum multitudinem in unum cogit ac paulatim consuefacit ordines habere, signa sequi, imperium observare, item alia militaria
3 facere. Praeterea regis Bocchi proxumos magnis muneribus et maioribus promissis ad studium sui perducit, quis adiutoribus regem aggressus, impellit
4 uti advorsus Romanos bellum incipiat. Id ea gratia facilius proniusque fuit, quod Bocchus initio huiusce belli legatos Romam miserat foedus et amicitiam
5 petitum, quam rem opportunissumam incepto bello pauci impediverant caeci avaritia, quis omnia honesta
6 atque inhonesta vendere mos erat. Etiam antea Iugurthae filia Boccho[1] nupserat. Verum ea necessitudo apud Numidas Maurosque levis ducitur, quia singuli pro opibus quisque quam plurumas uxores, denas alii, alii pluris habent, sed reges eo amplius.
7 Ita animus multitudine distrahitur; nulla pro socia optinet, pariter omnes viles sunt.

LXXXI. Igitur in locum ambobus placitum exercitus conveniunt. Ibi, fide data et accepta, Iugurtha Bocchi animum oratione accendit; Romanos iniustos, profunda avaritia communis omnium hostis esse; eandem illos causam belli cum Boccho habere, quam

[1] Bocchi, *A²CB n¹*.

LXXX. Since Jugurtha after the loss of Thala was convinced that nothing could resist Metellus, he journeyed through vast deserts with a few followers until he came to the Gaetulians, a wild and uncivilized race of men, who at that time had never heard the name of Rome. He mustered their population in one place and gradually trained them to keep ranks, follow the standards, obey orders, and perform the other duties of soldiers. He also won the favour of the nearest friends of King Bocchus by lavish gifts and still more lavish promises, and through their aid approached the king and induced him to make war upon the Romans. This was an easier and simpler matter, because at the beginning of this very war Bocchus had sent envoys to Rome, to ask for a treaty of alliance; but this arrangement, so advantageous for the war which was already under way, had been thwarted by a few men, blinded by greed, whose habit it was to traffic in everything, honourable and dishonourable. Even before that Bocchus had married a daughter of Jugurtha, but such a tie is not considered very binding among the Numidians and Moors, since each of them has as many wives as his means permit—some ten, others more, and kings a still greater number. Thus their affection is distributed among a large number; none of the wives is regarded as a consort, but all are equally misprised.

LXXXI. Now the armies met in a place mutually agreed upon. There, after an exchange of pledges, Jugurtha strove to inflame the heart of Bocchus by a speech. The Romans, he said, were unjust, of boundless greed, and the common foes of all mankind. They had the same motive for a war with Bocchus as

secum et cum aliis gentibus, lubidinem imperitandi,
quis omnia regna advorsa sint. Tum sese, paulo ante
Carthaginiensis, item regem Persen, post uti quisque
opulentissumus videatur, ita Romanis hostem fore.
2 Eis atque aliis talibus dictis ad Cirtam oppidum iter
constituunt, quod ibi[1] Metellus praedam captivosque
3 et impedimenta locaverat. Ita Iugurtha ratus aut
capta urbe operae pretium fore aut, si dux Romanus
4 auxilio suis venisset, proelio sese certaturos. Nam
callidus id modo festinabat, Bocchi pacem im-
minuere, ne moras agitando aliud quam bellum
mallet.

LXXXII. Imperator postquam de regum societate
cognovit, non temere neque, uti saepe iam victo
Iugurtha consueverat, omnibus locis pugnandi copiam
facit. Ceterum haud procul ab Cirta castris munitis
reges opperitur, melius esse ratus cognitis Mauris,
quoniam is novos hostis accesserat, ex commodo pug-
2 nam facere. Interim Roma per litteras certior fit
provinciam Numidiam Mario datam, nam consulem
factum ante acceperat. Quibus rebus supra bonum aut
honestum perculsus, neque lacrumas tenere neque
moderari linguam, vir egregius in aliis artibus nimis
3 molliter aegritudinem pati. Quam rem alii in superbiam vortebant, alii bonum ingenium contumelia

[1] ibiq(ue), *P l*; Q. Metellus, *the other mss.*, *Ah, Or.*

for one with himself and other nations, namely, the
lust for dominion, and their hatred of all monarchies.
Just now Jugurtha was their enemy, a short time
before it had been the Carthaginians and King Perses;
in the future it would be whoever seemed to them
most powerful. After he had spoken these and
similar words, the kings directed their march towards
the town of Cirta, because there Metellus had placed
his booty, his prisoners and his baggage. Hence
Jugurtha thought that if the city could be taken, it
would be worth the effort, while if the Roman leader
came to the help of his countrymen, there would be
a battle. And as a matter of fact, there was nothing
about which the wily king was in such haste as to
involve Bocchus in war, for fear that delay might lead
him to choose another course.

LXXXII. When the Roman general heard of the
league of the kings, he did not offer battle heedlessly
and in all places alike, as had been his custom with
Jugurtha after he had so often defeated him; but he
waited for them in a fortified camp not far from Cirta,
thinking it better to learn to know the Moors, since
this new enemy had appeared, and so to fight to
better advantage. Meanwhile he was informed by
letters from Rome that the province of Numidia
had been given to Marius; for he had already heard
of his election to the consulship. He was more
affected by this news than was right or becoming,
neither refraining from tears nor bridling his tongue;
although he had the other qualities of a great man,
he showed little fortitude in bearing mortification.
Some attributed his conduct on this occasion to arrogance; others declared that a noble spirit had been
exasperated by insult; many thought that it was due

accensum esse, multi, quod iam parta victoria ex manibus eriperetur. Nobis satis cognitum est illum magis honore Mari quam iniuria sua excruciatum neque tam anxie laturum fuisse, si adempta provincia alii quam Mario traderetur.

LXXXIII. Igitur eo dolore impeditus, et quia stultitiae videbatur alienam rem periculo suo curare, legatos ad Bocchum mittit postulatum ne sine causa hostis populo Romano fieret : habere tum magnam copiam societatis amicitiaeque coniungendae, quae potior bello esset, et quamquam opibus suis confideret, tamen non debere incerta pro certis mutare; omne bellum sumi facile, ceterum aegerrume desinere; non in eiusdem potestate initium eius et finem esse ; incipere cuivis, etiam ignavo licere, deponi, cum victores velint ; proinde sibi regnoque suo consuleret, neu florentis res suas cum Iugurthae perditis misceret.

2 Ad ea rex satis placide verba facit: sese pacem cupere, sed Iugurthae fortunarum misereri ; si eadem 3 illi copia fieret, omnia conventura. Rursus imperator contra postulata Bocchi nuntios mittit ; ille probare partim, alia abnuere. Eo modo saepe ab utroque missis remissisque nuntiis, tempus procedere et ex Metelli voluntate bellum intactum trahi.

to the fact that the victory which he had already won was snatched from his grasp. Personally, I feel confident that he was tormented more by the honour done to Marius than by the affront to himself, and that he would have felt less annoyance if the province had been taken from him to be given to any other man than Marius.

LXXXIII. Checked therefore as he was by this grievance and thinking it folly to promote another's interests at his own peril, Metellus sent envoys to Bocchus, to demand that he should not unprovoked become an enemy to the Roman people; he declared that in the crisis before them the king had a golden opportunity to form a friendly alliance, which was preferable to war, and that however much confidence he might feel in his strength, he ought not to exchange certainty for uncertainty. It was always easy to begin a war, but very difficult to stop one, since its beginning and end were not under the control of the same man. Anyone, even a coward, could commence a war, but it could be brought to an end only with the consent of the victors. Therefore the Moor ought to have regard to his own interests and those of his kingdom and ought not to unite his own prosperity with the desperate plight of Jugurtha.

To these words the king made a sufficiently conciliatory reply, saying that he desired peace, but pitied the misfortunes of Jugurtha; that if the same opportunity were offered his ally, agreement would be easy. Upon this, Metellus again sent envoys to object to the demands of Bocchus, who partly heeded and partly rejected his remonstrances. In this way, while messengers were continually being sent to and fro, time passed and, as Metellus wished, the war remained at a standstill.

LXXXIV. At Marius, ut supra diximus, cupientis-
suma plebe consul factus, postquam ei provinciam
Numidiam populus iussit, antea iam infestus nobili-
tati, tum vero multus atque ferox instare, singulos
modo, modo univorsos laedere, dictitare sese consulatum ex victis illis spolia cepisse, alia praeterea mag-
2 nifica pro se et illis dolentia. Interim quae bello
opus erant prima habere, postulare legionibus supplementum, auxilia a populis et regibus arcessere, praeterea ex Latio sociisque[1] fortissumum quemque,
plerosque militiae, paucos fama cognitos accire et
ambiundo cogere homines emeritis stipendiis secum
proficisci.

3 Neque illi senatus, quamquam advorsus erat, de
ullo negotio abnuere audebat. Ceterum supplementum etiam laetus decreverat, quia neque plebi militia
volenti putabatur et Marius aut belli usum aut studia
volgi amissurus. Sed ea res frustra sperata; tanta
4 lubido cum Mario eundi plerosque invaserat. Sese
quisque praeda locupletem fore, victorem domum
rediturum alia huiuscemodi animis trahebant, et eos
5 non paulum oratione sua Marius arrexerat. Nam
postquam omnibus quae postulaverat decretis milites
scribere volt, hortandi causa, simul et nobilitatem uti

[1] regibus sociisque, *mss., Or. Wirz placed* sociisque *after*
Latio, *followed by Ah.*

LXXXIV. Now Marius, as we have already said, was chosen consul with the ardent support of the commons. While even before his election he had been hostile to the nobles, as soon as the people voted him the province of Numidia he attacked the aristocracy persistently and boldly, assailing now individuals and now the entire party. He boasted that he had wrested the consulship from them as the spoils of victory, and made other remarks calculated to glorify himself and exasperate them. All the while he gave his first attention to preparation for the war. He asked that the legions should be reinforced, summoned auxiliaries from foreign nations and kings, besides calling out the bravest men from Latium and from our allies, the greater number of whom he knew from actual service but a few only by reputation. By special inducements, too, he persuaded veterans who had served their time to join his expedition.

The senate, although it was hostile to him, did not venture to oppose any of his measures; the addition to the legions it was particularly glad to vote, because it was thought that the commons were disinclined to military service and that Marius would thus lose either resources for the war or the devotion of the people. But such a desire of following Marius had seized almost everyone, that the hopes of the senate were disappointed. Each man imagined himself enriched by booty or returning home a victor, along with other visions of the same kind. Marius too had aroused them in no slight degree by a speech of his; for when all the decrees for which he had asked had been passed and he wished to enrol soldiers, in order to encourage men to enlist and at the same time,

consueverat exagitandi, contionem populi advocavit.
Deinde hoc modo disseruit.

LXXXV. "Scio ego, Quirites, plerosque non eisdem artibus imperium a vobis petere et postquam
adepti sunt gerere; primo industrios, supplices,
modicos esse, dein per ignaviam et superbiam aeta-
2 tem agere. Sed mihi contra ea videtur. Nam quo
pluris est univorsa res publica quam consulatus aut
praetura, eo maiore cura illam administrari quam haec
3 peti debere. Neque me fallit, quantum cum maxumo
benificio vostro negoti sustineam.[1] Bellum parare
simul et aerario parcere, cogere ad militiam eos quos
nolis offendere, domi forisque omnia curare et ea
agere inter invidos, occursantis, factiosos, opinione,
4 Quirites, asperius est. Ad hoc alii si deliquere, vetus
nobilitas, maiorum fortia facta, cognatorum et adfinium opes, multae clientelae, omnia haec praesidio
adsunt; mihi spes omnes in memet sitae, quas necesse est virtute et innocentia tutari. Nam alia
infirma sunt.

5 "Et illud intellego, Quirites, omnium ora in me convorsa esse, aequos bonosque favere, quippe mea bene
facta rei publicae procedunt, nobilitatem locum
6 invadendi quaerere. Quo mihi acrius adnitundum est

---

[1] sustineo, *P.*

according to his custom, to bait the nobles, he called an assembly of the people. Then he spoke in the following manner:

LXXXV. "I know, fellow citizens, that it is by very different methods that most men ask for power at your hands and exercise it after it has been secured; that at first they are industrious, humble and modest, but afterwards they lead lives of indolence and arrogance. But the right course, in my opinion, is just the opposite; for by as much as the whole commonwealth is of more value than a consulate or a praetorship, so much greater ought to be the care with which it is governed than that which is shown in seeking those offices. Nor am I unaware how great a task I am taking upon myself in accepting this signal favour of yours. To prepare for war and at the same time to spare the treasury; to force into military service those whom one would not wish to offend; to have a care for everything at home and abroad—to do all this amid envy, enmity and intrigue, is a ruder task, fellow citizens, than you might suppose. Furthermore, if others make mistakes, their ancient nobility, the brave deeds of their ancestors, the power of their kindred and relatives, their throng of clients, are all a very present help. My hopes are all vested in myself and must be maintained by my own worth and integrity; for all other supports are weak.

"This too I understand, fellow citizens, that the eyes of all are turned towards me, that the just and upright favour me because my services are a benefit to our country, while the nobles are looking for a chance to attack me. Wherefore I must strive the more earnestly that you may not be deceived and that

7 uti neque vos capiamini et illi frustra sint. Ita ad hoc
aetatis a pueritia fui, uti omnis labores et pericula
8 consueta habeam. Quae ante vostra benificia gratuito faciebam, ea uti accepta mercede deseram non est
9 consilium, Quirites. Illis difficile est in potestatibus
temperare, qui per ambitionem sese probos simula-
vere; mihi, qui omnem aetatem in optumis artibus
egi, bene facere iam ex consuetudine in naturam
10 vortit. Bellum me gerere cum Iugurtha iussistis,
quam rem nobilitas aegerrume tulit. Quaeso, reputate
cum animis vostris num id mutare melius sit, si quem
ex illo globo nobilitatis ad hoc aut aliud tale negotium
mittatis, hominem veteris prosapiae ac multarum
imaginum et nullius stipendi; scilicet ut in tanta re
ignarus omnium trepidet, festinet, sumat aliquem ex
11 populo monitorem offici sui. Ita plerumque evenit
ut quem vos imperari iussistis, is imperatorem alium
12 quaerat. Atque ego scio, Quirites, qui postquam
consules facti sunt et acta maiorum et Graecorum
militaria praecepta legere coeperint, praeposteri
homines; nam gerere quam fieri tempore posterius
re atque usu prius est.

13 "Comparate nunc, Quirites, cum illorum superbia
me hominem novum. Quae illi audire et[1] legere

_____

[1] aut, *VA, Ah, Or* ; et, *the other mss.*

_____

[1] That is to say, who reverse the natural order of events
or things.

[2] Sallust's brevity again makes his meaning obscure.
With *gerere* and *fieri* we must supply *magistratum*, meaning
"office" with the former and "official" with the latter.
Re atque usu, "in actual practice," is contrasted with

they may be disappointed. From childhood to my present time of life I have so lived that I am familiar with every kind of hardship and danger. As to the efforts, fellow citizens, which before your favours were conferred upon me I made without recompense, it is not my intention to relax them now that they have brought me their reward. To make a moderate use of power is difficult for those who from interested motives have pretended to be virtuous; for me, who have spent my entire life in exemplary conduct, habit has made right living a second nature. You have bidden me conduct the war against Jugurtha, a commission which has sorely vexed the nobles. I pray you, ponder well whether it would be better to change your minds and send on this or any similar errand one of that ring of nobles, a man of ancient lineage and many ancestral portraits—but no campaigns; in order, no doubt, that being wholly in ignorance of the duties of such an office, he might hurry and bustle about and select some one of the common people to act as his adviser. In fact, it very often happens that the man whom you have selected as a commander looks about for someone else to command him. I personally know of men, citizens, who after being elected consuls began for the first time to read the history of our forefathers and the military treatises of the Greeks, preposterous[1] creatures! for though in order of time administration follows election, yet in actual practice it comes first.[2]

"Compare me now, fellow citizens, a 'new man,' with those haughty nobles. What they know from

tempore. Election to an office precedes the administration of the office, but the training which fits one to administer an office _well_ comes before election.

solent, eorum partem vidi, alia egomet gessi; quae
14 illi litteris, ea ego militando didici. Nunc vos existu-
mate facta an dicta pluris sint. Contemnunt novita-
tem meam, ego illorum ignaviam; mihi fortuna, illis
15 probra obiectantur.[1] Quamquam ego naturam unam
et communem omnium existumo, sed fortissumum
16 quemque generosissumum. Ac si iam ex patribus
Albini aut Bestiae quaeri posset, mene an illos ex se
gigni maluerint, quid responsuros creditis, nisi sese
liberos quam optumos voluisse?

17 "Quod si iure me despiciunt, faciant[2] idem maioribus suis, quibus, uti mihi, ex virtute nobilitas coepit.
18 Invident honori meo; ergo invideant labori,[3] innocentiae, periculis etiam meis, quoniam per haec illum
19 cepi. Verum homines corrupti superbia ita aetatem
agunt, quasi vostros honores contemnant; ita hos
20 petunt, quasi honeste vixerint. Ne illi falsi sunt, qui
divorsissumas res pariter expectant, ignaviae volupta-
21 tem et praemia virtutis. Atque etiam, cum apud vos
aut in senatu verba faciunt, pleraque oratione maiores
suos extollunt, eorum fortia facta memorando clari-
22 ores sese putant. Quod contra est. Nam quanto vita
illorum praeclarior, tanto horum socordia flagitiosior.
23 Et profecto ita se res habet: maiorum gloria posteris
quasi lumen est, neque bona neque mala eorum in

---

[1] obiciuntur, VP^2.
[2] faciunt, PA^1; facient, n.
[3] labori innocentiae, VPM^2; l. et inn., $NKHM^1sm$; et l.
inn. A.

hearsay and reading, I have either seen with my own eyes or done with my own hands. What they have learned from books I have learned by service in the field; think now for yourselves whether words or deeds are worth more. They scorn my humble birth, I their worthlessness; I am taunted with my lot in life, they with their infamies. For my part, I believe that all men have one and the same nature, but that the bravest is the best born; and if the fathers of Albinus and Bestia could now be asked whether they would prefer to have me or those men for their descendants, what do you suppose they would reply, if not that they desired to have the best possible children?

"But if they rightly look down on me, let them also look down on their own forefathers, whose nobility began, as did my own, in manly deeds. They begrudge me my office; then let them begrudge my toil, my honesty, even my dangers, since it was through those that I won the office. In fact, these men, spoiled by pride, live as if they scorned your honours, but seek them as if their own lives were honourable. Surely they are deceived when they look forward with equal confidence to things which are worlds apart, the joys of idleness and the rewards of merit. Even when they speak to you or address the senate, their theme is commonly a eulogy of their ancestors; by recounting the exploits of their forefathers they imagine themselves more glorious. The very reverse is true. The more glorious was the life of their ancestors, the more shameful is their own baseness. Assuredly the matter stands thus: the glory of ancestors is, as it were, a light shining upon their posterity, suffering

24 occulto patitur. Huiusce rei ego inopiam fateor,[1]
Quirites, verum, id quod multo praeclarius est, mea-
25 met facta mihi dicere licet. Nunc videte quam iniqui
sint. Quod ex aliena virtute sibi arrogant, id mihi
ex mea non concedunt, scilicet quia imagines non
habeo et quia mihi nova nobilitas est, quam certe
peperisse melius est quam acceptam corrupisse.
26 "Equidem ego non ignoro, si iam mihi respondere
velint, abunde illis facundam et compositam orationem fore. Sed in vostro maxumo benificio cum
omnibus locis me[2] vosque maledictis lacerent, non
placuit reticere, ne quis modestiam in conscientiam
27 duceret. Nam me quidem ex animi mei sententia
nulla oratio laedere potest. Quippe vera necesse est
bene praedicent, falsa vita moresque mei superant.
28 Sed quoniam vostra consilia accusantur, qui mihi
summum honorem et maxumum negotium im-
posuistis, etiam atque etiam reputate num eorum
29 paenitendum sit. Non possum fidei causa imagines
neque triumphos aut consulatus maiorum meorum
ostentare, at, si res postulet, hastas, vexillum,
phaleras, alia militaria dona, praeterea cicatrices
30 adverso corpore. Hae sunt meae imagines, haec
nobilitas, non hereditate relicta, ut illa illis, sed quae
ego meis plurumis laboribus et periculis quaesivi.

[1] fateor, *Vs*; patior, *the other mss.* ("*fortasse recte,*" *Ah*).
[2] meque, *Vl n*; me, *the other mss.* (vos meque, *m*).

---

[1] That is, to a consciousness of my unworthiness for the
office.

neither their virtues nor their faults to be hidden. Of such glory I acknowledge my poverty, fellow citizens; but—and that is far more glorious—I have done deeds of which I have a right to speak. Now see how unfair those men are; what they demand for themselves because of others' merit they do not allow me as the result of my own, no doubt because I have no family portraits and because mine is a new nobility. And yet surely to be its creator is better than to have inherited and disgraced it.

" I am of course well aware that if they should deign to reply to me, their language would be abundantly eloquent and elaborate. But since after the great honour which you have done me they take every opportunity to rend us both with their invectives, I thought it best not to be silent, for fear that someone might interpret my reticence as due to a guilty conscience.[1] In point of fact, I am confident that I can be injured by no speech; for if they tell the truth, they cannot but speak well of me, and falsehood my life and character refutes. But since it is your judgment in giving me your highest office and a most important commission which they criticize, consider again and yet again whether you ought to regret those acts. I cannot, to justify your confidence, display family portraits or the triumphs and consulships of my forefathers; but if occasion requires, I can show spears, a banner, trappings and other military prizes,[2] as well as scars on my breast. These are my portraits, these my patent of nobility, not left me by inheritance as theirs were, but won by my own innumerable efforts and perils.

[2] Common military prizes were the *hasta pura*, or unused spear, and *phalerae*, ornamented discs of metal, which could be attached to a belt or a horse's harness.

31 "Non sunt composita verba mea; parvi[1] id facio.
Ipsa se virtus satis ostendit.   Illis artificio opus est,
32 ut turpia facta oratione tegant.   Neque litteras
Graecas didici; parum placebat eas discere, quippe
33 quae ad virtutem doctoribus nihil profuerant.   At
illa multo optuma rei publicae doctus sum: hostem
ferire, praesidia agitare, nihil metuere nisi turpem
famam, hiemem et aestatem iuxta pati, humi requi-
escere, eodem tempore inopiam et laborem tolerare.
34 His ego praeceptis milites hortabor, neque illos arte
colam, me opulenter, neque gloriam meam laborem
35 illorum faciam.   Hoc est utile, hoc civile imperium.
Namque cum tute per mollitiem[2] agas, exercitum
supplicio cogere, id est dominum, non imperatorem
36 esse.   Haec atque talia[3] maiores vostri faciundo
37 seque remque publicam celebravere.   Quis nobilitas
freta, ipsa dissimilis moribus, nos illorum aemulos
contemnit, et omnis honores non ex merito, sed
quasi debitos a vobis repetit.
38 "Ceterum homines superbissumi procul errant.
Maiores eorum omnia quae licebat illis reliquere:
divitias, imagines, memoriam sui praeclaram; virtutem non reliquere, neque poterant; ea sola neque
39 datur dono neque accipitur.   Sordidum me et in-
cultis moribus aiunt, quia parum scite convivium
exorno neque histrionem ullum neque pluris preti

---

[1] parvi, *VP*[2], *Nonius*, p. 257. 35 M (391. 35 L); parum, *the
other mss.*   [2] mollitiam, *VTn.*
[3] alia talia *Fabri, Ah*; alia, *VPCB*; talia, *the other
mss., Or.*

"My words are not well chosen; I care little for that. Merit shows well enough in itself. It is they who have need of art, to gloss over their shameful acts with specious words. Nor have I studied Grecian letters. I did not greatly care to become acquainted with them, since they had not taught their teachers virtue. But I have learned by far the most important lesson for my country's good—to strike down the foe, to keep watch and ward, to fear nothing save ill repute, to endure heat and cold alike, to sleep on the ground, to bear privation and fatigue at the same time. It is with these lessons that I shall encourage my soldiers; I shall not treat them stingily and myself lavishly, nor win my own glory at the price of their toil. Such leadership is helpful, such leadership is democratic [1]; for to live in luxury oneself but control one's army by punishments is to be a master of slaves, not a commander. It was by conduct like this that your forefathers made themselves and their country famous; but the nobles, relying upon such ancestors though themselves of very different character, despise us who emulate the men of old, and claim from you all honours, not from desert, but as a debt.

"But those most arrogant of men are greatly in error. Their ancestors have left them all that they could—riches, portrait busts, their own illustrious memory; virtue they have not left them, nor could they have done so; that alone is neither bestowed nor received as a gift. They say that I am common and of rude manners, because I cannot give an elegant dinner and because I pay no actor or cook

[1] *cf.* Suetonius, *Claud.* i. 4.

cocum quam vilicum habeo. Quae mihi lubet con-
40 fiteri, Quirites. Nam ex parente meo et ex aliis
sanctis viris ita accepi: munditias mulieribus, laborem viris convenire, omnibusque bonis oportere plus
gloriae quam divitiarum esse; arma, non supellec-
tilem decori esse.

41 "Quin ergo quod iuvat, quod carum aestumant, id
semper faciant: ament, potent; ubi adulescentiam
habuere ibi senectutem agant, in conviviis, dediti
ventri et turpissumae parti corporis. Sudorem, pul-
verem et alia talia relinquant nobis, quibus illa
42 epulis iucundiora sunt. Verum non ita est. Nam
ubi se flagitiis dedecoravere turpissumi viri, bonorum
43 praemia ereptum eunt. Ita iniustissume luxuria et
ignavia pessumae artes, illis qui coluere eas nihil
officiunt, rei publicae innoxiae cladi sunt.

44 "Nunc quoniam illis, quantum mei mores, non illorum flagitia poscebant, respondi, pauca de re publica
45 loquar. Primum omnium de Numidia bonum habete
animum, Quirites. Nam quae ad hoc tempus Iugurtham tutata sunt, omnia removistis, avaritiam, im-
peritiam atque superbiam. Deinde exercitus ibi est
locorum sciens, sed mehercule magis strenuus quam
46 felix. Nam magna pars eius avaritia aut temeritate
47 ducum attrita est. Quam ob rem vos, quibus militaris aetas est, adnitimini mecum et capessite rem
publicam neque quemquam ex calamitate aliorum
aut imperatorum superbia metus ceperit. Egomet

---

[1] "He feels it an injury to his own character even to have
to speak of their offences." Summers.

higher wages than I do my overseer. This I gladly admit, fellow citizens; for I learned from my father and other righteous men that elegance is proper to women but toil to men, that all the virtuous ought to have more fame than riches, and that arms and not furniture confer honour.

"Well then, let them continue to do what pleases them and what they hold dear; let them make love and drink; let them pass their old age where they have spent their youth, in banquets, slaves to their belly and the most shameful parts of their body. Sweat, dust, and all such things let them leave to us, to whom they are sweeter than feasts. But they will not; for when those most shameless of men have disgraced themselves by their crimes, they come to rob the virtuous of their rewards. Thus, most unjustly, their luxury and sloth, the most abominable of faults, in no wise injure those who practise them, but are the ruin of their blameless country.

"Now that I have replied to them to the extent that my character—but not their crimes—demanded[1] I shall say a few words about our country. First of all, be of good cheer as to Numidia, citizens; for you have put away everything which up to this time has protected Jugurtha—avarice, incompetence, and arrogance. Furthermore, there is an army in Africa familiar with the country, but by heaven! more valiant than fortunate; for a great part of it has perished through the greed or rashness of its leaders. Therefore do you, who are of military age, join your efforts with mine and serve your country, and let no one feel fear because of disasters to others or the arrogance of generals. I, Marius, shall be

in agmine aut in proelio consultor idem et socius
periculi vobiscum adero, meque vosque in omnibus
48 rebus iuxta geram. Et profecto dis iuvantibus omnia
matura sunt, victoria, praeda, laus. Quae si dubia
aut procul essent, tamen omnis bonos rei publicae
49 subvenire decebat. Etenim nemo ignavia immortalis
factus est neque quisquam parens liberis uti aeterni
forent optavit, magis uti boni honestique vitam exi-
50 gerent. Plura dicerem, Quirites, si timidis virtutem
verba adderent. Nam strenuis abunde dictum
puto."

LXXXVI. Huiuscemodi oratione habita Marius,
postquam plebis animos arrectos videt, propere commeatu, stipendio, armis, aliisque utilibus navis onerat;
2 cum his A. Manlium legatum proficisci iubet. Ipse
interea milites scribere, non more maiorum neque ex
classibus, sed uti cuiusque lubido erat, capite censos
3 plerosque. Id factum alii inopia bonorum, alii per
ambitionem consulis memorabant, quod ab eo genere
celebratus auctusque erat, et homini potentiam quae-
renti egentissumus quisque opportunissumus, cui
neque sua cara, quippe quae nulla sunt, et omnia
4 cum pretio honesta videntur. Igitur Marius, cum
aliquanto maiore numero quam decretum erat in
Africam profectus, paucis diebus Uticam advehitur.

---

[1] That is, the classes said to have been established by
Servius Tullius, based upon property qualifications. See
Livy 1. 43.
[2] The *capite censi* were those below the lowest Servian

with you on the march and in battle, at once your counsellor and the companion of your dangers, and I shall treat myself and you alike in all respects. And surely with the help of the gods everything is ripe for us—victory, spoils, glory; but even though these were uncertain or remote, yet all good men ought to fly to the aid of their fatherland. Truly, no one ever became immortal through cowardice, and no parent would wish for his children that they might live forever, but rather that their lives might be noble and honoured. I would say more, citizens, if words could make cowards brave. For the resolute I think I have spoken abundantly."

LXXXVI. After Marius had made a speech in these terms and saw that it had fired the spirits of the commons, he made haste to load his ships with provisions, money, arms, and other necessities, with which he bade his lieutenant Aulus Manlius set sail. He himself in the meantime enrolled soldiers, not according to the classes[1] in the manner of our forefathers, but allowing anyone to volunteer, for the most part the proletariat.[2] Some say that he did this through lack of good men, others because of a desire to curry favour, since that class had given him honour and rank. As a matter of fact, to one who aspires to power the poorest man is the most helpful, since he has no regard for his property, having none, and considers anything honourable for which he receives pay. The result was that Marius set sail for Africa with a considerably greater contingent than had been authorized. A few days later he arrived at Utica, where the army was handed over to him by the

class, without property and exempt from military service. They were entered on the censor's list only as regarded their persons (*caput*).

5 Exercitus **ei** traditur a P. Rutilio legato. Nam
Metellus conspectum Mari fugerat, ne videret ea
quae audita animus tolerare nequiverat.

LXXXVII. Sed consul expletis legionibus cohorti-
busque auxiliariis in agrum fertilem et praeda onus-
tum proficiscitur, omnia ibi capta militibus donat,
dein castella et oppida natura et viris parum munita
aggreditur, proelia multa, ceterum levia, alia[1] aliis
2 locis facere. Interim novi milites sine metu pugnae
adesse, videre fugientis capi aut occidi, fortissumum
quemque tutissumum, armis libertatem patriam
parentesque et alia omnia tegi, gloriam atque divi-
3 tias quaeri. Sic brevi spatio novi veteresque coaluere
et virtus omnium aequalis facta.

4 At reges ubi de adventu Mari cognoverunt, divorsi
in locos difficilis abeunt. Ita Iugurthae placuerat
speranti mox effusos hostis invadi posse, Romanos
sicuti plerosque remoto metu laxius licentiusque
futuros.

LXXXVIII. Metellus interea Romam profectus
contra spem suam laetissumis animis accipitur,[2]
plebi patribusque, postquam invidia decesserat, iuxta
2 carus. Sed Marius impigre prudenterque suorum et
hostium res pariter attendere, cognoscere quid boni

---

[1] levia alia, *Ciacconius* ; alia levia, *mss.*
[2] accipitur, $P^1A^1CN\,l$; *the other mss. have* excipitur.

---

[1] *cf.* Cat. lvi. 2.

second in command, Publius Rutilius. For Metellus had avoided meeting Marius, that he might not see what he had been unable even to hear of with composure.

LXXXVII. The consul, after having filled up[1] the ranks of the legions and the cohorts of auxiliaries, marched into a district which was fertile and rich in booty. There he gave to the soldiers everything that was taken, and then attacked some fortresses and towns not well defended by nature or by garrisons, fighting many battles, but slight ones and in various places. Meanwhile the raw soldiers learned to enter battle fearlessly and saw that those who ran away were either taken or slain, while the bravest were the safest; they realized that it was by arms that liberty, country, parents, and all else were protected, and glory and riches won. Thus in a short time the old and the new soldiers were assimilated and all became equally courageous.

But the two kings, on hearing of the arrival of Marius, withdrew each to a different place, difficult of access. This was a device of Jugurtha's, who hoped that the enemy could presently be divided and attacked, and that the Romans, like most soldiers, would have less restraint and discipline when they feared no danger.

LXXXVIII. Metellus meanwhile returned to Rome, where, contrary to his expectation, he was received with great rejoicing; for the feeling against him had died out and he found himself popular with people and senators alike. But Marius watched the conduct of his own men and of the enemy alike untiringly and sagaciously, learned what was to the advantage or disadvantage of both sides,

355

utrisque aut contra esset, explorare itinera regum,
consilia et insidias eorum antevenire, nihil apud se
3 remissum neque apud illos tutum pati. Itaque et
Gaetulos et Iugurtham ex sociis nostris praedas
agentis saepe aggressus in itinere fuderat, ipsumque
regem haud procul ab oppido Cirta armis exuerat.
4 Quae postquam gloriosa modo neque belli patrandi
cognovit, statuit urbis, quae viris aut loco pro hostibus et advorsum se opportunissumae erant, singulas
circumvenire; ita Iugurtham aut praesidiis nudatum,
5 si ea pateretur, aut proelio certaturum. Nam Bocchus nuntios ad eum saepe miserat, velle populi
6 Romani amicitiam, ne quid ab se hostile timeret. Id
simulaveritne, quo improvisus gravior accideret, an
mobilitate ingeni pacem atque bellum mutare solitus, parum exploratum est.

LXXXIX. Sed consul, uti statuerat, oppida castel-
laque munita adire, partim vi, alia metu aut praemia
2 ostentando avortere ab hostibus. Ac primo medio-
cria gerebat, existumans Iugurtham ob suos tutandos
3 in manus venturum. Sed ubi illum procul abesse
et aliis negotiis intentum accepit, maiora et magis
aspera aggredi tempus visum est.
4 Erat inter ingentis solitudines oppidum magnum
atque valens nomine Capsa, cuius conditor Hercules
Libys memorabatur. Eius cives apud Iugurtham

---

[1] That is, his troops threw away their arms and fled in
disorder.

observed the movements of the kings and anticipated
their plans and plots, allowing his soldiers no relaxation and the enemy no security. He made frequent
attacks on Jugurtha and the Gaetulians while they
were plundering our allies, routing them and compel-
ling the king himself to throw away his arms[1] not far
from the town of Cirta. But when he found that
such exploits merely brought him glory, but did not
tend to finish the war, he decided to invest one after
the other the cities which by reason of their garrison
or their situation were most serviceable to the enemy
and most detrimental to his own success. In that way
he thought that Jugurtha would either be deprived
of his defences, if he made no opposition, or would be
forced to fight. As for Bocchus, he had sent Marius
frequent messengers, saying that he desired the
friendship of the Roman people and bidding Marius
to fear no hostile act on his part. Whether he
feigned this, in order that he might strike an unexpected, and therefore a heavier blow, or from natural
instability of character was in the habit of wavering
between peace and war, is not altogether clear.

LXXXIX. But the consul, as he had planned, appeared before the fortified towns and strongholds,
and in some cases by force, in others by intimidation
or bribery, took them from the enemy. At first his
attempts were modest, since he thought that Jugurtha
would fight in defence of his subjects. But when he
learned that the king was far off and intent upon
other matters, he thought the time ripe for undertaking greater and harder tasks.

There was in the midst of a great desert a large
and strong town called Capsa, whose reputed founder
was the Libyan Hercules. Under Jugurtha's rule its

immunes, levi imperio et ob ea fidelissumi habebantur, muniti advorsum hostis non moenibus modo et
armis atque viris, verum etiam multo magis locorum
5 asperitate. Nam praeter oppido propinqua alia omnia vasta, inculta, egentia aquae, infesta serpentibus,
quarum vis sicuti omnium ferarum inopia cibi acrior.
Ad hoc natura serpentium ipsa perniciosa siti magis
6 quam alia re accenditur. Eius potiundi Marium
maxuma cupido invaserat, cum propter usum belli,
tum quia res aspera videbatur et Metellus oppidum
Thalam magna gloria ceperat, haud dissimiliter situm
munitumque, nisi quod apud Thalam non longe a
moenibus aliquot fontes erant, Capsenses una modo
atque ea intra oppidum iugi aqua, cetera pluvia ute-
7 bantur. Id ibique et[1] in omni Africa, quae procul a
mari incultius agebat,[2] eo facilius tolerabatur, quia
Numidae plerumque lacte et ferina corne vesce-
bantur et neque salem neque alia irritamenta gulae[3]
quaerebant; cibus illis advorsum[4] famem atque sitim,
non lubidini neque luxuriae erat.

XC. Igitur consul, omnibus exploratis, credo dis
fretus—nam contra tantas difficultates consilio satis
providere non poterat, quippe etiam frumenti inopia
temptabatur, quia Numidiae pabulo pecoris magis

---

[1] id ibique et, *CB and m²of AKHMD m* ; id ubique et, *the
other mss.* ; idque ibi ut, *Jordan.*

[2] quae . . . agebat, *mss.*; qua . . . agebatur, *Linker*; qua
. . . agebant, *Jordan.*

[3] gulae irritamenta, *Prisc.* ii. 147. 5 κ.

[4] adversus, *PH* ; advorsus, *Or.*

citizens were free from tribute and mildly treated, and were therefore counted upon as most loyal. They were protected from their enemies not only by walls and armed men, but still more by their inaccessible position; for except in the neighbourhood of the town the whole country was desolate, wild, without water, and infested by serpents, whose fierceness, like that of all wild animals, was made greater by scarcity of food. Moreover, the venom of serpents, which is always deadly, is especially aggravated by thirst. Marius was inspired with a great desire of taking this town, not only from its military importance, but also because the undertaking seemed hazardous and because Metellus had gained great renown by the capture of Thala. For Thala was similar in its situation and defences, except that there were some springs not far from the town, whereas the people of Capsa had but one flowing spring, which was within the walls, otherwise depending upon rain water. This condition was the more readily endured there and in all the less civilized part of Africa [1] remote from the sea, since the Numidians lived for the most part on milk and game, making no use of salt and other whets to the appetite; for in their opinion the purpose of food was to relieve hunger and thirst, not to minister to caprice and luxury.

XC. The consul then, after reconnoitring everywhere, must have put his trust in the gods; for against such great difficulties he could not make sufficient provision by his own wisdom. Indeed, he was even threatened with scarcity of grain, both because the Numidians give more attention to grazing

---

[1] *Quae*, referring to *Africa*, is used for the people; *cf.* the use of *civitas* in chap. lv.

quam arvo student et quodcumque natum fuerat
iussu regis in loca munita contulerant, ager autem
aridus et frugum vacuos ea tempestate, nam aestatis
extremum erat—tamen pro rei copia satis provi-
2 denter exornat : pecus omne quod superioribus diebus praedae fuerat equitibus auxiliariis agundum
attribuit, A. Manlium legatum cum cohortibus
expeditis ad oppidum Laris, ubi stipendium et commeatum locaverat, ire iubet dicitque se praedabun-
3 dum post paucos dies eodem venturum. Sic incepto
suo occultato pergit ad flumen Tanain.

XCI. Ceterum in itinere cotidie pecus exercitui
per centurias, item turmas aequaliter distribuerat et
ex coriis utres uti fierent curabat, simul inopiam
frumenti lenire et ignaris omnibus parare, quae mox
usui forent. Denique sexto die, cum ad flumen ven-
2 tum est, maxuma vis utrium effecta. Ibi castris levi
munimento positis, milites cibum capere atque uti
simul cum occasu solis egrederentur paratos esse
iubet; omnibus sarcinis abiectis aqua modo seque et
3 iumenta onerare. Dein, postquam tempus visum,
castris egreditur noctemque totam itinere facto consedit. Idem proxuma facit, dein tertia multo ante
lucis adventum pervenit in locum tumulosum ab
Capsa non amplius duum milium intervallo, ibique
quam occultissume potest cum omnibus copiis ope-

than to agriculture, and because such grain as there
was had been transported by the king's command to
fortified places. Moreover, the fields were dry and
stripped of their crops at that season, for it was the
end of summer. In spite of these difficulties, Marius
made the best possible provision under the circumstances. He gave all the cattle which had been
captured on previous days to the auxiliary cavalry to
drive, and directed his lieutenant Aulus Manlius to
go with the light-armed cohorts to the town of Laris,
where he had deposited his money and supplies,
telling him that a few days later he would himself
come to the same place to forage. Having thus
concealed his real purpose, he proceeded to the
river Tanaïs.

XCI. Now every day during the march Marius had
distributed cattle equally among the centuries and
the divisions of cavalry, taking care that bottles for
water should be made from the hides; thus at the
same time he made good the lack of grain and
without revealing his purpose provided something
which was soon to be useful. When they finally
reached the river on the sixth day, a great quantity
of bottles had been prepared. Having pitched his
camp by the river and fortified it slightly, he ordered
the soldiers to eat their dinners and be ready to
march at sunset, throwing aside all their baggage and
loading themselves and the pack-animals with water
only. Then, when he thought the proper time had
come, he left the camp and marched all night before
halting. He did the same thing the next night, and
on the third night long before daybreak he came to
a hilly tract, distant not more than two miles from
Capsa. There he waited with all his forces, keeping

4 ritur. Sed ubi dies coepit et Numidae nihil hostile metuentes multi oppido egressi, **repente omnem equitatum et cum eis velocissumos pedites cursu tendere ad Capsam et portas obsidere iubet. Deinde ipse intentus propere sequi neque milites praedari**
5 sinere. Quae postquam oppidani cognovere, res trepidae, metus ingens, malum improvisum, **ad hoc** pars civium extra moenia in hostium potestate co-
6 egere uti deditionem facerent. Ceterum oppidum incensum, Numidae puberes interfecti, alii omnes
7 venumdati, praeda militibus divisa. Id facinus contra ius belli non avaritia neque scelere consulis admissum, sed quia locus Iugurthae opportunus, nobis aditu difficilis, genus hominum mobile, infidum, ante neque benificio neque metu coercitum.

XCII. Postquam tantam rem peregit [1] Marius sine ullo suorum incommodo, magnus et clarus antea, maior
2 atque clarior haberi coepit. Omnia non bene consulta in virtutem trahebantur, milites modesto imperio habiti simul et locupletes ad caelum ferre, Numidae magis quam mortalem timere, postremo omnes, socii atque hostes, credere illi aut mentem divinam esse aut deorum nutu cuncta portendi.

[1] peregit, *A²CBn* ; *the other mss. omit.*

---

[1] Summers translates *modesto imperio* " strictly," comparing vii. 4. The two passages, however, are not parallel, since *modesto* is used of the commander, *modestissume* of the subordinate.

as much in concealment as possible. When day dawned and the Numidians, who had no fear of an attack, sallied forth in large numbers from the town, he suddenly ordered all the cavalry and with them the swiftest of the foot-soldiers to hasten at the double-quick to Capsa and beset the gates. Then he himself quickly followed, keeping on the alert and not allowing his soldiers to plunder. When the townspeople perceived what was going on, their disorder, their great panic, their unexpected plight and the fact that a part of their fellow citizens were outside the walls and in the power of the enemy, compelled them to surrender. But nevertheless the town was burned and the adult Numidians put to the sword; all the rest were sold and the proceeds divided among the soldiers. The consul was guilty of this violation of the laws of war, not because of avarice or cruelty, but because the place was of advantage to Jugurtha and difficult of access for us, while the people were fickle and untrustworthy and had previously shown themselves amenable neither to kindness nor to fear.

XCII. Marius was already great and famous, but after he had won this important success without loss to his own men he began to be regarded as still greater and more famous. All his rash acts, even when ill-advised, were regarded as proofs of his ability. The soldiers, who were kept under mild discipline [1] and at the same time enriched, extolled him to the skies, the Numidians feared him as if he were more than mortal; all, in short, friends and enemies alike, believed that he either possessed divine insight or that everything was revealed to him by the favour of the gods.

3   Sed consul, ubi ea res bene evenit, ad alia oppida pergit, pauca repugnantibus Numidis capit, plura deserta[1] propter Capsensium miserias igni corrumpit ; luctu atque caede omnia complentur.

4 Denique, multis locis potitus ac plerisque exercitu incruento, aliam rem aggreditur non eadem asperitate qua Capsensium, ceterum haud secus difficilem.

5   Namque haud longe a flumine Muluccha, quod Iugurthae Bocchique regnum diiungebat, erat inter ceteram planitiem mons saxeus mediocri castello satis patens, in immensum editus uno perangusto aditu relicto ; nam omnis natura velut opere atque

6 consulto praeceps. Quem locum Marius, quod ibi regis thesauri erant, summa vi capere intendit. Sed

7 ea res forte quam consilio melius gesta. Nam castello virorum atque armorum satis et magna vis frumenti[2] et fons aquae ; aggeribus turribusque et aliis[3] machinationibus locus importunus, iter castellanorum angustum admodum, utrimque praecisum.

8 Vineae cum ingenti periculo frustra agebantur. Nam cum eae paulo processerant, igni aut lapidibus

9 corrumpebantur, milites neque pro opere consistere propter iniquitatem loci neque inter vineas sine periculo administrare ; optumus quisque cadere aut sauciari, ceteris metus augeri.

   XCIII. At Marius, multis diebus et laboribus consumptis, anxius trahere cum animo suo omitteretne

---

[1] deserta, *found only in a few later integri.*
[2] magna vis et frumenti, *mss., Ah, Or* ; et m. v. f., *Jordan.*
[3] aliis, *Ys n* (*cf.* xxi. 3) ; altis, *X l* ; talibus, *m.*

After his success at Capsa the consul proceeded to other towns. A few he took in spite of the resistance of the Numidians, but the greater number were abandoned through dread of the wretched fate of Capsa, and burned; all Numidia was filled with bloodshed and lamentation. Finally, after capturing many places, for the most part without loss of life, he essayed another feat, not involving the same danger as the taking of Capsa, but no less difficult.

Not far from the river Muluccha, which separated the realms of Jugurtha and Bocchus, there was in the midst of a plain a rocky hill which was broad enough for a fortress of moderate size and very high, and accessible only by one narrow path; for the whole place was naturally steep, as if it had been made so by art and design. This place Marius aimed to take by a supreme effort, because it held the king's treasures, but in this case his success was the result of chance rather than of skill; for the fortress was well supplied with arms and men, besides having an abundance of grain and a spring of water. The situation was impracticable for mounds, towers, and other siege works, while the path to the fortifications was extremely narrow and had precipices on either side. Mantlets were pushed forward with extreme danger and to no purpose; for when they had gone but a short distance they were ruined by fire or by stones. The soldiers could not keep their footing before the works because of the steepness of the hill nor operate within the mantlets without peril; the bravest of them were killed or wounded, and the rest gradually lost courage.

XCIII. After Marius had spent many days in great labour, he was anxiously considering whether

inceptum, quoniam frustra erat, an fortunam opperi-
2 retur, qua saepe prospere usus fuerat. Quae cum
multos dies noctisque aestuans agitaret, forte quidam
Ligus ex cohortibus auxiliariis miles gregarius, castris
aquatum egressus haud procul ab latere castelli quod
avorsum proeliantibus erat, animum advortit inter
saxa repentis cocleas; quarum cum unam atque alteram, dein plures peteret, studio legundi paulatim
3 prope ad summum montis egressus est. Ubi postquam
solitudinem intellexit, more ingeni humani cupido
4 difficilia faciundi animum adorta. Et forte in eo
loco grandis ilex coaluerat inter saxa, paulum modo
prona, deinde inflexa atque aucta in altitudinem, quo
cuncta gignentium natura fert. Cuius ramis modo,
modo eminentibus saxis nisus, Ligus in castelli
planitiem pervenit, quod cuncti Numidae intenti
5 proeliantibus aderant. Exploratis omnibus quae mox
usui fore ducebat, eadem regreditur non temere, uti
adscenderat, sed temptans omnia et circumspiciens.
6 Itaque Marium propere adit, acta edocet, hortatur
ab ea parte qua ipse adscenderat castellum temptet,
pollicetur sese itineris periculique ducem.
7 Marius cum Ligure promissa eius cognitum ex
praesentibus misit, quorum uti cuiusque ingenium
erat, ita rem difficilem aut facilem nuntiavere. Con-
8 sulis animus tamen paulum arrectus. Itaque ex
copia tubicinum et cornicinum numero quinque quam

---

[1] On which the fortress was situated.

he should abandon the attempt as fruitless or await
the favour of fortune, which he had so often enjoyed.
For many days and nights he had been a prey to
indecision, when it chanced that a Ligurian, a
common soldier of the auxiliary cohorts, who had
left the camp to fetch water, noticed near the side
of the fortress which was farthest from the besiegers
some snails creeping about among the rocks. Picking
up one or two of these and then looking for more, in
his eagerness to gather them he gradually made his
way almost to the top of the mountain.[1] When he
found that he was alone there, the love of overcoming
difficulties which is natural to mankind seized him.
It happened that a great oak tree had grown up
there among the rocks; it bent downward for a little
way, then turned and grew upward, as is the nature
of all plants. With the help, now of the branches of
this tree and now of projecting rocks, the Ligurian
mounted to the plateau about the fortress, while all
the Numidians were intent upon the combatants.
After examining everything that he thought would be
useful later, he returned by the same way, not
heedlessly, as he had gone up, but testing and
observing everything. Then he hastened to Marius,
told him what he had done, and urged him to make
an attempt on the fortress at the point where he
himself had mounted, offering himself as a guide for
the ascent and leader in the dangerous undertaking.

Marius thereupon ordered some of his staff to go
with the Ligurian and look into his proposal, and each
of them, according to his temperament, pronounced
the attempt difficult or easy; on the whole, however,
the consul was somewhat encouraged. Accordingly,
out of all his horn-blowers and trumpeters he chose

velocissumos delegit et cum eis praesidio qui forent
quattuor centuriones,[1] omnisque Liguri parere iubet
et ei negotio proxumum diem constituit.

XCIV. Sed ubi ex praecepto tempus visum, paratis
compositisque omnibus ad locum pergit. Ceterum
illi, qui escensuri[2] erant, praedocti ab duce arma
ornatumque mutaverant, capite atque pedibus nudis,
uti prospectus nisusque per saxa facilius foret; super
terga gladii et scuta, verum ea Numidica ex coriis,
ponderis gratia simul et offensa quo levius streperent.
2 Igitur praegrediens Ligus saxa et si quae vetustae[3]
radices eminebant laqueis vinciebat, quibus allevati
milites facilius escenderent,[4] interdum timidos insolentia itineris levare manu, ubi paulo asperior
ascensus erat singulos prae[5] se inermos mittere,
deinde ipse cum illorum armis sequi, quae dubia nisui
videbantur potissumus temptare ac saepius eadem
ascendens descendensque, dein statim digrediens,
3 ceteris audaciam addere. Igitur diu multumque
fatigati tandem in castellum perveniunt, desertum
ab ea parte, quod omnes sicut aliis diebus advorsum
hostis aderant.

[1] centuriones, *mss.*; centuriatos, *Eussner.*
[2] escensuri erant, *Carrio*; ascensuri erant, $A^1T^2F^2$; e centuriis erant, P ; centuriis praeerant, $A^2CB\ n$; et centuriae
praeerant, Ys ; centuriones erant, *l.*
[3] vetustae, P ; vetustate, *the other mss., Ah, Or.*
[4] escenderent, PAN^1; ascenderent, *the other mss.*
[5] prae, KTs ; pro, P^1; per, *the other mss.*

the five who were most agile, and with them four centurions [1] as a protection. He put them all under command of the Ligurian and set the next day for the attempt.

XCIV. Now, when the Ligurian thought the appointed [2] time had come, he made all his preparations and went to the spot. Those who were going to make the ascent, following the previous instructions of their guide had changed their arms and accoutrements, baring their heads and feet so as to be able to see better and climb among the rocks more easily. They carried their swords and shields on their backs, but took Numidian shields of hide, because they were lighter and would make less noise when struck. Then the Ligurian led the way, fastening ropes to the rocks or to old projecting roots, in order that with such help the soldiers might more easily make the ascent. Sometimes he lent a hand to those whom the unusual nature of the route alarmed, and where the ascent was unusually difficult, he would send men ahead one by one unarmed and then follow himself, bringing the arms. He was first to try the places which it seemed dangerous to attempt, and by often climbing up and returning the same way, and then at once stepping aside, he lent courage to the rest. In this way, after a long time and great exertion, they at last reached the fortress, which was deserted at that point because all the men, as on other days, were face to face with the enemy.

---

[1] The reading and the sense are uncertain ; see the critical notes. It is obvious from the account that a certain number of soldiers accompanied the centurions.

[2] Namely, the time which he had arranged with Marius.

Marius ubi ex nuntiis quae Ligus egerat cognovit, quamquam toto die intentos proelio Numidas habuerat, tum vero cohortatus milites et ipse extra vineas egressus, testudine acta succedere et simul hostem tormentis sagittariisque et funditoribus eminus ter-

4 rere. At Numidae, saepe antea vineis Romanorum subvorsis item incensis, non castelli moenibus sese tutabantur, sed pro muro dies noctisque agitare, male dicere Romanis ac Mario vecordiam obiectare, militibus nostris Iugurthae servitium minari, secundis rebus feroces esse.

5 Interim omnibus Romanis hostibusque proelio intentis, magna utrimque vi pro gloria atque imperio his, illis pro salute certantibus, repente a tergo signa canere. Ac primo mulieres et pueri, qui visum processerant, fugere, deinde uti quisque muro proxu-

6 mus erat, postremo cuncti armati inermesque. Quod ubi accidit, eo acrius Romani instare, fundere ac plerosque tantum modo sauciare, dein super occisorum corpora vadere, avidi gloriae certantes murum petere neque quemquam omnium praeda morari. Sic forte correcta Mari temeritas gloriam ex culpa invenit.

XCV. Ceterum dum ea res geritur, L. Sulla quaestor cum magno equitatu in castra venit, quos

---

1 In this formation the soldiers held their shields above their heads in such a way that they overlapped and made a continuous covering.

Marius had devoted the whole day to keeping the Numidians intent upon the battle; but as soon as he heard that the Ligurian had accomplished his purpose, he began to urge on his soldiers. He himself went outside the mantlets, formed the tortoise-shed,[1] and advanced to the wall, at the same time trying to terrify the enemy at long range with artillery, archers and slingers. But the Numidians, since they had often before overturned the mantlets of the enemy and set fire to them, no longer protected themselves within the walls of the fortress, but spent day and night outside, reviling the Romans and taunting Marius with madness. Emboldened by their successes, they threatened our soldiers with slavery at the hands of Jugurtha.

In the meantime, while all the Romans and all the enemy were intent upon the conflict, and both sides were exerting themselves to the utmost, the one for glory and dominion and the other for safety, suddenly the trumpets sounded in the rear of the foe. Then the women and children, who had come out to look on, were the first to flee, followed by those who were nearest the wall, and finally by all, armed and unarmed alike. Upon this the Romans pressed on with greater vigour, routing the enemy, but for the most part only wounding them. Then they rushed on over the bodies of the slain, eager for glory and each striving to be first to reach the wall; not one stayed to plunder. Thus Marius's rashness was made good by fortune and he gained glory through an error in judgment.

XCV. During the attack on the fortress the quaestor Lucius Sulla arrived in camp with a large force of horsemen which he had mustered from Latium and

uti ex Latio et a sociis cogeret Romae relictus erat.
2 Sed quoniam nos tanti viri res admonuit, idoneum
visum est de natura cultuque eius paucis dicere.
Neque enim alio loco de Sullae rebus dicturi sumus
et L. Sisenna, optume et diligentissume omnium qui
eas res dixere persecutus, parum mihi libero ore
locutus videtur.

3 Igitur Sulla gentis patriciae nobilis fuit, familia
prope iam extincta maiorum ignavia, litteris Graecis
et Latinis iuxta atque doctissume[1] eruditus, animo
ingenti, cupidus voluptatum sed gloriae cupidior, otio
luxurioso esse; tamen ab negotiis numquam voluptas
remorata, nisi quod de uxore potuit honestius consuli;
facundus, callidus, et amicitia facilis; ad simulanda
negotia altitudo ingeni incredibilis; multarum rerum
4 ac maxume pecuniae largitor. Atque illi, felicissumo
omnium ante civilem victoriam, numquam super
industriam fortuna fuit, multique dubitavere fortior
an felicior esset. Nam postea quae fecerit, incertum
habeo pudeat an pigeat magis disserere.

XCVI. Igitur Sulla, uti supra dictum est, postquam in Africam atque in castra Mari cum equitatu
venit, rudis antea et ignarus belli, sollertissumus
2 omnium in paucis tempestatibus factus est. Ad hoc

---

[1] atque doctissume, *mss.*; *omitted by Ah (Vogel).*

---

[1] A younger contemporary of Sulla and an adherent of the
aristocratic party. He wrote a history in at least twenty-
three books, from the beginning of the Social War to the end
of the Civil War of Marius and Sulla, preceded by a brief
sketch of the early history of Rome.

the allies, having been left in Rome for that purpose. And since the event has brought that great man to our attention, it seems fitting to say a few words about his life and character; for we shall not speak elsewhere of Sulla's affairs, and Lucius Sisenna,[1] whose account of him is altogether the best and most careful, has not, in my opinion spoken with sufficient frankness.

Sulla, then, was a noble of patrician descent, of a family almost reduced to obscurity through the degeneracy of his ancestors. He was well versed alike in Grecian and Roman letters, of remarkable mental power,[2] devoted to pleasure but more devoted to glory. In his leisure hours he lived extravagantly, yet pleasure never interfered with his duties, except that his conduct as a husband might have been more honourable. He was eloquent, clever, and quick to make friends. He had a mind deep beyond belief in its power of disguising his purposes, and was generous with many things, especially with money. Before his victory in the civil war he was the most fortunate of all men, but his fortune was never greater than his deserts, and many have hesitated to say whether his bravery or his good luck was the greater. As to what he did later, I know not if one should speak of it rather with shame or with sorrow.

XCVI. Now Sulla, as I have already said, after he came with his cavalry to Africa and the camp of Marius, although he was without previous experience and untrained in war, soon became the best soldier in the whole army. Moreover, he was

---

[2] *cf.* Tac. *Ann.* 1. 69. 2; Sall. *Hist.* 3. 91 *Maur., ingens virium atque animi* (of Mithridates).

milites benigne appellare, multis rogantibus, aliis per
se ipse dare benificia, invitus accipere, sed ea properantius quam aes mutuum reddere, ipse ab nullo
repetere, magis id laborare ut illi quam plurumi
3 deberent; ioca atque seria cum humillumis agere, in
operibus, in agmine atque ad vigilias multus adesse
neque interim, quod prava ambitio solet, consulis aut
cuiusquam boni famam laedere, tantum modo neque
consilio neque manu priorem alium pati, plerosque
antevenire. Quibus rebus et artibus brevi Mario
militibusque carissumus factus.

XCVII. At Iugurtha, postquam oppidum Capsam
aliosque locos munitos et sibi utilis, simul et magnam
pecuniam amiserat, ad Bocchum nuntios misit, quam
primum in Numidiam copias adduceret, proeli faciundi
2 tempus adesse. Quem ubi cunctari accepit et
dubium belli atque pacis rationes trahere, rursus uti
antea proxumos eius donis corrupit, ipsique Mauro
pollicetur Numidiae partem tertiam, si aut Romani
Africa expulsi aut integris suis finibus bellum con-
3 positum foret. Eo praemio illectus Bocchus cum
magna multitudine Iugurtham accedit. Ita amborum
exercitu coniuncto, Marium iam in hiberna proficiscentem vix decuma parte die reliqua invadunt, rati
noctem, quae iam aderat, et victis sibi munimento

---

[1] *cf.* Ovid, *Met.* 3. 319, *agitasse iocos. Ioca atque seria*
is formulaic; see Cic. *Fin.* 2. 26. 85, *quicum ioca seria, ut
dicitur.*

courteous in his language to the soldiers, granted
favours to many at their request and to others of
his own accord, unwilling himself to accept favours
and paying them more promptly than a debt of
money. He himself never asked for payment, but
rather strove to have as many men as possible in
his debt. He talked in jest or earnest[1] with the
humblest, was often with them at their work, on
the march, and on guard duty, but in the meantime
did not, like those who are actuated by depraved
ambition, try to undermine the reputation of the
consul or of any good man. His only effort was not
to suffer anyone to outdo him in counsel or in
action, and as a matter of fact he surpassed almost
all. Such being his character and conduct, he was
soon greatly beloved by both Marius and the soldiers.

XCVII. Now, Jugurtha, having lost Capsa and
other fortified places which were helpful to his cause,
as well as a great sum of money, sent messengers to
Bocchus, urging him to lead his troops into Numidia
as soon as possible, since the time for a battle was at
hand. But when he learned that Bocchus was
hesitating and doubtfully weighing the advantages of
peace and war, he once more bribed the king's
intimates with gifts and promised the Moor himself
a third part of Numidia, if the Romans should be
driven from Africa or the war brought to a close
without any loss of his own territory. Tempted by
this prize, Bocchus joined Jugurtha with a great
throng. Then the kings united their forces and
attacked Marius just as he was going into winter
quarters, when scarcely a tenth part of the day was
left; for they thought that the approaching night
would be a protection to them if they were

345

fore et, si vicissent nullo impedimento, quia locorum
scientes erant, contra Romanis utrumque casum in
4 tenebris difficiliorem fore. Igitur simul consul ex
multis de hostium adventu cognovit et ipsi hostes aderant, et priusquam exercitus aut instrui aut sarcinas
colligere, denique antequam signum aut imperium
ullum accipere quivit, equites Mauri atque Gaetuli,
non acie neque ullo more proeli sed catervatim, uti
quosque fors conglobaverat, in nostros incurrunt.

5 Qui omnes trepidi improviso metu ac tamen virtutis
memores aut arma capiebant aut capientis alios ab
hostibus defensabant ; pars equos ascendere,[1] obviam
ire hostibus, pugna latrocinio magis quam proelio
similis fieri, sine signis, sine ordinibus equites peditesque permixti cedere alii, alii[2] obtruncari, multi[3]
contra advorsos acerrume pugnantes ab tergo circumveniri ; neque virtus neque arma satis tegere,
quia hostes numero plures et undique circumfusi
erant. Denique Romani novi veteresque[4] et ob ea
scientes belli, si quos locus aut casus coniunxerat,
orbis fecere atque ita ab omnibus partibus simul tecti
et instructi hostium vim sustentabant.

XCVIII. Neque in eo tam aspero negotio Marius
territus aut magis quam antea demisso animo fuit,

[1] ascendere (scandere, A^1), *mss.*, *Or* ; esc. N^1, *Arus.* vii.
472. 12 κ, *Ah.*
[2] alii alii, *Linker, Ah* ; alios alios, *mss.* ; alius alius, *Or*
(*Klotz*).
[3] multi, *Dietsch* ; multa, A^1N ; multos, *the other mss.*
[4] n. veteresque, *Wölfflin* ; v. novique, *mss.* ; veteres, *Ah, Or*

unsuccessful and would be no hindrance if they conquered, because of their familiarity with the region; while to the Romans darkness would be more dangerous in either victory or defeat. Then, at the very moment that the consul learned from many of his scouts of the coming of the enemy, the foe themselves appeared, and before the army could be drawn up or the baggage piled, in fact before any signal or order could be given, the Moorish and Gaetulian cavalry fell upon the Romans, not in order or with any plan of battle but in swarms, just as chance had brought them together.

Our men were all bewildered by the unlooked for danger, but nevertheless did not forget their valour. Some took arms, while others kept off the enemy from their comrades who were arming; a part mounted their horses and charged the foe. The combat was more like an attack of brigands than a battle. Without standards and in disorder, horse and foot massed together, some gave ground, others slew their opponents; many who were bravely fighting against their adversaries were surrounded from the rear. Valour and arms were no sufficient protection against a foe who were superior in numbers and attacked on every side. At last the Romans, both the raw recruits and the veterans (who as such were skilled in warfare), if the nature of the ground or chance brought any of them together, formed a circle, thus at once protecting themselves on every side and presenting an orderly front to the attacks of the enemy.

XCVIII. In so dangerous a crisis Marius was neither frightened nor less confident than before, but with his bodyguard of cavalry, which he had

sed cum turma sua, quam ex fortissumis magis quam
familiarissumis paraverat, vagari passim ac modo
laborantibus suis succurrere, modo hostis, ubi con-
fertissumi obstiterant, invadere ; manu consulere
militibus, quoniam imperare conturbatis omnibus non

2 poterat. Iamque dies consumptus erat, cum tamen
barbari nihil remittere atque, uti reges praeceperant,

3 noctem pro se rati, acrius instare. Tum Marius ex
copia rerum consilium trahit, atque uti suis receptui
locus esset, collis duos propinquos inter se occupat,
quorum in uno, castris parum amplo, fons aquae magnus erat, alter usui opportunus, quia magna parte
editus et praeceps pauca munimenta quaerebat.[1]

4 Ceterum apud aquam Sullam cum equitibus noctem
agitare iubet, ipse paulatim dispersos milites neque
minus hostibus conturbatis in unum contrahit, dein

5 cunctos pleno gradu in collem subducit. Ita reges
loci difficultate coacti proelio deterrentur, neque
tamen suos longius abire sinunt, sed utroque colle
multitudine circumdato effusi consedere.

6 Dein, crebris ignibus factis, plerumque noctis barbari more suo laetari, exultare, strepere vocibus et
ipsi duces feroces, quia non fugerant,[2] pro victoribus

7 agere. Sed ea cuncta Romanis ex tenebris et edi-
tioribus locis facilia visu magnoque hortamento
erant.

---

[1] quaerebat, *editors*; gerebant, XDl; gerebat, $K^2HTFsnm$;
regebant, $A^1(?)N^1K^1$; regebat, M.
[2] fugerant, A^2C^2; fugere aut, *the other mss.*

formed of the bravest soldiers rather than of his most intimate friends, he went from place to place, now succouring those of his men who were in difficulty, now charging the enemy where they were pressing on in greatest numbers. He directed the soldiers by gestures, since in the general confusion his orders could not be heard. And now the day was spent, yet the barbarians did not at all relax their efforts, but thinking that darkness would favour them, as the kings had declared, they attacked with greater vigour. Then Marius, adapting his tactics to the situation and wishing to provide a place of refuge for his men, took possession of two neighbouring hills, one of which was too small for a camp but had a large spring of water, while the other was adapted to his purpose because it was for the most part high and steep and required little fortification. But he ordered Sulla to pass the night with the cavalry beside the spring, while he himself gradually rallied his scattered forces and the enemy were in no less disorder, and then led them all at the double quick to the hill. Thus the kings were compelled by the strength of his position to cease from battle. However, they did not allow their men to go far away, but encompassing both hills with their huge army, they bivouacked in loose order.

Then, after building many fires, the barbarians, as is their usual habit, spent the greater part of the night in rejoicing, in exultation and in noisy demonstrations, while even their leaders, who were filled with confidence because they had not been put to flight, acted as if they were victorious. Now, all this was clearly visible to the Romans from their higher position in the darkness and encouraged them greatly

349

XCIX. Plurumum vero Marius imperitia hostium confirmatus, quam maxumum silentium haberi iubet, ne signa quidem, uti per vigilias solebant, canere. Deinde, ubi lux adventabat, defessis iam hostibus ac paulo ante somno captis, de improviso vigiles,[1] item cohortium, turmarum, legionum tubicines simul omnis signa canere, milites clamorem tollere atque portis 2 erumpere iubet.   Mauri atque Gaetuli, ignoto et horribili sonitu repente exciti, neque fugere neque arma capere neque omnino facere aut providere 3 quicquam poterant ; ita cunctos strepitu, clamore, nullo subveniente, nostris instantibus, tumultu, formidine,[2] terrore [3] quasi vecordia ceperat.   Denique omnes fusi fugatique, arma et signa militaria pleraque capta, pluresque eo proelio quam omnibus superioribus interempti. Nam somno et metu insolito impedita fuga.

C. Dein Marius, uti coeperat, in hiberna proficiscitur, nam[4] propter commeatum in oppidis maritumis agere decreverat.   Neque tamen victoria socors aut insolens factus, sed pariter atque in conspectu hostium quadrato agmine incedere.

---

[1] vigiles, *Korrte*; vectigales, *mss.*
[2] formido, *MT, Or, omitting* terrore.   [3] terror, A^2, *Ah.*
[4] *The mss. omit* proficiscitur *and* nam (Nipperdey); in hiberna it : propter, *Ah (CB m)*; in h.—nam, *Or.*

---

[1] *cf.* Livy 7. 35. 1 : *ubi secundae vigiliae bucina datum signum esset* . . . .

XCIX. Marius, who was particularly heartened by the enemy's lack of discipline, ordered the utmost possible silence to be kept and not even the customary signals to be sounded to mark the night watches.[1] Then, as daylight was drawing near and the enemy having at length become exhausted had just yielded to sleep, on a sudden he ordered the watch and at the same time the horn-blowers of the cohorts,[2] of the divisions of cavalry and of the legions to sound the signal together, and the soldiers to raise a shout and burst forth from the gates of their camp. The Moors and Gaetulians, being suddenly awakened by the strange and terrible sound, could not flee, arm themselves, or do or provide for anything at all; into such a panic, all but frenzy, were they thrown by the clash of arms, the shouting, the lack of help, the charge of our men, the confusion and terror. To make a long story short, they were all routed and put to flight, the greater number of their arms and military standards were taken, and in that one battle more of the enemy fell than in all those that had gone before; for sleep and the unlooked-for danger hampered flight.

C. Then Marius proceeded, as he had been about to do, to his winter quarters, for he had decided to winter in the coast towns for the sake of supplies. His victory, however, did not make him careless or over-confident, but he advanced in square formation,[3] as though he were under the

---

[2] When contrasted with the legions, as here, "cohort" refers to the auxiliary troops.

[3] That is, with the baggage in the centre, surrounded by the heavy-armed troops, and with front, rear, and flanks protected by cavalry and light-armed soldiers.

2 Sulla cum equitatu apud dextumos,[1] in sinistra
parte A. Manlius cum funditoribus et sagittariis,
praeterea cohortis Ligurum curabat.   Primos et
extremos cum expeditis manipulis tribunos loca-
3 verat.   Perfugae, minume cari et regionum scientis-
sumi, hostium iter explorabant.   Simul consul quasi
nullo imposito omnia providere, apud omnis adesse,
4 laudare et increpare merentis.   Ipse armatus inten-
tusque item milites cogebat.   Neque secus atque iter
facere, castra munire, excubitum in porta cohortis
ex legionibus, pro castris equites auxiliarios mittere,
praeterea alios super vallum in munimentis locare,
vigilias ipse circumire, non tam diffidentia futurum
quae imperavisset, quam uti militibus exaequatus
5 cum imperatore labor volentibus esset.   Et sane
Marius illoque aliisque temporibus Iugurthini belli
pudore magis quam malo exercitum coercebat.
Quod multi per ambitionem fieri aiebant[2]; a pueritia
consuetam duritiam, et alia, quae ceteri miserias
vocant, voluptati habuisse ;[3] nisi tamen res publica[4]

[1] dextumos, *P²ACBK²Ts n*; *Prisc.* ii. 95. 5, 98. 14 κ;
extimos, *m* ; extremos, *the other mss.*
[2] aiebant; a pueritia, *Eussner*; aiebant quod a pueritia, *mss.*
[3] habuisse, *PA¹NK¹*; habuisset, *the other mss.*
[4] res publica (R.P. *or* r.p.), *CNKMsm*; *Fronto,* p. 110 *N*;
reip. *PA²BHTDF* ; remp., *A¹*.

[1] *cf.* Ter. *Adelph.* 69:

Malo coactus qui suom officium facit,
dum id rescitum iri credit, tantisper pavet.

eyes of the enemy. Sulla had charge of the right, together with the cavalry, on the left was Aulus Manlius with the slingers, the archers and the cohorts of Ligurians, while in front and in the rear Marius had stationed the tribunes with the light-armed companies. The deserters, who were least esteemed and best acquainted with the region, reconnoitred the enemy's line of march. At the same time the consul was as careful as if he had no officers, looking out for everything, being everywhere present, and distributing praise or blame where each was deserved. He himself was armed and alert, and he compelled the soldiers to follow his example. With the same care that he showed in making his march he fortified his camp, sent cohorts from the legions to keep ward at the gate and the auxiliary cavalry to perform the like duty before the camp, and in addition stationed others on the ramparts above the palisade. He personally inspected the guards, not so much because he feared that his orders would not be executed, as to make the soldiers willing to endure labour of which their commander did his full share. Obviously Marius at that time, and at other times during the war with Jugurtha controlled his army rather by appealing to their sense of shame than by punishment.[1] Many said that he did this through a desire for popularity; that [2] he himself took pleasure in hardship, to which he had been accustomed from childhood, and in other things which the rest of mankind call afflictions. But at all events, its service to our country [3]

[2] The meaning and the text are uncertain; see the critical note.

[3] cf. Caes. Bell. Civ. 1. 7. 7: *hortatur cuius imperatoris ductu viiii annis rem publicam felicissime gesserint . . . ut eius existimationem ab inimicis defendant.*

pariter ac saevissumo imperio bene atque decore
gesta.

CI. Igitur quarto denique die haud longe ab oppido
Cirta undique simul speculatores citi sese ostendunt,
2 qua re hostis adesse intellegitur.   Sed quia divorsi re-
deuntes alius ab alia parte atque omnes idem significa-
bant, consul incertus quonam modo aciem instrueret,
nullo ordine commutato, advorsum omnia paratus
3 ibidem opperitur.   Ita Iugurtham spes frustrata, qui
copias in quattuor partis distribuerat, ratus ex omnibus aeque aliquos ab tergo hostibus venturos.
4 Interim Sulla, quem primum hostes attigerant,
cohortatus suos turmatim et quam maxume confertis
equis ipse aliique Mauros invadunt, ceteri in loco
manentes ab iaculis eminus emissis corpora tegere, et
5 si qui in manus venerant, obtruncare.   Dum eo modo
equites proeliantur, Bocchus cum peditibus, quos
Volux filius eius adduxerat neque in priore pugna
in itinere morati affuerant, postremam Romanorum
6 aciem invadunt.   Tum Marius apud primos agebat,[1]
quod ibi Iugurtha cum plurumis erat.   Dein Numida
cognito Bocchi adventu clam cum paucis ad pedites
convortit.   Ibi Latine—nam apud Numantiam loqui
didicerat—exclamat nostros frustra pugnare, paulo
ante Marium sua manu interfectum.   Simul gladium

---

[1] agebat, *CBH*; agitabat, A^2n; erat, *the other mss.*

---

[1] That is, Jugurtha secretly left the van, where he was
leading his cavalry against Marius, and went back to the
rear where Bocchus and his infantry were attacking the
Romans from behind.

was as great and as glorious as it could have been
with the severest discipline.

CI. Finally on the fourth day, when they were not
far from the town of Cirta, the scouts quickly appeared from all sides at once, showing that the
enemy were at hand. But since the different parties,
though returning from various quarters, all made the
same report, the consul was in doubt what order of
battle to take; he therefore waited where he was,
without changing his formation, but prepared for any
emergency. In this way he disappointed Jugurtha,
who had made four divisions of his troops, in the expectation that if they attacked from all quarters
alike, some of them at least would take the Romans
in the rear. Meanwhile Sulla, whom the enemy
had reached first, after encouraging his men attacked the Moors with a part of his force, charging
by squadrons and in as close order as possible;
the rest of his troops held their ground, protecting themselves from the javelins which were hurled
at long range, and slaying all who succeeded in
reaching them. While the cavalry were fighting
thus, Bocchus with the infantry brought by his son
Volux, which had been delayed on the way and had
not taken part in the former battle, charged the
Roman rear. Marius at the time was busy with the
van, since Jugurtha was there with the greater part
of his forces. Then the Numidian, on learning of the
arrival of Bocchus, made his way secretly with a few
followers to the king's infantry.[1] When he reached
them, he cried out in Latin (for he had learned to
speak the language at Numantia) that our men were
fighting in vain, since he had a short time before slain
Marius with his own hand. And with these words

355

sanguine oblitum ostendere, quem in pugna satis
7 impigre occiso pedite nostro cruentaverat. Quod ubi
milites accepere, magis atrocitate rei quam fide
nuntii terrentur, simulque barbari animos tollere et
8 in perculsos Romanos acrius incedere. Iamque
paulum a fuga aberant, cum Sulla, profligatis eis
quos advorsum ierat, rediens ab latere Mauris
9 incurrit. Bocchus statim avortitur. At Iugurtha,
dum sustentare suos et prope iam adeptam victoriam
retinere cupit, circumventus ab equitibus, dextra,
sinistra[1] omnibus occisis, solus inter tela hostium
10 vitabundus erumpit. Atque interim Marius fugatis
equitibus accurrit auxilio suis, quos pelli iam
11 acceperat. Denique hostes iam undique fusi. Tum
spectaculum horribile in campis patentibus : sequi,
fugere, occidi, capi, equi atque viri afflicti, ac multi
volneribus acceptis neque fugere posse neque quietem
pati, niti modo ac statim concidere, postremo omnia,
qua visus erat, constrata telis, armis, cadaveribus, et
inter ea humus infecta sanguine.

CII. Post ea loci consul haud dubie iam victor
pervenit in oppidum Cirtam, quo initio profectus
2 intenderat. Eo post diem quintum quam iterum
barbari male pugnaverant legati a Boccho veniunt,
qui regis verbis ab Mario petivere, duos quam fidissu-
mos ad eum mitteret: velle de suo[2] et de populi

---

[1] sinistraque, K^2m, Ah.   [2] se, A^2CB.

---

[1] Some take *pedite* as collective, but *satis impigre* seems to
be sarcastic.

he displayed a sword smeared with blood, which
he had made gory during the battle by valiantly
slaying one of our foot-soldiers.[1] When our men
heard this, they were shocked rather by the horror
of the deed than because they believed the report,
while at the same time the barbarians were encouraged and charged upon the appalled Romans with
greater vigour. And our men were just on the point
of flight, when Sulla, who had routed his opponents,
returned and fell upon the flank of the Moors.
Bocchus at once gave way. As for Jugurtha, while
he was trying to hold his men and grasp the victory
which he had all but won, he was surrounded by the
cavalry; but though all on his right and left were
slain, he broke through alone, escaping amid a shower
of hostile weapons. Marius in the meantime, after
putting the cavalry to flight, was hastening to the
aid of his men, of whose imminent defeat he had
now heard. Finally the enemy were everywhere
routed. Then there was a fearful sight in the open
plains—pursuing, fleeing, killing, capturing, horses
and men dashed to the ground, many of the wounded
unable either to flee or remain quiet, now making
an effort to rise and at once collapsing; in short,
wherever the eye could reach, the ground was
soaked in blood and strewn with weapons, arms,
and corpses.

CII. After this the consul, now beyond all question
victor, came to the town of Cirta, which had been
his destination from the first. Thither came envoys
from Bocchus five days after the second defeat of the
barbarians, to ask of Marius in the king's name that
he should send him two of his most trusty officers;
they said that Bocchus wished to confer with them

3 Romani commodo cum eis disserere. Ille statim L.
Sullam et A. Manlium ire iubet. Qui quamquam ac-
citi ibant, tamen placuit verba apud regem facere:
ingenium aut avorsum flecterent aut cupidum pacis
4 vehementius accenderent. Itaque Sulla, cuius facun-
diae, non aetati a Manlio concessum, pauca verba
huiuscemodi locutus.

5 " Rex Bocche, magna laetitia nobis est, cum te
talem virum di monuere uti aliquando pacem quam
bellum malles, neu te optumum cum pessumo omnium Iugurtha miscendo commaculares, simul nobis
demeres acerbam necessitudinem, pariter te er-
6 rantem atque illum sceleratissumum persequi. Ad
hoc populo Romano iam a principio imperi[1] melius
visum amicos quam servos quaerere, tutiusque rati
7 volentibus quam coactis imperitare. Tibi vero nulla
opportunior nostra amicitia, primum quia procul ab-
sumus, in quo offensae minumum, gratia par ac si
prope adessemus; dein, quia parentis abunde habemus, amicorum neque nobis neque cuiquam omnium
8 satis fuit. Atque hoc utinam a principio tibi placuis-
set; profecto ex populo Romano ad hoc tempus
multo plura bona accepisses, quam mala perpessus es.[2]
9 Sed quoniam humanarum rerum fortuna pleraque

---

[1] imperi, *Selling*; inopi, $VP^2A^2CBK^2H$ *s n, Ah, Or.*
[2] esses, *mss.* (esse, *V*); es, *Fabri, Or* ("*fort. recte,*" *Ah*).

---

[1] They had been summoned to hear the king's proposal,
not to speak.

about his own interests and those of the Roman
people. Marius immediately selected Lucius Sulla
and Aulus Manlius, and they, although they had been
sent for by the king,[1] decided to address him, with
the view of changing his purpose, if unfavourable,
or of making him more eager for peace if he already
desired it. Therefore Sulla, to whom Manlius gave
place, not because of his years, but because of his
eloquence, spoke briefly to the following purport:

"King Bocchus, it gives us much joy that the
gods have led you, so great a man, at last to prefer
peace to war; to refuse to contaminate yourself, one
of the best of men, by association with Jugurtha,
the very worst; and at the same time to relieve
us of the bitter necessity of meting out the same
treatment to your error and to his crimes. I may
add that the Roman people from the beginning of
their rule have preferred to seek friends rather than
slaves, and have thought it safer to govern by consent
than by compulsion. For you, indeed, no friendship
is more desirable than ours: first, because we are at
a distance from you, a condition which offers less
friction than if we were near at hand, with no less
power[2]; and secondly, because we already have
more than enough subjects, while neither we nor
anyone else ever had friends enough. I only wish
that you had felt thus disposed from the first! In
that event, the favours which by this time you
would have received from the Roman people would
far outnumber the misfortunes which you have suffered. But since Fortune has the chief control of
human destiny, and since it seems to have been her

---

[2] That is, "our alliance will be as powerful as if we were
nearer neighbours."

regit, cui scilicet placuit et vim et gratiam nostram te
experiri, nunc quando per illam licet, festina atque
10 ut coepisti perge. Multa atque opportuna habes,
11 quo facilius errata officiis superes. Postremo hoc in
pectus tuum demitte, numquam populum Romanum
benificiis victum esse. Nam bello quid valeat tute
scis."

12   Ad ea Bocchus placide et benigne, simul pauca
pro delicto suo verba facit : se non hostili animo, sed
13 ob regnum tutandum arma cepisse. Nam Numidiae
partem unde vi Iugurtham expulerit iure belli suam
factam. Eam vastari a Mario pati nequivisse. Praeterea missis antea Romam legatis repulsum ab
14 amicitia. Ceterum vetera omittere, ac tum,[1] si per
15 Marium liceret, legatos ad senatum missurum. Dein,
copia facta, animus barbari ab amicis flexus, quos
Iugurtha, cognita legatione Sullae et Manli, metuens
id quod parabatur, donis corruperat.

CIII. Marius interea, exercitu in hibernaculis composito, cum expeditis cohortibus et parte equitatus
proficiscitur in loca sola obsessum turrim regiam, quo
Iugurtha perfugas omnis praesidium imposuerat.
2 Tum rursus Bocchus, seu[2] reputando quae sibi duobus
proeliis venerant seu admonitus ab aliis amicis, quos
incorruptos Iugurtha reliquerat, ex omni copia
necessariorum quinque[3] delegit, quorum et fides

---

[1] actutum, *Jordan.*
[2] Bocchus seu, *C l s*; Bocchus, feliciter seu, *the other mss.*
[3] *The codices mutili omit from* quinque *to* pacem, cxii. 3.

---

[1] Returning to the plans mentioned in cii. 2.

pleasure that you should experience both our power and our kindness, make haste now that she allows it and follow the course which you have begun. You have many opportunities easily to atone for your mistakes by good offices. Finally, let this thought sink into your heart, that the Roman people has never been outdone in kindness; its prowess in war you know by experience."

To these words Bocchus made a conciliatory and courteous reply, at the same time offering a brief defence of his conduct, declaring that he had taken arms, not in a spirit of hostility, but to protect his kingdom; for the part of Numidia from which he had driven Jugurtha, he said, was his by right of conquest and he could not allow it to be laid waste by Marius. Furthermore, he had previously sent envoys to Rome, but his friendship had been rejected. He waived the past, however, and if Marius would allow him, he would again send ambassadors to the senate. But after the consul had granted his request, the barbarian's purpose was changed by some of his friends, whom Jugurtha had bribed; for he knew of the embassy of Sulla and Manlius and feared its effects.

CIII. Meanwhile Marius, having settled his army in winter quarters, went with the light-armed cohorts and a part of the cavalry into the desert, in order to besiege a stronghold of the king, which Jugurtha had garrisoned with deserters only. Then Bocchus again,[1] led either by the recollection of what had happened to him in two battles or by the warnings of other friends of his whom Jugurtha had failed to bribe, chose out of the whole body of his relatives five of those whom he knew to be faithful and of pre-

3 cognita et ingenia validissuma erant. Eos ad
Marium ac deinde, si placeat, Romam legatos ire
iubet ; agundarum rerum et quocumque modo belli
4 componundi licentiam ipsis permittit. Illi mature
ad hiberna Romanorum proficiscuntur ; deinde in
itinere a Gaetulis latronibus circumventi spoliatique,
pavidi sine decore ad Sullam perfugiunt, quem
consul in expeditionem proficiscens pro praetore
5 reliquerat. Eos ille non pro vanis hostibus, uti
meriti erant, sed accurate ac liberaliter habuit.
Qua re barbari et famam Romanorum avaritae
falsam et Sullam ob munificentiam in sese amicum
6 rati. Nam etiam tum largitio multis ignota erat ;
munificus nemo putabatur nisi pariter volens, dona
7 omnia in benignitate habebantur. Igitur quaestori
mandata Bocchi patefaciunt ; simul ab eo petunt uti
fautor consultorque sibi adsit ; copias, fidem, magnitudinem regis sui et alia, quae aut utilia aut benevolentiae[1] esse credebant, oratione extollunt. Dein
Sulla omnia pollicito, docti quo modo apud Marium,
item apud senatum verba facerent, circiter dies
quadraginta ibidem opperiuntur.

CIV. Marius postquam confecto[2] quo[3] intenderat
negotio Cirtam redit et de adventu legatorum
certior factus est, illosque et Sullam ab Utica venire
iubet, item L. Bellienum praetorem Utica,[4] praeterea

[1] benevolentia, *H R l*; benevolentiam, *C T s n*; benevolentiae,
the other mss., Ah, Or.
[2] infecto, *K H M T D¹ m π, Ah*; confecto, *the other mss., Or.*
[3] quod, *K T D Q m.*
[4] praetorem, *M D Q m π, Ah, Or*; praetorem Utica(m), *the
other mss.*

eminent ability. These he ordered to go as envoys to Marius and then, if it seemed advisable, to Rome, giving them complete freedom of action and permission to make peace on any terms. These envoys left betimes for the Roman winter quarters, but on the way they were set upon and robbed by Gaetulian brigands and fled in terror and disgrace to Sulla, whom the consul had left in command when beginning his expedition. Sulla did not treat them as liars and enemies, as he might well have done,[1] but received them with a sympathy and generosity which led the barbarians to think that the Romans' reputation for avarice was unmerited and that Sulla because of his liberality towards them was really their friend. For even then many men did not know the significance of largess; no one who was generous was suspected of insincerity, and all gifts were regarded as indications of kind feeling. Therefore they confided to the quaestor what Bocchus had ordered and at the same time begged him to help them with his favour and advice. They exaggerated the wealth, integrity and might of their sovereign and everything else which they thought would help them or ensure kind treatment. Then, after Sulla had promised to do all that they asked and had instructed them how to address Marius and the senate, they tarried with him about forty days.[2]

CIV. After finishing the task which he had set himself, Marius returned to Cirta. There being informed of the arrival of the envoys, he ordered them to come from Utica with Sulla; he also summoned Lucius Bellienus the praetor from Utica, as well as

[1] Their appearance belied the assertion that they were envoys of the king.

[2] Apparently waiting for Marius to return.

omnis undique senatorii ordinis; quibuscum mandata
2 Bocchi cognoscit. In quis [1] legatis potestas Romam
eundi fit,[2] et ab consule interea indutiae postulabantur. Ea Sullae et plerisque placuere; pauci
ferocius decernunt, scilicet ignari humanarum rerum,
quae fluxae et mobiles semper in advorsa mutantur.
3 Ceterum Mauri, impetratis omnibus rebus, tres
Romam profecti cum Cn. Octavio Rusone, qui quaestor stipendium in Africam portaverat, duo ad regem
redeunt. Ex eis Bocchus cum cetera, tum maxume
benignitatem et studium Sullae lubens accepit.
4 Romaeque legatis eius, postquam errasse regem et
Iugurthae scelere lapsum deprecati sunt, amicitiam et
5 foedus petentibus hoc modo respondetur: "Senatus
et populus Romanus benefici et iniuriae memor esse
solet. Ceterum Boccho, quoniam paenitet, delicti
gratiam facit; foedus et amicitia dabuntur, cum
meruerit."

CV. Quis rebus cognitis, Bocchus per litteras a
Mario petivit [3] uti Sullam ad se mitteret, cuius
2 arbitratu communibus [4] negotiis consuleretur. Is
missus cum praesidio equitum atque funditorum [5]
Balearum; praeterea iere sagittarii et cohors Pae-
ligna cum velitaribus armis, itineris properandi causa,
neque his secus atque aliis armis advorsum tela
hostium, quod ea levia sunt, muniti.

---

[1] legatis, $F\pi$, Ah, Or; in (*om.* Q; a, M) quibus (quis, n)
legatis, *the other mss.*
[2] fit *omitted by* C; fuit, R^1; fieret, *Dietsch.*
[3] petiverat, $\Pi T D Q m$.
[4] de communibus, KF.
[5] atque peditum (p. item f., $TQ m$) *mss.*; p. *deleted by Korrte.*

every member of the senatorial order to be found in all parts of the province. In consultation with these men he considered the proposals of Bocchus. Among these proposals the consul was asked to give the envoys permission to go to Rome, and in the meantime a truce was requested. This met the approval of the majority, including Sulla; a few hot-heads were for rejecting them, doubtless unaware that human affairs, which are shifting and unstable, are always changing for better or worse.

Now when the Moors had obtained everything that they desired, three of them departed for Rome with Gnaeus Octavius Ruso, the quaestor who had brought the soldiers' pay to Africa, while two returned to the king. Bocchus heard the report of the latter with joy, especially the friendly interest of Sulla. And at Rome his envoys, after urging in excuse that their king had made a mistake and been led astray by the wickedness of Jugurtha, asked for a treaty of friendship and received this reply: " The Senate and People of Rome are wont to remember both a benefit and an injury. But since Bocchus repents, they forgive his offence; he shall have a treaty of friendship when he has earned it."

CV. Upon receiving news of this, Bocchus wrote to Marius to send Sulla to him with power to adjust their common interests. He was accordingly sent with a guard of horsemen and Balearic slingers, also taking with him the archers and a cohort of Paelignians, who wore light armour for the sake of speed and because they were as well protected by this as by any other armour against the weapons of the enemy, which are also light.

3 Sed in itinere quinto denique die Volux, filius
Bocchi, repente in campis patentibus cum mille non
amplius equitibus sese ostendit, qui temere et effuse
euntes Sullae aliisque omnibus et numerum am-
4 pliorem vero et hostilem metum efficiebant. Igitur
se quisque expedire, arma atque tela temptare,
intendere; timor aliquantus, sed spes amplior, quippe
victoribus et advorsum eos quos saepe vicerant.
5 Interim equites exploratum praemissi rem, uti erat,
quietam nuntiant.

CVI. Volux adveniens quaestorem appellat dicitque se a patre Boccho obviam illis simul et praesidio
missum. Deinde eum et proxumum diem sine metu
2 coniuncti eunt. Post, ubi castra locata et diei vesper
erat, repente Maurus incerto voltu pavens ad Sullam
accurrit dicitque sibi ex speculatoribus cognitum
Iugurtham haud procul abesse; simul uti noctu clam
3 secum profugeret rogat atque hortatur. Ille animo
feroci negat se totiens fusum Numidam pertimescere:
virtuti suorum satis credere; etiamsi certa pestis
adesset, mansurum potius quam, proditis quos ducebat, turpi fuga incertae ac forsitan post paulo morbo
4 interiturae vitae parceret. Ceterum ab eodem moni-
tus uti noctu proficiscerentur, consilium approbat ac

On the fifth day of their march Volux, the son of Bocchus, suddenly appeared in the open plains with not more than a thousand horsemen; but since they were riding in disorder and widely scattered, they seemed to Sulla and all the rest much more numerous and excited fear of an attack. Therefore each man prepared himself, tried his arms and weapons, and was on the alert; there was some anxiety, but greater confidence, as was natural to victors in the presence of those whom they had often vanquished. Meanwhile the horsemen who had been sent to reconnoitre announced that the intentions of the newcomers were peaceful, as in fact they were.

CVI. When he came up, Volux addressed the quaestor, saying that he had been sent by his father Bocchus to meet them and act as their escort. Then they went on in company that day and the next without any cause for alarm. Later in the day, when the camp was pitched and evening came on, the Moor on a sudden with a troubled countenance ran in terror to Sulla and said that he had learned from his scouts that Jugurtha was not far off; at the same time he begged and implored Sulla to make his escape with him secretly during the night. But the Roman boldly declared that he did not fear the Numidian whom he had so often routed and that he had absolute trust in the valour of his men; he added that even if inevitable destruction threatened, he would rather stand his ground than betray the men under his command, and by cowardly flight save a life that he might perhaps be fated soon to lose from natural causes. When, however, Volux recommended that they continue their march during the night, he approved the plan, ordered the soldiers

statim milites cenatos esse, in castris ignis quam
creberrumos fieri, dein prima vigilia silentio egredi
iubet.

5 Iamque nocturno itinere fessis omnibus, Sulla
pariter cum ortu solis castra metabatur, cum equites
Mauri nuntiant Iugurtham circiter duum milium
6 intervallo ante eos consedisse. Quod postquam
auditum est, tum vero ingens metus nostros invadit ;
credere se proditos a Voluce et insidiis circumventos.
Ac fuere qui dicerent manu vindicandum neque
apud illum tantum scelus inultum relinquendum.

CVII. At Sulla, quamquam eadem existumabat,
tamen ab iniuria Maurum prohibet. Suos hortatur
uti fortem animum gererent : saepe antea a paucis
strenuis advorsum multitudinem bene pugnatum ;
quanto sibi in proelio minus pepercissent, tanto
tutiores fore, nec quemquam decere, qui manus
armaverit, ab inermis pedibus auxilium petere, in
maxumo metu nudum et caecum corpus ad hostis
2 vortere. Dein Volucem, quoniam hostilia faceret,
Iovem maxumum obtestatus, ut sceleris atque perfidiae Bocchi testis adesset, ex castris abire iubet.
3 Ille lacrumans orare ne ea crederet : nihil dolo
factum, ac magis calliditate Iugurthae, cui videlicet
4 speculanti iter suum cognitum esset. Ceterum
quoniam neque ingentem multitudinem haberet et
spes opesque eius ex patre suo penderent, credere
illum nihil palam ausurum, cum ipse filius testis
5 adesset. Qua re optumum factu videri per media

---

[1] cf. Xen. *Cyrop*. **3. 3.** 45.

to have their dinners at once, to build as many fires in the camp as possible, and at the first watch to withdraw in silence.

And now, when all were wearied from the night march, Sulla was measuring off his camp at sunrise, when suddenly the Moorish horsemen reported that Jugurtha was encamped about two miles in advance of them. Upon hearing this, the Romans were at last seized with great fear; they believed that they had been betrayed by Volux and led into a trap. Some said that he ought to be put to death and not allowed to escape the penalty of such a crime.

CVII. Although Sulla shared this opinion, he forbade them to harm the Moor. He urged his men to keep a stout heart, saying that often before a handful of valiant soldiers had worsted a multitude. The less they spared themselves in the fight the safer they would be. It was not seemly for any man who had weapons in his hands to resort to the help of his unarmed feet and in time of great fear to turn towards the enemy the defenceless and blind part of his body.[1] Then calling upon great Jupiter to witness the crime and perfidy of Bocchus, he ordered Volux to quit the camp, since he was playing a hostile part. The young man begged Sulla with tears not to believe such a thing; he insisted that the situation was due to no treachery on his part, but to the cunning of Jugurtha, who had evidently learned from spies of their expedition. But since the Numidian had no great force and all his hopes and resources depended upon Bocchus, Volux was sure, he said, that he would venture upon no open attempt when the king's son was present as a witness. He therefore advised that they should march fearlessly through the midst

eius castra palam transire; sese, vel praemissis vel
ibidem relictis Mauris, solum cum Sulla iturum.

6   Ea res uti in tali negotio probata; ac statim profecti, quia de improviso acciderant, dubio atque
7 haesitante Iugurtha incolumes transeunt. Deinde
paucis diebus quo ire intenderant perventum est.

CVIII. Ibi cum Boccho Numida quidam Aspar
nomine multum et familiariter agebat, praemissus ab
Iugurtha, postquam Sullam accitum audierat, orator
et subdole speculatum Bocchi consilia; praeterea
Dabar Massugradae filius, ex gente Masinissae,
ceterum materno genere impar—nam pater eius ex
concubina ortus erat—Mauro ob ingeni multa bona
2 carus acceptusque.   Quem Bocchus fidum esse
Romanis multis ante tempestatibus expertus, ilico ad
Sullam nuntiatum mittit paratum sese facere quae
populus Romanus vellet: colloquio diem, locum,
tempus ipse deligeret, neu Iugurthae legatum per-
timesceret; consulto sese omnia cum illo integra
habere, quo res communis licentius gereretur; nam
ab insidiis eius aliter caveri nequivisse.

3   Sed ego comperior Bocchum magis Punica fide
quam ob ea quae praedicabat simul Romanum et
Numidam spe pacis attinuisse multumque cum animo
suo volvere solitum, Iugurtham Romanis an illi Sullam
traderet; lubidinem advorsum nos, metum pro nobis
suasisse.

---

[1] Except by receiving Jugurtha's envoy and pretending
friendship with the king. Text and meaning are somewhat
uncertain.

of Jugurtha's camp; he said that he himself would accompany Sulla alone, whether his Moors were sent ahead or left behind.

This plan seemed the best possible one under the circumstances. They set out at once, and because their action was unexpected, Jugurtha wavered and hesitated and they passed through unscathed. A few days later they reached their destination.

CVIII. There was in that place a Numidian called Aspar, who was on very familiar terms with Bocchus. He had been sent on by Jugurtha, after he heard of the summoning of Sulla, to plead for the Numidian and craftily spy upon Bocchus' designs. There was also a certain Dabar, son of Massugrada, of the family of Masinissa, a man of inferior birth on his mother's side (for her father was the son of a concubine), but dearly beloved by the Moor because of many good qualities. Having found Dabar faithful to the Romans on many previous occasions, Bocchus at once sent him to Sulla, to report that he was ready to do what the Roman people wished. He suggested that Sulla should select the day, place and hour for a conference and told him to have no fear of Jugurtha's envoy, declaring that he was purposely maintaining friendly relations with the Numidian, in order that they might discuss their common interests more freely; in no other way could he have guarded against his plots.[1]

But I believe that it was rather with Punic faith than for the reasons which he made public that Bocchus beguiled both the Roman and the Numidian with the hope of peace, and that he pondered for a long time whether to betray Jugurtha to the Romans or Sulla to Jugurtha; that his inclination counselled against us, but his fears in our favour.

371

CIX. Igitur Sulla respondit pauca se coram Aspare locuturum, cetera occulte aut nullo aut quam paucissumis praesentibus; simul edocet quae sibi responderentur. 2 Postquam sicuti voluerat congressi, dicit se missum a consule venisse quaesitum ab eo pacem 3 an bellum agitaturus foret. Tum rex, uti praeceptum fuerat, post diem decumum redire iubet: ac nihil etiam nunc decrevisse, sed illo die responsurum. 4 Deinde ambo in sua castra digressi. Sed ubi plerumque noctis processit, Sulla a Boccho occulte accersitur; ab utroque tantum modo fidi interpretes adhibentur, praeterea Dabar internuntius, sanctus vir et ex sententia ambobus. Ac statim sic rex incipit.

CX. "Numquam ego ratus sum fore uti rex maxumus in hac terra et omnium, quos novi, privato 2 homini gratiam deberem. Et mehercule, Sulla, ante te cognitum multis orantibus, aliis ultro egomet opem 3 tuli, nullius indigus! Id imminutum, quod ceteri dolere solent, ego laetor; fuerit mihi eguisse aliquando pretium tuae amicitiae, qua apud animum meum 4 nihil carius habeo. Id adeo experiri licet: arma, viros, pecuniam, postremo quidquid animo lubet, sume, utere et, quoad vives, numquam tibi redditam gratiam putaveris, semper apud me integra erit;

---

[1] He is willing to put up with the loss of his former independence for the sake of Sulla's friendship.

CIX. Now Sulla replied to the king's proposal, that he would speak briefly in the presence of Aspar, but would discuss other matters privately with Bocchus either with no one else present or before as few as possible; at the same time he instructed the envoys what reply was to be made to him. When the meeting had been arranged according to his wishes, Sulla said that he had been sent by the consul to ask of Bocchus whether he desired peace or war. Then the king, as had been arranged, directed him to return ten days later, saying that even yet he had made no decision, but would give his answer at that time. Then they both withdrew to their camps. But when a good part of the night had passed, Sulla was secretly summoned by Bocchus; both were attended only by trustworthy interpreters in addition to Dabar as mediator, an upright man who was trusted by both of them. Then the king immediately began as follows:

CX. "I never believed it possible that I, the greatest monarch in these lands and of all kings whom I know, should owe gratitude to a man of private station. And by Heaven! Sulla, before I knew you many have prayed for my help, which I gave often to their prayers, often unasked, needing no man's help myself. At such a curtailment of independence others are wont to grieve, but I rejoice in it; let the need which I at last feel be the price that I pay for your friendship;[1] for in my heart I hold nothing dearer. As a proof of this, take arms, men, money, in short whatever you like; use them, and as long as you live never think that you are repaid; for I shall always feel a fresh sense of obligation towards you. In short, there will be

5 denique nihil me sciente frustra voles. Nam, ut
ego aestumo, regem armis quam munificentia vinci
minus flagitiosum est.

6 "Ceterum de re publica vostra, cuius curator huc
missus es, paucis accipe. Bellum ego populo Romano neque feci neque factum umquam volui; at
7 finis meos advorsum armatos armis tutatus sum. Id
omitto, quando vobis ita placet; gerite quod voltis
8 cum Iugurtha bellum. Ego flumen Muluccham,
quod inter me et Micipsam fuit, non egrediar neque
id intrare Iugurtham sinam. Praeterea siquid meque vobisque dignum petiveris, haud repulsus abibis."

CXI. Ad ea Sulla pro se breviter et modice, de
pace et de communibus rebus multis disseruit.
Denique regi patefacit,[1] quod polliceatur, senatum
et populum Romanum, quoniam armis amplius valu-
issent, non in gratia habituros. Faciundum aliquid,
quod illorum magis quam sua retulisse videretur; id
adeo in promptu esse, quoniam copiam Iugurthae
haberet. Quem si Romanis tradidisset, fore ut illi
plurumum deberetur; amicitiam, foedus, Numidiae
partem quam nunc peteret, tum ultro adventuram.

2   Rex primo negitare: cognationem, affinitatem,
praeterea foedus intervenisse; ad hoc metuere ne
fluxa fide usus popularium animos avorteret, quis et

---

[1] patefacit *Fπ, Ah*; patefecit, *the other mss., Or.*

nothing for which you can wish in vain, provided your desires are known to me. For in my opinion it is less disgraceful for a king to be vanquished in war than to be outdone in gratitude.

"Now hear a few words with regard to your country, as whose representative you have been sent hither. I did not make war on the Roman people and I never wished to do so; but I defended my realm with arms against armed invaders. Even that I now cease to do, since it is your wish. Carry on the war with Jugurtha as you think best. I shall not pass the river Muluccha, which was the boundary between Micipsa and myself, nor will I allow Jugurtha to do so. If you have anything further to ask which is honourable for us both, you shall not go away disappointed."

CXI. To these words Sulla replied on his own account briefly and modestly; he spoke at length about peace and their common interests. Finally, he made it clear to the king that the senate and people of Rome would feel no gratitude for his promises, since they had shown themselves his superior in arms. He must do something which would clearly be for their interests rather than his own. This would be easy, since he could get control of Jugurtha; if he would deliver the king into the hands of the Romans, they would be greatly indebted to him. Then friendship, alliance, and the part of Numidia which he now desired would freely be given him.

At first the king refused, saying that relationship and kinship forbade, as well as a treaty; moreover, he feared that if he showed treachery he would alienate his subjects to whom Jugurtha was dear

3 Iugurtha carus et Romani invisi erant. Denique saepius fatigatus lenitur et ex voluntate Sullae om-
4 nia se facturum promittit. Ceterum ad simulandam pacem, cuius Numida defessus bello avidissumus erat, quae utilia visa constituunt. Ita composito dolo digrediuntur.

CXII. At rex postero die Asparem Iugurthae legatum appellat dicitque sibi per Dabarem ex Sulla cognitum, posse condicionibus bellum poni : quam ob
2 rem regis sui sententiam exquireret. Ille laetus in castra Iugurthae proficiscitur; deinde ab illo cuncta edoctus, properato itinere post diem octavum redit ad Bocchum et ei nuntiat Iugurtham cupere omnia quae imperarentur facere, sed Mario parum confidere; saepe antea cum imperatoribus Romanis
3 pacem conventam frustra fuisse. Ceterum Bocchus si ambobus consultum et ratam pacem vellet, daret operam ut una ab omnibus quasi de pace in colloquium veniretur ibique sibi Sullam traderet. Cum talem virum in potestatem habuisset, tum fore uti iussu senatus aut populi foedus fieret; neque hominem nobilem, non sua ignavia, sed ob rem publicam in hostium potestate relictum iri.

CXIII. Haec Maurus secum ipse diu volvens tandem promisit, ceterum dolo an vere cunctatus parum comperimus. Sed plerumque regiae voluntates ut vehementes sic mobiles, saepe ipsae sibi advorsae.
2 Postea tempore et loco constituto in colloquium uti de pace veniretur, Bocchus Sullam modo, modo

and the Romans hateful. At last, after many importunities, he gave way and promised to do all that Sulla desired. They also took the necessary steps for pretending to make the peace which was most desired by the Numidian, who was weary of war. Having thus perfected their plot, they parted.

CXII. Now, on the following day the king summoned Aspar, Jugurtha's envoy, and said that he had learned from Sulla through Dabar that terms of peace could be arranged; he therefore desired him to find out the intentions of his king. The envoy joyfully departed to Jugurtha's camp; then after eight days he returned in haste to Bocchus with full instructions from the king and reported to him that Jugurtha was willing to do anything that he desired, but put little trust in Marius. He said that peace had often before been agreed upon with Roman generals to no purpose; but that Bocchus, if he wished to consult for the interests of both and to have a lasting peace, ought to arrange for a general interview under pretext of agreeing upon conditions and there deliver Sulla to him. When he had so important a man in his power, a treaty would surely be made by order of the senate or of the people; for a man of rank would not be left in the power of the enemy when he had fallen into it, not through his own cowardice, but in the service of the country.

CXIII. After long consideration, the Moor at last promised this. Whether his hesitation was feigned or genuine I cannot say; but as a rule the desires of kings, although strong, are changeable and often contradictory. Afterwards, when time and place were agreed upon for holding the peace conference, Bocchus addressed now Sulla and now the envoy of

377

Iugurthae legatum appellare, benigne habere, idem ambobus polliceri. Illi pariter laeti ac spei bonae pleni esse.

3 Sed nocte ea, quae proxuma fuit ante diem colloquio decretum, Maurus, adhibitis amicis ac statim immutata voluntate remotis ceteris, dicitur secum ipse multum agitavisse, voltu[1] et oculis pariter atque animo varius; quae scilicet tacente ipso occulta 4 pectoris patefecisse. Tamen postremo Sullam accersi iubet et ex illius sententia Numidae insidias tendit.

5 Deinde ubi dies advenit et ei nuntiatum est Iugurtham haud procul abesse, cum paucis amicis et quaestore nostro quasi obvius honoris causa procedit 6 in tumulum facillumum visu insidiantibus. Eodem Numida cum plerisque necessariis suis inermis, uti dictum erat, accedit ac statim signo dato undique simul ex insidiis invaditur. Ceteri obtruncati, Iugurtha Sullae vinctus traditur et ab eo ad Marium deductus est.

CXIV. Per idem tempus advorsum Gallos ab ducibus nostris Q. Caepione et Cn. Manlio male 2 pugnatum. Quo metu Italia omnis contremuit. Illique et inde usque ad nostram memoriam Romani sic habuere, alia omnia virtuti suae prona esse, 3 cum Gallis pro salute non pro gloria certari. Sed postquam bellum in Numidia confectum et Iugur-

---

[1] vultu corporis, *mss.*; vultu et oculis, *Serv. Aen.* vii. 251; *Klotz regards both* corporis *and* et oculis *as glosses.*

Jugurtha, received both courteously and made them the same promises. Both alike were joyful and full of good hope.

That night, however, which was the one preceding the day appointed for the conference, the Moor summoned his friends and at once changed his purpose and dismissed all others; then he is said to have had a long struggle with himself, during which the conflict in his mind was reflected in his expression and eyes, which, though he was silent, revealed the secrets of his heart. At last, however, he ordered Sulla to be summoned and yielding to his wish, set a trap for the Numidian.

When day came and he was told that Jugurtha was not far off, he proceeded with a few friends and the Roman quaestor[1] to a mound in full sight of those who were in ambush, as if he were honouring Jugurtha by going to meet him. Jugurtha came to the same place unarmed and with only a few followers, as had been agreed, and immediately on a given signal those who were in concealment rushed upon him from all sides at once. His companions were killed; the king himself was bound and delivered to Sulla, who took him to Marius.

CXIV. At this same time our generals Quintus Caepio and Gnaeus Manlius were defeated by the Gauls[2] and terror at this had made all Italy tremble. The Romans of that time and even down to our own day believed that all else was easy for their valour, but that with the Gauls they fought for life and not for glory. But when it was announced that the war in Numidia was ended and that Jugurtha was being

---

[1] Sulla.
[2] In 105 B.C. Really by the Cimbri, a Germanic tribe.

tham Romam vinctum adduci nuntiatum est, Marius consul absens factus est et ei decreta provincia Gallia, isque kalendis Ianuariis magna gloria consul 4 triumphavit. Et ea tempestate spes atque opes civitatis in illo sitae.

---

¹ January 1st, 105 B.C.

brought a captive to Rome, Marius was made consul in his absence and Gaul was assigned him as his province. On the Kalends of January[1] he entered upon his office and celebrated a triumph of great magnificence. At that time the hopes and welfare of our country were in his hands.[2]

[2] Jugurtha was taken to Rome, where, after being led with his two sons before Marius's chariot in the triumphal procession, he was starved to death, or, according to some, strangled, in the Tullianum.

ORATIONS AND LETTERS FROM THE HISTORIES

ORATIONES ET EPISTULAE EX-CERPTAE DE HISTORIIS

ORATIO LEPIDI COS. AD POPULUM ROMANUM [1]

1 CLEMENTIA et probitas vostra, Quirites, quibus per ceteras gentis maxumi et clari estis, plurumum timoris mihi faciunt advorsum tyrannidem L. Sullae, ne, quae ipsi nefanda aestumatis, ea parum credundo de aliis circumveniamini—praesertim cum illi spes omnis in scelere atque perfidia sit neque se aliter tutum putet, quam si peior atque intestabilior metu vostro fuerit, quo captis libertatis curam miseria eximat—aut, si provideritis, in tutandis [2] periculis magis quam ulciscendo teneamini.

2 Satellites quidem eius, homines maxumi nominis optumis maiorum exemplis, nequeo satis mirari, qui dominationis in vos servitium suum mercedem

---

[1] *Histories*, i. 55 ; see Introd. pp. xv. ff. *V* = Codex Vaticanus, 3864 ; ς = copies of *V*.
[2] tutandis, *V* : vitandis, *Asulanus.*

---

[1] This attack on Sulla's rule was made in 78 B.C., the year of the consulship of Q. Lutatius Catulus and M. Aemilius Lepidus.

ORATIONS AND LETTERS FROM THE HISTORIES

SPEECH OF THE CONSUL LEPIDUS TO THE ROMAN PEOPLE. [1]

Your mercy and your honesty, fellow citizens,[2] which make you supreme and renowned throughout all nations, cause me the greatest apprehension in the face of the tyranny of Lucius Sulla. On the one hand, I fear that you may be outwitted through not believing others capable of acts which you yourselves regard as abominable; especially since all Sulla's hopes depend upon crime and treachery, and since he thinks that he cannot be safe, unless he has shown himself even worse and more detestable than you fear, so that when you are enslaved to him, you may cease because of your wretchedness to think of freedom. On the other hand, if you are on your guard, I fear that you may be more occupied in avoiding danger than in taking vengeance.

As to his satellites, I cannot sufficiently wonder that men bearing great names, made great by the deeds of distinguished ancestors, are willing to purchase dominion over you with their own slavery, and

---

[2] With the beginning of this speech compare that of the Corinthians to the Lacedaemonians, Thuc. 1. 68.

dant et utrumque per iniuriam malunt quam
3 optumo iure liberi agere, praeclara Brutorum atque
Aemiliorum et Lutatiorum proles, geniti ad ea
4 quae maiores virtute peperere subvortunda. Nam
quid a Pyrrho, Hannibale, Philippoque et Antiocho
defensum est aliud quam libertas et suae cuique
5 sedes, neu cui nisi legibus pareremus? Quae
cuncta scaevos[1] iste Romulus quasi ab externis
rapta tenet, non tot exercituum clade neque consulum et aliorum principum, quos fortuna belli con-
sumpserat, satiatus, sed tum crudelior, cum plerosque
6 secundae res in miserationem ex ira vortunt. Quin
solus omnium post memoriam humani generis[2]
supplicia in post futuros composuit, quis prius iniuria
quam vita certa esset, pravissumeque per sceleris
immanitatem adhuc tutus fuit, dum vos metu
gravioris serviti a repetunda libertate terremini.
7 Agundum atque obviam eundum est, Quirites, ne
spolia vostra penes illum[3] sint, non prolatandum
neque votis paranda auxilia. Nisi forte speratis
taedium iam aut pudorem tyrannidis Sullae esse et
eum per scelus occupata periculosius dimissurum.
8 At ille eo processit, ut nihil gloriosum nisi tutum et

---

[1] scaevus, *V*; saevus, *Serv. Ecl.* 3. 13.
[2] generis, *supplied by Orelli*; hominum, *Aldus.*
[3] illum, *Korte*; illos, *V, Ah.*

---

[1] He refers to D. Junius Brutus, consul in 77, his colleague
Mam. Aemilius Lepidus and Q. Lutatius Catulus, consul
in 78.
[2] Since Sulla planned a reorganization of the state, he is
compared with the founder of Rome.

prefer these two things joined with injustice to living free with the best of right. Glorious scions of the Bruti, Aemilii, and Lutatii,[1] born to overthrow what their ancestors won by their prowess! For what did their forefathers defend against Pyrrhus, Hannibal, Philip and Antiochus, if not our liberty and our own hearthstones, and our privilege of submitting to nothing but the laws? All these things that caricature of Romulus[2] holds in his possession, as if they had been wrested from foreigners; and not content with the destruction of so many armies, consuls, and other leading men, whom the fortune of war had swept away, he grows more cruel at a time when success turns most men from wrath to pity. Nay, he alone of all within the memory of man has devised punishment for those yet unborn,[3] who are thus assured of outrage before they are of life. Worst of all, he has hitherto been protected by the enormity of his crimes, while you are deterred from trying to recover your liberty by the fear of a still more cruel slavery.

You must rouse yourselves, fellow citizens, and resist the tyrant, in order that he may not possess your spoils. You must not delay or look for help from prayers to the gods; unless haply you hope that Sulla is now weary or ashamed of his tyranny and that what he has criminally seized he will with still greater peril[4] resign. On the contrary, he has sunk so low that he thinks nothing glorious

---

[3] By providing that the children of the proscribed should not be allowed to hold office; see Velleius, 2. 28. 4 and *Cat.* xxxvii. 9.

[4] That is, greater than the risk which he ran in usurping his power.

omnia retinendae dominationis honesta aestumet.
9 Itaque illa quies et otium cum libertate, quae multi
probi potius quam laborem cum honoribus capesse-
10 bant, nulla sunt ; hac tempestate serviundum aut
imperitandum, habendus metus est aut faciundus,
11 Quirites.   Nam quid ultra ?   Quaeve humana
superant aut divina impolluta sunt ? Populus Romanus, paulo ante gentium moderator, exutus imperio,[1] gloria, iure, agitandi inops despectusque, ne
12 servilia quidem alimenta reliqua habet.   Sociorum
et Lati magna vis civitate pro multis et egregiis
factis a vobis data per unum prohibentur et plebis
innoxiae patrias sedes occupavere pauci satellites
13 mercedem scelerum.   Leges, iudicia, aerarium,
provinciae, reges penes unum, denique necis civium
14 et vitae licentia.   Simul humanas hostias vidistis et
15 sepulcra infecta sanguine civili.   Estne viris reliqui
aliud quam solvere iniuriam aut mori per virtutem ?
Quoniam quidem unum omnibus finem natura vel
ferro saeptis statuit neque quisquam extremam
necessitatem nihil ausus nisi muliebri ingenio
exspectat.
16   Verum ego seditiosus, uti Sulla ait, qui praemia
turbarum queror, et bellum cupiens, qui iura pacis

[1] imperii, *Mommsen.*

---

[1] Since Sulla had repealed the laws which gave cheap
grain to the populace.
[2] Since Sulla confined the right of serving as jurors to the
senatorial order, taking it from the knights.

which is not safe, and regards every means of retaining his supremacy as honourable. Hence that state of repose and tranquillity combined with freedom, which many good men prized more highly than honours attended with toil, is a thing of the past; in these times one must either be slave or master, one must feel fear, citizens, or inspire it. For what else is left us? What human laws survive? What divine laws have not been violated? The Roman people, lately ruler of the nations, now stripped of power, repute and rights, without the means to live [1] and an object of contempt, does not even retain the rations of slaves. A great part of our allies and of the people of Latium to whom you gave citizenship in return for many distinguished services are robbed of it by one man, while a few of his minions, as a recompense for their crimes, have seized upon the ancestral homes of the guiltless commons. The laws, the courts,[2] the treasury, the provinces, the kings, in fact, the power of life and death over our citizens are in the hands of one man. You have even beheld human sacrifices [3] and tombs stained with the blood of citizens. If you are men, is anything left to you except to put an end to oppression or to die valiantly? For of a truth Nature has appointed one and the same end for all, even for those encased in steel, and no one awaits the last necessity, daring nothing, unless he has the heart of a woman.

But Sulla says that I am a sower of sedition, because I protest against the rewards paid to civil commotion; a lover of war, because I would reclaim

---

[3] Marius Gratidianus was immolated at the tomb of the Lutatian gens; see Valerius Maximus, 9. 2. 1.

17 repeto. Scilicet, quia non aliter salvi satisque tuti
in imperio eritis, nisi Vettius Picens et scriba
Cornelius aliena bene parata [1] prodegerint; nisi
approbaritis omnes proscriptionem innoxiorum ob
divitias, cruciatus virorum illustrium, vastam urbem
fuga et caedibus, bona civium miserorum quasi
18 Cimbricam praedam venum aut dono datam. At
obiectat mihi possessiones ex bonis proscriptorum;
quod quidem scelerum illius vel maxumum est, non
me neque quemquam omnium satis tutum fuisse,
si recte faceremus. Atque illa, quae tum formidine
mercatus sum, pretio soluto iure dominis tamen
restituo, neque pati consilium est ullam ex civibus
19 praedam esse. Satis illa fuerint, quae rabie contracta toleravimus, manus conserentis inter se
Romanos exercitus et arma ab externis in nosmet
vorsa; scelerum et contumeliarum omnium finis sit;
quorum adeo Sullam non paenitet, ut et facta in
gloria numeret et, si liceat, avidius fecerit.

20 Neque iam quid existumetis de illo, sed quantum
audeatis vereor, ne alius alium principem expec-
tantes ante capiamini, non opibus eius, quae futiles
et corruptae sunt, sed vostra socordia, qua raptum
ire [2] licet et quam audeat,[3] tam videri Felicem.
21 Nam praeter satellites commaculatos quis eadem

---

[1] parta, *Orelli.*
[2] qua raptum ire, *Madvig*; quam raptum iri, *V.*
[3] quam audeat, *Korrte*; quam audeas, *V, Ah.*

---

[1] According to Cicero (*Off.* 2. 29) he was a clerk in Sulla's
dictatorship and a quaestor in Caesar's.

the rights of peace. Of course! since you cannot be safe and fully protected under Sulla's dominion, unless Vettius of Picenum and the clerk Cornelius [1] may squander the goods which others have honestly acquired; unless you all approve the proscription of innocent men because of their wealth, the tortures of distinguished citizens, a city depopulated by exile and murder, the goods of wretched citizens sold or given away as if they were the spoils of the Cimbri. Sulla blames me for having possessions which are derived from the goods of the proscribed. But in fact it is the very greatest of his crimes that neither I nor anyone else would have been safe if we did what was right. Moreover, the property which at that time I bought through fear and paid for I nevertheless restore now to its rightful owners, and it is not my purpose to allow any booty to be taken from the citizens. Let it be enough to have endured what our frenzy has brought about—Roman armies pitted against each other, our arms turned away from the enemy and against ourselves. Let there be an end to crimes and all outrages; of which, however, Sulla is so far from repenting that he counts them among his titles to glory, and, if he were allowed, would more eagerly do them again.

But now I care no longer what you think of him, but what you dare; for while you are all waiting for someone else to assume the lead, I fear lest you may be caught, not by his forces, which are insignificant and degenerate, but through your own indifference, which allows him to continue his course of rapine and to seem fortunate [2] in proportion to his audacity. For with the exception of his crime-stained minions,

---

[2] Playing upon Sulla's surname of Felix.

volt aut quis non omnia mutata praeter victoriam[1]?
Scilicet milites, quorum sanguine Tarulae Scirtoque,
22 pessumis servorum, divitiae partae sunt? An quibus
praelatus in magistratibus capiundis Fufidius, ancilla
turpis, honorum omnium dehonestamentum? Itaque
maxumam mihi fiduciam parit victor exercitus, cui
per tot volnera et labores nihil praeter tyrannum
23 quaesitum est. Nisi forte tribuniciam potestatem
evorsum profecti sunt per arma, conditam a maioribus suis, utique iura et iudicia sibimet extorquerent,
egregia scilicet mercede, cum relegati in paludes et
silvas contumeliam atque invidiam suam, praemia
penes paucos intellegerent.[2]
24   Quare igitur tanto agmine atque animis incedit?
Quia secundae res mire sunt vitiis optentui, quibus
labefactis,[3] quam formidatus est, tam contemnetur.
Nisi forte specie concordiae et pacis, quae sceleri et
parricidio suo nomina indidit. Neque aliter rem
publicam et belli finem ait, nisi maneat expulsa agris
plebes, praeda civilis acerbissuma, ius iudiciumque
omnium rerum penes se, quod populi Romani fuit.
25 Quae si vobis pax et composita intelleguntur, maxuma turbamenta rei publicae atque exitia probate,

---

[1] praeter victoriam, *Müller, Ah*; propter victoriam, **V**;
victorem, *Kritz* ("*an* victorem *scribendum,*" *Ah*).
[2] intellegerent, *V* ; intellegerint, *Orelli.*
[3] labefactis, *Mähly* ; labefacti, *mss.*

---

[1] The meaning is that even the members of Sulla's own
party (*praeter satellites commaculatos*) are dissatisfied with

who is on his side or who does not desire a complete change, retaining only the victory?[1] Think you it is the soldiers, at the price of whose blood riches are won for vile slaves such as Tarula and Scirtus? Or is it those who in suing for office were thought less worthy than Fufidius, a vile wench, the dishonour of all honours? It is because of acts like these that I rest my greatest confidence in the victorious army, which has gained nothing by so many wounds and hardships save a tyrant. Unless haply they took the field to overthrow the power of the tribunes, which their forefathers had established, and to rob themselves with their own hands of their rights and their jurisdiction[2]; richly rewarded, no doubt, when, banished to swamps and woods, they find that insult and hatred are their portion, that a handful of men gain the prizes!

Why then does the tyrant walk abroad with so great a following and with such assurance? Because success is a wonderful screen for vices; but let a reverse come, and he will be despised as much as he is now feared. Or perhaps he does it to make a pretence of peace and harmony, which are the names which he has applied to his guilt and treason. Furthermore, he declares that the republic cannot be established, and war ended, unless the commons are for ever driven from their lands, the citizens cruelly plundered, and all rights and jurisdiction, once belonging to the Roman people, placed in his own hands. If this seems to you to be peace and order, show your approval of the utter demoralization and overthrow of the republic, bow to the laws which

everything except their victory (in the civil war), and would gladly see everything else changed.

[2] See note on § 13, above.

annuite legibus impositis, accipite otium cum servitio et tradite exemplum posteris ad rem publicam
suimet sanguinis mercede circumveniundam!

26 Mihi quamquam per hoc summum imperium satis
quaesitum erat nomini maiorum, dignitati atque
etiam praesidio, tamen non fuit consilium privatas
opes facere, potiorque visa est periculosa libertas
27 quieto servitio. Quae si probatis, adeste, Quirites,
et bene iuvantibus divis M. Aemilium consulem
ducem et auctorem sequimini ad recipiundam
libertatem!

have been imposed upon you, accept a peace combined with servitude and teach future generations how to ruin their country at the price of their own blood.

For my own part, although by attaining this the highest of offices [1] I had done enough to live up to the fame of my ancestors as well as to secure my own dignity, and even my safety, yet it was not my intention to pursue my private interests, but I looked upon freedom united with danger as preferable to peace with slavery. If you are of the same mind, citizens of Rome, rouse yourselves and with the kindly aid of the gods follow Marcus Aemilius, your consul, who will be your leader and champion in recovering your freedom!

[1] The consulship.

ORATIO PHILIPPI IN SENATU [1]

1   MAXUME vellem, patres conscripti, rem publicam
quietam esse aut in periculis a promptissumo quoque
defendi, denique prava incepta consultoribus noxae
esse.   Sed contra seditionibus omnia turbata sunt et
ab eis quos prohibere magis decebat; postremo, quae
pessumi et stultissumi decrevere, ea bonis et sapienti-
2   bus faciunda sunt.   Nam bellum atque arma, quamquam vobis invisa, tamen quia Lepido placent,
sumunda sunt, nisi forte cui pacem praestare et
bellum pati consilium est.

3   Pro di boni, qui hanc urbem omissam cura nostra [2]
adhuc tegitis, M. Aemilius, omnium flagitiosorum
postremus, qui peior an ignavior sit deliberari non
potest, exercitum opprimundae libertatis habet et
se e contempto metuendum effecit; vos mussantes
et retractantes verbis et vatum carminibus pacem
optatis magis quam defenditis, neque intellegitis

[1] *Histories*, i. 77.
[2] omissam cura nostra, *Opitz*; omissa cura nostra, *Wirtz*;
omissa cura, *V, Ah*; amissa curia, *Haupt*; o. consulum c.,
Steup.

[1] When Lepidus demanded a second consulship and the
restitution of the powers of the tribunes, the leader of the
aristocracy, L. Marcius Philippus, opposed his demands and
convinced the senate that Lepidus ought to be punished.

THE SPEECH OF PHILIPPUS IN THE SENATE.[1]

I COULD wish above everything, Fathers of the Senate, that our country might be at peace, or that amidst dangers, it might be defended by its ablest citizens; or at any rate that evil designs should prove the ruin of their contrivers. But on the contrary, everything is in disorder as the result of civil dissensions, which are aroused by those whose duty it rather was to suppress them; and finally, the wise and good are forced to do what the worst and most foolish of men have resolved. For even though you may detest war and arms, yet you must take them up because it is the will of Lepidus, unless haply anyone is disposed to grant him peace and at the same time to suffer war.[2]

O ye good gods, who still watch over this city, for which we take no thought, Marcus Aemilius, the lowest of all criminals—and it is not easy to say whether he is more vicious or more cowardly—has an army for the purpose of overthrowing our liberties, from contemptible has made himself terrible! You,[3] meanwhile, muttering and shrinking, trusting to the predictions and incantations of soothsayers,[4] pray rather than fight for peace, and you do not

---

[2] cf. Livy 42. 13. 5, *videbam quam impar esset sors, cum ille vobis bellum pararet, vos ei securam pacem praestaretis.*

[3] Addressed to the senators.

[4] The Sybilline books had been burned with the Capitol in 83 B.C., but many other prophetic writings were in circulation; see Suet. *Aug.* 31. 1.

mollitia decretorum vobis dignitatem, illi metum
4 detrahi. Atque id iure; quoniam ex rapinis consulatum, ob seditionem provinciam cum exercitu
adeptus est, quid ille ob bene facta cepisset, cuius
sceleribus tanta praemia tribuistis?

5 At scilicet eos, qui ad postremum usque legatos,
pacem, concordiam, et alia huiuscemodi decreverunt,
gratiam ab eo peperisse! Immo despecti et indigni
re publica habiti praedae loco aestumantur, quippe
metu pacem repetentes, quo habitam amiserant.

6 Equidem a principio, cum Etruriam coniurare, pro-
scriptos arcessi, largitionibus rem publicam lacerari
videbam, maturandum putabam et Catuli consilia
cum paucis secutus sum ; ceterum illi qui gentis
Aemiliae bene facta extollebant et ignoscundo populi
Romani magnitudinem auxisse, nusquam etiam tum
Lepidum progressum aiebant, cum privata arma
opprimundae libertatis cepisset, sibi quisque opes
aut patrocinia quaerundo consilium publicum cor-
ruperunt.

7 At tum erat Lepidus latro cum calonibus et paucis
sicariis, quorum nemo diurna mercede vitam mutaverit;
nunc est pro consule cum imperio non empto sed
dato a vobis, cum legatis adhuc iure parentibus, et
ad eum concurrere homines omnium ordinum cor-
ruptissumi, flagrantes inopia et cupidinibus, scelerum

---

[1] That is, divided into opposing factions.
[2] On the inversion of the price and the object bought see
Horace, *Serm.* 2. 7. 109, with the notes of Lejay, Palmer,
and others.

realise that by your irresolute decrees you are losing your prestige, he his fear. And naturally enough, for since his robberies have made him consul, his acts of sedition have given him a province and an army, what might he not have gained by good conduct, when you have rewarded his crimes so generously?

But perhaps it is those who up to the very last have voted for embassies, for peace, for harmony, and the like, that have won his favour. Nay, despised, held unworthy of a share in the state, they are regarded as plunder, since fear makes them sue for peace, which fear had made them lose. For my own part, at the very outset, when I saw Etruria conspiring, the proscribed recalled, and the state rent asunder[1] by bribery, I thought that there was no time to be lost and with a few others I followed the standard of Catulus. But those who lauded the great deeds of the Aemilian family, and the clemency which had made the Roman people great, said that even then Lepidus had taken no decisive step, although he had taken up arms on his own responsibility to crush out liberty; and thus while seeking power or protection for themselves each of them perverted the public counsels.

At that time, however, Lepidus was a mere brigand at the head of a few camp-followers and cut-throats, any one of whom would have sold his life for a day's wages[2]; now he is a proconsul with military power which he did not buy, but which you gave him, with subordinates who are still[3] bound by law to obey him; the most vicious characters of every class flock to his standard, inflamed by poverty

[3] Since Lepidus has not yet been outlawed by the senate.

consientia exagitati, quibus quies in seditionibus, in pace turbae sunt. Hi tumultum ex tumultu, bellum ex bello serunt, Saturnini olim, post Sulpici, dein

8 Mari Damasippique, nunc Lepidi satellites. Praeterea Etruria atque omnes reliquiae belli arrectae, Hispaniae armis sollicitae, Mithridates in latere vectigalium nostrorum quibus adhuc sustentamur, diem bello circumspicit ; quin praeter idoneum ducem nihil abest ad subvortundum imperium.

9 Quod ego vos oro atque obsecro, patres conscripti, ut animadvortatis neu [1] patiamini licentiam scelerum quasi rabiem ad integros contactu procedere ; nam ubi malos praemia secuntur, haud facile quisquam

10 gratuito bonus est. An expectatis dum exercitu rursus admoto ferro atque flamma urbem invadat ? Quod multo propius est ab eo quo agitat statu, quam

11 ex pace et concordia ad arma civilia. Quae ille advorsum divina et humana omnia cepit, non pro sua aut quorum simulat iniuria, sed legum ac libertatis subvortundae. Agitur enim ac laceratur animi cupidine et noxarum metu, expers consili, inquies, haec atque illa temptans, metuit otium, odit bellum,

---

[1] neu, *Carrio* ; ne, *V.*

---

[1] In 100 B.C. Lucius Saturninus, who was then tribune of the commons, set on foot a rebellion and was condemned to death by Marius.

and greed, driven on by the consciousness of their crimes, men who find repose in discord, disquiet in time of peace. These are the men who rouse rebellion after rebellion, war after war, followers now of Saturninus,[1] then of Sulpicius,[2] next of Marius and Damasippus,[3] and now of Lepidus. Moreover, Etruria is aroused, as well as all the other smouldering fires of war; the Spanish provinces are stirred to revolt, Mithridates, who is close beside those of our tributaries from whom we still receive support, is watching for an opportunity for war; in short, for the overthrow of our empire nothing is lacking save a competent leader.

Therefore, Fathers of the Senate, take heed, I beg and implore you, and do not allow the licence of crime, like a madness, to infect those who are as yet sound. For when the wicked are rewarded, it is not easy for anyone to be virtuous without price. Or are you waiting for Lepidus to come again with an army and enter our city with fire and sword? Verily, such an act is much nearer the condition in which he now finds himself than are peace and concord to civil arms. And these arms he took up in defiance of all human and divine law, not in order to avenge his own wrongs or the wrongs of those whom he pretends to represent, but to overthrow our laws and our liberty. For he is hounded and tormented in mind by ambition and terror because of his crimes, uneasy and at his wits' end, resorting now to this plan, now to that. He fears peace, hates war; he sees that he must sacrifice

---

[2] Sulpicius, tribune in 88 B.C., proposed and carried through the bill by which the command of the war against Mithridates was taken from Sulla and given to Marius. He was put to death at Laurentum.   [3] See *Cat.* li. 32.

luxu **atque licentia** carendum **videt** atque interim
abutitur vostra socordia.

12 Neque mihi satis consili est, metum an ignaviam **an**
dementiam **eam** appellem, qui videmini tanta mala
quasi fulmen optare se quisque **ne** attingat, sed prohibere ne conari quidem.

13 Et quaeso considerate quam convorsa rerum natura
sit; antea malum publicum occulte, auxilia palam
instruebantur et eo boni malos facile anteibant : nunc
pax et concordia disturbantur palam, defenduntur
occulte ; quibus illa placent in armis sunt, vos in
metu. Quid expectatis ? Nisi forte pudet aut piget
14 recte facere. An Lepidi mandata animos movere ?
Qui placere ait sua cuique reddi et aliena tenet, belli
iura rescindi, cum ipse armis cogat, civitatem confirmari, quibus ademptam negat, concordiae gratia
tribuniciam potestatem restitui, ex qua omnes discordiae accensae.

15 Pessume omnium atque impudentissume, tibine
egestas civium et luctus curae sunt ? Cui nihil est
domi nisi armis partum aut per iniuriam ! Alterum
consulatum petis, quasi primum reddideris, bello concordiam quaeris quo parta disturbatur, nostri proditor,
istis infidus, hostis omnium bonorum ! Ut te neque

luxury and licence, and meanwhile he takes advantage of your indolence.

As to your conduct, I lack sufficient wisdom to know whether to call it cowardice, weakness or madness, when each one of you seems to pray that the evils which threaten you like a thunderbolt may not touch him, and yet makes not the slightest effort to prevent them.

I pray you consider how the order of things is inverted; formerly public mischief was planned secretly, public defence openly; and hence the good easily forestalled the wicked. Nowadays peace and harmony are disturbed openly, defended secretly; those who desire disorder are in arms; you are in fear. What are you waiting for, unless perchance you are ashamed or weary of well doing? Are you influenced by the demands of Lepidus? He says that he wishes to render unto each his own, and keeps the property of others; to annul laws established in time of war, while he uses armed compulsion; to establish the citizenship of those from whom he denies that it has been taken, and in the interests of peace to restore the power of the tribunes, from which all our discords were kindled.

O vilest and most shameless of all men, do you take to heart the poverty and grief of the citizens, when you have nothing in your possession which was not seized by arms or by injustice! You ask for a second consulship, as if you had ever given up your first. You seek harmony through war, by which the harmony which we had attained is broken, a traitor to us, unfaithful to your party, the enemy of all good citizens. Are you not ashamed either before

403

hominum neque deorum pudet, quos per fidem aut
periurio violasti!

16 Qui quando talis es, maneas in sententia et retineas arma te hortor, neu prolatandis seditionibus,
inquies ipse, nos in sollicitudine attineas; neque
te provinciae neque leges neque di penates civem
patiuntur; perge qua coeptas, ut quam maturrume
merita invenias.

17 Vos autem, patres conscripti, quo usque cunctando
rem publicam intutam patiemini et verbis arma
temptabitis? Dilectus advorsus vos habiti, pecuniae
publice et privatim extortae, praesidia deducta atque
imposita, ex lubidine leges imperantur, cum interim
vos legatos et decreta paratis. Quanto mehercule
avidius pacem petieritis, tanto bellum acrius erit,
cum intelleget se metu magis quam aequo et bono

18 sustentatum. Nam qui turbas et caedem civium
odisse ait et ob id armato Lepido vos inermos retinet,
quae victis toleranda sunt ea, cum facere possitis,
patiamini potius censet; ita illi a vobis pacem, vobis

19 ab illo bellum suadet. Haec si placent, si tanta torpedo animos obrepsit,[1] ut obliti scelerum Cinnae,
cuius in urbem reditu decus ordinis huius interiit,
nihilo minus vos atque coniuges et liberos Lepido

[1] obrepsit, *F*[1] *Non.* p. 229. 4 M; obprepsit, *F*[2]; oppressit, *V, Ah.*

---

[1] During the proscriptions of 87 B.C.

men or before the gods, whom you have insulted by your perfidy or perjury?

Since such is your character, I urge you to be true to your purpose and to retain your arms, lest by deferring your rebellious plans you may be uneasy yourself and keep us in a ferment. Neither the provinces, nor the laws, nor your country's gods tolerate you as a citizen. Continue as you have begun, in order that as soon as possible you may meet with your deserts.

But you, Fathers of the Senate, how long will your hesitation leave your country undefended, and how long will you meet arms with words? Forces have been levied against you, money extorted from individuals and from the treasury, garrisons removed from one place and stationed in another, the laws interpreted in accordance with caprice, and in the meantime you are preparing to send envoys and make decrees. But, by Heaven! the more eagerly you seek peace, the more cruel will the war be, when he finds that he can more safely rely upon your fears than upon the justice and righteousness of his cause. In truth, whoever says that he hates disturbance and the death of citizens, and therefore keeps you unarmed while Lepidus is in arms, is in reality advising you to suffer what the conquered must endure, when you might yourselves visit it upon others. Such counsellors advise you to keep peace with him and encourage him to make war upon you. If this is your intention, if such torpor has stolen upon your spirits that forgetting the crimes of Cinna, upon whose return to our city the flower of this order perished,[1] you will nevertheless entrust yourselves, your wives, and your children to Lepidus, what

permissuri sitis, quid opus decretis, quid auxilio
Catuli? Quin is et alii boni rem publicam frustra
curant.

20 Agite ut lubet, parate vobis Cethegi atque alia
proditorum patrocinia, qui rapinas et incendia instau-
rare cupiunt et rursus advorsum deos penatis manus
armare. Sin libertas et vera magis placent, decernite
digna nomine et augete ingenium viris fortibus.

21 Adest novus exercitus, ad hoc coloniae veterum
militum, nobilitas omnis, duces optumi ; fortuna
meliores sequitur ; iam illa quae socordia nostra[1]
collecta sunt, dilabentur.

22 Quare ita censeo : quoniam M.[2] Lepidus exercitum
privato consilio paratum cum pessumis et hostibus rei
publicae contra huius ordinis auctoritatem ad urbem
ducit, uti Ap. Claudius interrex cum Q. Catulo pro
consule et ceteris, quibus imperium est, urbi praesidio
sint operamque dent nequid res publica detrimenti
capiat.

[1] vostra, *Dietsch.*   [2] M *added by Orelli.*

need is there of decrees? What need of Catulus'
help? Surely it is in vain that he and other good
citizens are taking thought for the republic.

But have your way! Gain the protection of
Cethegus and the other traitors, who are eager to
renew the reign of pillage and fire and once more
to arm their hands against our country's gods. Or
if you prefer liberty and justice, pass decrees worthy
of your reputation, and thus increase the courage
of your brave defenders. A new army is ready,
besides the colonies of veterans, all the nobles, and
the best leaders; fortune attends the stronger;
soon the forces which our negligence has assembled
will melt away.

Therefore this is my recommendation: whereas
Marcus Lepidus, in defiance of the authority of this
body and in concert with the worst enemies of their
country, is leading against this city an army raised
on his own authority, therefore be it resolved that
Appius Claudius the interrex,[1] with Quintus Catulus,
the proconsul and others who have military power,
shall defend the city and see to it that no harm
come to our countr y.[2]

---

[1] Taking the place of the consuls for 77 B.C., who at this
time (the end of January) had not yet been elected.

[2] See *Cat.* xxix. 2-3.

ORATIO C. COTTAE AD POPULUM ROMANUM[1]

1 QUIRITES, multa mihi pericula domi militiaeque, multa advorsa fuere, quorum alia toleravi, partim reppuli deorum auxiliis et virtute mea[2]; in quis omnibus numquam animus negotio defuit neque decretis labos; malae secundaeque res opes, non 2 ingenium mihi mutabant. At contra in his miseriis cuncta me cum fortuna deseruere; praeterea senectus, per se gravis, curam duplicat, cui misero acta iam aetate ne mortem quidam honestam sperare 3 licet. Nam, si parricida vostri sum et bis genitus hic deos penatis meos patriamque et summum imperium vilia habeo, quis mihi vivo cruciatus satis est aut quae poena mortuo? Quin omnia memorata apud inferos supplicia scelere meo vici.

4 A prima adulescentia in ore vostro privatus et in magistratibus egi; qui lingua, qui consilio meo,

---

[1] *Histories*, ii. 47.
[2] *The words* Quirites . . . virtute mea *are found in the fragg. Berol. and Aurel*; see Introd. p. xvi.

---

[1] During the year 75 B.C. there was civil discord at Rome and attacks were made upon the nobles by the commons.

SPEECH OF GAIUS COTTA TO THE ROMAN PEOPLE.[1]

I HAVE encountered many dangers, fellow citizens, at home and abroad, and many adversities, some of which I have endured, some averted by the gods' help and my own courage; in all these I never lacked resolution to decide or energy to act. Adversity and prosperity changed my resources, not my character. But in these present troubles it is different, and along with Fortune everything else has deserted me. Furthermore, old age, which is in itself an affliction, redoubles my anxiety, since it is my wretched lot, when near the end of life, not even to be able to hope for an honourable death. For if I am a traitor to you, and although twice born into this state,[2] hold cheap my country's gods, my fatherland, and its highest magistracy, what torture is enough for me while I live, and what punishment after death? Surely I have committed a crime too great to be expiated by all the torments related of the Nether World.

From early youth I have passed my life before your eyes both as a private citizen and in office; those who needed my voice, my counsel, my purse,

Alarmed by the dangerous outlook, Gaius Cotta, one of the consuls, put on mourning garb and made an address designed to calm the people.

[2] His recall from exile is regarded as a second birth; so Cicero, ad Att. 6. 6. 4, calls his recall a παλιγγενεσία.

qui pecunia voluere, usi sunt : neque ego callidam [1]
facundiam neque ingenium ad male faciundum
exercui ; avidissumus privatae gratiae maxumas
inimicitias pro re publica suscepi, quis victus cum
illa simul, cum egens alienae opis plura mala ex-
pectarem, vos, Quirites, rursus mihi patriam deosque
5 penatis cum ingenti dignitate dedistis.   Pro quibus
beneficiis vix satis gratus videar, si singulis animam
quam nequeo concesserim ; nam vita et mors iura
naturae sunt ; ut sine dedecore cum civibus fama et
fortunis integer agas, id dono datur atque accipitur.

6   Consules nos fecistis, Quirites, domi bellique
impeditissuma re publica ; namque imperatores
Hispaniae stipendium, milites, arma, frumentum
poscunt—et id res cogit, quoniam defectione sociorum et Sertori per montis fuga neque manu
7 certare possunt neque utilia parare—exercitus in
Asia Ciliciaque ob nimias opes Mithridatis aluntur,
Macedonia plena hostium est, nec minus Italiae
marituma et provinciarum, cum interim vectigalia
parva et bellis incerta vix partem sumptuum [2] sustinent ; ita classe, quae commeatus tuebatur, minore
quam antea navigamus.

8   Haec si dolo aut socordia nostra contracta sunt,
agite ut monet ira, supplicium sumite ; sin fortuna

---

[1] callidam, *mss.* ; caninam, *Carrio.*
[2] sumptum, *V.*

have had them. I have not practised a calculating eloquence or used my talents for evil-doing. Most covetous of private friendships, I have incurred the bitterest public enmities for my country. When these had overcome me along with my country, when in need of others' help, I looked for still greater calamities, you, fellow citizens, gave me back my country and my fathers' gods, and added to them your highest mark of distinction. For such favours I should seem hardly grateful enough if I could give my life for each one of you. That I cannot do, since life and death are subject to natural laws; but to live unashamed among one's fellow citizens, and with unblemished reputation and fortune, is something that may be given and received.

You have elected us to the consulship, Romans, at a time when our country is in dire straits at home and abroad; for our generals in Spain are calling for money, men, arms, and supplies—and they are forced to do so by circumstances, since the defection of our allies and the retreat of Sertorius over the mountains prevent them from either contending in battle or providing for their necessities. Armies are maintained in Asia and in Cilicia because of the excessive power of Mithridates, Macedonia is full of foes, as is also the sea-coast of Italy and of the provinces. In the meantime our revenues, made scanty and uncertain by war, barely suffice for a part of our expenditures; hence the fleet which we keep upon the sea is much smaller than the one which formerly safeguarded our supplies.

If such a state of affairs has been brought about by treason or negligence on our part, follow the promptings of your anger and inflict punishment

communis asperior est, quare indigna vobis nobisque
9 et re publica incipitis? Atque ego, cuius aetati
mors propior est, non deprecor, si quid ea vobis
incommodi demitur; neque mox ingenio corporis
honestius quam pro vostra salute finem vitae fecerim.
10 Adsum en C. Cotta consul! Facio quod saepe
maiores asperis bellis fecere, voveo dedoque me pro
re publica! Quam deinde cui mandetis circum-
11 spicite; nam talem honorem bonus nemo volet, cum
fortunae et maris et belli ab aliis acti ratio reddunda
12 aut turpiter moriundum sit. Tantum modo in
animis habetote non me ob scelus aut avaritiam
caesum, sed volentem[1] pro maxumis benificiis
13 animam dono dedisse. Per vos, Quirites, et gloriam
maiorum, tolerate advorsa et consulite rei publicae!
14 Multa cura summo imperio inest, multi ingentes
labores, quos nequiquam abnuitis et pacis opulentiam
quaeritis, cum omnes provinciae, regna, maria,
terraeque aspera aut fessa bellis sint.

[1] volente, *V.*

upon us; but if fortune, which is common to all, frowns upon us, why do you resort to acts unworthy of you, of us, and of our country? I, to whom death is nearer because of my years, am ready to meet it, if that will lessen any of your ills; nor could I end my life (as in the course of nature I soon must) with more honour than in securing your safety. Behold, here I stand, Gaius Cotta, your consul! I do what our ancestors often did in adverse wars; I consecrate myself and offer my life for my country. It is your task to find someone to whom you may entrust the state; for no good man will desire such an honour, when one must render an account for the vagaries of fortune, for the uncertainties of the sea, and for war brought on by others, or else must die a shameful death. Only bear in mind that it was not for crime or avarice that I was put to death, but that I willingly gave my life as a gift in return for your great favours. In your own name,[1] fellow-citizens, and by the glory of your ancestors, I conjure you to endure adversity and take thought for your country. The price of supreme power is great anxiety, many heavy burdens. It is vain for you to attempt to avoid them and to look for peace and prosperity, when all the provinces and realms, all lands and seas, are devastated or exhausted by wars.

[1] *cf. Jug.* xiv. 25.

EPISTULA CN. POMPEI AD SENATUM[1]

1   Si adversus vos patriamque et deos penatis tot
labores et pericula suscepissem, quotiens a prima
adulescentia ductu meo scelestissumi hostes fusi et
vobis salus quaesita est, nihil amplius in absentem
me statuissetis quam adhuc agitis, patres conscripti,
quem contra aetatem proiectum ad bellum saevis-
sumum cum exercitu optume merito, quantum est in
vobis, fame, miserruma omnium morte, confecistis.

2   Hacine spe populus Romanus liberos suos ad bellum
misit? Haec sunt praemia pro volneribus et totiens
ob rem publicam fuso sanguine? Fessus scribundo
mittundoque legatos omnis opes et spes privatas
meas consumpsi, cum interim a vobis per triennium

3   vix annuus sumptus datus est. Per deos immortalis, utrum censetis me vicem aerari praestare an
exercitum sine frumento et stipendio habere posse?

4   Equidem fateor me ad hoc bellum maiore studio
quam consilio profectum, quippe qui nomine modo

---

[1] *Histories*, ii. 98, from exercitum (3) to end preserved in
Frag. Aur.; see Introd. p. xvi.

---

[1] In the autumn of 75 B.C. Sertorius by avoiding pitched
battles and resorting to guerilla warfare cut off Pompey's
supplies. Since Pompey had long since exhausted his own

LETTER OF GNAEUS POMPEIUS TO THE SENATE.[1]

IF I had been warring against you, against my country, and against my fathers' gods, when I endured such hardships and dangers as those amid which from my early youth the armies under my command have routed the most criminal of your enemies and insured your safety; even then, Fathers of the Senate, you could have done no more against me in my absence than you are now doing. For after having exposed me, in spite of my youth,[2] to a most cruel war, you have, so far as in you lay, destroyed me and a faithful army by starvation, the most wretched of all deaths. Was it with such expectations that the Roman people sent its sons to war? Are these the rewards for wounds and for so often shedding our blood for our country? Wearied with writing letters and sending envoys, I have exhausted my personal resources and even my expectations, and in the meantime for three years you have barely given me the means of meeting a year's expenses. By the immortal gods! do you think that I can play the part of a treasury or maintain an army without food and pay?

I admit that I entered upon this war with more zeal than discretion; for within forty days of the time when I received from you the empty title of

means, he wrote this letter to the senate, asking for reinforcements and money.

[2] Pompey was only twenty-eight years old at the time and had held no civil office.

415

imperi a vobis accepto, diebus quadraginta exercitum paravi hostisque in cervicibus iam Italiae
agentis ab Alpibus in Hispaniam submovi; per eas
iter aliud atque Hannibal, nobis opportunius, pate-
5 feci. Recepi Galliam, Pyrenaeum, Lacetaniam, In-
digetis et primum impetum Sertori victoris novis
militibus et multo paucioribus sustinui hiememque
castris inter saevissumos hostis, non per oppida
neque ex ambitione mea egi.

6 Quid deinde proelia aut expeditiones hibernas,
oppida excisa aut recepta enumerem ? Quando res
plus valet quam verba : castra hostium apud Su-
cronem capta et proelium apud flumen Turiam et
dux hostium C. Herennius cum urbe Valentia et
exercitu deleti satis clara vobis sunt; pro quis, o
grati patres, egestatem et famem redditis. Itaque
meo et hostium exercitui par condicio est; namque
7 stipendium neutri datur, victor uterque in Italiam
8 venire potest. Quod ego vos moneo quaesoque ut
animadvortatis neu cogatis necessitatibus privatim
9 mihi consulere. Hispaniam citeriorem, quae non ab
hostibus tenetur, nos aut Sertorius ad internecionem
vastavimus praeter maritumas civitates, ultro nobis
sumptui onerique ; Gallia superiore anno Metelli
exercitum stipendio frumentoque aluit et nunc malis
fructibus ipsa vix agitat; ego non rem familiarem

---

[1] By indulging the soldiers; for the same use of *ambitio*
see *Jug.* xlv. 1.

commander I had raised and equipped an army and driven the enemy, who were already at the throat of Italy, from the Alps into Spain; and over those mountains I had opened for you another and more convenient route than Hannibal had taken. I recovered Gaul, the Pyrenees, Lacetania, and the Indigetes; with raw soldiers and far inferior numbers I withstood the first onslaught of triumphant Sertorius; and I spent the winter in camp amid the most savage of foes, not in the towns or in adding to my own popularity.[1]

Why need I enumerate our battles or our winter campaigns, the towns which we destroyed or captured? Actions speak louder than words. The taking of the enemy's camp at Sucro, the battle at the River Turia, and the destruction of Gaius Herennius, leader of the enemy, together with his army and the city of Valentia, are well enough known to you. In return for these, grateful fathers, you give me want and hunger. Thus the condition of my army and of that of the enemy is the same; for neither is paid and either can march victorious into Italy.[2] Of this situation I warn you and I beg you to give it your attention; do not force me to provide for my necessities on my own responsibility. Hither Spain, so far as it is not in the possession of the enemy, either we or Sertorius have devastated to the point of ruin, except for the coast towns, so that it is actually an expense and a burden to us. Gaul last year supplied the army of Metellus with pay and provisions and can now scarcely keep alive itself because of a failure of the crops; I

[2] The meaning is, that Pompey can lead his victorious army into Italy (*i.e.*, return home) and then Sertorius would be able to march into Italy unopposed.

417

10 modo, verum etiam fidem consumpsi. Reliqui vos
estis : qui nisi subvenitis, invito et praedicente me
exercitus hinc et cum eo omne bellum Hispaniae
in Italiam transgredientur.[1]

Hae litterae principio sequentis anni recitatae
in senatu. Sed consules decretas a patribus provincias inter se paravere[2]; Cotta Galliam citeriorem
habuit, Ciliciam Octavius. Dein proxumi consules,
L. Lucullus et M. Cotta, litteris nuntiisque Pompei
graviter perculsi, cum summae rei gratia tum ne
exercitu in Italiam deducto neque laus sua neque
dignitas esset, omni modo stipendium et supplementum paravere, adnitente maxime nobilitate,
cuius plerique iam tum lingua ferociam suam et
dicta factis sequebantur.[3]

[1] The letter ends at this point. The *Frag. Aur.* adds the
following paragraph from the *Histories.*
[2] partivere, *Wölfflin.*
[3] seque (bantur), *Hauler.*

myself have exhausted not only my means, but even my credit. You are our only resource; unless you come to our rescue, against my will, but not without warning from me, our army will pass over into Italy, bringing with it all the war in Spain.

This letter was read in the senate at the beginning of the following year. But the consuls distributed the provinces which had been decreed by the senate, Cotta taking Hither Gaul and Octavius taking Cilicia. Then the next consuls, Lucius Lucullus and Marcus Cotta, who were greatly agitated by Pompey's letters and messages, both because of the interests of the state and because they feared that, if he led his army into Italy, they would have neither glory nor position, used every means to provide him with money and reinforcements. And they were aided especially by the nobles, the greater number of whom were already giving expression to their confidence and adapting their conduct to their words.

ORATIO MACRI TR. PL. AD PLEBEM [1]

1 Sɪ, Quirites, parum existumaretis, quid inter ius a
maioribus relictum vobis et hoc a Sulla paratum
servitium interesset, multis mihi disserundum fuit
docendique, quas ob iniurias et quotiens a patribus
armata plebes secessisset utique vindices paravisset

2 omnis iuris sui tribunos plebis : nunc hortari modo
relicum est et ire primum via, qua capessundam

3 arbitror libertatem.   Neque me praeterit, quantas
opes nobilitatis solus, impotens inani specie magistratus pellere dominatione incipiam, quantoque tu-

4 tius factio noxiorum agat quam soli innocentes. Sed
praeter spem bonam ex vobis, quae metum vicit,
statui certaminis advorsa pro libertate potiora esse
forti viro quam omnino non certavisse.

5   Quamquam omnes alii creati pro iure vostro vim
cunctam et imperia sua gratia aut spe aut praemiis

[1] *Histories*, iii. 48.

---

[1] In the year 73 B.C. the strife between the nobles and the
commons continued. In the course of these dissensions the

THE SPEECH OF MACER, TRIBUNE OF THE COMMONS TO THE COMMONS.[1]

IF you did not realize, fellow citizens, what a difference there is between the rights left you by your forefathers and this slavery imposed upon you by Sulla, I should be obliged to make a long speech and to inform you because of what wrongs, and how often, the plebeians took up arms and seceded from the patricians; and how they won the tribunes of the commons as the defenders of all their rights. But as it is, I have only to encourage you and to precede you on the road which, in my opinion, leads to the recovery of your liberties. I am not unaware how great is the power of the nobles, whom I alone, powerless, am trying to drive from their tyranny by the empty semblance of a magistracy [2]; and I know how much more secure a faction of wicked men is than any upright man alone. But in addition to the fair hopes which you have inspired and which have dispelled my fear, I have decided that defeat in a struggle for liberty is for a brave man better than never to have struggled at all.

And yet all the others who were elected to maintain your rights have been led by personal interest, by hope, or by bribery to turn all their

[1] tribune C. Licinius Macer assailed the rule of the optimates in this long speech.

[2] Since the tribunes of the commons had been deprived of their real power by Sulla.

in vos convortere, meliusque habent mercede delin-
6 quere quam gratis recte facere. Itaque omnes
concessere iam in paucorum dominationem, qui per
militare nomen aerarium, exercitus, regna, provincias
occupavere et arcem habent ex spoliis vostris, cum
interim more pecorum vos, multitudo, singulis habendos fruendosque praebetis, exuti omnibus quae
maiores reliquere; nisi quia vobismet ipsi[1] per
suffragia, ut praesides olim, nunc dominos destinatis.
7 Itaque concessere illuc omnes, at mox,[2] si vostra
receperitis, ad vos plerique; raris enim animus est
ad ea, quae placent, defendunda, ceteri validiorum
8 sunt. An dubium habetis, num officere quid vobis
uno animo pergentibus possit, quos languidos socor-
desque pertimuere? Nisi forte C. Cotta, ex factione
media consul, aliter quam metu iura quaedam tribunis plebis restituit; et quamquam L. Sicinius,
primus de potestate tribunicia loqui ausus, mussanti-
bus vobis circumventus erat, tamen prius illi invidiam metuere, quam vos iniuriae pertaesum est.
Quod ego nequeo satis mirari, Quirites, nam spem
9 frustra fuisse intellexistis. Sulla mortuo, qui sce-
lestum imposuerat servitium, finem mali credebatis;

---

[1] vobismet ipsi, *Korrte*; vobismet ipsis, *V.*
[2] at mox, *Kritz*; et mox, *V.*

---

[1] That is, the spoils taken from you.

power and authority against you; and they consider
it better to do wrong for hire than to do right
without recompense. Therefore they have now, one
and all, submitted to the mastery of a few men, who,
under the pretext of carrying on a war, have taken
possession of the treasury, the armies, the kingdoms
and the provinces. These men have made themselves a stronghold from your spoils,[1] while in the
meantime you, like so many cattle, yield yourselves,
a multitude, to single owners for use and enjoyment;
and that, too, after being stripped of every privilege
which your forefathers left you, save that by your
ballots you may yourselves choose, as once your defenders, so now your masters.

Therefore all men have now gone over to their
side, but presently, if you regain what is yours, most
of them will return to you, for few have courage to
defend their independence, the rest belong to the
stronger. Can you fear that anything will be able
to resist you, if you advance with a united purpose,
when they have feared you even in your weakness
and indifference? Unless haply it was from another
motive than fear that Gaius Cotta, a consul chosen
from the heart of the aristocratic party, restored
some of their rights to the people's tribunes. In
fact, although Lucius Sicinius, who was the first to
dare to speak about the tribunician power, was cut
off while you only murmured, yet his slayers feared
your displeasure even before you resented your
wrongs. At that patience of yours, citizens, I cannot sufficiently marvel; for you knew that your
hopes had often been disappointed. On the death
of Sulla, who had imposed this infamous slavery
upon you, you believed that your troubles were

10 ortus est longe saevior Catulus. Tumultus inter-
cessit Bruto et Mamerco consulibus, dein C. Curio
ad exitium usque insontis tribuni dominatus est.

11   Lucullus superiore anno quantis animis ierit in
L. Quintium vidistis: quantae denique mihi turbae
concitantur ! Quae profecto incassum agebantur, si
prius quam vos serviundi finem, illi dominationis
facturi erant, praesertim cum his civilibus armis
dicta alia, sed certatum utrimque de dominatione in
12 vobis sit. Itaque cetera ex licentia aut odio aut
avaritia in tempus arsere, permansit una res modo,
quae utrimque quaesita est et erepta in posterum :
vis tribunicia, telum a maioribus libertati paratum.

13 Quod ego vos moneo quaesoque ut animadvortatis
neu nomina rerum ad ignaviam mutantes otium pro
servitio appelletis. Quo iam ipso frui, si vera et
honesta flagitium superaverit, non est condicio ;
fuisset, si omnino quiessetis. Nunc animum advortere et, nisi viceritis, quoniam omnis iniuria
gravitate tutior est, artius habebunt.

14   "Quid censes igitur?" aliquis vostrum subiecerit.
Primum omnium omittundum morem hunc quem
agitis impigrae linguae, animi ignavi, non ultra con-

---

¹ 77 B.C.

ended; up rose Catulus, a tyrant far crueller than
Sulla. There was an outbreak in the consulship of
Brutus and Mamercus,[1] and after it Gaius Curio was
long enough your master to cause the death of a
guiltless tribune.

You saw with what passion Lucullus last year
assailed Lucius Quintius; what tempests are now
roused against me! But these acts they certainly
committed in vain, if it was their intention to put
an end to their mastery before you did to your
slavery; especially since in these civil dissensions,
although other motives were alleged, the real object of the contest on both sides was to determine
who should be your masters. Therefore the other
struggles, inspired as they were by licence, by
hatred, or by avarice, blazed up for a time only;
one issue only has persisted, which has been the aim
of both sides and has been taken away from you for
the future: the tribunician power, a weapon given
you by your ancestors, with which to defend your
liberties. Of this fact I warn you and I beg you to
bear it in mind; do not change the names of things
to suit your own cowardice and give to slavery the
title of peace. Even peace you will not be allowed
to enjoy, if wickedness triumph over right and
honour; you might have done so, if you had never
roused yourselves. As it is, they are on their guard,
and if you do not gain the victory, they will hold
you in tighter bonds, since the greater the injustice
the greater its safety.

What then do you advise? some one of you will say.
First of all, you must give up this habit which you
have, ye men of active tongue but of weak spirit, not
to retain the thought of liberty outside of the place

425

15 tionis locum memores libertatis. Deinde—ne vos ad
virilia illa vocem, quo tribunos plebei, modo patri-
cium magistratum, libera ab auctoribus patriciis
suffragia maiores vostri paravere—cum vis omnis,
Quirites, in vobis sit et quae iussa nunc pro aliis
toleratis pro vobis agere aut non agere certe possitis,
Iovem aut alium quem deum consultorem expectatis?

16 Magna illa consulum imperia et patrum decreta vos
exsequendo rata efficitis, Quirites, ultroque licentiam

17 in vos auctum atque adiutum properatis. Neque
ego vos ultum iniurias hortor, magis uti requiem
cupiatis, neque discordias, uti illi criminantur, sed
earum finem volens iure gentium res repeto; et si
pertinaciter retinebunt, non arma neque secessionem,
tantum modo ne amplius sanguinem vostrum prae-

18 beatis censebo. Gerant habeantque suo modo
imperia, quaerant triumphos, Mithridatem, Ser-
torium et reliquias exsulum persequantur cum ima-
ginibus suis, absit periculum et labos, quibus nulla
pars fructus est.

19 Nisi forte repentina ista frumentaria lege munia
vostra pensantur; qua tamen quinis modiis liber-

---

[1] That is, while they are being reminded of it by popular
orators.

[2] For *quo*, instead of *quibus*, *cf. Jug.* cii. 10.

[3] That is, a share in a magistracy which had previously
(*modo*) been confined to the patricians. The reference is to

of assembly.[1] Then (not to attempt to urge you to those manly deeds [2] by which your ancestors gained their tribunes of the commons, a magistracy previously patrician,[3] and a suffrage independent of the sanction of the patricians) since all the power is in your hands, citizens, and since you undoubtedly can execute or fail to execute on your own account the orders to which you now submit for the profit of others, I would ask you whether you are waiting for the advice of Jupiter or some other one of the gods. That supreme power of the consuls, and those potent decrees of the senate, you yourselves ratify, citizens, by executing them; and you hasten voluntarily to increase and strengthen their despotism over you. I do not urge you to avenge your wrongs, but rather to seek quiet; and it is not because I desire discord, as they charge, but because I wish to put an end to it, that I demand restitution according to the law of nations. If they persist in refusing this, I do not advise war or secession, but merely that you should refuse longer to shed your blood for them. Let them hold their offices and administer them in their own way, let them seek triumphs, let them lead their ancestral portraits[4] against Mithridates, Sertorius, and what is left of the exiles, but let those who have no share in the profits be free also from dangers and toil.

But perhaps your services have been paid for by that hastily enacted law for the distribution of grain, a law by which they have valued all your liberties

the consulship, to which plebeians became eligible by the bill of Licinius and Sextius in 377 B.C.

[4] That is to say, let them lead the portraits of their ancestors against the enemy, in lieu of soldiers.

tatem omnium aestumavere, qui profecto non
amplius possunt alimentis carceris. Namque ut
illis exiguitate mors prohibetur, senescunt vires, sic
neque absolvit[1] cura familiari tam parva res et
20 ignavi cuiusque tenuissumas spes frustratur. Quae
tamen quamvis ampla quoniam serviti pretium
ostentaretur, cuius torpedinis erat decipi et vostra-
rum rerum ultro iniuriae[2] gratiam debere? Cavendus
21 dolus est[3]; namque alio modo neque valent in univorsos neque conabuntur.[3] Itaque simul comparant
delenimenta et differunt vos in adventum Cn.
Pompei, quem ipsum ubi pertimuere, sublatum in
22 cervices suas, mox dempto metu lacerant. Neque
eos pudet, vindices uti se ferunt libertatis, tot viros
sine uno aut remittere iniuriam non audere aut ius
23 non posse defendere. Mihi quidem satis spectatum
est Pompeium, tantae gloriae adulescentem, malle
principem volentibus vobis esse quam illis dominationis socium auctoremque in primis fore tribuniciae
potestatis.
24 Verum, Quirites, antea singuli cives in pluribus,
non in uno cuncti praesidia habebatis. Neque
mortalium quisquam dare aut eripere talia unus
25 poterat. Itaque verborum satis dictum est; neque
26 enim ignorantia res claudit, verum occupavit nescio

[1] absolvi, *V.*
[2] iniuriae, *Kritz*; iniuria, *V.*   [3] *Transp. by Fabri.*

---

[1] Like slaves (*lecticarii*) carrying their master in a litter.

at five pecks per man, an allowance actually not much greater than the rations of a prison. For just as in the case of prisoners that scanty supply keeps off death, but yet their strength wanes, so this small amount relieves you of no financial care and disappoints the slenderest hopes of the idle. But even though the allowance were a great one, what lethargy it would show, since it was offered as the price of your slavery, to be deceived by it and actually to owe gratitude to your oppressors for your own property. You must guard against craft; for by no other means can they prevail against the people as a whole, and in that way only will they attempt to do so. It is for this reason that they are making plans to soothe you and at the same time to put you off until the coming of Gnaeus Pompeius, the very man whom they bore upon their necks[1] when they feared him, but presently, their fear dispelled, they tear to pieces. Nor are these self-styled defenders of liberty, many as they are, ashamed to need one man before they dare to right a wrong or can defend a right. For my own part I am fully convinced that Pompey, a young man of such renown, prefers to be the leading man of the state with your consent, rather than to share in their mastery, and that he will join you and lead you in restoring the power of the tribunes.

There was once a time, fellow countrymen, when each of you citizens found protection in the many[2] and not the community in one man, and when no single mortal was able to give or to take away such things from you. I have therefore said enough; for it is not through ignorance that the matter halts,

[2] In the collective strength of the community.

quae[1] vos torpedo, qua non gloria movemini neque
flagitio, cunctaque praesenti ignavia mutavistis,
abunde libertatem rati, quia tergis abstinetur et huc
ire licet atque illuc, munera ditium dominorum
27 Atque haec eadem non sunt agrestibus, sed cae-
duntur inter potentium inimicitias donoque dantur
in provincias magistratibus. Ita pugnatur et vin-
citur paucis, plebes, quodcumque accidit, pro victis
est et in dies magis erit, si quidem maiore cura
dominationem illi retinuerint, quam vos repetiveritis
libertatem.

[1] nescio quae, *Carrio* ; nescio qua, *V.*

but a kind of lethargy has laid hold upon
you, because of which neither glory nor disgrace
moves you. You have given up everything in exchange for your present slothfulness, thinking that
you have ample freedom because your backs are
spared, and because you are allowed to go hither
and thither by the grace of your rich masters. Yet
even these privileges are denied to the country
people, who are cut down in the quarrels of the
great, and sent to the provinces as gifts to the
magistrates. Thus they fight and conquer for the
benefit of a few, but whatever happens, the commons
are treated as vanquished; and this will be more
so every day, so long as your oppressors make
greater efforts to retain their mastery than you do
to regain your freedom.

EPISTULA MITHRIDATIS[1]

1   Rex Mithridates regi Arsaci salutem. Omnes qui secundis rebus suis ad belli societatem orantur considerare debent liceatne tum pacem agere, dein quod quaesitur satisne pium, tutum, gloriosum an 2 indecorum sit. Tibi si perpetua pace frui licet, nisi hostes opportuni et scelestissumi, ni[2] egregia fama, si Romanos oppresseris, futura est, neque petere audeam societatem et frustra mala mea cum 3 bonis tuis misceri sperem. Atque ea, quae te morari posse videntur, ira in Tigranem recentis belli et meae res parum[3] prosperae, si vera existumare 4 voles, maxume hortabuntur. Ille enim obnoxius qualem tu voles societatem accipiet, mihi fortuna multis rebus ereptis usum dedit bene suadendi et, quod florentibus optabile est, ego non validissumus praebeo exemplum, quo rectius tua componas.

[1] *Histories*, iv. 69.   [2] ni *inserted by Madvig*.
[3] parum, *Aldus*; rarum, V.

---

[1] In 69 B.C. Mithridates and Tigranes, both of whom had been decisively defeated by Lucullus, tried to add to their

LETTER OF MITHRIDATES[1]

KING MITHRIDATES to King Arsaces, Greeting. All those who in the time of their prosperity are asked to form an offensive alliance ought to consider, first, whether it is possible for them to keep peace at that time; and secondly, whether what is asked of them is wholly right and safe, honourable or dishonourable. If it were possible for you to enjoy lasting peace, if no treacherous foes were near your borders, if to crush the Roman power would not bring you glorious fame, I should not venture to sue for your alliance, and it would be vain for me to hope to unite my misfortunes with your prosperity. But the considerations which might seem to give you pause, such as the anger against Tigranes inspired in you by the recent war, and my lack of success, if you but consent to regard them in the right light, will be special incentives. For Tigranes is at your mercy and will accept an alliance on any terms which you may desire, while so far as I am concerned, although Fortune has deprived me of much, she has bestowed upon me the experience necessary for giving good advice; and since I am no longer at the height of my power,[2] I shall serve as an example of how you may conduct your own affairs with more prudence, a lesson highly advantageous to the prosperous.

forces. Mithridates wrote this letter to Arsaces, king of the Parthians, to induce him to become his ally.

[2] A euphemistic expression for one who had suffered total defeat.

433

5 Namque Romanis cum nationibus, populis, regibus
cunctis una et ea vetus causa bellandi est, cupido
profunda imperi et divitiarum ; qua primo cum rege
Macedonum Philippo bellum sumpsere, dum a Car-
6 thaginiensibus premebantur amicitiam simulantes.
Ei subvenientem Antiochum concessione Asiae per
dolum avortere, ac mox fracto Philippo Antiochus
omni cis Taurum agro et decem milibus talentorum
7 spoliatus est. Persen deinde, Philippi filium, post
multa et varia certamina apud Samothracas deos
acceptum in fidem, callidi et repertores perfidiae,
quia pacto vitam dederant, insomniis occidere.
8 Eumenen, cuius amicitiam gloriose ostentant, initio
prodidere Antiocho, pacis mercedem : post, habitum
custodiae agri captivi, sumptibus et contumeliis ex
rege miserrumum servorum effecere, simulatoque
impio testamento filium eius Aristonicum, quia
patrium regnum petiverat, hostium more per trium-
9 phum duxere. Asia ab ipsis obsessa est, postremo
Bithyniam Nicomede mortuo diripuere, cum filius
Nysa, quam reginam appellaverat, genitus haud
dubie esset.
10 Nam quid ego me appellem ? Quem diiunctum
undique regnis et tetrarchiis ab imperio eorum, quia

---

[1] Namely, his own kingdom, which he nominally ruled,
while really governing it as a province of Rome.

In fact, the Romans have one inveterate motive for making war upon all nations, peoples and kings; namely, a deep-seated desire for dominion and for riches. Therefore they first began a war with Philip, king of Macedonia, having pretended to be his friends as long as they were hard pressed by the Carthaginians. When Antiochus came to his aid, they craftily diverted him from his purpose by the surrender of Asia, and then, after Philip's power had been broken, Antiochus was robbed of all the territory this side Taurus, and of ten thousand talents. Next Perses, the son of Philip, after many battles with varying results, was formally taken under their protection before the gods of Samothrace; and then those masters of craft and artists in treachery caused his death from want of sleep, since they had made a compact not to kill him. Eumenes, whose friendship they boastfully parade, they first betrayed to Antiochus as the price of peace; later, having made him the guardian of a captured territory,[1] they transformed him by means of imposts and insults from a king into the most wretched of slaves. Then, having forged an unnatural will,[2] they led his son Aristonicus in triumph like an enemy, because he had tried to recover his father's realm. They took possession of Asia, and finally, on the death of Nicomedes, they seized upon all Bithynia, although Nysa, whom Nicomedes had called queen, unquestionably had a son.

Why should I mention my own case? Although I was separated from their empire on every side by kingdoms and tetrarchies, yet because it was reported

---

[2] So called because in it Attalus III, son of Eumenes II, bequeathed his kingdom to the Romans. The throne was claimed by Aristonicus, a natural son of Eumenes.

fama erat divitem neque serviturum esse, per Nicomedem bello lacessiverunt, sceleris eorum haud
ignarum et ea, quae accidere, testatum antea Cretensis, solos omnium liberos ea tempestate, et regem
11 Ptolemaeum. Atque ego ultus iniurias Nicomedem
Bithynia expuli Asiamque spolium regis Antiochi
12 recepi et Graeciae dempsi grave servitium. Incepta
mea postremus servorum Archelaus exercitu prodito
impedivit, illique, quos ignavia aut prava calliditas,
ut meis laboribus tuti essent, armis abstinuit, acer-
bissumas poenas solvunt, Ptolemaeus pretio in dies
bellum prolatans, Cretenses impugnati semel iam
13 neque finem nisi excidio habituri.[1] Equidem cum
mihi ob ipsorum interna mala dilata proelia magis
quam pacem datam intellegerem, abnuente Tigrane,
qui mea dicta sero probat, te remoto procul, omnibus
aliis obnoxiis, rursus tamen bellum coepi Marcumque
Cottam, Romanum ducem, apud Chalcedona[2] terra
14 fudi, mari exui classe pulcherruma. Apud Cyzicum
magno cum exercitu in obsidio moranti frumentum
defuit, nullo circum adnitente; simul hiems mari
prohibebat. Ita, sine vi hostium regredi conatus in
patrium regnum, naufragiis apud Parium et Hera-

---

[1] habitur, V.   [2] Calchedona, V, Ah.

that I was rich and that I would not be a slave, they provoked me to war through Nicomedes. And I was not unaware of their design, but I had previously given warning of what afterwards happened, both to the Cretans, who alone retained their freedom at that time, and to king Ptolemy. But I took vengeance for the wrongs inflicted upon me; I drove Nicomedes from Bithynia, recovered Asia, the spoil taken from king Antiochus, and delivered Greece from cruel servitude. Further progress was frustrated by Archelaus, basest of slaves, who betrayed my army; and those whom cowardice or misplaced cunning kept from taking up arms, since they hoped to find safety in my misfortunes, are suffering most cruel punishment. For Ptolemy is averting hostilities from day to day by the payment of money, while the Cretans have already been attacked once and will find no respite from war until they are destroyed. As for me, I soon learned that the peace afforded by civil dissensions at Rome was really only a postponement of the struggle, and although Tigranes refused to join with me (he now admits the truth of my prediction when it is too late), though you were far away, and all the rest had submitted, I nevertheless renewed the war and routed Marcus Cotta, the Roman general, on land at Chalcedon, while on the sea I stripped him of a fine fleet. During the delay caused by my siege of Cyzicus with a great army provisions failed me, since no one in the neighbourhood rendered me aid and at the same time winter kept me off the sea. When I, therefore, without compulsion from the enemy, attempted to return into my kingdom, I lost the best of my

15 cleam militum optumos cum classibus amisi. Resti-
tuto deinde apud Cabiram[1] exercitu et variis inter
me atque Lucullum proeliis, inopia rursus ambos
incessit; illi suberat regnum Ariobarzanis bello intactum, ego vastis circum omnibus locis, in Ar-
meniam concessi; secutique Romani non me, sed
morem suum omnia regna subvortundi, quia multitudinem artis locis pugna prohibuere, imprudentiam
Tigranis pro victoria ostentant.

16   Nunc, quaeso, considera nobis oppressis utrum
firmiorem te ad resistundum, an finem belli futurum
putes? Scio equidem tibi magnas opes virorum
armorum et auri esse; et ea re a nobis ad societatem
ab illis ad praedam peteris. Ceterum consilium
est, Tigranis regno integro, meis militibus belli
prudentibus, procul ab domo, parvo labore per
nostra corpora bellum conficere, quo[2] neque vincere
17 neque vinci sine tuo periculo possumus. An ignoras
Romanos, postquam ad occidentem pergentibus finem
Oceanus fecit, arma huc convortisse? Neque quicquam a principio nisi raptum[3] habere, domum,
coniuges, agros, imperium? Convenas olim sine
patria, parentibus, pestem conditos orbis terrarum,
quibus non humana ulla neque divina obstant, quin

---

[1] Cabiram, *Carrio*; Caberam, *V, Ah.*
[2] quo, *Gerlach*; quō, *V.*
[3] raptum, *Ciacconius*; partum, *V.*

soldiers and my fleets by shipwrecks at Parium and at Heraclea. Then when I had raised a new army at Cabira and engaged with Lucullus with varying success, scarcity once more attacked us both. He had at his command the kingdom of Ariobarzanes, unravaged by war, while I, since all the country about me had been devastated, withdrew into Armenia. Thereupon the Romans followed me, or rather followed their custom of overthrowing all monarchies, and because they were able to keep from action a huge force hemmed in by narrow defiles, boasted of the results of Tigranes' imprudence as if they had won a victory.

I pray you, then, to consider whether you believe that when we have been crushed you will be better able to resist the Romans, or that there will be an end to the war. I know well that you have great numbers of men and large amounts of arms and gold, and it is for that reason that I seek your alliance and the Romans your spoils. Yet my advice is, while the kingdom of Tigranes is entire, and while I still have soldiers who have been trained in warfare with the Romans, to finish far from your homes and with little labour, at the expense of our bodies, a war in which we cannot conquer or be conquered without danger to you. Do you not know that the Romans turned their arms in this direction only after Ocean had blocked their westward progress? That they have possessed nothing since the beginning of their existence except what they have stolen: their home, their wives, their lands, their empire? Once vagabonds without fatherland, without parents, created to be the scourge of the whole world, no laws, human or divine, prevent them from seizing

socios, amicos, procul iuxta sitos, inopes potentisque trahant excindant, omniaque non serva et maxume regna hostilia ducant.

18   Namque pauci libertatem, pars magna iustos dominos volunt, nos suspecti sumus aemuli et in tem-
19 pore vindices affuturi.   Tu vero, cui Seleucea,
maxuma urbium, regnumque Persidis inclutis divitiis
est, quid ab illis nisi dolum in praesens et postea
20 bellum expectas?   Romani arma in omnis habent,
acerruma in eos, quibus victis spolia maxuma;
audendo et fallundo et bella ex bellis serundo magni
21 facti.   Per hunc morem extinguent omnia aut
occident ... quod haud difficile est, si tu Mesopotamia, nos Armenia circumgredimur exercitum sine
frumento, sine auxiliis, fortuna aut nostris vitiis
22 adhuc incolumem.   Teque illa fama sequetur, auxilio profectum magnis regibus latrones gentium
23 oppressisse.   Quod uti facias moneo hortorque, neu
malis pernicie nostra tuam prolatare quam societate
victor fieri.

---

1 That is, of planning to arise at some future time (*affuturi*) and avenge mankind.

and destroying allies and friends, those near them
and those afar off, weak or powerful, and from considering every government which does not serve
them, especially monarchies, as their enemies.

Of a truth, few men desire freedom, the greater
part are content with just masters; we are suspected
of being rivals of the Romans and future avengers.[1]
But you, who possess Seleucea, greatest of cities,
and the realm of Perses famed for its riches, what
can you expect from them other than guile in the
present and war in the future? The Romans have
weapons against all men, the sharpest where victory
yields the greatest spoils; it is by audacity, by
deceit, and by joining war to war that they have
grown great. Following their usual custom, they
will destroy everything or perish in the attempt . . .[2]
and this is not difficult if you on the side of
Mesopotamia and we on that of Armenia surround
their army, which is without supplies and without
allies, and has been saved so far only by its good
fortune or by our own errors. You will gain the
glory of having rendered aid to great kings and of
having crushed the plunderers of all the nations.
This is my advice and this course I urge you to
follow; do not prefer by our ruin to put off your
own for a time rather than by our alliance to
conquer.

[2] There is a lacuna at this point. Obviously Mithridates
urged Arsaces to join him in an attack upon the Romans.

DOUBTFUL WORKS

AD CAESAREM SENEM DE RE PUBLICA ORATIO.[1]

I. Pro vero antea optinebat regna atque imperia fortunam dono dare, item alia quae per mortaleis[2] avide cupiuntur, quia et apud indignos saepe erant quasi per libidinem data neque cuiquam incorrupta 2 permanserant. Sed res docuit id verum esse, quod in carminibus Appius ait, fabrum esse suae quemque fortunae, atque in te maxume, qui tantum alios praegressus es, ut prius defessi sint homines laudando 3 facta tua quam tu laude digna faciundo. Ceterum ut fabricata sic virtute parta quam magna industria haberei decet, ne incuria deformentur aut corruant 4 infirmata. Nemo enim alteri imperium volens concedit, et quamvis bonus atque clemens sit, qui plus 5 potest tamen, quia malo esse licet, formeidatur. Id eo evenit, quia plerique rerum potentes pervorse consulunt et eo se munitiores putant, quo illei quibus imperitant nequiores fuere. 6 bus imperitant nequiores fuere. At contra id eniti

---

[1] See Introd. pp. xviii ff. $V =$ codex Vaticanus, 3864;
$\varsigma =$ copies of V.
[2] *The writer frequently has* ei *for long* i *and indulges in other archaic spellings ;* see Introd. p. xvii.

---

[1] Appius Claudius Caecus, consul in 307 B.C., the earliest Roman writer known to us. He composed *Sententiae* in the

SPEECH ON THE STATE, ADDRESSED TO CAESAR IN HIS LATER YEARS

I. It was accounted true formerly that Fortune gave as gifts kingdoms and empires, as well as the other possessions which are eagerly coveted among mortal men ; for they were often found in the hands of the undeserving, as if given capriciously, and they did not remain unspoiled in anyone's hands. But experience has shown that to be true which Appius[1] says in his verses, that every man is the architect of his own fortune ; and this proverb is especially true of you, who have excelled others to such a degree that men are sooner wearied in singing the praises of your deeds than you in doing deeds worthy of praise. But as the work of an architect, so the achievements of virtue ought to be guarded with all possible care, in order that they may not be injured by neglect or fall in ruins through weakness. For no one willingly yields empire to another ; and however virtuous and merciful one may be, one who has more power is nevertheless feared, since it is lawful for him to be wicked. The reason for this is, that potentates for the most part have perverted ideas and think themselves the more strongly entrenched the greater the wickedness of their subjects.[2] But on the contrary, this should be one's endeavour, to

Saturnian measure in imitation of the "Golden Verses" of Pythagoras ; see Cic. *Tusc. Disp.* 4. 2. 4.
[2] See *Cat.* vii. 1 ; Pliny, *Paneg.* 45.

445

decet, cum ipse bonus atque strenuus sis, uti quam
optimis imperites. Nam pessumus quisque asper-
rume rectorem patitur.

7   Sed tibi hoc gravius est, quam ante te omnibus,
8 armis parta componere, quod bellum aliorum pace
mollius gessisti. Ad hoc victores praedam petunt,
victi cives sunt. Inter has difficultates evadendum
est tibi atque in posterum firmanda res publica non
armis modo neque advorsum hostis, sed, quod multo
9 multoque asperius est, pacis bonis artibus. Ergo
omnes magna, mediocri[1] sapientia res huc vocat,
10 quae quisque optuma potest, utei dicant. Ac mihi
sic videtur: qualeicumque modo tu victoriam com-
posuereis, ita alia omnia futura.

II. Sed iam, quo melius faciliusque constituas,
paucis quae me animus monet accipe.

2   Bellum tibi fuit, imperator, cum homine claro,
magnis opibus, avido potentiae, maiore fortuna quam
sapientia, quem secuti sunt pauci per suam iniuriam
tibi inimici, item quos adfinitas aut alia necessitudo
3 traxit. Nam particeps dominationis neque fuit quisquam neque, si pati potuisset, orbis terrarum bello
4 concussus foret. Cetera multitudo volgi more magis

---

[1] mediocri, *Asulanus*; mediocris, *V*.

---

[1] *cf.* Tacitus, *Agr.* 42, *proprium humani ingenii est odisse
quem laeseris.*

be virtuous and valiant oneself and rule over subjects the best possible; for the worst men most bitterly resent a ruler.

But for you it is harder than for all before you to administer your conquests, because your war was more merciful than their peace. Moreover, the victors demand booty, the vanquished are fellow citizens. Amidst these difficulties you have to make your way, and strengthen the state for the future, not in arms only and against the enemy, but also in the kindly arts of peace, a task far, far thornier. Therefore the situation calls upon all men, whether of great or of moderate wisdom, to offer you the best advice of which each is capable. And this is my opinion: even as you use your victory, so will the whole future be.

II. But now, to enable you the better and more easily to arrange matters, let me give you in a few words what my mind prompts.

You waged war, Caesar, with a distinguished antagonist, of great prowess, greedy for power, but not wise so much as favoured by fortune. He was followed by a small party, those who were your enemies because of the wrongs which they had done you [1] and those whom relationship or some other tie had attached to him. For no one of them had any share in his power, and if he had been able to brook a rival, the world would not have been convulsed by war.[2] The rest took his side rather after the usual custom of the multitude than from

---

[1] cf. Lucan, *Pharsalia*, 1. 125:

*Nec quemquam iam ferre potest Caesarve priorem
Pompeiusve parem.*

quam iudicio, post alius alium quasi prudentiorem
5 secuti. Per idem tempus maledictis ineiquorum
occupandae rei publicae in spem adducti homines,
quibus omnia probro ac luxuria polluta erant, concurrere in castra tua et aperte quieteis mortem,
rapinas, postremo omnia quae corrupto animo lube-
6 bat, minitari. Ex queis magna pars, ubi neque
creditum condonarei[1] neque te civibus sicuti hostibus uti vident, defluxere, pauci restitere, quibus
maius otium in castris quam Romae futurum erat;
7 tanta vis creditorum impendebat. Sed ob easdem
causas immane dictust quanti et quam multi mortales postea ad Pompeium discesserint, eoque per
omne tempus belli quasi sacro atque inspoliato fano
debitores usi.

III. Igitur quoniam tibi victori de bello atque
pace agitandum est, hoc uti civiliter deponas, illa
ut[2] quam iustissima et diuturna sit, de te ipso
primum, qui ea compositurus es, quid optimum factu
2 sit existima. Equidem ego cuncta imperia crudelia
magis acerba quam diuturna arbitror, neque quemquam multis metuendum esse, quin ad eum ex
multis formido reccidat; eam vitam bellum aeter-
num et anceps gerere, quoniam neque adversus
neque ab tergo aut lateribus tutus sis, semper in
3 periculo aut metu agites. Contra qui benignitate
et clementia imperium temperavere iis laeta et

---

[1] condonari, *Korrte*; condonare, *V*.
[2] ut *Aldus*; *omitted by V*.

deliberate choice, each man following his neighbour, as if he were wiser than himself. At the same time, the slanders of unfair critics inspired men whose whole lives were stained with infamy and debauchery with the hope of getting control of the state. They accordingly flocked into your camp and openly threatened peaceable citizens with death, robbery, in short, with everything that a perverted mind could imagine. The greater number of these, however, when they saw that there was no repudiation of debts and that you did not treat your fellow citizens as enemies, gradually dispersed; a few remained, expecting to find more repose in your camp than in Rome, so great was the throng of creditors that there awaited them. But an enormous number of prominent men afterwards went over to Pompey from those same motives, and debtors during the whole course of the war found in him a sacred and inviolable asylum.

III. Therefore, since you must deal as victor with both war and peace, in order that you may end the one in the spirit of a good citizen, and make the other as just and as lasting as possible, first consider what your own conduct should be, since the settlement of the state is your task. For my own part, I believe that a cruel rule is always more bitter than lasting, and that no one is fearful to the many but fear from the many recoils upon his head; that such a life is engaged in an eternal and dangerous warfare, in which there is no safety in front, in the rear, or on the flanks, but always peril or fear. On the contrary, those who have tempered their rule with kindness and mercy have found everything happy and

candida omnia visa, etiam hostes aequiores quam
aliis[1] cives.

4   Haud scio an qui me his dictis corruptorem
victoriae tuae nimisque in victos bona voluntate
praedicent.   Scilicet quod ea, quae externis nationibus, natura nobis hostibus, nosque maioresque nostri
saepe tribuere, ea civibus danda arbitror, neque
barbaro ritu caede caedem et sanguinem sanguine
expianda.

    IV. An illa, quae paulo ante hoc bellum in Cn.
Pompeium victoriamque Sullanam increpabantur,
oblivio interfecit[2]: Domitium, Carbonem, Brutum
alios item, non armatos neque in proelio belli iure,
sed postea supplices per summum scelus interfectos,
plebem Romanam in villa publica pecoris modo
2 conscissam?   Eheu quam illa occulta civium funera
et repentinae caedes, in parentum aut liberorum
sinum fuga mulierum et puerorum, vastatio domuum
ante partam a te victoriam saeva atque crudelia
3 erant!   Ad quae te idem illi hortantur; scilicet[3] id
certatum esse, utrius vestrum arbitrio iniuriae fierent, neque receptam sed captam a te rem publicam
et ea causa exercitus stipendiis confectis optimos et

---

[1] aequiores quam aliis, *Carrio*; nequiores quam alii, *V.*
[2] intercepit, *Gronov.*
[3] et scilicet, *V* ; et *deleted by Jordan.*

---

[1] A building in the Campus Martius, the headquarters of
state officials when taking the census or levying troops.   In
it were lodged foreign ambassadors and generals applying

prosperous; even their enemies are more friendly than their countrymen to others.

Probably some will declare that with these words I am the ruiner of your victory, and that I am too well disposed towards the vanquished. Doubtless because I believe that the same privileges which we and our forefathers have often granted to foreign nations, our natural enemies, ought to be allowed to our fellow citizens, and that murder should not, after the manner of barbarians, be atoned for by murder, and blood by blood.

IV. Or has oblivion destroyed the murmurs which, a short time before this war, were directed against Gnaeus Pompeius and the victory of Sulla; when it was said that Domitius, Carbo, Brutus and others were slain, not in arms nor in battle according to the laws of war, but afterwards with the utmost barbarity, while they were begging for mercy; and that the Roman commons were slaughtered like so many cattle in the Villa Publica?[1] Alas! before your victory was won, how savage and cruel were the secret deaths of citizens and their sudden murder, the flight of women or boys to the bosom of their parents or children, and the devastation of homes! It is to such atrocities that these same men are urging you, declaring indeed that the purpose of the contest was to determine which of you two should have the right to commit outrages, and maintaining that you did not restore the state, but took it captive. It was for this reason, these men say, that after finishing their term of service

for the honour of a triumph; here Sulla massacred the 4,000 prisoners taken in the battle at the Colline Gate; see Platner, *Topogr. of Rome*, p. 345.

veterrimos omnium advorsum fratres parentisque[1]
armis contendere; ut ex alienis malis deterrumi
mortales ventri atque profundae lubidini sumptus
quaererent atque essent opprobria victoriae, quorum
4 flagitiis commacularetur bonorum laus. Neque enim
te praeterire puto, quali quisque eorum more aut
modestia, etiam tum dubia victoria, sese gesserit
quoque modo in belli administratione scorta aut
convivia exercuerint non nulli, quorum aetas ne
per otium quidem talis voluptatis sine dedecore
attingerit.

V. De bello satis dictum. De pace firmanda
quoniam tuque et omnes tui agitatis, primum id
quaeso, considera quale sit de quo consultas; ita
bonis malisque dimotis patenti via ad verum perges.
2 Ego sic existimo: quoniam orta omnia intereunt,
qua tempestate urbi Romanae fatum excidii adven-
tarit, civis cum civibus manus conserturos, ita defessos et exsanguis regi aut nationi praedae futuros.
Aliter non orbis terrarum neque cunctae gentes
conglobatae movere aut contundere queunt hoc
3 imperium. Firmanda igitur sunt vel concordiae
4 bona et discordiae mala expellenda. Id ita eveniet,
si sumptuum et rapinarum licentiam dempseris,
non ad vetera instituta revocans, quae iam pridem
corruptis moribus ludibrio sunt, sed si suam quoique
5 rem familiarem finem sumptuum statueris; quoniam

---

[1] parentisque alii liberos, *V*; alii liberos *deleted by Jordan.*

---

[1] The *evocati*, reservists or volunteer veterans.

the best and oldest soldiers of our armies [1] contended in battle against their brothers and parents; namely, that through others' woes the worst of men might acquire the means to gratify their belly and their fathomless lust, and be a disgrace to your victory by staining with their crimes the patriots' glory. For I think you did not fail to observe with what manners and discipline each one of them conducted himself while the victory was even then uncertain; and while directing the war how some of them gave themselves up to harlots or gluttony, whose age could not touch such pleasures without disgrace even in time of peace.

V. Of war enough has been said. Since it is peace that you and all your followers are planning to establish, first, I pray you, consider what the aim is which you have in view; in that way, after separating the good from the evil, you will open a broad highway to the truth. My own opinion is this: since everything which has a beginning must also have an end, when the day destined for the destruction of Rome shall come, citizen will battle with citizen; that thus worn out and enfeebled, they will fall a prey to some king or nation. Otherwise not the whole world, nor all the nations banded together, can move or crush this empire. You must establish therefore even harmony with all its blessings, and cast out the evils of discord. And this can be done, if you will check the frenzied indulgence in extravagance and pillage, not by calling men back to the old standards, which from the corruption of our morals have long since become a farce, but by fixing the amount of each man's income as the limit of his expenditure. For it has become the custom

is incessit mos, ut homines adulescentuli sua atque
aliena consumere, nihil libidinei atque aliis rogantibus denegare pulcherrimum putent, eam virtutem
et magnitudinem animi, pudorem atque modestiam
6 pro socordia aestiment. Ergo animus ferox prava
via ingressus, ubi consueta non suppetunt, fertur
accensus in socios modo, modo in civis, movet com-
7 posita et res novas veteribus aeque conquirit.[1] Quare
tollendus est fenerator in posterum, uti suas quisque
8 res curemus. Ea vera atque simplex via est magistratum populo, non creditori gerere et magnitudinem animi in addendo non demendo rei publicae
ostendere.

VI. Atque ego scio quam aspera haec res in principio futura sit, praesertim is, qui se in victoria
licentius liberiusque quam artius futuros credebant.
Quorum si saluti potius quam lubidini consules, illosque nosque et socios in pace firma constitues ; sin
eadem studia artesque iuventuti erunt, ne ista
egregia tua fama simul cum urbe Roma brevi
concidet.

2 Postremo sapientes pacis causa bellum gerunt,
laborem spe otii sustentant. Nisi illam firmam
3 efficis, vinci an vicisse quid retulit ? Quare capesse,
per deos, rem publicam et omnia aspera, uti soles,
4 pervade. Namque aut tu mederi potes aut omit-

---

[1] veteribus aec conquirit (a *in* aec *erased*), *V* ; *corrected by*
Hauler ; *cf. Plaut. Amph.* 293, *Curc.* 141.

---

[1] The text is corrupt and the meaning consequently uncertain.

for mere youths to think it a fine thing to waste their own substance and that of others, to refuse nothing to their own lust and the demands of their fellows, to regard such conduct as evidence of manliness and high spirit, but to consider modesty and self-restraint as cowardice. Therefore the headstrong spirit, entering upon the wrong course, when he finds his habits no longer supplied hurls himself madly now upon our allies and now upon the citizens, subverts the established order of things, and is eager for a revolution.[1] We must therefore for the future rid ourselves of the moneylender, to the end that each one of us may take care of his own property. This is the only right way to administer a magistracy for the people and not for the creditor, and to show greatness of soul by enriching the state, not by pillaging it.

VI. I am well aware how objectionable this step will be at first, especially to those who expected to find in the hour of victory more licence and freedom than restraint. But if you have regard to the welfare of such men rather than to their desires, you will establish both them and us, along with our allies, upon a solid foundation of peace. But if our youth continue to have the same desires and habits as at present, beyond doubt that eminent renown of yours will come to a speedy end, along with the city of Rome.

Finally, wise men wage war only for the sake of peace and endure toil in the hope of quiet; unless you bring about a lasting peace, what mattered victory or defeat? Therefore, I conjure you by the gods, take the commonwealth in hand and surmount all difficulties, as you always do. For either you can

tenda est cura omnibus. Neque quisquam te ad
crudelis poenas aut acerba iudicia invocat, quibus
civitas vastatur magis quam corrigitur, sed ut pravas
5 artis malasque libidines ab iuventute prohibeas. Ea
vera clementia erit, consuluisse ne merito cives
patria expellerentur, retinuisse ab stultitia et falssi
voluptatibus, pacem et concordiam stabilivisse, non
si flagitis opsecutus, delicta perpessus praesens
gaudium cum [1] mox futuro malo concesseris.

VII. Ac mihi animus, quibus rebus alii timent,
maxume fretus est: negoti magnitudine et quia
tibi terrae et maria simul omnia componenda sunt.
Quippe res parvas [2] tantum ingenium attingere
2 nequeiret, magnae curae magna merces est. Igitur
provideas oportet, uti pleps, largitionibus et publico
frumento corrupta, habeat negotia sua, quibus ab
malo publico detineatur; iuventus probitati et
industriae, non sumptibus neque divitiis studeat.
3 Id ita eveniet, si pecuniae, quae maxuma omnium
4 pernicies est, usum atque decus [3] dempseris. Nam
saepe ego cum animo meo reputans quibus quisque
rebus clari viri magnitudinem invenissent quaeque
res populos nationesve magnis auctibus [4] auxissent,
ac deinde quibus causis amplissima regna et imperia
conruissent, eadem semper bona atque mala reperie-
bam, omnesque victores divitias contempsisse et

[1] quom, V.   [2] parvas, *ed. Rom.* 1475; pravas, V.
[3] decus, *Asulanus*; dedecus, V.
[4] auctibus, *Ciacconius*; auctoribus, V.

456

cure our ills, or else all must give up the attempt.
No one, however, urges you to cruel punishments or
harsh sentences, by which our country is rather
ravaged than corrected, but rather to keep depraved
practices and evil passions far from our youth. True
mercy will consist in taking care that citizens may
not deserve to be banished from their country, in
keeping them from folly and deceptive pleasures, in
establishing peace and harmony; not in being in-
dulgent to crime and tolerant of offences, and in
allowing them a temporary gratification at the
expense of inevitable evil in the near future.

VII. And for my own part, the things which cause
fear to others give me a special confidence; I mean
the greatness of the task and the fact that you have
the whole world to set in order by land and by sea.
For a mind as great as yours could not touch
small matters, and great responsibilities have great
rewards. Therefore you ought to provide that the
commons, who are demoralized by largess and by
the free distribution of grain, shall have their occupations, by which they may be kept from public
mischief; and that our young men may cultivate
honesty and industry, not extravagance and the
pursuit of wealth. This will come to pass, if you
deprive money, which is the root of all evil, of its
advantage and honour. For when I have meditated,
as I often do, on the means by which various eminent
men acquired greatness, and have asked myself what
it is that has greatly advanced peoples and nations,
and then have inquired what causes have brought
about the downfall of kingdoms and empires, I
invariably found the same virtues and the same
vices: that the victors always despised riches, the

5 victos cupivisse. Neque aliter quisquam extollere
sese et divina mortalis attingere potest, nisi omissis
pecuniae et corporis gaudiis, animo indulgens non
adsentando neque concupita praebendo, pervorsam
gratiam gratificans, sed in labore, patientia, bonisque
praeceptis et factis fortibus exercitando.

VIII. Nam domum aut villam exstruere, eam
signis, aulaeis, alieisque operibus exornare et omnia
potius quam semet visendum efficere, id est non
divitias decori habere, sed ipsum illis flagitio esse.
2 Porro ei,[1] quibus bis die ventrem onerare, nullam
noctem sine scorto quiescere mos est, ubi animum
quem dominari decebat, servitio oppressere, nequei-
quam eo postea hebeti atque claudo pro exercito uti
3 volunt. Nam imprudentia pleraque et se praecipitat.
Verum haec et omnia mala pariter cum honore
pecuniae desinent, si neque magistratus neque alia
volgo cupienda venalia erunt.
4 Ad hoc providendum est tibi, quonam modo Italia
atque provinciae tutiores sint; id quod factu haud
5 obscurum est. Nam idem omnia vastant, suas
deserendo domos et per iniuriam alienas occupando.
6 Item ne, uti adhuc, militia iniusta aut inaequalis sit,
cum alii triginta, pars nullum stipendium facient.[2]
Et frumentum id, quod antea praemium ignaviae
fuit, per municipia et colonias illis dare conveniet,
qui stipendiis emeritis domos reverterint.

---

[1] eis, *V*.
[2] *Perhaps* faciunt *is the correct reading, as suggested by Jordan.*

vanquished coveted them. In fact, a mortal cannot exalt himself and draw near to the gods unless he cast away the delights of wealth and bodily pleasure, and invite his soul, not by flattery, by indulging its desires, by allowing it a perverse gratification, but by exercising it in labour, in patience, in virtuous precepts and in meritorious deeds.

VIII. In fact, to build a mansion or a country house, to adorn it with statues, tapestries, and other works of art, to make everything in it better worth seeing than its owner, is not to make one's riches an honour, but to be a disgrace to one's own riches. Moreover, when those whose habit it is to overload their stomachs twice a day, and to pass no night without a harlot, have enslaved the mind, which ought to have ruled, it is vain for them to hope to find it ready for action after they have dulled and crippled it. For folly ruins most things, and even itself. But these and all other evils will come to an end with the worship of money, when neither magistracies nor any of the other things which the vulgar desire are for sale.

Besides this, you must provide that Italy and the provinces may be safer, which it is not difficult to accomplish ; for it is these same men who commit devastation everywhere, by abandoning their own homes and wrongfully appropriating those of others. You must also provide that military service may not be unjust and unequal, as it has been hitherto, when some serve thirty campaigns and some none at all. It will be right too that the grain which was once made the reward of idleness be taken to the free towns and colonies and distributed to those soldiers who have returned to their homes after having served their time.

7 Quae rei publicae necessaria tibique gloriosa ratus
8 sum, quam paucissimis apsolvi. Non peius[1] videtur
9 pauca nunc de facto meo disserere. Plerique mortales ad iudicandum satis ingenii habent aut
simulant; verum enim ad reprehendunda aliena
facta aut dicta ardet omnibus animus, vix satis
apertum os aut lingua prompta videtur, quae
meditata pectore evolvat.[2] Quibus me subiectum
10 haud paenitet, magis reticuisse pigeret. Nam sive
hac seu meliore alia via perges, a me quidem pro
virili parte dictum et adiutum fuerit. Relicuum est
optare uti quae tibi placuerint ea di immortales
adprobent beneque evenire sinant.

[1] *Considered corrupt by Jordan* ; ineptum, *Wirz, Zeitschr. f.
Gymn.-w.* xxxi, p. 286.
[2] quae medita pectore evolat, *V* ; quem edita pectore
evolat, *ed. Rom.* 1475.

I have set forth in the fewest possible words the conduct which I think will benefit our country and bring glory to you. It now seems in place to say a word or two about my act.[1] Most men have, or pretend to have, sufficient ability to sit in judgment; indeed, all are so eager to censure the doings or sayings of other men that hardly any mouth is sufficiently open,[2] or any tongue sufficiently ready, to give utterance to the thoughts of their hearts. I do not regret having subjected myself to the criticism of such men; I should feel more regret for having kept silence. For whether you take this course or some better one, I shall have the consciousness of having advised and aided you to the best of my ability. It only remains to pray that the immortal gods may approve your decision and grant it a happy issue.

[1] Namely, the motives which have led me to give you advice.

[2] That is, apparently, can be quickly enough opened.

AD CAESAREM SENEM DE RE PUBLICA
EPISTULA

I. Scio ego quam difficile atque asperum factu sit consilium dare regi aut imperatori, postremo quoiquam mortali, quoius opes in excelso sunt; quippe cum et illis consultorum copiae adsint neque de futuro quisquam satis callidus satisque prudens sit.

2 Quin etiam saepe prava magis quam bona consilia prospere eveniunt, quia plerasque res fortuna ex libidine sua agitat.

3 Sed mihi studium fuit adulescentulo rem publicam capessere, atque in ea cognoscenda multam magnamque curam habui; non ita ut magistratum modo caperem, quem multi malis artibus adepti erant, sed etiam ut rem publicam domi militiaeque quantumque armis, viris, opulentia posset cognitum habuerim.

4 Itaque mihi multa cum animo agitanti consilium fuit famam modestiamque meam post tuam dignitatem haberei et quoius rei lubet periculum facere,

5 dum quid tibi ex eo gloriae acciderit. Idque non temere neque ex fortuna tua decrevi, sed quia in te praeter ceteras artem unam egregie mirabilem comperi, semper tibi maiorem in adversis quam in

6 secundis rebus animum esse. Sed per ceteros morta-

LETTER TO CAESAR ON THE STATE

I. I FULLY realize how difficult and dangerous a task it is to give counsel to a king or to a ruler, indeed, to anyone who possesses supreme authority; for such men have an abundance of counsellors, and besides, no one can be sufficiently clever and sufficiently wise with regard to the future. Nay, more, bad counsel often has a better result than good, since Fortune commonly directs the course of events according to her own caprice.

In my early youth [1] I had a desire to embark upon a political career and in preparing for it I spent long and diligent labour, hoping not merely to be elected to office, which many had attained through dishonourable means, but also to make myself familiar with the administration of public business at home and abroad and with the resources of our country in arms, men, and money. In consequence of this I have determined, after much counsel with myself, to subordinate my own reputation and modesty to your honour, and to venture upon anything whatever, provided only that it will contribute something to your glory. And I have come to this decision, not lightly or from regard for your fortune, but because in you I found, in addition to other qualities, one unusually admirable, that your spirit was always greater in adversity than in prosperity. But that

[1] cf. Cat. iii.

lis illa res clarior est, quod prius defessi sunt homines
laudando atque admirando munificentiam tuam,
quam tu in [1] faciundo quae gloria digna essent.

II. Equidem mihi decretum est nihil tam ex alto
reperiri [2] posse, quod non cogitanti tibi in promptu sit.
2 Neque eo quae visa sunt de re publica tibi scripsi,
quia mihi consilium atque ingenium meum amplius
aequo probaretur, sed inter labores militiae interque
proelia, victorias, imperium statui admonendum
3 te de negotiis urbanis. Namque tibi si id modo in
pectore consilii est, ut te ab inimicorum impetu
vindices, quoque modo contra adversum consulem
beneficia populi retineas, indigna virtute tua cogitas.
4 Sin in te ille animus est qui iam a principio nobilitatis factionem disturbavit, [3] plebem Romanam ex
gravi servitute in libertatem restituit, in praetura
inimicorum arma inermis disiecit, domi militiaeque
tanta et tam praeclara facinora fecit, ut ne inimici
quidem queri quicquam audeant nisi de magnitudine
tua: quin tu accipe ea quae dicam de summa re
publica. Quae profecto aut vera invenies aut certe
haud procul a vero.

III. Sed quoniam Cn. Pompeius, aut animi pravi-
tate aut quia nihil eo maluit quod tibi obesset, ita

---

[1] *Rom. ed. omits* in.
[2] repeti, *Ciacconius*.   [3] disturbabit, *V*.

---

[1] In particular, the extension of his military command
and the privilege of becoming a candidate for the consulship
in his absence from Rome.

464

is made more manifest by the rest of the world, because men are sooner wearied in praising and admiring your munificence than you are in doing deeds worthy of praise.

II. For my own part, I am convinced that nothing so deep can be found that your thoughts cannot easily grasp it; and I have written you my views upon public affairs, not because I thought more highly than is proper of my own counsel and my own ability, but because it seemed to me that during the toil of war, amid battles, victories and the duties of a commander, you ought to be reminded of the interests of our city. For if you have in your heart this consideration only, how you may protect yourself against the assaults of your enemies and retain the favours of the people[1] in opposition to a hostile consul,[2] your thoughts are unworthy of your manhood. But if you have in you the spirit which has from the very beginning dismayed the faction of the nobles, which restored the Roman commons to freedom after a grievous slavery, which in your praetorship routed your armed enemies without resort to arms,[3] which has achieved so many and such glorious deeds at home and abroad that not even your enemies dare to make any complaint except of your greatness : if you have that spirit, pray give ear to what I shall say about our country's welfare. You will assuredly find it either true or at all events not far from the truth.

III. Now, since Gnaeus Pompeius, either from perversity of spirit or because he desired above all

---

[2] Referring to Lucius Cornelius Lentulus Crus, consul in 49 b.c., or his colleague Gaius Claudius Marcellus. This seems to be the time assumed by the writer of the letter.

[3] See Suet. *Jul.* 16.

lapsus est ut hostibus tela in manus iaceret, quibus
ille rebus rem publicam conturbavit, eisdem tibi
2 restituendum est. Primum omnium summam potestatem moderandi de vectigalibus, sumptibus, iudiciis
senatoribus paucis tradidit, plebem Romanam, quoius
antea summa potestas erat, ne aequeis quidem
3 legibus in servitute reliquit. Iudicia tametsi, sicut
antea, tribus ordinibus tradita sunt, tamen idem illi
factiosi regunt, dant, adimunt quae lubet,[1] innocentis
4 circumveniunt, suos ad honorem extollunt. Non
facinus, non probrum aut flagitium obstat, quo minus
magistratus capiant. Quos commodum est trahunt,
rapiunt; postremo tamquam urbe capta libidine ac
5 licentia sua pro legibus utuntur. Ac me quidem
mediocris dolor angeret, si virtute partam victoriam
6 more suo per servitium exercerent. Sed homines
inertissimi, quorum omnis vis virtusque in lingua
sita est, forte atque alterius socordia dominationem
7 oblatam insolentes agitant. Nam quae[2] seditio aut
dissensio civilis tot tam illustris familias ab stirpe
evertit? Aut quorum umquam in victoria animus
tam praeceps tamque immoderatus fuit?

IV. L. Sulla, cui omnia in victoria lege belli
licuerunt, tametsi supplicio hostium partis suas
muniri intellegebat, tamen paucis interfectis ceteros

---

[1] luget, *V.*   [2] namque, *V.*

things to injure you, has fallen so low as to put arms into the hands of the enemy, you must restore the government by the same means by which he has overthrown it. To begin with, he gave a few senators the absolute power of regulating the revenues, the expenditures and the courts, leaving the commons of Rome, who once held the supreme power, in slavery, under laws which are not even alike for all. For even though the courts, as before, have been entrusted to the three orders,[1] yet that same faction controls them, gives and takes away whatever it pleases, defrauds the innocent, elevates its members to high positions. Neither crime nor shame nor disgrace bars them from holding office. They rob and pillage where it suits them; finally, just as if they had taken the city captive, they regard their own will and caprice as law. And so far as I am concerned, I should feel but moderate resentment, if they had won by valour that victory which, according to their custom, they are making an instrument of slavery. But these most cowardly of men, whose whole power and courage lies in the tongue, are insolently exercising a tyranny which they have acquired by chance and through the incapacity of another. For what rebellion or civil dissension has utterly destroyed so many illustrious families? Or who ever had in victory a spirit so frenzied and so unbridled.

IV. Lucius Sulla, to whom the laws of war allowed unrestrained power in his victory, although he knew that by the execution of his foes he could strengthen his party, yet put but few to death, preferring to

---

[1] The senators, knights, and *tribuni aerarii*; *cf.* Suet. *Jul.* 41. 2.

SALLUST

2 beneficio quam metu retinere maluit. At hercule a M. Catone,[1] L. Domitio, ceterisque eiusdem factionis quadraginta senatores, multi praeterea cum spe bona adulescentes sicutei hostiae mactati sunt, quom interea importunissuma genera hominum tot miserorum civium sanguine satiari nequiere[2]; non orbi liberi, non parentes exacta aetate, non luctus, gemitus virorum mulierum immanem eorum animum inflexit, quein acerbius in dies male faciundo ac dicundo dignitate alios, alios civitate eversum irent.

3 Nam quid ego de te dicam? cuius contumeliam homines ignavissimi vita sua commutare volunt, si liceat. Neque illis tantae voluptati est, tametsi insperantibus accidit, dominatio quanto maerori tua dignitas; quein optatius habent ex tua calamitate periculum libertatis facere, quam per te populi

4 Romani imperium maximum ex magno fieri. Quo magis tibi etiam atque etiam animo prospiciendum

5 est, quonam modo rem stabilias communiasque. Mihi quidem quae mens suppetit eloqui non dubitabo. Ceterum tuei erit ingenii probare, quae vera atque utilia factu putes.

V. In duas partes ego civitatem divisam arbitror, sicut a maioribus accepi, in patres et plebem. Antea in patribus summa auctoritas erat, vis multo maxuma

2 in plebe. Itaque saepius in civitate secessio fuit

[1] at hercule a M. Catone, *Mommsen*; at hercule M. Catoni, *Orelli*; atherculem catonem, *V.*   [2] nequier, *V.*

---

[1] Referring to the censorship of Appius Claudius, to which Sallust fell a victim; see Introd. p. viii.

hold the rest by kindness rather than by intimidation. But, by Heaven! Marcus Cato, Lucius Domitius, and the others of that faction, have butchered forty senators and many young men of excellent promise like so many sacrificial victims; and yet meanwhile the blood of so many wretched citizens has not been enough to sate those most ruthless of men. Not orphans and aged parents, not the grief and lamentation of men and women, could turn them from their inhuman purpose; nay, harsher in deed and word day by day, they have deprived some of their rank,[1] others of their citizenship.[2] What shall I say of you, whose humiliation, if it were possible, those basest of creatures would buy at the cost of their own lives? And they do not feel so much pleasure in their supremacy, although it is more than they had hoped for, as they do chagrin at your glory. Nay, they would prefer to endanger liberty by your downfall, rather than that through you the empire of the Roman people from being merely great should become the greatest. Therefore it behooves you again and again to consider by what means you may strengthen and fortify your country. For myself, I shall not hesitate to utter what my mind prompts, but it will be for your judgment to determine which of my suggestions you think wise and helpful.

V. I believe, as I have learned from our forefathers, that our commonwealth is divided into two bodies, the patricians and the plebeians. In days of old the patricians had the chief authority, but the commons by far the greatest numerical strength. Therefore secessions occurred on several occasions[3]

---

[1] By driving them into exile.   [2] See p. 56, note 2.

semperque nobilitatis opes deminutae sunt et ius
3 populi amplificatum. Sed plebs eo libere agitabat,
quia nullius potentia super leges erat neque divitiis
aut superbia sed bona fama factisque fortibus nobilis
ignobilem anteibat; humillimus quisque in arvis[1]
aut in militia nullius honestae rei egens satis sibi
satisque patriae erat.

4 Sed ubi eos paulatim expulsos agris inertia atque
inopia incertas domos habere subegit, coepere alienas
opes petere, libertatem suam cum re publica venalem
5 habere. Ita paulatim populus, qui dominus erat,
cunctis gentibus imperitabat, dilapsus est et pro
communi imperio privatim sibi quisque servitutem
6 peperit. Haec igitur multitudo primum malis moribus imbuta, deinde in artis vitasque varias dispalata,
nullo modo inter se congruens, parum mihi quidem
idonea videtur ad capessendam rem publicam
7 Ceterum additis novis civibus magna me spes
tenet fore ut omnes expergiscantur ad libertatem;
quippe cum illis libertatis retinendae, tum his ser-
8 vitutis amittendae cura orietur. Hos ego censeo
permixtos cum veteribus novos in coloniis constituas; ita et res militaris opulentior erit et plebs
bonis negotiis impedita malum publicum facere
desinet.

[1] arvis, *Dousa*; armis, *V.*

and the power of the nobles was constantly curtailed, while the privileges of the commons were extended. But in those days the reason why the commons enjoyed freedom was because no man's power was superior to the laws, and because the noble surpassed the commoner, not in riches or ostentation, but in good repute and valiant deeds; while the humblest citizen lacked nothing for which he could honourably wish either in the fields or in military service, but was sufficient for himself and for his country.

When, however, idleness and poverty gradually drove the commons from the fields and forced them to live without a fixed abode, they began to covet the riches of other men and to regard their liberty and their country as objects of traffic. Thus little by little the people, which had been sovereign and had exercised authority over all nations, became degenerate, and each man bartered his share of the common sovereignty for slavery to one man. Hence this population of ours, at first acquiring evil habits and then divided by different employments and modes of life, since it has no bond of union, seems to me quite unfitted to govern the state. But if new citizens should be added to their number, I have high hopes that all would be aroused to a sense of freedom; for the new citizens will feel a desire to retain their liberty, those who are already citizens will long to throw off the yoke of slavery. I therefore advise you to settle these newcomers, along with the earlier citizens, in colonies; for in this way our military power will be the greater, and the commons, being occupied with useful occupations, will cease to work public mischief.

VI. Sed non inscius neque imprudens sum, quom ea res agetur, quae saevitia quaeque tempestates hominum nobilium futurae sint, quom indignabuntur, omnia funditus misceri, antiquis civibus hanc servitutem imponi, regnum denique ex libera civitate futurum, ubi unius munere multitudo ingens in 2 civitatem pervenerit. Equidem ego sic apud animum meum statuo : malum facinus in se admittere, qui incommodo rei publicae gratiam sibi conciliet; ubi bonum publicum etiam privatim usui est, id vero dubitare aggredi, socordiae atque ignaviae duco.

3 M. Druso semper consilium fuit in tribunatu summa ope niti pro nobilitate ; neque ullam rem in principio agere intendit, nisi illei auctores fuerant. 4 Sed homines factiosi, quibus dolus atque malitia fide cariora erant, ubi intellexerunt per unum hominem maxumum beneficium multis mortalibus dari, videlicet sibi quisque conscius malo atque infido animo esse, de M. Druso iuxta se[1] existumaverunt. 5 Itaque metu ne per tantam gratiam solus rerum poteretur, contra eam nisi, sua et ipseius consilia 6 disturbaverunt. Quo tibı, imperator, maiore[2] cura fideique amici et multa praesidia paranda sunt.

VII. Hostem adversum deprimere strenuo homini haud difficilest ; occulta pericula neque facere neque

---

[1] iuxta se, *Jordan*; iuxta ac se, *V*; iuxta ac de se, *Gerlach*.   [2] maiore, *Gerlach*; maior, *V*.

---

[1] Tribune in 91 B.C. He attempted to carry out reforms which would have been advantageous both to the nobles and

VI. I am not, however, ignorant or unaware what rage and what tempests the execution of this project will rouse among the nobles, who will cry out that the very foundations of society are being undermined, that this is the same as enslaving the original citizens; in short, that a free state will be transformed into a monarchy, if citizenship is conferred upon a great multitude through the bounty of one man. But while it is my firm conviction that he commits a crime who tries to win popular favour at the cost of his country's welfare, yet when a public service is at the same time to the advantage of one man, to hesitate on that account to undertake it I consider a mark of folly and cowardice.

Marcus Drusus[1] always intended to exert his every power during his tribunate for the nobles, and at first he took no step without their sanction. But a faction to whom treachery and dishonesty were dearer than honour perceived that the greatest of benefits[2] was being conferred upon many by one man; and just because all of them were conscious of having evil and disloyal minds, they judged Marcus Drusus to be like themselves. Fearing therefore that by conferring such a favour he might acquire supreme power, they strove to prevent it and thus ruined his plans and their own as well. With this example before you, my general, it behooves you the more carefully to surround yourself with loyal friends and with many defences.

VII. An enemy in front can be overthrown without difficulty by a stout-hearted man, but hidden snares

to the people, and to extend the franchise to all the Italians; but he fell victim to an unknown assassin.

[2] Namely, citizenship; see the preceding note.

2 vitare bonis in promptu est. Igitur, ubi eos in
civitatem adduxeris, quoniam quidem renovata plebs
erit, in ea re maxume animum exerceto, ut colantur
boni mores, concordia inter veteres et novos coal-
3 escat. Sed multo maxumum bonum patriae, civibus,
tibi, liberis, postremo humanae genti pepereris, si
studium pecuniae aut sustuleris aut, quoad res feret,[1]
minueris. Aliter neque privata res neque publica
4 neque domi neque militiae regi potest. Nam ubi
cupido divitiarum invasit, neque disciplina neque
artes bonae neque ingenium ullum satis pollet, quin
animus magis aut minus mature, postremo tamen
5 succumbat. Saepe iam audivi, qui reges, quae civitates et nationes per opulentiam magna imperia
amiserint, quae per virtutem inopes ceperant; id
6 adeo[2] haud mirandum est. Nam ubi bonus de-
teriorem divitiis magis clarum magisque acceptum
videt, primo aestuat multaque in pectore volvit; sed
ubi gloria honorem magis in dies, virtutem opulentia
7 vincit, animus ad voluptatem a vero deficit. Quippe
gloria industria alitur, ubi eam dempseris ipsa per se
8 virtus amara atque aspera est. Postremo ubi divitiae
clarae habentur, ibi omnia bona vilia sunt, fides,
9 probitas, pudor, pudicitia. Nam ad virtutem via
ardua[3] est, ad pecuniam qua cuique lubet nititur;
et malis et bonis rebus ea creatur.

[1] feret, *Aldus* ; referet, *V*.
[2] id adeo, *Asulanus* ; ideo, *V*.
[3] una ardua via (*superscribed*) est, *V* ; una et ardua via est,
Aldus ; via ardua est, *Jordan*.

are not commonly laid or readily avoided by the honourable. Since therefore by the introduction of new citizens into the commonwealth the commons will be regenerated, you should devote particular attention to the problem of fostering good morals and establishing harmony between the old and the new burgesses. But by far the greatest blessing which you can confer upon your country and fellow citizens, upon yourself and your children, in short, upon all mankind, will be either to do away with the pursuit of wealth or to reduce it so far as circumstances permit. Otherwise, neither public nor private affairs can be regulated at home or abroad. For wherever the desire for riches has penetrated, neither education, nor good qualities, nor talents, can prevent the mind from at last yielding to it sooner or later. Often before this I have heard how kings, how cities and nations have lost mighty empires through opulence, which they had won through valour when in poverty; and such a loss is not at all surprising. For when the good sees the baser by riches made more renowned and more beloved, at first he boils with anger and feels much perplexed; but when more and more each day vainglory prevails over honour, opulence over merit, his mind turns to pleasure and forsakes the truth. In fact, endeavour feeds upon glory; take that away, and virtue by itself is bitter and harsh. Finally, wherever riches are regarded as a distinction, there honour, uprightness, moderation, chastity and all the virtues are lightly rated. For the only path to virtue is steep; to riches one may mount wherever one chooses, and they may be won by means either honourable or dishonourable.

10 Ergo in primis auctoritatem pecuniae demito.
Neque de capite neque de honore ex copiis quisquam
magis aut minus iudicaverit, sicut neque praetor
neque consul ex opulentia verum ex dignitate
11 creetur. Sed de magistratu facile populi iudicium
fit; iudices a paucis probari regnum est, ex pecunia
legi inhonestum. Quare omnes primae classis iu-
dicare placet, sed numero plures quam iudicant.
12 Neque Rhodios neque alias civitates unquam iudi-
ciorum suorum paenituit, ubi promiscue dives et
pauper, ut cuique fors tulit, de maximis rebus iuxta
ac de minimis disceptat.

VIII. Sed magistratibus creandis haud mihi
quidem apsurde placet lex, quam C. Gracchus in
tribunatu promulgaverat, ut ex confusis quinque
2 classibus sorte centuriae vocarentur. Ita coae-
quatur[1] dignitate pecunia, virtute anteire alius
3 alium properabit. Haec ego magna remedia contra
divitias statuo. Nam perinde omnes res laudantur
atque appetuntur, ut earum rerum usus est. Malitia praemiis exercetur; ubi ea dempseris, nemo
4 omnium gratuito malus est. Ceterum avaritia belua
fera, immanis, intoleranda est; quo intendit, oppida,
agros, fana atque domos vastat, divina cum humanis
permiscet, neque exercitus neque moenia obstant,
quo minus vi sua penetret; fama, pudicitia, liberis,

<hr>

[1] coaequantur, V.

<hr>

[1] See *Jug.* lxxxvi. 2, and the note.
[2] To give their votes; instead of having all the centuries
of the first-class vote first, and so on.

First of all then, deprive money of its importance. Let no one be given greater or less opportunity according to his wealth to serve as a juror in cases involving life or honour; just as no consul or praetor should be chosen because of his riches, but because of his worth. In the case of a magistrate, however, the people can easily decide; but for jurors to be selected by a faction is tyranny, for them to be chosen on the basis of money is shameful. It therefore seems to me fitting that all citizens of the first class [1] should be eligible as jurors, but that they should serve in somewhat greater numbers than at present. Neither the Rhodians nor the citizens of any other state have ever had occasion to be ashamed of their courts, where rich and poor alike, according to the fortune of the lot, decide indiscriminately matters of greatest or of slight importance.

VIII. As regards the election of magistrates, I for my part very naturally approve the law which Gaius Gracchus proposed in his tribunate, that the centuries should be called up by lot [2] from the five classes without distinction. In this way money and worth are put on an equality [3] and each man will strive to outdo his fellow in merit. These are the great safeguards which I have to propose against the power of riches; for everything is valued and sought for according to the advantages which it offers. Wickedness is practised for gain; take that away, and no one at all is wicked for nothing. But avarice is a wild beast, monstrous and irresistible; wherever it goes, it devastates town and country, shrines and homes, and lays low everything human and divine; no army and no walls can withstand it; it robs all

[3] Text and meaning are uncertain.

patria atque parentibus cunctos mortalis spoliat.

5 Verum, si pecuniae decus ademeris, magna illa vis

6 avaritiae facile bonis moribus vincetur. Atque haec ita sese habere tametsi omnes aequi atque iniqui memorant, tamen tibi cum factione nobilitatis haut mediocriter certandum est. Quoius si dolum

7 caveris, alia omnia in proclivi erunt. Nam ii, si virtute satis valerent, magis aemuli bonorum quam invidi essent. Quia desidia et inertia, stupor eos atque torpedo invasit, strepunt, obtrectant, alienam famam bonam suum dedecus aestumant.

IX. Sed quid ego plura quasi de ignotis memorem? M. Bibuli fortitudo atque animi vis in consulatum erupit; hebes lingua, magis malus quam callidus

2 ingenio. Quid ille audeat, quoi[1] consulatus, maximum imperium, maxumo dedecori fuit? An L. Domiti magna vis est? Quoius nullum membrum a flagitio aut facinore vacat, lingua vana, manus cruentae, pedes fugaces; quae honeste nominari nequeunt inhonestissima.

3 Unius tamen M. Catonis ingenium versutum, loquax, callidum haud contemno. Parantur haec disciplina Graecorum. Sed virtus, vigilantia, labor apud Graecos nulla sunt. Quippe qui domi libertatem suam per inertiam amiserint, censesne eorum praeceptis imperium haberi posse?

[1] qui, V.

---

[1] Ironical, of course. He was Caesar's colleague in 59 B.C. Wags referred to it as the consulate of Julius and Caesar (Suet. *Jul.* 20. 2). For *erupit in cf.* Ter. *Phorm.* 324 f.

men of their repute, their chastity, their children, country and parents. Yet if you take away the honour paid to money, the power of avarice, great as it is, will readily yield to good morals. But although all men, just and unjust alike, admit the truth of this, yet your struggle with the nobles will be no light one. If, however, you avoid their snares, all else will be easy; for if merit made them strong enough, they would emulate the virtuous instead of envying them. It is because sloth and indolence, dullness and torpor, have taken possession of their minds, that they resort to abuse and slander and consider the glory of others a disgrace to themselves.

IX. But why should I say more of the nobles, as if you did not know them well. It was Marcus Bibulus' courage and force of character that landed him in the consulship:[1] dull of speech, rather wicked than clever by nature. What would a man dare to do who found in the consulship, the supreme power, his supreme disgrace? Has Lucius Domitius[2] great strength? A man whose every member is stained with disgrace or crime, of lying tongue, blood-stained hands, fleeing feet, most dishonourable in those parts which cannot honourably be named.

There is one of them, however, Marcus Cato, whose versatile, eloquent and clever talents I do not despise. Training such as his comes from the Greeks; but among that people manliness, vigilance and industry are wholly lacking. Pray do you think that a government can be upheld by the precepts of those who through incapacity have lost their freedom at home?

[2] Lucius Domitius Ahenobarbus, brother-in-law of Cato Uticensis and consul in 54 B.C.

4 Reliqui de factione sunt inertissimi nobiles, in
quibus sicut in titulo [1] praeter bonum nomen nihil
est additamenti.   L. Postumii M. Favonii mihi
videntur quasi magnae navis supervacuanea onera
esse; ubi salvi pervenere, usui sunt; siquid adversi
coortum est, de illeis potissimum iactura fit, quia
pretii minimi sunt.

X. Nunc quoniam, sicut mihi videor, de plebe
renovanda corrigendaque satis disserui, de senatu
2 quae tibi agenda videntur, dicam.   Postquam mihi
aetas ingeniumque adolevit, haud ferme armis atque
equis corpus exercui, sed animum in litteris agitavi;
3 quod natura firmius erat, id in laboribus habui.
Atque ego in ea vita multa legendo atque audiendo
ita comperi, omnia regna, item civitates et nationes
usque eo prosperum imperium habuisse, dum apud
eos vera consilia valuerunt; ubicumque gratia
timor, voluptas ea corrupere, post paulo imminutae
opes, deinde ademptum imperium, postremo servitus
imposita est.

4 Equidem ego sic apud animum meum statuo:
cuicumque in sua civitate amplior illustriorque locus
quam aliis est, ei magnam curam esse rei publicae.
5 Nam ceteris salva urbe tantum modo libertas tuta
est; qui per virtutem sibi divitias, decus, honorem
pepererunt, ubi paulum inclinata res publica agitari

----

1 in titulo, *Jordan*; instituto, *V*; in statua nihil praeter
nomen, *Lipsius.*

In addition to those whom I have mentioned the party consists of nobles of utter incapacity, who, like an inscription, contribute nothing but a famous name. Men like Lucius Postumius and Marcus Favonius[1] seem to me like the superfluous deckload of a great ship. When they arrive safely, some use can be made of them; if any disaster occurs, they are the first to be jettisoned because they are of least value.

X. Having now, as it seems to me, said enough about the regeneration and reformation of the commons, let me tell you what I think you ought to do about the senate. Ever since years have matured my mind, I have seldom exercised my body with arms and horses, but I have busied my mind with reading, thus employing the part of my being which was by nature the stronger. Spending my life in that way, I have learned by abundant reading and instruction that all kingdoms, as well as states and nations, have enjoyed prosperity and power for so long a time as wise counsel has reigned among them; but just so soon as this was vitiated by favour, fear or pleasure, their strength rapidly waned, then their supremacy was wrested from them, and finally they were reduced to slavery.

Personally, I have made up my mind that whenever a man has in his own state a higher and more conspicuous position than his fellows, he takes a great interest in the welfare of his country. For to other citizens the safety of the state merely assures their personal liberty; but those who by their talents have won riches, respect and renown are filled with

[1] Famous as an imitator of Cato; see Suet. *Aug.* 13. 2. Postumius is unknown except for this reference.

coepit, multipliciter animus curis atque laboribus
fatigatur; aut gloriam aut libertatem aut rem familiarem defensat, omnibus locis adest, festinat,
quanto in secundis rebus florentior fuit, tanto in
adversis asperius magisque anxie agitat.

6 Igitur ubi plebs senatui sicuti corpus animo
oboedit eiusque consulta exsequitur, patres [1] consilio
valere decet, populo supervacuanea est calliditas.

7 Itaque maiores nostri, cum bellis asperrumis pre-
merentur, equis, viris, pecunia amissa, numquam
defessi sunt armati de imperio certare. Non inopia
aerarii, non vis hostium, non adversa res ingentem
eorum animum subegit quin, quae [2] virtute ceperant,

8 simul cum anima retinerent. Atque ea magis fortibus consiliis quam bonis proeliis patrata sunt.
Quippe apud illos una res publica erat, ei omnes
consulebant, factio contra hostis parabatur, corpus
atque ingenium patriae, non suae quisque potentiae

9 exercitabat. At hoc tempore contra ea homines
nobiles, quorum animos socordia atque ignavia
invasit, ignarei laboris, hostium, militiae, domi factione instructi per superbiam cunctis gentibus
moderantur.

XI. Itaque patres, quorum consilio antea dubia
res publica stabiliebatur, oppressi ex aliena libidine
huc atque illuc fluctuantes agitantur; interdum alia
deinde alia decernunt; uti eorum, qui dominantur,

---

[1] patris, *V.*
[2] quin quae, *ed. Mant.*, 1476–1478; quique, *V.*

manifold anxiety and trouble if the state begins
to decline and totter ever so little. He flies to the
defence of his repute, or his freedom, or his property; he is to be seen everywhere and makes haste;
the more prosperous he was in prosperity, the more
cruelly is he harried and worried in adversity.

Therefore, since the commons submit to the
senate as the body does to the soul, and carry out its
decrees, the fathers ought to be strong in counsel,
but for the people cleverness is superfluous. Accordingly our forefathers, when they were harassed
by the most difficult wars, although they suffered
loss of horses, men and money, never wearied in
their efforts to maintain their supremacy by arms.
Not a depleted treasury, no strength of their enemies,
no disaster could daunt their great souls or prevent
them, while they had breath, from defending what
they had won by their valour. And their success was
due rather to firmness in the council-chamber than
to victories in the field; for in their day the commonwealth was united, for its welfare all citizens had
regard; leagues were formed only against the enemy,
each man exerted body and mind for his country,
not for his own power. To-day, on the contrary,
certain of the nobles, whose minds are possessed by
indolence and cowardice, although they are ignorant
of hardship, of the enemy, and of military life, have
formed a faction within the state and arrogantly
claim sovereignty over all nations.

XI. Thus the Fathers, by whose wisdom the
wavering state was formerly steadied, are over-
powered and tossed to and fro according to the
caprice of others; they decree now one measure
and now another, determining what is helpful or

ʒimultas aut gratia fert,[1] ita bonum malumque publicum aestumant.

2 Quodsi aut libertas aequa omnium aut sententia obscurior esset, maioribus opibus res publica et 3 minus potens nobilitas esset. Sed quoniam coaequari gratiam[2] omnium difficile est, quippe cum illis maiorum virtus partam reliquerit gloriam, dignitatem, clientelas, cetera multitudo pleraque insiticia sit, sententias eorum a metu libera; ita in occulto 4 sibi quisque alterius potentia carior erit. Libertas iuxta bonis et malis, strenuis atque ignavis optabilis est. Verum eam plerique metu deserunt. Stultissimi mortales, quod in certamine dubium est, quorsum accidat, id per inertiam in se quasi victi recipiunt.

5 Igitur duabus rebus confirmari posse senatum puto: si numero auctus per tabellam sententiam feret. Tabella obtentui erit, quo magis animo libero facere audeat; in multitudine et praesidii plus et 6 usus amplior est. Nam fere his tempestatibus alii iudiciis publicis, alii privatis suis atque amicorum negotiis implicati, haud sane rei publicae consiliis adfuerunt; neque eos magis occupatio quam superba imperia distinuere. Homines nobiles cum paucis

---

[1] fert, *Aldus*; fertur, *V.*   [2] gratia, *V.*

harmful to the public from the enmity or favour of their masters.

But if all the senators had equal freedom of action, or if their voting were done less openly, the state would have greater strength and the nobles[1] less power. Now, since it is not easy to make the influence of all equal (for the prowess of their ancestors has left the nobles[1] a heritage of glory, prestige and patronage, while the rest are for the most part grafted upon the state), at least free the votes of the latter from the effects of fear; thus each man, if assured of secrecy, will value his own judgment more highly than the authority of another. Independence is desirable alike to good and bad, to hero and coward; but many men, most foolish of mortals, sacrifice independence to fear, and are led by cowardice to accept defeat, when a struggle would make the issue doubtful.

There are then, in my judgment, two ways by which the senate may be given greater strength: by an increase in its numbers and by permission to vote by ballot. The ballot will serve as a screen, giving courage to act with more independence, while the increase in numbers will furnish greater protection and an opportunity for larger usefulness. As a matter of fact, in these days some of the senators are habitually occupied with the public courts and others with their own business and that of their friends, and hence they do not attend deliberations on matters of public moment; although in reality it is the insolence of power which has kept them away, rather than outside interests. Hence certain of the nobles, in conjunction with a

---

[1] That is, the faction of the nobles mentioned in x. 9.

senatoriis, quos additamenta factionis habent, quaecumque libuit probare,[1] reprehendere, decernere, ea,
7 uti lubido tulit, fecere. Verum ubi numero senatorum aucto per tabellam sententiae dicentur, ne
illi superbiam suam dimittent, ubi iis oboediendum
erit, quibus antea crudelissime imperitabant.

XII. Forsitan, imperator, perlectis litteris de-
sideres quem numerum senatorum fieri placeat,
quoque modo is in multa et varia officia distribuatur ;
iudicia quoniam omnibus primae classis committenda
putem, quae discriptio, quei numerus in quoque
2 genere futurus sit. Ea mihi omnia generatim dis-
cribere haud difficile factu fuit ; sed prius laboran-
dum visum est de summa consilii, idque tibi pro-
bandum verum esse. Si hoc itinere uti decreveris,
3 cetera in promptu erunt. Volo ego consilium meum
prudens maxumeque usui esse ; nam ubicumque tibi
4 res prospere cedet, ibi mihi bona fama eveniet. Sed
me illa magis cupido exercet, ut quocumque modo
5 quam primum res publica adiutetur. Libertatem
gloria cariorem habeo, atque ego te oro hortorque
ne clarissumus imperator Gallica gente subacta
populi Romani summum atque invictum imperium
6 tabescere vetustate ac per summam socordiam dilabi
patiaris. Profecto, si id accidat neque tibi nox
neque dies curam animi sedaverit, quin insomniis
exercitus, furibundus atque amens alienata mente
7 feraris. Namque mihi pro vero constat omnium

---

[1] probari, V.

few men of senatorial rank who support their faction, approve, censure, or decree whatever their caprice suggests. But when the number of the senators is increased and the voting is done by ballot, these men will surely lay aside their insolence when they shall be forced to obey those over whom they formerly exercised a merciless sway.

XII. Perhaps, my general, after reading this letter you may wish to know what number of senators I would recommend and in what way their many varied duties should be distributed; also, since I believe that jury duty should be entrusted to all the members of the first class, how I would apportion them and what number there should be in each division. It would not be at all difficult for me to go into all these details, but it has seemed to me that I ought first to work out the general plan and convince you that it is a reasonable one. If you decide to follow the course which I have suggested, the rest will be easy. For my own part, I desire my plans to be wise and above all practicable; for wherever you carry them out successfully, I shall gain fame. But the strongest desire which actuates me is that somehow or other, and as soon as possible, our country may be helped. I hold freedom dearer than glory, and I beg and implore you, illustrious general that you are, after subduing the Gallic nation not to allow the great and unconquered dominion of the Roman people to waste away through decay and fall asunder through excess of negligence. If that should happen, you surely could not escape remorse either by day or by night, but tormented with sleeplessness, mad and beside yourself, you would fall a victim to frenzy. As for me, I am firmly convinced that a divine power

mortalium vitam divino numine invisier; neque
bonum neque malum facinus quoiusquam pro nihilo
haberi, sed ex natura divorsa[1] praemia bonos ma-
8 losque sequi. Interea si forte ea tardius procedunt,
suus quoique animus ex conscientia spem praebet.

XIII. Quodsi tecum patria atque parentes possent
loqui, scilicet haec tibi dicerent: " O Caesar, nos te
genuimus fortissimi viri, in optima urbe, decus
2 praesidiumque nobis, hostibus terrorem. Quae
multis laboribus et periculis ceperamus, ea tibi
nascenti cum anima simul tradidimus: patriam
maxumam in terris, domum familiamque in patria
clarissimam, praeterea bonas artis, honestas divitias,
postremo omnia honestamenta pacis et praemia
3 belli. Pro iis amplissimis beneficiis non flagitium a
te neque malum facinus petimus, sed utei libertatem
4 eversam restituas. Qua re patrata profecto per
5 gentes omnes fama virtutis tuae volitabit. Namque
hac tempestate tametsi domi militiaeque praeclara
facinora egisti, tamen gloria tua cum multis viris
fortibus aequalis est. Si vero urbem amplissimo
nomine et maxumo imperio prope iam ab occasu
restitueris, quis te clarior, quis maior in terris fuerit?
6 Quippe si morbo iam aut fato huic imperio secus
accidat, cui dubium est quin per orbem terrarum
vastitas, bella, caedes oriantur? Quodsi tibi bona
lubido fuerit patriae parentibusque gratificandi,
posteroque tempore re publica restituta super omnis

---

[1] diversa, *Aldus*; divisa, *V*.

watches over the life of all mortals; that no one's good or evil action is overlooked, but that by a law of nature their different rewards await the good and the bad. Meanwhile, retribution and reward, if they are slow in coming, are held up to each man's mind by his own conscience.

XIII. If your country and your forefathers could address you, this would assuredly be their language: "We, bravest of men, have begotten you, O Caesar, in the most excellent of cities, to be our glory and defence and a terror to our enemies. What we had won at the cost of great hardship and peril we transmitted to you at your birth along with the breath of life: a fatherland the mightiest in the world, a house and family the most distinguished in that fatherland, and in addition, eminent talents, honourable riches, in short, all the rewards of peace and all the prizes of war. In return for these splendid gifts we ask of you, not disgrace or crime, but the restoration of our prostrate freedom. This accomplished, the fame of your prowess will surely wing its way to all nations. At present, although your exploits are brilliant at home and abroad, yet your glory is but on a par with that of many a hero. But if you rescue almost from the brink of ruin the most famous and powerful of cities, who upon the face of this earth will be more famous than you, who will be greater? For if this empire should succumb to decay or to fate, can anyone doubt but that all over the world devastation, wars, and bloodshed would ensue? But if you are inspired by the noble passion of showing gratitude to your forefathers and your fatherland, in days to come you will tower above all men in glory as the saviour of

mortalis gloria agitabis[1] tuaque unius mors vita
7 clarior erit.   Nam vivos interdum fortuna, saepe
invidia fatigat; ubi anima naturae cessit, demptis
obtrectatoribus, ipsa se virtus magis magisque
extollit."

8   Quae mihi utilissima factu visa sunt quaeque tibi
usui fore credidi, quam paucissimis potui perscripsi.
Ceterum deos immortales obtestor uti, quocumque
modo ages, ea res tibi reique publicae prospere
eveniat.

[1] gloria agitabis, *Jordan* ; gloria agnita, *earlier editors.*

your country, and you alone of all mortals will enjoy greater fame after death than was yours during your lifetime. For the living are sometimes harried by fortune, often by envy; but when the debt of nature has been paid, detraction is silent and merit lifts its head higher and higher."

I have written in the fewest possible words what I thought it helpful for you to do, and what I believed would be to your advantage. It remains to implore the immortal gods that whatever you decide, the result may be propitious to you and to your country.

[C. SALLUSTII CRISPI] IN M. TULLIUM CICERONEM ORATIO [1]

I. GRAVITER et iniquo animo maledicta tua paterer, M. Tulli, si te scirem iudicio magis quam morbo animi petulantia ista uti. Sed quoniam [2] in te neque modum neque modestiam ullam animadverto, respondebo tibi, ut, si quam male dicendo voluptatem cepisti, eam male audiendo amittas.

Ubi querar, quos implorem, patres conscripti, diripi rem publicam atque audacissimo cuique esse praedae [3]? Apud populum Romanum? qui ita largitionibus corruptus est, ut se ipse ac fortunas suas venales habeat. An apud vos, patres conscripti? quorum auctoritas turpissimo cuique et sceleratissimo ludibrio est. Ubiubi M. Tullius, leges, iudicia, rem publicam [4] defendit atque in hoc ordine ita moderatur, quasi unus reliquus e familia viri clarissimi, Scipionis Africani, ac non reperticius ac

[1] Sigla :—
α { A = cod. Guelferbytanus Gud. 335, s. x.
    Hᵃ = cod. Harleianus 2682, s. xi.
    TB = codd. Monacenses 19472, 4611, s. xi, xii.
β { HHᵇ = codd. Harleiani 2716, 3859, s. ix. or x, xii.
    EM = codd. Monacenses 14714, 19474, s. xii., xii.–xiii.
    P = cod. Admontensis 383, s. xii.
    V = cod. Vaticanus, 1747, s. xiii.
Kur. = Kurfess' ed., Teubner text, 1914.

AN INVECTIVE AGAINST MARCUS TULLIUS (ATTRIBUTED TO SALLUST)[1]

I. I SHOULD be troubled and angered by your abuse, Marcus Tullius, if I were sure that your impudence was the result of intention rather than of a disordered mind. But since I perceive in you neither moderation nor any modesty, I shall answer you; so that if you have derived any pleasure from reviling, you may lose it by listening to censure.

Where shall I make complaint, Fathers of the Senate, that our country is being rent asunder and is the victim of all the most reckless of men; to whom shall I appeal? Shall I turn to the Roman people, who are so corrupted by largess that they offer themselves and all their fortunes for sale? Shall I appeal to you, Fathers of the Senate, whose authority is the plaything of all the basest and most criminal of men? Wherever Marcus Tullius is, is he the defender of the laws, the courts and the state, and does he lord it in this assembly as if he were the sole survivor of the family of the illustrious Scipio Africanus and not a parvenu citizen

---

[1] See Introd. pp. xviii. f.

---

[2] quoniam, *Halm*; cum, *mss., Kur.*
[3] praedae, *Eussner, Kur.*; perfidiae, *mss.*
[4] R.P. audacia, *A*; audacia r.p., *H^aTB*; iudicia r.p., *HEMP*; iudiciaque r.p., *H^b*; iuditiaque rei p., *V.*

2 paullo ante insitus huic urbi civis? An vero, M.
Tulli, facta tua ac dicta obscura sunt? An non
ita a pueritia vixisti, ut nihil flagitiosum corpori
tuo putares quod alicui collibuisset? At[1] scilicet
istam immoderatam eloquentiam apud M. Pisonem
non pudicitiae iactura perdidicisti? Itaque minime
mirandum est, quod eam flagitiose venditas, quam
turpissime parasti.

II. Verum, ut opinor, splendor domesticus tibi
animos tollit, uxor sacrilega ac periuriis delibuta,
filia matris paelex, tibi iucundior atque obsequentior
quam parenti par est. Domum ipsam tuam vi et
rapinis funestam tibi ac tuis comparasti; videlicet,
3 ut nos commonefacias quam conversa res sit, cum in
ea domo habites,[2] homo flagitiosissime, quae P. Crassi,
viri clarissimi, fuit. Atque haec cum ita sint, tamen
Cicero se dicit in concilio deorum immortalium
fuisse, inde missum huic urbi civibusque custodem
absque carnificis nomine, qui civitatis incommodum
in gloriam suam ponit. Quasi vero non illius coniurationis causa fuerit consulatus tuus et idcirco
res publica disiecta eo tempore, quod te custodem
habebat.

Sed, ut opinor, illa te magis extollunt, quae post
consulatum cum Terentia uxore de re publica con-

---

[1] at, *Wirz*; aut, *mss.*
[2] habites, *Halm*; habitas, H^b; habitares, *Kur.*

---

[1] *cf.* Cass. Dio 46. 20. 2, καίτοι πολλὰ μὲν περὶ τῶν νόμων,
πολλὰ δὲ περὶ τῶν δικαστηρίων ἀεὶ καὶ πανταχοῦ (= *ubiubi*)
θρυλῶν.

but recently grafted upon this city [1]? Or pray, Marcus Tullius, are your deeds and words unknown to us? Have you not lived such a life from childhood, that you thought nothing a disgrace to your body which any other's desire prompted? Did you not in fact learn all your unchecked torrent of language under Marcus Piso at the expense of your chastity? It is, therefore, not at all surprising that you trade upon it shamefully, when you acquired it most shamefully.

II. But, I suppose, your spirits are raised by the brilliance of your home, by a wife guilty of sacrilege and dishonoured by perjury, by a daughter who is her mother's rival and is more compliant and submissive to you than a daughter should be to a parent. Even your house, fatal to yourself and your family, you obtained by violence and robbery; doubtless in order to remind us how our country has changed, when you, vilest of men that you are, live in the house which was once the property of that most distinguished man Publius Crassus. And in spite of all this, Cicero declares that he was present at the council of the immortal gods,[2] from which he, a man who makes disaster to his country the means of his own glorification, was sent as a protector to this city and its citizens, and not as its executioner. As if, forsooth, your consulship was not the cause of that conspiracy, and as if the reason why the commonwealth was not rent asunder at that time was because it had you for a protector.

But, I suppose, you are raised to a higher pinnacle by what you planned for the state after your consulship, in company with your wife Terentia, when you

[2] A sarcastic allusion to Cicero's recognition of the help of the gods; *e.g. in Cat.* 2. 13. 29, etc.

suluisti, cum legis Plautiae iudicia domo faciebatis,
ex coniuratis aliquos[1] pecunia condemnabas, cum
tibi alius Tusculanam, alius Pompeianam villam
exaedificabat, alius domum emebat; qui vero nihil
poterat, is erat calumniae proximus, is aut domum
tuam oppugnatum venerat aut insidias senatui
4 fecerat, denique de eo tibi compertum erat. Quae
si tibi falsa obicio, redde rationem quantum patri-
monii acceperis, quid tibi litibus accreverit, qua ex
pecunia domum paraveris, Tusculanum et Pompei-
anum infinito sumptu aedificaveris, aut, si retices,
cui dubium potest esse, quin[2] opulentiam istam ex
sanguine et miseriis civium pararis[3]?

III. Verum, ut opinor, homo novus Arpinas, ex
M. Crassi[4] familia, illius virtutem imitatur, contemnit
simultatem hominum nobilium, rem publicam caram
5 habet, neque terrore neque gratia removetur a vero,[5]
amicitia tantum ac virtus est animi. Immo vero
homo levissimus, supplex inimicis, amicis contu-
meliosus, modo harum, modo illarum partium, fidus
nemini, levissimus senator, mercennarius patronus,
cuius nulla pars corporis a turpitudine vacat, lingua
vana, manus rapacissimae, gula immensa, pedes
fugaces; quae honeste nominari non possunt, in-

---

[1] aliquos, *Kur.*; alios, *mss.*
[2] *Om. by H, Kur.*   [3] *Jordan*; parasti (parasses, *V*), *mss.*
[4] C. Marii, *Glareanus.*
[5] a vero, *Reitzenstein*; aliud vero, *mss.* (et id vero, *V*).

---

[1] See *Cat.* xxxi. 4.
[2] That is, furnished the money for them through the fines
which they paid.

were holding trials under the Plautian law[1] at your own home and condemning some of the conspirators to pay fines; when one built your country house at Tusculum, another that at Pompeii, and still another bought your house for you.[2] But the man who could do nothing for you was the most liable to false accusation; he it was who had come to attack your house, or who had plotted against the senate; in short, you were quite convinced of his guilt. If my charges are false, render an account of the amount of the patrimony which you inherited, and of what has come to you from lawsuits, and tell us where you got the money to buy your house and build your villas at Tusculum and Pompeii regardless of expense. If you are silent, who can doubt but that you amassed that wealth from the blood and wretchedness of the citizens?

III. But, I suppose, a parvenu Arpinate of the breed of Marcus Crassus[3] imitates that great man's merits, scorns the enmity of the nobles, holds the state dear, and is deflected from the truth neither by fear nor by favour, such are his loyalty and virtuous spirit. On the contrary, he is the most unstable of men, a suppliant to his enemies, insulting to his friends, an adherent now of this party and now of that, loyal to no one, an unstable senator, a mercenary counsel, free from disgrace in no member of his body, with a false tongue, thievish hands, a bottomless gullet, fleeing feet; most dishonoured in that part of his body which cannot honourably be named.[4]

---

[3] He is called " of the breed of Crassus," because he gained money in any and every way. *cf.* Velleius 2. 46. 2 (Crassus) *vir cetera sanctissimus immunisque voluptatibus neque in pecunia neque in gloria concupiscenda aut modum norat aut capiebat terminum.* [4] *cf.* the *Epistle to Caesar,* ix. 2.

honestissima. Atque is cum eius modi sit, tamen audet dicere: "O fortunatam natam me consule Romam!" "Te consule fortunatam," Cicero? Immo vero infelicem et miseram, quae crudelissimam proscriptionem eam perpessa est, cum tu perturbata re publica metu perculsos omnes bonos parere crudelitati tuae cogebas, cum omnia iudicia, omnes leges in tua libidine erant, cum tu sublata lege Porcia, erepta libertate omnium nostrum vitae necisque

6 potestatem ad te unum revocaveras. Atque parum quod impune fecisti, verum etiam commemorando exprobras neque licet oblivisci his servitutis suae. Egeris, oro te, Cicero, perfeceris quid libet; satis est perpessos esse; etiamne aures nostras odio tuo onerabis, etiamne molestissimis verbis insectabere? "Cedant arma togae, concedat laurea linguae." Quasi vero togatus et non armatus ea, quae gloriaris, confeceris, atque inter te Sullamque dictatorem praeter nomen imperii quicquam interfuerit.

IV. Sed quid ego plura de tua insolentia comme-

7 morem? quem Minerva omnis artis edocuit, Iuppiter Optumus Maxumus in concilio deorum admisit, Italia exsulem humeris suis reportavit. Oro te, Romule Arpinas, qui egregia tua virtute omnis Paulos, Fabios, Scipiones superasti, quem tandem locum in

---

[1] A line from Cicero's poem "On his Consulship," ridiculed by Juvenal (x. 123) and others because of the jingle *fortunatam natam*.

And although such is his character, he yet has the assurance to say, "Fortunate Rome, born in my consulate." [1] "Fortunate in having you for her consul," Cicero? Nay, ill-starred and wretched in having endured that most ruthless proscription, when after embroiling your country and filling all virtuous citizens with fear, you forced them to obey your cruel mandates ; when all the courts and all the laws were subservient to your will ; when after annulling the Porcian law [2] and robbing us all of our freedom, you alone took the power of life and death over all of us into your own hands. And not content with having done all this with impunity, you even insult us by recalling it, and you do not allow these men to forget their slavery. Do, Cicero, I beseech you, have done, have accomplished, what you wish : it is enough for us to have endured it ; will you also burden our ears with your hatred, and even pursue us with the tiresome refrain, "Let arms yield to the toga, the laurel to the tongue"? [3] Just as if it were in the toga and not in arms that you did what you boast of, and as if there were any difference between you and a dictator like Sulla except the mere title of your office.

IV. But why should I enlarge upon your presumption, when you declare that Minerva taught you all the arts, that Jupiter, greatest and kindest of the gods, admitted you to their council, and that Italy brought you back from exile upon its shoulders? I beseech you, O Romulus of Arpinum, who by your transcendent merit surpass every Paulus, Fabius and Scipio, what place, pray, do you hold in this

[2] See *Cat.* li. 22.
[3] Another line from Cicero's poem "On his Consulship."

hac civitate obtines? Quae tibi partes rei publicae placent? Quem amicum, quem inimicum habes? Cui in civitate insidias fecisti, ancillaris. Quo auctore[1] de exsilio tuo Dyrrhachio redisti, eum sequeris. Quos tyrannos appellabas, eorum potentiae faves! Qui tibi ante optimates videbantur, eosdem dementes ac furiosos vocas! Vatini causam agis, de Sestio male existimas. Bibulum petulantissimis verbis laedis, laudas Caesarem. Quem maxime odisti, ei maxime obsequeris. Aliud stans, aliud sedens sentis de re publica. His male dicis, illos odisti, levissime transfuga, neque in hac neque in illa parte fidem habens.

[1] auctore, *Wirz*; iure cum, *mss.*

state? What part in public life do you desire? Who is your friend and who your enemy? You play maidservant to the man against whom you plotted in the state. You follow the one through whose influence you returned from your exile at Dyrrachium. You truckle to the power of those whom you formerly called tyrants. Those who once seemed to you the best of citizens you now call mad and frenzied. You plead the cause of Vatinius, you think ill of Sestius, you assail Bibulus with impudent language, you praise Caesar, you are most obsequious to him whom you most hated; you think one thing about the state when you stand up, another when you sit; you revile some, hate others, vile turncoat that you are, showing loyalty neither to one side nor to the other.

[M. TULLII CICERONIS] IN SALLUSTIUM
CRISPUM ORATIO

I. Ea demum magna voluptas est, C. Sallusti,
aequalem ac parem verbis vitam agere, neque quicquam tam obscaenum dicere cui non ab initio
pueritiae omni genere facinoris aetas tua respondeat,
ut omnis oratio moribus consonet. Neque enim qui
ita vivit, ut tu, aliter ac tu loqui potest, neque qui
tam inloto sermone utitur vita honestior est.

Quo me praevertam, patres conscripti, unde
initium sumam? Maius enim mihi dicendi onus
imponitur, quo notior est uterque nostrum, quod aut
si de mea vita atque actibus huic conviciatori re-
spondero, invidia gloriam consequetur, aut, si huius
facta, mores, omnem aetatem nudavero, in idem
vitium incidam procacitatis, quod huic obicio. Id
vos si forte offendimini, iustius huic quam mihi
2 succensere debetis, qui initium introduxit. Ego
dabo operam ut et pro me minimo cum fastidio
respondeam et in hunc minime mentitum esse
videatur.

Scio me, patres conscripti, in respondendo non
habere magnam exspectationem, quod nullum vos
sciatis novum crimen in Sallustium audituros, sed

AN INVECTIVE AGAINST SALLUSTIUS CRISPUS (ATTRIBUTED TO CICERO)

I. IT surely must be a great satisfaction to you, Gaius Sallustius, that you lead a life similar in all respects to your words, and that you say nothing so foul that your conduct from earliest childhood does not match it with every species of vice; so that your language is wholly consistent with your character. For neither can one who lives as you do speak otherwise than as you speak, nor can one who uses such filthy language be any more respectable in his life.

Whither shall I turn first, Fathers of the Senate, where shall I begin? For the more thoroughly you know each of us, the greater difficulty I find in addressing you; for if I defend my life and conduct against this slanderer, envy will result from boasting; or if I lay bare his conduct, character, and entire life, I shall be liable to the same charge of shamelessness that I bring against him. But in this if haply I should offend you, you ought more justly to be angry with him than with me, since he set the example.[1] I shall do my best to justify myself with the least possible vainglory, and to say nothing about him that is not true.

I realize, Fathers of the Senate, that my reply to his attack awakens no great expectations, since you are conscious that you can hear no new accusation against Sallust, but that you will merely pass in

[1] That is, of talking of such matters.

omnia vetera recognituros, quis et meae et vestrae
iam et ipsius aures calent. Verum eo magis odisse
debetis hominem, qui ne incipiens quidem peccare
minimis rebus posuit rudimentum, sed ita ingressus
est, ut neque ab alio vinci possit neque ipse se omnino
3 reliqua aetate praeterire. Itaque nihil aliud studet
nisi ut lutulentus cum quovis volutari. Longe vero
fallitur opinione. Non enim procacitate linguae
vitae sordes eluuntur, sed est quaedam calumnia,
quam unus quisque nostrum testante animo suo
fert. Quod si vita istius memoriam vicerit, illam,
patres conscripti, non ex oratione, sed ex moribus
suis spectare debebitis. Iam dabo operam quam
maxime potuero breve ut id faciam. Neque haec
altercatio nostra vobis inutilis erit, patres conscripti.
Plerumque enim res publica privatis crescit inimi-
citiis, ubi nemo civis qualis sit vir potest latere.

4 II. Primum igitur, quoniam omnium maiores
C. Sallustius ad unum exemplum et regulam quaerit,
velim mihi respondeat num quid his quos protulit
Scipiones et Metellos ante fuerit aut opinionis aut
gloriae quam eos res suae gestae et vita innocen-
tissime acta commendavit. Quod si hoc fuit illis
initium nominis et dignitatis, cur non aeque de nobis
existimetur, cuius et res gestae illustres et vita
integerrime acta? Quasi vero tu sis ab illis, Sallusti,
ortus. Quod si esses, non nullos iam tuae turpi-
5 tudinis pigeret. Ego meis maioribus virtute mea

---

[1] Because his crimes are so many that no one could remember all of them.

review all the old ones, with which your ears and mine, as well as his own, are burning. But you ought to hate the man all the more bitterly, because he did not begin with slight offences even at the outset of his career of crime, but at once set such a standard, that he could neither be outdone by anyone else nor even outdo himself during the remainder of his life. Hence his only aim is to wallow in the mire with anyone and everyone. But he is very much mistaken. For no wanton words can remove the stains upon a life, but there are accusations which each one of us makes according to the testimony of his own mind. But if this man's life defies recollection,[1] you ought to examine it, Fathers of the Senate, not from a speech, but from his own character. I shall take care to be as brief as I possibly can, and this our war of words, Fathers of the Senate, will not be without profit to you; for as a rule the state is advanced by the quarrels of individuals, which allow the character of no citizen to be hidden.

II. Well then, to begin with, since Gaius Sallustius weighs and measures the ancestors of all men according to the same standard and rule, I should like him to tell me whether those Scipios and Metelluses whom he cites had any renown or glory, before their own exploits and blameless lives commended them to notice. But if this was for them the beginning of repute and rank, why should the case not be similar with me, whose deeds are noble and whose life is well spent? As if you too, Sallust, were sprung from those heroes of old! If you were, some of them would now be sick at heart at your baseness. I have outshone my ancestors in

praeluxi, ut, si prius noti non fuerunt, a me accipiant
initium memoriae suae; tu tuis vita, quam turpiter
egisti, magnas offudisti tenebras, ut, etiam si fuerint
egregii cives, certe venerint in oblivionem. Qua re
noli mihi antiquos viros obiectare. Satius est enim
me meis rebus gestis florere quam maiorum opinione
niti et ita vivere, ut sim posteris meis nobilitatis
initium et virtutis exemplum.

Neque me cum iis conferri decet, patres conscripti, qui iam decesserunt omnique odio carent
et invidia, sed cum eis, qui mecum una in re
6 publica versati sunt. Sed fuerim aut in honoribus
petendis nimis ambitiosus—non hanc dico popu-
larem ambitionem, cuius me principem confiteor,
sed illam perniciosam contra leges, cuius primos
ordines Sallustius duxit—, aut in gerundis magistratibus aut in vindicandis maleficiis tam severus
aut in tuenda re publica tam vigilans, quam tu
proscriptionem vocas, credo, quod non omnes tui
similes incolumes in urbe vixissent; at quanto
meliore loco res publica staret, si tu par ac similis
scelestorum civium una cum illis adnumeratus esses?
7 An ego tunc falso scripsi, "cedant arma togae," qui
togatus armatos et pace bellum oppressi? An illud
mentitus sum, "fortunatam me consule Romam,"
qui tantum intestinum bellum ac domesticum urbis
incendium exstinxi?

merit, so that if they were not known before, I would give them fame for the first time; but you by the base life which you have led have enveloped yours in thick darkness, so that even if they were once eminent citizens, they assuredly have fallen into oblivion. Do not then taunt me with the men of bygone days; for rather than depend upon the reputation of my forefathers, I prefer to win success by my own efforts, and to live in such fashion as to be for my posterity the beginning of their rank and an incentive to virtue.

It is not just, Fathers of the Senate, to compare me with those who have already passed away, and who are free from all hatred or envy; I should rather be matched against those who have been associated with me in public life. If I have been too ambitious in seeking preferment (I do not refer to the ambition which aims at the good of the people, in which I admit that I have always been among the foremost, but to that ruinous and lawless kind in which Sallust is a leader), or if I have been so strict in administering the offices which I have held or in punishing evil-doing, or so vigilant in the defence of our country, that you, Sallust, call it a proscription (I suppose because not all who are like you were allowed to live in our city), yet in how much better condition would the state be if you, who are like those wicked citizens and on a par with them, had been numbered with them? Did I speak falsely when I wrote, "Let arms give place to the toga," I who, clad in the toga, laid low armed men and put a peaceful end to war? Did I lie when I said, "Rome fortunate in my consulship," when I ended such a civil war and extinguished the fire of rebellion raging within our city?

507

III. Neque te tui piget, homo levissime, cum ea culpas, quae historiis mihi gloriae ducis? An turpius est scribentem mentiri quam vel[1] palam hoc ordine dicentem? Nam quod in aetatem increpuisti, tantum me abesse puto ab impudicitia, quantum tu a pudicitia.

8 Sed quid ego de te plura querar? Quid enim mentiri turpe ducis, qui mihi ausus sis eloquentiam ut vitium obicere? Cuius semper nocens eguisti patrocinio. An ullum existimas posse fieri civem egregium, qui non his artibus et disciplinis sit eruditus? An ulla alia putas esse rudimenta et incunabula virtutis, quibus animi ad gloriae cupiditatem aluntur? Sed minime mirum est, patres conscripti, si homo, qui desidiae ac luxuriae plenus sit, haec ut nova atque inusitata miratur.

9 Nam quod ista inusitata rabie petulanter in uxorem et in filiam meam invasisti, quae facilius mulieres se a viris abstinuerunt quam tu vir a viris, satis docte ac perite fecisti. Non enim me sperasti mutuam tibi gratiam relaturum, ut vicissim tuos compellarem. Unus enim satis es materiae habens; neque quicquam domi tuae turpius est quam tu.

Multum vero te, opinor,[2] fallit, qui mihi parare putasti invidiam ex mea re familiari, quae mihi multo minor est quam habere dignus sum. Atque

---

[1] vel, *Norden*; ullum, *HMPV* (*in margin*); illud, E ; illam, *T* ; illic, *H*b ; *the others*, illum.

[2] ut opinor, *A* ; opinio, *H*b (?), *Jordan*.

III. Are you not ashamed, most inconsistent of men, to censure conduct for which you glorify me in your own histories? Is it more shameful, senators, to lie in writing or in open speech before this body? As to the charges which you have made against my life, I believe that I am as far from unchastity as you are from chastity.

But why should I make further complaint of your calumnies? For what falsehood would you consider shameful, when you have dared to make my eloquence an accusation against me, that eloquence whose protection you have always required because of your guilt? Or do you think that anyone can become an eminent citizen who has not been trained in these arts and studies? Do you think that there are any other elements and nursery of virtue in which the mind is trained to desire glory? But it is not to be marvelled at, Fathers of the Senate, if a man who is full of extravagance and sloth should express surprise at these pursuits as if they were new and unusual.

As for the unheard of virulence of your attacks upon my wife and daughter (who, women though they are, have more successfully avoided the attentions of men than you have those of your own sex) in assailing them you showed both cleverness and cunning. For you could not expect me to retaliate by attacking your family in turn, since you alone furnish enough material and have in your home nothing more shameful than yourself.

You are greatly mistaken, I think, if you hoped to rouse enmity against me because of the amount of my property, which in reality is much less than I deserve to have. Yet I could wish that it were not as great

utinam ne tanta quidem esset quanta est, ut potius amici mei viverent quam ego testamentis eorum locupletior essem !

10   Ego fugax, C. Sallusti? Furori tribuni plebis cessi; utilius duxi quamvis fortunam unus experiri quam universo populo Romano civilis essem dissensionis causa. Qui postea quam ille suum annum in re publica perbacchatus est omniaque, quae commoverat, pace et otio resederunt, hoc ordine revocante atque ipsa re publica manu retrahente me reverti. Qui mihi dies, si cum omni reliqua vita conferatur, animo quidem meo superet, cum universi vos populusque Romanus frequens adventu meo gratulatus est; tanti me, fugacem, mercennarium patronum, hi aestimaverunt.

11   IV. Neque hercle mirum est, si ego semper iustas omnium amicitias aestimavi. Non enim uni privatim ancillatus sum neque me addixi, sed, quantum quisque rei publicae studuit, tantum mihi fuit aut amicus aut adversarius. Ego nihil plus volui valere quam pacem; multi privatorum audacias nutriverunt. Ego nihil timui nisi leges; multi arma sua timeri voluerunt. Ego numquam volui quicquam posse nisi pro vobis; multi ex vobis potentia freti in vos suis viribus abusi sunt. Itaque non est mirum, si nullius amicitia usus sum qui non perpetuo rei publicae

12 amicus fuit. Neque me paenitet, si aut petenti Vatinio reo patrocinium pollicitus sum aut Sesti

---

[1] Cicero tells us that he received over £200,000, about a million dollars, in bequests.

as it is, that my friends might still be alive, rather than that I should be the richer through their wills.[1]

Am I a runaway, Gaius Sallustius? I bowed to the madness of a tribune of the commons; I considered it more expedient to endure any lot as an individual, rather than be the cause of civil strife among the entire Roman people. And after that tribune had rioted out his year in public life, and all the disturbance which he had stirred up had subsided into peace and quiet, I returned at the summons of this assembly, my country herself leading me by the hand. To my mind, that day is the crowning glory of my whole life, when all my colleagues in the senate, and the Roman people in throngs, congratulated me on my return; so highly did these men rate me, the runaway and mercenary counsel.

IV. And by Heaven! it is small wonder if I have always thought that I merited the friendship of all mankind; for I have not waited upon one person privately or made myself his slave, but every man was my friend or my foe according to the degree of his devotion to the commonwealth. My highest desire was peace; many men have fostered the reckless designs of individuals. I have feared nothing save the laws; many have wished their arms to be feared. I never coveted power except for your sakes; many even of your own number, relying upon their personal influence, have misused their power to do you harm. And so it is not surprising if I have enjoyed the friendship of no one who was not for all time the friend of our country. Nor have I regret for having promised Vatinius my services when he was accused and appealed to me, for having checked the insolence of Sestius, censured

insolentiam repressi aut Bibuli patientiam culpavi aut virtutibus Caesaris favi. Hae enim laudes egregii civis et unicae sunt. Quae si tu mihi ut vitia obicis, temeritas tua reprehendetur, non mea vitia culpabuntur.

Plura dicerem, si apud alios mihi esset disserendum, patres conscripti, non apud vos, quos ego habui omnium actionum mearum monitores. Sed ubi rerum testimonia adsunt, quid opus est verbis?

13   V. Nunc ad te revertar, Sallusti, patremque tuum praeteream, qui si nunquam in vita sua peccavit, tamen maiorem iniuriam rei publicae facere non potuit quam quod te talem filium genuit; neque tu si qua in pueritia peccasti exsequar, ne parentem tuum videar accusare, qui eo tempore summam tui potestatem habuit, sed qualem adolescentiam egeris; hac enim demonstrata facile intelligetur quam petulanti pueritia tam impudicus et procax adoleveris. Postea quam immensae gulae impudicissimi corporis quaestus sufficere non potuit et aetas tua iam ad ea patienda, quae alteri facere collibuisset, exoleverat, cupiditatibus infinitis efferebaris, ut quae ipse corpori tuo turpia non duxisses in aliis experireris. Ita
14   non est facile exputare, patres conscripti, utrum inhonestioribus corporis partibus rem quaesierit an amiserit.

Domum paternam vivo [1] patre venalem habuit. Et cuiquam dubium potest esse quin mori coëgerit eum, quo hic nondum mortuo pro herede gesserit

---

[1] turpissime (*before* patre), β, *Kur.*

the indifference of Bibulus, or applauded the valour of Caesar. For this last is the praise of an eminent citizen and is unique. If you charge it against me as a fault, it is your audacity that will be censured rather than my fault.

I would speak on, if I had to address others, Fathers of the Senate, and not you, whom I have always regarded as the prompters of all my acts. Moreover, when we have the evidence of facts, what need is there for words?

V. I shall now return to you, Sallust, saying nothing of your father; for even if he never committed a sin in all his life, he could not have inflicted a greater injury upon his country than in begetting such a son. Nor shall I inquire into any sins of your boyhood, lest I may seem to criticize your father, who had full control of you at that time, but how you spent your youth. For if this be shown, it will readily be understood how vicious was the childhood which led up to a manhood so shameless and lawless. When the profit derived from your vile body could no longer suffice for your bottomless gullet, and when you were too old to endure what another's passion prompted, you were incited by an unbounded desire of trying upon others what you had not considered disgraceful to your own person. Therefore, Fathers of the Senate, it is not easy to determine whether he acquired his property or squandered it with more dishonourable members.

He offered his father's house for sale while his father still lived. And can anyone doubt that he drove his sire to his death, when he made himself heir to all his property even before the decease of

513

omnia? Neque pudet eum a me quaerere quis
in P. Crassi domo habitet, cum ipse respondere
nequeat[1] quis in ipsius habitet paterna domo. "At
hercules, lapsus aetatis tirocinio postea se correxit."
Non ita est, sed abiit in sodalicium sacrilegi Nigi-
diani; bis iudicis ad subsellia attractus, extrema
fortuna stetit et ita discessit, ut non hic innocens
esse, sed iudices peierasse existimarentur.

15   Primum honorem in quaestura adeptus hunc
locum et hunc ordinem despectu habuit,[2] cuius
aditus sibi quoque sordidissimo homini patuisset.
Itaque timens ne facinora eius clam vos essent, cum
omnibus matrum familiarum viris opprobrio esset,
confessus est vobis audientibus adulterium neque
erubuit ora vestra.

VI. Vixeris ut libet, Sallusti, egeris quae volueris;
satis sit unum te tuorum scelerum esse conscium,
noli nobis languorem et soporem nimium exprobrare.
Sumus diligentes in tuenda pudicitia uxorum nos-
trarum, sed ita experrecti non sumus, ut a te cavere
16 possimus. Audacia tua vincit studia nostra. Ecquod
hunc movere possit, patres conscripti, factum aut
dictum turpe, quem non puduerit palam vobis
audientibus adulterium confiteri? Quod si tibi per

---

[1] nequeat, *H*ᵇ*BTM*; non querat, *V*; non queat, *the other
mss.*   [2] *Added by Norden.*

---

[1] Referring to P. Nigidius Figulus, who, besides being the
most learned Roman of his day next to Varro, was interested
in the occult; see Suet. *Aug.* 94. 5, and Hieron. *Chron.*

his parent? And yet he is not ashamed to ask me who lives in the house of Publius Crassus, when he himself is unable to answer the question who it is that lives in the house of his very father. Perhaps you may say (save the mark!) that he fell through the inexperience of youth and afterwards reformed. Not so! On the contrary, he became an associate in the sacrilege of Nigidius,[1] he was twice haled before the tribunal of a judge, he was all but condemned, and such was his escape, that he was not thought to be innocent, but the jurors to have committed perjury.

When he obtained the quaestorship as his first office, he brought contempt upon this place and upon this assembly, by showing that it was open even to him, the meanest of mankind. As a matter of fact, through fear that his crimes should not be known to you, although he was a reproach to the husbands of all our matrons, he pleaded guilty to adultery in your hearing and did not blush in your presence.

VI. Be content, Sallust, with having lived as you pleased, and with having acted as you wished; be it enough that you alone are conscious of your guilt, and do not charge us with indifference and with too sound sleep. We are vigilant in defending the chastity of our wives, but we are not sufficiently wide awake to guard against you. Your audacity defeats our diligence. Can any reproach in word or deed, Fathers of the Senate, affect this man, who was not ashamed to confess adultery openly in your hearing? If I should decide to make no reply to

yr. Abr. 1972 (= 45 B.C.), *Nigidius Figulus, Pythagoricus et magus, moritur.*

me nihil respondere voluissem, sed illud censorium eloquium Appii Claudii et L. Pisonis, integerrimorum virorum, quo usus est quisque eorum, pro lege palam universis recitarem, nonne tibi viderer aeternas inurere maculas, quas reliqua vita tua eluere non posset? Neque post illum dilectum senatus umquam te vidimus, nisi forte in ea te castra coniecisti, quo omnis sentina rei publicae con-
17 fluxerat. At idem Sallustius, qui in pace ne senator quidem manserat, postea quam res publica armis oppressa est, idem a victore, qui exsules reduxit, in senatum per[1] quaesturam est reductus. Quem honorem ita gessit, ut nihil in eo non venale habuerit, cuius aliquis emptor fuerit, et[2] ita egit, ut nihil non aequum ac verum duxerit, quod ipsi facere collibuisset, neque aliter vexavit ac debuit, si quis
18 praedae loco magistratum accepisset. Peracta quaestura, postea quam magna pignora eis dederat cum quibus similitudine vitae se coniunxerat, unus iam ex illo grege videbatur. Eius enim partis erat Sallustius, quo tamquam in unam voraginem coetus omnium vitiorum excesserat; quidquid impudicorum, cilonum, parricidarum, sacrilegorum, debitorum fuit in urbe, municipiis, coloniis, Italia tota, sicut in fretis subsederant, nominis perditi ac notissimi, nulla

---

[1] per, *Mommsen*; post, *mss.*   [2] et *added by Kurfess.*

---

[1] Their sentence and the speech in which they justified it.
[2] Referring to the expulsion of many senators by Appius and Piso.

you on my own account, but, to show what the law
is, should read to this whole body the famous
pronouncement[1] of those most irreproachable of men,
Appius Claudius and Lucius Piso, in which they both
concurred, should I not seem to brand you with in-
effaceable stains, of which you could not rid yourself
for the rest of your life? And after that revision of
the senate[2] we saw you no more, unless haply you
threw yourself into that camp into which all the dregs
of the commonwealth had flowed.[3] But that same
Sallust, who in time of peace could not even remain
a senator, that same man after the republic was conquered by arms[4] was returned to the senate, through
the medium of a quaestorship, by the same victor
who recalled the exiles. That office he administered
in such a manner that there was nothing connected
with it which he did not offer for sale, provided any
purchaser could be found for it; and he conducted
himself as if he considered everything just and
proper which he himself had desired to do, abusing
his authority as completely as anyone might have
done who had received the office by way of booty.
Having finished his quaestorship and having given
heavy pledges to those with whom, because of their
similar manner of life, he had joined himself, he now
appeared to be one of that faction. For Sallust
belonged to that party into which, as into a common
sewer, a flood of all the vices had flowed; whatever
wantons, catamites, traitors, committers of sacrilege,
and debtors were to be found in the city or in the
free towns, in the colonies or in all Italy, were en-
gulfed there as in a sea, abandoned and infamous

[3] Namely Caesar's.
[6] Referring to Caesar's supremacy.

in parte castris apti nisi licentia vitiorum et cupiditate rerum novarum.

19   VII. "At postea quam praetor est factus, modeste se gessit et abstinenter." Non ita; provinciam vastavit, ut nihil neque passi sint neque exspectaverint gravius in bello socii nostri quam experti sunt in pace, hoc Africam inferiorem obtinente. Unde tantum hic exhausit, quantum potuit aut fide nominum traici aut in naves contrudi; tantum, inquam, exhausit, patres conscripti, quantum voluit. Ne causam diceret, sestertio duodeciens cum Caesare paciscitur. Quod si quippiam eorum falsum est, his palam refelle, unde, qui modo ne paternam quidem domum reluere[1] potueris, repente tamquam somnio beatus hortos pretiosissimos, villam Tiburti C.
20   Caesaris, reliquas possessiones paraveris. Neque piguit quaerere cur ego P. Crassi domum emissem, cum tu vetus[2] villae dominus sis cuius paulo ante fuerat Caesar? Modo, inquam, patrimonio non comesso, sed devorato, quibus rationibus repente factus es tam adfluens et tam beatus? Nam quis te faceret heredem, quem ne amicum quidem suum satis honestum quisquam sibi ducit nisi similis ac par tui?

21   VIII. At hercules, egregia facta maiorum tuorum te extollunt; quorum sive tu similis es sive illi

[1] reluere, *V* (elu *in an erasure*), *Heraeus*; relinire *or* relinere, *the other codices*; redimere, *Aldus*; retinere, *Vogel*.
[2] netus, *M*; veteris, *the other mss., Aldus*; eius, *Baiter.*

518

characters, in no wise fit for a camp except in the licence of their vices and their love of disorder.

VII. "But perhaps he conducted himself with moderation and integrity after he became a praetor." Not so; he so pillaged his province that our allies never suffered or looked for anything worse in time of war than they experienced during peace while he was governor of lower Africa. He drained from that province as much as could be carried off on credit or crammed into ships; he drained, I say, Fathers of the Senate, as much as he wished. He bargained with Caesar for twelve hundred thousand sesterces[1] that he should not be brought to trial. If any of these statements is false, refute it by telling us how it was that a man who a short time before could not even buy back his father's house, suddenly became rich beyond the dreams of avarice and acquired those precious gardens, and the Tiburtine residence of Gaius Caesar, and the rest of your possessions. And were you not ashamed to ask why I had bought the house of Publius Crassus, when you were the old established master of the villa in which the master had once been Caesar? Tell me, I repeat, when you had, not devoured, but gorged your patrimony, by what means you suddenly became so prosperous and wealthy. Who, pray, made an heir of you, a man whom no one considered it respectable to have even for a friend, except of those who are like and similar to yourself?

VIII. But, good heavens! I suppose the great deeds of your ancestors exalt you, when it is true that if you resemble them or they resemble you,

---

[1] See Index, *s.v.* sestertius.

tui, nihil ad omnium scelus ac nequitiam addi
potest.

Verum, ut opinor, honores tui te faciunt insolen-
tem. Tu, C. Sallusti, idem putas esse bis senatorem
et bis quaestorem fieri quod bis consularem et bis
triumphalem? Carere decet omni vitio qui in
alterum dicere parat. Is demum male dicit, qui
non potest verum ab altero audire. Sed tu, omnium
mensarum assecula, omnium cubiculorum in aetate
paelex et idem postea adulter, omnis ordinis tur-
22 pitudo es et civilis belli memoria. Quid enim hoc
gravius pati potuimus quam quod te incolumem in
hoc ordine videmus? Desine bonos petulantissima
consectari lingua, desine morbo procacitatis isto uti,
desine unum quemque moribus tuis aestimare. His
moribus amicum tibi facere non potes; videris velle
inimicum habere.

Finem dicendi faciam, patres conscripti. Saepe
enim vidi gravius offendere animos auditorum eos,
qui aliena flagitia aperte [1] dixerunt, quam eos, qui
commiserunt. Mihi quidem ratio habenda est, non
quae Sallustius merito debeat audire, sed ut ea
dicam, si qua ego honeste effari possim.

[1] apte, *HH*ᵃ*T*.

nothing can be added to the wickedness and baseness of all of them.

Perhaps it is your own political offices which make
you insolent. Do you imagine, Gaius Sallustius, that
to be twice a senator and twice a quaestor is the
same thing as to be twice a consular and twice a
triumphator?[1] One ought oneself to be wholly
free from fault who is making ready to speak against
another. He only has a right to utter reproaches
who cannot hear a just reproach from another's lips.
But you, the parasite of all tables, the harlot of all
chambers in your youth and in later years their
adulterer, are the disgrace of our whole order and a
memory of the civil war. For what worse affliction
could we endure as a result of that strife than to see
you reinstated in this assembly? Cease, then, to
assail good men with your most wanton tongue,
cease to make use of that disease of calumny from
which you suffer, cease to measure all men by the
standard of your own character. By such conduct
you cannot gain a single friend; but you appear to
wish to add to the number of your enemies.[2]

I shall cease speaking, Fathers of the Senate, for
I have often seen men more grievously offend the
minds of their hearers by descanting openly on
others' crimes than by committing crimes themselves.
I must therefore consider, not what Sallust ought
by rights to hear, but how I may say what I have to
say, if it is at all possible, in an honourable manner.

[1] The title applied to one who had been granted a triumph.
[2] In the person of Cicero.

INDEX

The following abbreviations are used : *C* = Catiline ; *J.* = Jugurtha ; *H.* = Histories (i. 55, The Speech of Lepidus ; i. 77, The Speech of Philippus ; ii. 47, The Speech of Cotta ; ii. 98, The Letter of Pompey ; iii. 48, The Speech of Macer ; iv. 69, The Letter of Mithridates) ; *O.* = The Oration to Caesar ; *E.* = The Epistle to Caesar ; *Inv. I.* = The Invective of Sallust against Cicero ; *Inv. II.* = The Invective of Cicero against Sallust.

Aborigines, *C.* vi. 1. A name applied to the primitive inhabitants of Italy.

Adherbal, *J.* v. 7 ; ix. 4 ; x. 8 ; xi. 3 ; xiii. 1 (*bis*), 3, 9 ; xv. 1, 2, 3 ; xvi. 2, 5 ; xx. 1, 4 ; xxi. 1, 2, 8 ; xxii. 4, 5 ; xxv. 1, 10 ; xxvi. 1, 3 ; xxxv. 1 ; xlviii. 3.

Aefulanus ager, *C.* xliii. 1. A district of Latium.

Aegyptus, *J.* xix. 3 (*bis*). Egypt.

Aemilii, *H.* i. 55. 3.

Aemilius, -a, -um, adj. : *gens*, *H.* i. 77. 6.

Aemilius Lepidus, M., *H.* i. 55. 27 ; 77. 2, 3, 6, 7 (*bis*), 14, 18, 19, 22. Father of the Triumvir ; consul in 78 B.C.

Aemilius Lepidus Livianus, Mamercus, *H.* iii. 48. 10. Consul in 77 B.C.

Aemilius Lepidus, M'., *C.* xviii. 2. Consul in 66 B.C.

Aemilius Paulus, L., *C.* xxxi. 4. Brother of the Triumvir Lepidus and consul in 50 B.C.

Aemilius Scaurus, M., *J.* xv. 4 ; xxv. 4, 10 ; xxviii. 4 ; xxix. 2, 3, 5 ; xxx. 2 ; xxxii. 1 ; xl. 4. Consul in 115 B.C.

Aeneas, *C.* vi. 1.

Aethiopes, *J.* xix. 6. The people of Aethiopia in Central Africa.

Afri, *J.* xviii. 3. The people of Africa.

Africa, *J.* v. 4 ; xiii. 1 ; xiv. 10 ; xvii. 1, 3 (*bis*), 7 ; xviii. 1 ; 4, 12 ; xix. 3, 8 ; xx. 1 ; xxi. 4 ; xxii. 1 ; xxiii. 1 ; xxv. 1, 4 ; xxvii. 5 ; xxviii. 7 ; xxx. 1 ; xxxvi. 1 ; xxxix. 4 ; xliv. 1 ; lxvi. 2 ; lxxviii. 2 ; lxxix. 2 ; lxxxvi. 4 ; lxxxix. 7 ; xcvi. 1 ; xcvii. 2 ; civ. 3 ; *Inferior*, *Inv. II.* vii. 19.

Africanus, surname of P. Cornelius Scipio Africanus, *J.* v. 4 ; *Inv. I.* i. 1.

Africus, -a, -um, adj. to Africa : *mare*, *J.* xviii. 9. A name applied to the southern part of the Mediterranean.

Albinus, *see* Postumius.

Allobroges, *C.* xl. 1, 4 ; xli. 1 ; xliv. 1, 3 ; xlv. 1 ; xlix. 1, 4 ; l. 1 ; lii. 36. A Gallic people, whose territories extended from Lake Geneva south-west to the Rhone.

Alpes, *H.* ii. 98. 4.

Annius, C., *J.* lxxvii. 4. Prefect of Leptis Magna.

Annius, Q., *C.* xvii. 3 ; A friend of Catiline.

Antiochus, *H.* i. 55. 4 ; iv. 69. 6 (*bis*), 8, 11. Antiochus III., king of Syria, defeated by the Romans in a war lasting from 192 to 190 B.C.

Antonius (Hybrida), C., *C.* xxi. 3 ; xxiv. 1 ; xxvi. 1, 4 ; xxxvi. 3 ; lvi. 4 ; lvii. 4, 5 ; lix. 4. Consul

INDEX

525

INDEX

INDEX

Cyzicus, *H.* iv. 69, 14. A city of Mysia on the Propontis (Sea of Marmora).

Dabar, *J.* cviii. 1; cix. 4; cxii. 1. Son of Massugrada and grandson of Masinissa.

Damasippus, *C.* li. 32, 34; *H.* i. 77. 7. Surname of L. Iunius Brutus, a follower of Marius. When praetor in 82 B.C., he put to death many of Sulla's followers. He was himself slain in Sulla's massacre after the victory at the Colline Gate.

December, -bris, -bre, adj.: *nonas, C.* xviii. 5.

Domitius Ahenobarbus, Cn., *O.* iv. 1 Consul in 87 B.C.

Domitius Ahenobarbus, L., *E.* iv. 2; ix. 2. Consul in 94 B.C.

Drusus, *see* Livius.

Dyrrachium, *Inv. I.* iv. 7. A town in southern Illyricum, nearly opposite Brundisium.

Etruria, *C.* xxvii. 1; xxviii. 4; *H.* i. 77. 6, 8.

Eumenes, *H.* iv. 69. 8. Eumenes II. king of Pergamum, an ally of the Romans in their war with Antiochus.

Europa, *J.* xvii. 3 (*bis*).

Fabii, *Inv. I.* iv. 7.

Fabius Maximus (Cunctator), Q., *J.* iv. 5. The famous "shield of Rome," whose "Fabian policy" wore out Hannibal.

Fabius Sanga, Q., *C.* xli. 4, 5. Patron of the Allobroges at Rome in the time of Cicero.

Faesulae, *C.* xxiv. 2; xxvii. 1; xxx. 1, 3. A town of Etruria, modern Fiesole, near Florence.

Faesulanus, -a, -um, adj. from Faesu ae. As subst., Faesulanus, an inhabitant of Faesulae, *C.* lix. 3; lx. 6.

Favonius, M., *E.* ix. 4.

Februarius, -a, -um, adj.; *nonas, C.* xviii. 6.

Felix, *H.* i. 55. 20. Surname of L. Cornelius Sulla.

Figulus, *see* Marcius.

Flaccus, *see* Fulvius and Valerius.

Flaminius, C., *C.* xxxvi. 1.

Fufidius, *H.* i. 55. 22. A centurion of Sulla.

Fulvia, *C.* xxiii. **3, 4**; xxvi. 3; xxviii. 2.

Fulvius Flaccus, M., *J.* xvi. 2; xxxi. 7; xlii. 1. A follower of the Gracchi, slain in 121 B.C.

Fulvius Nobilior, M., *C.* xvii. 4. A Roman knight, a follower of Catiline.

Fulvius, A., *C.* xxxix. 5. Son of a senator; a member of Catiline's conspiracy.

Furius, P., *C.* l. 4. A native of Faesulae.

Gabinius Capito, P., *C.* xvii. 4; xl. 6; xliii. 2; xlvi. 3; xlvii. 1 (*bis*), 4; lii. 34; lv. 6. A Roman knight, a follower of Catiline.

Gaetuli, *J.* xviii. 1, 7, 9, 12; xix. 5, 7; lxxx. 1; lxxxviii. 3; xcvii. 4; xcix. 2; ciii. 4. A people of north-eastern Africa, south of the Numidians.

Galli, *C.* xlv 3; xlvii. 2; lii. 24; liii. 3; *J.* cxiv. 1, 2.

Gallia, *C.* xl. 2; lvi. 4; lvii. 3; lviii. 4, 6; *J.* cxiv. 3; *H.* ii. 98. 5, 9; iv. 40. *Citerior, C.* xlii. 1 (should be Ulterior), 3; *Ulterior, C.* xlii. 1. *Transalpina, C.* lvii. 1.

Gallicus, -a, -um, adj. to Gallia: *bellum, C.* lii. 30; *gens, C.* xl. 1; *E.* xii. 5.

Gauda, *J.* lxv. 1. Brother of Jugurtha.

Gracchi, *J.* xlii. 1, 2. Tiberius and Gaius Gracchus; *see* Sempronius.

Gracchus, *see* Sempronius.

Graeci, *C.* liii. 3; *J.* lxxix. 8; lxxxv. 12; *E.* ix. 3 (*bis*).

Graecia, *C.* ii. 2; li. 39; *H.* iv. 69. 11.

Graecus, -a, -um, adj. to Graecia: *facundia, J.* lxiii. 3; *litterae, C.* xxv. 2; *J.* lxxxv. 32; xcv. 3.

Gulussa, *J.* v. 6; xxxv. 1. Son of Masinissa.

527

INDEX

Hadrumetum, *J.* **xix. 1.** A city on the northern coast of Africa, modern Susa.

Hamilcar, *J.* lxxvii. 1. A prominent citizen of Leptis Magna.

Hannibal, *J.* v. 4; *H.* i. 55. 4; ii. 98. 4. The famous Carthaginian general.

Heraclea, *H.* iv. 69. 14. A city of Pontus.

Hercules, *J.* xviii. 3; Libyan, *J.* lxxxix. 4.

Herennius, C., *H.* ii. 98. 6. A general under Sertorius.

Hiempsal, *J.* v. 7; ix. 4; x. 8; **xi. 3,** 6, 9; xii. 3 (*bis*), 5; **xv.** 1, 3; xxiv. 6; xxviii. 1. Son of Micipsa.

Hiempsal, *J.* xvii. 7. Greatgrandson of Masinissa, son of Gauda and father of Juba.

Hippo, *J.* xix. 1. The name of two cities on the northern coast of Africa, west of Carthage, distinguished as H. Regius and H. Zarytus. The latter is probably meant, modern Biserta.

Hispani, *C.* xix. 5; *J.* xviii. 5.

Hispania, *J.* vii. 2; x. 2; xviii. 3, 9; xix. 4; *H.* ii. 47. 6; 98. 4, 10; *Citerior*, *C.* **xix. 1**; xxi. 3; *H.* ii. 98. 9.

Hispaniae, *C.* xviii. 5.

Hispanus, -a, -um, adj. to Hispania : *equites*, *C.* xix. 3.

Ianuarius, -a, -um, adj. : *kalendae*, *C.* xviii. 5; *J.* cxiv. 3; *mensis*, *J.* xxxvii. 3.

Indigetes, *H.* ii. 98. 5. A people dwelling in the north-eastern corner of Spain on the slope of the Pyrenees.

Italia, *C.* xxiv. 2; lii. 15; *J.* v. 2, 4; xxvii. 3; xxviii. 2, 6; **xxxv. 9**; cxiv. 2; *H.* ii. 47. 7, 98. 4, 7, 10; *O.* viii. 4; *Inv. I.* iv. 7; *Inv. II.* vi. 18.

Italicus, -a, -um, adj. to Italia : *genus*, *J.* xlvii. 1; *socii*, *J.* xl. 2. As subst. Italici, *J.* xxvi. 1, 2; lxvii. 3. Natives of Italy.

Iugurtha, *J.* v. 1, 7; vi. 2, 3; vii. **4, 6**; viii. 1; ix. 2, 3, 4;

x. 1, 7; xi. 1, **3** (*bis*), 5, 7; xii. 4, 5; xiii. 2, 5; xiv. 2, 4, 11, 14, 15, 20; xv. 1 (*bis*), 2; xvi. 2, 3, 5; xix. 7; xx. 1, 5, 6; xxi. 1, 3; xxii. 2; xxiii. 1; xxiv. 2, 4, 10; xxv. 1, 5; xxvi. 1, 3; xxvii. 2; xxviii. 1, 3; xxix. 1, 3, 4; xxxi. 18, 19; xxxii. 1, 3, 5; xxxiii. 1, 4; xxxiv. 1, 2; xxxv. 1, 2, 4, 8; xxxvi. 2; xxxviii. 1; xlvi. 1, 4, 8; xlvii. 3; xlviii. 1; xlix. 1; l. 3, 5; li. 5; lii. 2; liv. 2; lv. 1, 4, 8; lvi. 1; lviii. 1, 6; lix. 2; lx. 4 ; lxi. 1, 4, 5; lxii. 1, 3, 5, 8; lxiv. 5; lxvi. 1, 2; lxix. 1; lxx. 1, 2, 5; lxxii. 2; lxxiii. 7; lxxiv. 1, 2; lxxv. 1, 9; lxxx. 1, 6; lxxxi. 1, 3; lxxxii. 1; lxxxiii. 1, 2; lxxxv. 10, 45; lxxxvii. 4; lxxxix. 2, 4; xci. 7; xcvii. 1, 3; ci. 3, 6, 9; cii. 5, 13; ciii. 2; civ. 4; cvi. 2, 5; cvii. 6; cviii. 1, 2, 3; cx. 7, 8; cxi. 1, 2; cxii. 1, 2 (*bis*); cxiii. 2, 5, 6; cxiv. 3.

Iugurthinus, -a, -um, adj. from Jugurtha : *bellum*, *J.* xix. 7; lxxvii. 2; c. 5; *milites*, *J.* xxi. 2; lvi. 6.

Iulius Caesar, C., *C.* xlvii. 4; xlix. 1, 2, 4; l. 4, 5; li. 1, 13; liii. 6; liv. 2, 3, 4; *E.* xiii. 1; *Inv. I.* iv. 7; *Inv. II.* iv. 12; vii. 19 (*bis*), 20.

Iulius Caesar, L., *C.* xvii. 1. Consul in 64 B.C.

Iulius, C., *C.* xxvii. 1. One of the Catilinarian conspirators.

Iunius, -a, -um, adj. : *kalendae*, *C.* xvii. 1.

Iunius Brutus, D., *C.* xl. 5 (*bis*); *H.* iii. 48. 10. Consul in 77 B.C., husband of Sempronia.

Iunius Brutus, M., *O.* iv. 1.

Iunius Silanus, D., *C.* l. 4; **li. 16, 18.** Consul elect for 62 B.C.

Iunius Silanus, M., *J.* xliii. 1. Consul with Metellus Numidicus in 107 B.C.

Iuppiter, *J.* cvii. 2; *H.* iii. 48. 15; *Inv. I.* iv. 7.

Lacedaemonii, *C.* ii. 2; li. 28. The people of Lacedaemon (Sparta).

528

INDEX

Lacetania, *H.* ii. 98. 5. The country of the Lacetani, just south of the Pyrenees.

Laeca, *see* Porcius.

Lares, *J.* xc. 2. A city of Numidia between Sicca and Zama.

Latine, *J.* ci. 6. Adv. meaning "in Latin."

Latinus, -a, -um, adj. meaning "Latin": *litterae, C.* xxv. 2; *J.* xcv. 3; *nomen, J.* xxxix. 2; xl. 2; xlii. 1; xliii. 4.

Latium, *J.* lxix. 4; lxxxiv. 2; xcv. 1; *H.* i. 55. 12.

Lentulus, *see* Cornelius.

Lepcis, *J.* xix. 1, 3; lxxvii. 1. The name of two cities on the northern coast of Africa, distinguished as Lepcis Magna and Lepcis Minor; see notes on the two passages.

Lepcitani, *J.* lxxvii. 2; lxxix. 1. The inhabitants of Lepcis.

Lepidus, *see* Aemilius.

Libys, -yos, adj. from Libya: *Hercules, J.* lxxxix. 4. As subst. Libyes, *J.* xviii. 1, 9, 10, 12. The inhabitants of Libya.

Licinius Crassus, M., *C.* xvii. 7; xix. 1; xxxviii. 1; xlvii. 4; xlviii. 4, 5 (*bis*), 7, 8, 9; *Inv. I.* iii. 4. The Triumvir, celebrated for his wealth.

Licinius Crassus, P., *Inv. I.* ii. 3; *Inv. II.* v. 14; vii. 20. Father of M. Crassus.

Licinius Crassus, P., *J.* xxxvii. 2.

Licinius Lucullus, L., *H.* iii. 48. 11; iv. 69. 15. Consul in 74 B.C., celebrated for his victories over Mithridates and Tigranes, as well as for his wealth and luxurious habits.

Licinius Macer, C., Speech of, p. 420.

Licinius Murena, C., *C.* xlii. 3. Governor of Farther Gaul in 63 B.C.

Ligus, *J.* xciii. 2, 4, 7, 8; xciv. 2, 3.

Ligures, *J.* xxxviii. 6; lxxvii. 4; c. 2. Dwellers in Liguria, a district of Cisalpine Gaul in the neighbourhood of modern Genoa.

Limetanus, *see* Mamilius.

Livius Drusus, M., *E.* vi. 3, 4.

Longinus, *see* Cassius.

Lucullus, *see* Licinius.

Lutatii, *H.* i. 55. 3. A distinguished Roman family.

Lutatius Catulus, Q., *C.* xxxiv. 3; xxxv. 1; xlix. 1, 2; *H.* i. 77. 6, 19, 22; iii. 48. 9. Consul with Lepidus in 78 B.C. Son of the victor over the Cimbri in 101.

Macedones, *H.* iv. 69. 5. The people of Macedonia.

Macedonia, *J.* xxxv. 3; *H.* ii. 47. 7. A country north of Greece at the north-western end of the Aegean Sea; made a Roman province in 148 B.C.

Macedonicus, -a, -um, adj. to Macedonia: *bellum, C.* li. 5. The war with Perses (171–168 B.C.).

Macer, *see* Licinius.

Mamilius Limetanus, C., *J.* xl. 1. Tribune of the commons in 110 B.C.

Mamilius, -a, -um, adj. to (C.) Mamilius (Limetanus): *lex, J.* lxv. 5; *rogatio, J.* xl. 4.

Manlianus, -a, -um, adj. to (C.) Manlius: *castra, C.* xxxii. 1.

Mancinus, *see* Manlius.

Manlius, A., *J.* lxxxvi. 1; xc. 2; c. 2; cii. 3, 4, 15. A *legatus* of Marius.

Manlius, C., *C.* xxiv. 2; xxvii. 1, 4; xxviii. 4; xxix. 1; xxx. 1; xxxii. 3; xxxvi. 1, 2; lvi. 1; lix. 3; lx. 6. A colonist of Faesulae who aided Catiline in his conspiracy.

Manlius (Maximus), Cn., *J.* cxiv. 1. Consul in 105 B.C.

Manlius Mancinus, T., *J.* lxxiii. 7. Tribune of the commons in 107 B.C.

Manlius Torquatus, A. (should be T.), *C.* lii. 30.

Manlius Torquatus, L., *C.* xviii. 5. Consul in 65 B.C.

Marcius Figulus, C., *C.* xvii. 1. Consul in 64 B.C.

Marcius Philippus, L., Speech of, p. 396. Consul in 91 B.C., and

529

INDEX

princeps senatus in 78, when he opposed Lepidus.

Marcius Rex, Q., *C.* xxx. 3; xxxii. 3; xxxiv. 1.

Marius, C., *C.* lix. 3; *J.* xlvi. 7; l. 2; lv. 4, 8; lvi. 3, 5; lvii. 1; lviii. 5; lx. 5; lxiii. 1; lxiv. 1, 3, 4; lxv. 3, 4, 5; lxxiii. 2, 3, 5, 6, 7; lxxxii. 2, 3 (*bis*); lxxxiv. 1, 3 (*bis*), 4; lxxxvi. 1, 4, 5; lxxxvii. 4; lxxxviii. 2; lxxxix. 6; xcii. 1, 6; xciii. 1, 6, 7; xciv. 3, 4, 6; xcvi. 1, 3; xcvii. 3; xcviii. 1, 3; xcix. 1; c. 1, 5; ci. 6 (*bis*), 10; cii. 2, 13, 14; ciii. 1, 3, 7; civ. 1; cv. 1; cxii. 2; xciii. 6; cxiv. 3; *H.* i. 77. 7.

Masinissa, *J.* v. 4, 5, 7; ix. 2; xiv. 2, 6, 18; xxiv. 10; xxxv. 1, 2; lxv. 1, 3; cviii. 1. King of Numidia. He became the ally of the Romans in 204 and died in 149 B.C.

Massilia, *C.* xxxiv. 2. A city in the southern part of Gaul, modern Marseilles.

Massiva, *J.* xxxv. 1, 4 (*bis*), 6; lxi. 4. Son of Gulussa and grandson of Masinissa.

Massugrada, *J.* cviii. 1. Probably a son of Masinissa.

Mastanabal, *J.* v. 6, 7; lxv. 1. A natural son of Masinissa.

Mauretania, *C.* xxi. 3; *J.* xvi. 5; xix. 4; lxii. 7. The kingdom of Bocchus in north-western Africa, modern Morocco.

Maurus, *J.* xcvii. 2; cvi. 2; cvii. 1; cviii. 1; cxii. 1, 3; plur. Mauri, *J.* xviii. 10; xix. 4, 7; lxxx. 6; lxxxii. 1; xcix. 2; ci. 4, 8; cvii. 5. Inhabitants of Mauretania; Moors.

Maurus, -a, -um, adj. to Maurus: *equites*, *J.* xcvii. 4; cvi. 5.

Maxumus, *see* Fabius.

Medi, *J.* xviii. 4, 9, 10. A people of Asia east of the Tigris River.

Memmius, C., *J.* xxvii. 2; xxx. 3, 4; xxxii. 1, 5; xxxiii. 3. Tribune of the commons in 111 B.C.

Mesopotamia, *H.* iv. 69. 21. A country of Asia between the Tigris and Euphrates rivers.

Metelli, *Inv. II.* ii. 4. A distinguished Roman family.

Metellus, *see* Caecilius.

Micipsa, *J.* v. 6; vi. 2; vii. 2; viii. 1; ix. 1; xi. 2, 5; xiv. 1, 9; xvi. 2; xxii. 2; xxiv. 3; lxv. 1; cx. 8. Son and successor of Masinissa, king of Numidia.

Minerva, *Inv. I.* iv. 7.

Minucius Rufus, Q. (probably for M.), *J.* xxxv. 2, 4. Consul in 110 B.C. with Spurius Albinus.

Mithridates, *H.* i. 77. 8; ii. 47. 7; iii. 48. 18; iv. 69. 1. Mithridates VI, king of Pontus, surnamed the Great. Letter of, p. 433.

Mithridaticus, -a, -um, adj. to Mithridates: *bellum*, *C.* xxxix. 1.

Muluccha, *J.* xix. 7; xcii. 5; cx. 8. A river which formed the boundary between Numidia and Mauretania.

Mulvis pons, *C.* xlv. 1. The Mulvian bridge, which carried the via Flaminia across the Tiber, north of Rome. The modern Ponte Molle.

Murena, *see* Licinius.

Muthul, *J.* xlviii. 3. A river of Numidia, the modern Mellèque. It flows into the Bagradas (modern Medjerda).

Nabdalsa, *J.* lxx. 2, 4; lxxi. 1, 5. A Numidian.

Nasica, *see* Cornelius.

Nero, *see* Claudius.

Nicomedes, *H.* iv. 69. 9, 10, 11. Nicomedes III, king of Bithynia. In 74 B.C. he bequeathed his kingdom to the Romans.

Nigidianus, -a, -um, adj. from (P.) Nigidius (Figulus): *Inv. II.* v. 14; see note.

Nobilior, *see* Fulvius.

Nomades, *J.* xviii. 7. The Greek name for the inhabitants of Northern Africa, from which Numidae is supposed to be derived.

November, -bris, -bre, adj.: *kalendae*, *C.* xxx. 1.

Nucerinus, -a, -um, adj. from Nuceria, a city of Campania not

INDEX

533

INDEX

but was defended by Cicero and acquitted. Later he sided with Caesar against Cicero.

Sextius, *J.* xxix. 4. A quaestor during the war with Jugurtha.

Sibyllini libri, *C.* xlvii. 2. A collection of prophetic utterances in Greek, preserved in the temple of Jupiter on the Capitoline Hill. Tradition said that they were sold to King Tarquinius Priscus, or to Tarquinius Superbus, by a sibyl. See also Suet, *Aug.* xxxi.

Sicca, *J.* lvi. 3. A city in the interior of Numidia.

Siccenses, *J.* lvi. 4, 5. The people of Sicca.

Sicilia, *J.* xxviii. 6 (*bis*).

Sicinius, L., *H.* iii. 48. 8. Tribune in 76 B.C. He tried to restore the powers of the tribunes, which Sulla had curtailed.

Sidonicus, -a, -um, adj. to Sidon, the Phoenician city : *pleraque, J.* lxxviii.

Sidonii, *J.* lxxviii. 1. The people of Sidon.

Silanus, *see* Iulius and Turpilius.

Sisenna, *see* Cornelius.

Sittius, P., *C.* xxi. 3. A native of Nuceria in Campania, who in 63 B.C. commanded an army of mercenaries in Mauretania.

Spinther, *see* Cornelius Lentulus.

Statilius, L., *C.* xvii. 3 ; xliii. 2 ; xliv. 1 ; xlvi. 4 ; xlvii. 4 ; lii. 34 ; iv. 6. A Roman knight ; a member of Catiline's conspiracy.

Sucro, *H.* ii. 98. 6. A town on the eastern coast of Spain.

Sulla, *see* Cornelius.

Sullanus, -a, -um. adj. from Sulla : *coloniae, C.* xxviii. 4 ; *milites, C.* xvi. 4 ; *victoria, C.* xxi. 4 ; xxxvii. 6 ; *O.* iv. 1.

Sulpicius Rufus, P., *H.* i. 77. 7. Tribune of the commons in 88 B.C. ; he caused the command of the war with Mithridates to be transferred from Sulla to Marius.

Sura, *see* Cornelius Lentulus.

Suthul, *J.* xxxvii. 3 ; xxxviii. 2. A city of Numidia.

Syphax, *J.* v. 4 ; xiv. 8. King of

western Numidia. He was defeated by the Romans in 203 B.C. and his kingdom given to Masinissa.

Syrtes, *J.* xix. 3 ; lxxviii. 1, 3. Two large shallow bays on the northern coast of Africa (*see J.* lxxviii.).

Tanais, *J.* xc. 3. A river of Numidia.

Tarquinius, L., *C.* xlviii. 3, 5, 6, 8. One of Catiline's associates.

Tarracinensis, -e, adj. from Tarracina, a town in the southern part of Latium, near the Pomptine Marshes : *C.* xlvi. 3.

Tarrula, *H.* i. 55. 21. A follower of Sulla.

Taurus, *H.* iv. 69. 6. A range of mountains in the south-eastern part of Asia Minor.

Terentia, *Inv. I.* ii. 3. Wife of Cicero.

Terentius, Cn., *C.* xlvii. 4. A Roman senator.

Thala, *J.* lxxv. 1, 2, 6, 9 ; lxxvii. 1 ; lxxx. 1 ; lxxxix. 6 (*bis*). A city of Numidia.

Theraei, *J.* xix. 3.

Thirmida, *J.* xii. 3. A town of Numidia.

Thraces, *J.* xxxviii. 6. The people of Thrace.

Tiburs, *Inv. II.* vii. 19. The territory about Tibur, a hill town on the Anio, north-east of Rome ; modern Tivoli.

Tigranes, *H.* iv. 69. 3, 13, 15, 16. King of Armenia and son-in-law of Mithridates.

Tisidium, *J.* lxii. 8. A town of Numidia.

Torquatus, *see* Manlius.

Transpadanus, -a, -um, adj. : *quidam, C.* xlix. 2. A man of Transpadine Gaul.

Troiani, *C.* vi. 1.

Tullianum, *C.* lv. 3. The lower room of the *carcer*, or dungeon, on the southern slope of the Capitoline Hill. *See* note.

Tullius Cicero, M., *C.* xxii. 3 ; xxiii. 5 ; xxiv. 1 ; xxvii. 4 ;

Printed in Great Britain by
Richard Clay (The Chaucer Press), Ltd.,
Bungay, Suffolk

THE LOEB CLASSICAL LIBRARY

VOLUMES ALREADY PUBLISHED

Latin Authors

1

CICERO: DE SENECTUTE, DE AMICITIA, DE DIVINATIONE. W. A. Falconer.

CICERO: IN CATILINAM, PRO FLACCO, PRO MURENA, PRO SULLA. Louis E. Lord.

CICERO: LETTERS to ATTICUS. E. O. Winstedt. 3 Vols.

CICERO: LETTERS TO HIS FRIENDS. W. Glynn Williams. 3 Vols.

CICERO: PHILIPPICS. W. C. A. Ker.

CICERO: PRO ARCHIA POST REDITUM, DE DOMO, DE HARUSPICUM RESPONSIS, PRO PLANCIO. N. H. Watts.

CICERO: PRO CAECINA, PRO LEGE MANILIA, PRO CLUENTIO, PRO RABIRIO. H. Grose Hodge.

CICERO: PRO CAELIO, DE PROVINCIIS CONSULARIBUS, PRO BALBO. R. Gardner.

CICERO: PRO MILONE, IN PISONEM, PRO SCAURO, PRO FONTEIO, PRO RABIRIO POSTUMO, PRO MARCELLO, PRO LIGARIO, PRO REGE DEIOTARO. N. H. Watts.

CICERO: PRO QUINCTIO, PRO ROSCIO AMERINO, PRO ROSCIO COMOEDO, CONTRA RULLUM. J. H. Freese.

CICERO: PRO SESTIO, IN VATINIUM. R. Gardner.

CICERO: TUSCULAN DISPUTATIONS. J. E. King.

CICERO: VERRINE ORATIONS. L. H. G. Greenwood. 2 Vols.

CLAUDIAN. M. Platnauer. 2 Vols.

COLUMELLA: DE RE RUSTICA. DE ARBORIBUS. H. B. Ash, E. S. Forster and E. Heffner. 3 Vols.

CURTIUS, Q.: HISTORY OF ALEXANDER. J. C. Rolfe. 2 Vols.

FLORUS. E. S. Forster; and CORNELIUS NEPOS. J. C. Rolfe.

FRONTINUS: STRATAGEMS and AQUEDUCTS. C. E. Bennett and M. B. McElwain.

FRONTO: CORRESPONDENCE. C. R. Haines. 2 Vols.

GELLIUS, J. C. Rolfe. 3 Vols.

HORACE: ODES AND EPODES. C. E. Bennett.

HORACE: SATIRES, EPISTLES, ARS POETICA. H. R. Fairclough.

JEROME: SELECTED LETTERS. F. A. Wright.

JUVENAL and PERSIUS. G. G. Ramsay.

LIVY. B. O. Foster, F. G. Moore, Evan T. Sage, and A. C. Schlesinger and R. M. Geer (General Index). 14 Vols.

LUCAN. J. D. Duff.

LUCRETIUS. W. H. D. Rouse.

MARTIAL. W. C. A. Ker. 2 Vols.

MINOR LATIN POETS: from PUBLILIUS SYRUS TO RUTILIUS NAMATIANUS, including GRATTIUS, CALPURNIUS SICULUS, NEMESIANUS, AVIANUS, and others with " Aetna " and the " Phoenix." J. Wight Duff and Arnold M. Duff.

OVID: THE ART OF LOVE and OTHER POEMS. J. H. Mozley.

OVID: FASTI. Sir James G. Frazer.
OVID: HEROIDES and AMORES. Grant Showerman.
OVID: METAMORPHOSES. F. J. Miller. 2 Vols.
OVID: TRISTIA and EX PONTO. A. L. Wheeler.
PERSIUS. Cf. JUVENAL.
PETRONIUS. M. Heseltine; SENECA; APOCOLOCYNTOSIS. W. H. D. Rouse.
PHAEDRUS AND BABRIUS (Greek). B. E. Perry.
PLAUTUS. Paul Nixon. 5 Vols.
PLINY: LETTERS, PANEGYRICUS. Betty Radice. 2 Vols.
PLINY: NATURAL HISTORY.
    10 Vols. Vols. I.–V. and IX. H. Rackham. Vols. VI.–VIII. W. H. S. Jones. Vol. X. D. E. Eichholz.
PROPERTIUS. H. E. Butler.
PRUDENTIUS. H. J. Thomson. 2 Vols.
QUINTILIAN. H. E. Butler. 4 Vols.
REMAINS OF OLD LATIN. E. H. Warmington. 4 Vols. Vol. I. (ENNIUS AND CAECILIUS.) Vol. II. (LIVIUS, NAEVIUS, PACUVIUS, ACCIUS.) Vol. III. (LUCILIUS and LAWS OF XII TABLES.) Vol. IV. (ARCHAIC INSCRIPTIONS.)
SALLUST. J. C. Rolfe.
SCRIPTORES HISTORIAE AUGUSTAE. D. Magie. 3 Vols.
SENECA: APOCOLOCYNTOSIS. Cf. PETRONIUS.
SENECA: EPISTULAE MORALES. R. M. Gummere. 3 Vols.
SENECA: MORAL ESSAYS. J. W. Basore. 3 Vols.
SENECA: TRAGEDIES. F. J. Miller. 2 Vols.
SIDONIUS: POEMS and LETTERS. W. B. ANDERSON. 2 Vols.
SILIUS ITALICUS. J. D. Duff. 2 Vols.
STATIUS. J. H. Mozley. 2 Vols.
SUETONIUS. J. C. Rolfe. 2 Vols.
TACITUS: DIALOGUS. Sir Wm. Peterson. AGRICOLA and GERMANIA. Maurice Hutton.
TACITUS: HISTORIES AND ANNALS. C. H. Moore and J. Jackson. 4 Vols.
TERENCE. John Sargeaunt. 2 Vols.
TERTULLIAN: APOLOGIA and DE SPECTACULIS. T. R. Glover. MINUCIUS FELIX. G. H. Rendall.
VALERIUS FLACCUS. J. H. Mozley.
VARRO: DE LINGUA LATINA. R. G. Kent. 2 Vols.
VELLEIUS PATERCULUS and RES GESTAE DIVI AUGUSTI. F. W. Shipley.
VIRGIL. H. R. Fairclough. 2 Vols.
VITRUVIUS: DE ARCHITECTURA. F. Granger. 2 Vols.

Greek Authors

ACHILLES TATIUS. S. Gaselee.

AELIAN: ON THE NATURE OF ANIMALS. A. F. Scholfield. 3 Vols.

AENEAS TACTICUS, ASCLEPIODOTUS and ONASANDER. The Illinois Greek Club.

AESCHINES. C. D. Adams.

AESCHYLUS. H. Weir Smyth. 2 Vols.

ALCIPHRON, AELIAN, PHILOSTRATUS: LETTERS. A. R. Benner and F. H. Fobes.

ANDOCIDES, ANTIPHON, Cf. MINOR ATTIC ORATORS.

APOLLODORUS. Sir James G. Frazer. 2 Vols.

APOLLONIUS RHODIUS. R. C. Seaton.

THE APOSTOLIC FATHERS. Kirsopp Lake. 2 Vols.

APPIAN: ROMAN HISTORY. Horace White. 4 Vols.

ARATUS. Cf. CALLIMACHUS.

ARISTOPHANES. Benjamin Bickley Rogers. 3 Vols. Verse trans.

ARISTOTLE: ART OF RHETORIC. J. H. Freese.

ARISTOTLE: ATHENIAN CONSTITUTION, EUDEMIAN ETHICS, VICES AND VIRTUES. H. Rackham.

ARISTOTLE: GENERATION OF ANIMALS. A. L. Peck.

ARISTOTLE: HISTORIA ANIMALIUM. A. L. Peck. Vols. I.–II.

ARISTOTLE: METAPHYSICS. H. Tredennick. 2 Vols.

ARISTOTLE: METEOROLOGICA. H. D. P. Lee.

ARISTOTLE: MINOR WORKS. W. S. Hett. On Colours, On Things Heard, On Physiognomies, On Plants, On Marvellous Things Heard, Mechanical Problems, On Indivisible Lines, On Situations and Names of Winds, On Melissus, Xenophanes, and Gorgias.

ARISTOTLE: NICOMACHEAN ETHICS. H. Rackham.

ARISTOTLE: OECONOMICA and MAGNA MORALIA. G. C. Armstrong; (with Metaphysics, Vol. II.).

ARISTOTLE: ON THE HEAVENS. W. K. C. Guthrie.

ARISTOTLE: ON THE SOUL. PARVA NATURALIA. ON BREATH. W. S. Hett.

ARISTOTLE: CATEGORIES, ON INTERPRETATION, PRIOR ANALYTICS. H. P. Cooke and H. Tredennick.

ARISTOTLE: POSTERIOR ANALYTICS, TOPICS. H. Tredennick and E. S. Forster.

ARISTOTLE: ON SOPHISTICAL REFUTATIONS.
On Coming to be and Passing Away, On the Cosmos. E. S. Forster and D. J. Furley.

ARISTOTLE: PARTS OF ANIMALS. A. L. Peck; MOTION AND PROGRESSION OF ANIMALS. E. S. Forster.

ARISTOTLE: PHYSICS. Rev. P. Wicksteed and F. M. Cornford. 2 Vols.

ARISTOTLE: POETICS and LONGINUS. W. Hamilton Fyfe; DEMETRIUS ON STYLE. W. Rhys Roberts.

ARISTOTLE: POLITICS. H. Rackham.

ARISTOTLE: PROBLEMS. W. S. Hett. 2 Vols.

ARISTOTLE: RHETORICA AD ALEXANDRUM (with PROBLEMS. Vol. II). H. Rackham.

ARRIAN: HISTORY OF ALEXANDER and INDICA. Rev. E. Iliffe Robson. 2 Vols.

ATHENAEUS: DEIPNOSOPHISTAE. C. B. GULICK. 7 Vols.

BABRIUS AND PHAEDRUS (Latin). B. E. Perry.

ST. BASIL: LETTERS. R. J. Deferrari. 4 Vols.

CALLIMACHUS: FRAGMENTS. C. A. Trypanis.

CALLIMACHUS, Hymns and Epigrams, and LYCOPHRON. A. W. Mair; ARATUS. G. R. MAIR.

CLEMENT of ALEXANDRIA. Rev. G. W. Butterworth.

COLLUTHUS. Cf. OPPIAN.

DAPHNIS AND CHLOE. Thornley's Translation revised by J. M. Edmonds; and PARTHENIUS. S. Gaselee.

DEMOSTHENES I.: OLYNTHIACS, PHILIPPICS and MINOR ORATIONS. I.-XVII. AND XX. J. H. Vince.

DEMOSTHENES II.: DE CORONA and DE FALSA LEGATIONE. C. A. Vince and J. H. Vince.

DEMOSTHENES III.: MEIDIAS, ANDROTION, ARISTOCRATES, TIMOCRATES and ARISTOGEITON, I. AND II. J. H. Vince.

DEMOSTHENES IV.-VI.: PRIVATE ORATIONS and IN NEAERAM. A. T. Murray.

DEMOSTHENES VII.: FUNERAL SPEECH, EROTIC ESSAY, EXORDIA and LETTERS. N. W. and N. J. DeWitt.

DIO CASSIUS: ROMAN HISTORY. E. Cary. 9 Vols.

DIO CHRYSOSTOM. J. W. Cohoon and H. Lamar Crosby. 5 Vols.

DIODORUS SICULUS. 12 Vols. Vols. I.-VI. C. H. Oldfather. Vol. VII. C. L. Sherman. Vol. VIII. C. B. Welles. Vols. IX. and X. R. M. Geer. Vol. XI. F. Walton. Vol. XII. F. Walton. General Index. R. M. Geer.

DIOGENES LAERTIUS. R. D. Hicks. 2 Vols.

DIONYSIUS OF HALICARNASSUS: ROMAN ANTIQUITIES. Spelman's translation revised by E. Cary. 7 Vols.

EPICTETUS. W. A. Oldfather. 2 Vols.

EURIPIDES. A. S. Way. 4 Vols. Verse trans.

EUSEBIUS: ECCLESIASTICAL HISTORY. Kirsopp Lake and J. E. L. Oulton. 2 Vols.

GALEN: ON THE NATURAL FACULTIES. A. J. Brock.

THE GREEK ANTHOLOGY. W. R. Paton. 5 Vols.

GREEK ELEGY AND IAMBUS with the ANACREONTEA. J. M. Edmonds. 2 Vols.

THE GREEK BUCOLIC POETS (THEOCRITUS, BION, MOSCHUS). J. M. Edmonds.

GREEK MATHEMATICAL WORKS. Ivor Thomas. 2 Vols.

HERODES. Cf. THEOPHRASTUS: CHARACTERS.

HERODIAN. C. R. Whittaker. 2 Vols.

HERODOTUS. A. D. Godley. 4 Vols.

HESIOD AND THE HOMERIC HYMNS. H. G. Evelyn White.

HIPPOCRATES and the FRAGMENTS OF HERACLEITUS. W. H. S. Jones and E. T. Withington. 4 Vols.

HOMER: ILIAD. A. T. Murray. 2 Vols.

HOMER: ODYSSEY. A. T. Murray. 2 Vols.

ISAEUS. E. W. Forster.

ISOCRATES. George Norlin and LaRue Van Hook. 3 Vols.

[ST. JOHN DAMASCENE]: BARLAAM AND IOASAPH. Rev. G. R. Woodward, Harold Mattingly and D. M. Lang.

JOSEPHUS. 9 Vols. Vols. I.–IV.; H. Thackeray. Vol. V.; H. Thackeray and R. Marcus. Vols. VI.–VII.; R. Marcus. Vol. VIII.; R. Marcus and Allen Wikgren. Vol. IX. L. H. Feldman.

JULIAN. Wilmer Cave Wright. 3 Vols.

LIBANIUS. A. F. Norman. Vol. I.

LUCIAN. 8 Vols. Vols. I.–V. A. M. Harmon. Vol. VI. K. Kilburn. Vols. VII.–VIII. M. D. Macleod.

LYCOPHRON. Cf. CALLIMACHUS.

LYRA GRAECA. J. M. Edmonds. 3 Vols.

LYSIAS. W. R. M. Lamb.

MANETHO. W. G. Waddell: PTOLEMY: TETRABIBLOS. F. E. Robbins.

MARCUS AURELIUS. C. R. Haines.

MENANDER. F. G. Allinson.

MINOR ATTIC ORATORS (ANTIPHON, ANDOCIDES, LYCURGUS, DEMADES, DINARCHUS, HYPERIDES). K. J. Maidment and J. O. Burtt. 2 Vols.

NONNOS: DIONYSIACA. W. H. D. Rouse. 3 Vols.

OPPIAN, COLLUTHUS, TRYPHIODORUS. A. W. Mair.

PAPYRI. NON-LITERARY SELECTIONS. A. S. Hunt and C. C. Edgar. 2 Vols. LITERARY SELECTIONS (Poetry). D. L. Page.

PARTHENIUS. Cf. DAPHNIS and CHLOE.

PAUSANIAS: DESCRIPTION OF GREECE. W. H. S. Jones. 4 Vols. and Companion Vol. arranged by R. E. Wycherley.

PHILO. 10 Vols. Vols. I.–V.; F. H. Colson and Rev. G. H. Whitaker. Vols. VI.–IX.; F. H. Colson. Vol. X. F. H. Colson and the Rev. J. W. Earp.

6

PHILO: two supplementary Vols. (*Translation only*.) Ralph Marcus.

PHILOSTRATUS: THE LIFE OF APOLLONIUS OF TYANA. F. C. Conybeare. 2 Vols.

PHILOSTRATUS: IMAGINES; CALLISTRATUS: DESCRIPTIONS. A. Fairbanks.

PHILOSTRATUS and EUNAPIUS: LIVES OF THE SOPHISTS. Wilmer Cave Wright.

PINDAR. Sir J. E. Sandys.

PLATO: CHARMIDES, ALCIBIADES, HIPPARCHUS, THE LOVERS, THEAGES, MINOS and EPINOMIS. W. R. M. Lamb.

PLATO: CRATYLUS, PARMENIDES, GREATER HIPPIAS, LESSER HIPPIAS. H. N. Fowler.

PLATO: EUTHYPHRO, APOLOGY, CRITO, PHAEDO, PHAEDRUS. H. N. Fowler.

PLATO: LACHES, PROTAGORAS, MENO, EUTHYDEMUS. W. R. M. Lamb.

PLATO: LAWS. Rev. R. G. Bury. 2 Vols.

PLATO: LYSIS, SYMPOSIUM, GORGIAS. W. R. M. Lamb.

PLATO: REPUBLIC. Paul Shorey. 2 Vols.

PLATO: STATESMAN, PHILEBUS. H. N. Fowler; ION. W. R. M. Lamb.

PLATO: THEAETETUS and SOPHIST. H. N. Fowler.

PLATO: TIMAEUS, CRITIAS, CLITOPHO, MENEXENUS, EPISTULAE. Rev. R. G. Bury.

PLOTINUS: A. H. Armstrong. Vols. I.–III.

PLUTARCH: MORALIA. 16 Vols. Vols. I.–V. F. C. Babbitt. Vol. VI. W. C. Helmbold. Vols. VII. and XIV. P. H. De Lacy and B. Einarson. Vol. VIII. P. A. Clement and H. B. Hoffleit. Vol. IX. E. L. Minar, Jr., F. H. Sandbach, W. C. Helmbold. Vol. X. H. N. Fowler. Vol. XI. L. Pearson and F. H. Sandbach. Vol. XII. H. Cherniss and W. C. Helmbold. Vol. XV. F. H. Sandbach.

PLUTARCH: THE PARALLEL LIVES. B. Perrin. 11 Vols.

POLYBIUS. W. R. Paton. 6 Vols.

PROCOPIUS: HISTORY OF THE WARS. H. B. Dewing. 7 Vols.

PTOLEMY: TETRABIBLOS. Cf. MANETHO.

QUINTUS SMYRNAEUS. A. S. Way. Verse trans.

SEXTUS EMPIRICUS. Rev. R. G. Bury. 4 Vols.

SOPHOCLES. F. Storr. 2 Vols. Verse trans.

STRABO: GEOGRAPHY. Horace L. Jones. 8 Vols.

THEOPHRASTUS: CHARACTERS. J. M. Edmonds. HERODES, etc. A. D. Knox.

THEOPHRASTUS: ENQUIRY INTO PLANTS. Sir Arthur Hort, Bart. 2 Vols.

THUCYDIDES. C. F. Smith. 4 Vols.

Tryphiodorus. Cf. Oppian.
Xenophon: Cyropaedia. Walter Miller. 2 Vols.
Xenophon: Hellenica. C. L. Brownson. 2 Vols.
Xenophon: Anabasis. C. L. Brownson.
Xenophon: Memorabilia and Oeconomicus. E. C. Marchant. Symposium and Apology. O. J. Todd.
Xenophon: Scripta Minora. E. C. Marchant and G. W. Bowersock.

IN PREPARATION

Greek Authors

Aristides: Orations. C. A. Behr.
Musaeus: Hero and Leander. T. Gelzer and C. H. Whitman.
Theophrastus: De Causis Plantarum. G. K. K. Link and B. Einarson.

Latin Authors

Asconius: Commentaries on Cicero's Orations. G. W. Bowersock.
Benedict: The Rule. P. Meyvaert.
Justin-Trogus. R. Moss.
Manilius. G. P. Goold.

DESCRIPTIVE PROSPECTUS ON APPLICATION

London
Cambridge, Mass.

WILLIAM HEINEMANN LTD
HARVARD UNIVERSITY PRESS